LISTENING TO MUSIC

Jay Zorn

**University of Southern California
Thornton School of Music**

with

June August

PRENTICE HALL
Upper Saddle River, New Jersey 07458

Library of Congress Cataloging-in-Publication Data
Zorn, Jay D.
    Listening to music / Jay Zorn ; with June August. —3rd ed.
    p.   cm.
    Includes bibliographical references and index.
    ISBN 0-13-907346-9
    1. Music appreciation.   I. August, June.   II. Title.
MT90.Z65   2000
781.1'7—dc21   99-15105
                                                   CIP

I dedicate this book to my wife,
June August.
Her continuous encouragement, editing
expertise, musical advice and many hours
of work eased the project from its
inception to its completion.

Editorial Director: CHARLYCE JONES OWEN
Publisher: BUD THERIEN
Senior Acquisitions Editor:
 CHRISTOPHER T. JOHNSON
Editorial Assistant: LAKSHMI BALASUBRAMANIAN
Marketing Manager: SHERYL ADAMS
AVP, Director of Production & Manufacturing:
 BARBARA KITTLE
Manufacturing Manager: NICK SKLITSIS
Manufacturing Buyer: BENJAMIN D. SMITH

Production Editor: JEAN LAPIDUS
Creative Design Director: LESLIE OSHER
Interior & Cover Designer: ANNE BONANNO NIEGLOS
Photo Research Supervisor: MELINDA REO
Interior Image Specialist: BETH BOYD
Photo Researcher: TERI STRATFORD
Photo Permissions Coordinator: MICHELINA VISCUSI
Copy Editor: MICHELE LANSING
Text Permissions Specialist: ELSA PETERSON LTD.
Cover Photo: MICHAEL SHAY/FPG INTERNATIONAL

This book was set in 11/13 Cochin by Stratford Publishing
Services, Inc. and printed and bound by Courier Corpora-
tion. The cover was printed by Phoenix Color Corpora-
tion.

Printed in the United States of America
10 9 8 7 6 5 4 3 2 1 0

ISBN 0-13-907346-9

Prentice-Hall International (UK) Limited, London
Prentice-Hall of Australia Pty. Limited, Sydney
Prentice-Hall Canada Inc., Toronto
Prentice-Hall Hispanoamericana, S.A., Mexico
Prentice-Hall of India Private Limited, New Delhi
Prentice-Hall of Japan, Inc., Tokyo
Pearson Education Asia Pte. Ltd., Singapore
Editora Prentice-Hall do Brasil, Ltda., Rio de Janeiro

Contents

7 Music Before 1600   64

8 The Baroque Style Period (1600–1750)   79

9 Baroque Style Music (1600–1750)   84

14 Early-Romantic Music   160

15 Romantic Opera   190

PART FOUR: ADJUNCT MUSIC

25   North American Popular Music   351

26   Broadway Musical Theater   361

27   Music in the Movies   390

Preface

Perhaps the words that best describe **Listening to Music** are *accessible* and *reader-friendly*. The information and the music are accessible; the language and presentation are reader-friendly. According to one reader, "It's a book you can't get lost in."

The **Third Edition** of *Listening to Music* has been substantially shaped by its advocates: those instructors across North America who have been using it successfully in the classroom as a framework for their courses. Their reactions and opinions, along with those of their teaching assistants and students, are represented in the **Third Edition**.

Among the most popular features have been the composer's biographies. As a result, this new edition includes more than 60 biographies, complete with lists of principal works and their dates. Other additions provide more opportunities for enhancing instruction by introducing diversity and critical thinking issues.

The art of teaching music appreciation has many dedicated and passionate practitioners, all sharing the belief that music is a vital component of a civilized society. *Listening to Music* continues to be a dynamic and still-evolving tool for the study of music in its historical and social contexts.

A close reading of the Table of Contents will clarify the exact sequence of instruction.

Part 1 The Musical Process opens with ways of listening to music, then offers a guide for attending a concert

- where to buy tickets
- how to prepare for the performance
- how to interpret the printed program
- what orchestra members, soloists, and conductors do
- when to applaud.

Further discussions include explanations of typical performing media.

Part 2 The Materials of Music is a multimedia presentation of the elements of music and the introduction of basic concepts and terminology. By allowing students to self-pace their learning, the presentation frees valuable class time for in-depth instruction and discussion.

Part 3 The Common Style Periods in Music progresses chronologically from Gregorian Chant to the present. The music examples chosen to illustrate the style periods have proven their effectiveness over years of actual class use and are representative of today's concert programming. Instruction is reinforced with detailed listening guides and listening insights.

Part 4 Adjunct Music highlights diversity issues in American popular music, Broadway musical theater, music for the movies, and music of world cultures. These topics have been greatly expanded for the **Third Edition**.

NEW TO THE THIRD EDITION

Several Listening Guides are new to this edition. Both the scope and content of the musical examples have been broadened. Additions include performances of works by Clara Schumann, Giuseppe Verdi, Giacomo Puccini, Scott Joplin, and Charles Ives.

We have also expanded coverage of key topics in a number of areas:

- becoming an active concertgoer (audience development)
- exploring the contributions of music to film
- appreciating the important cultural diversity that led to the creation and development of Broadway Musicals.

Another new feature of the **Third Edition** is the inclusion of *Challenge Your Expertise* activities in each chapter. These questions stimulate critical thinking and encourage thorough reading of the chapters.

Also new to **Third Edition** are two exciting supplements for the student: Prentice Hall's exclusive *Companion Website*™ that accompanies **Listening to Music** offers unique tools and support that make it easy for students and instructors to integrate this online study guide with the text: www.prenhall.com/zorn

We are also proud to introduce the Critical Review Guide to the supplements program. Packaged at no additional cost to the student, this 96-page manual contains chapter review material and activities designed to promote critical thinking about music.

SUPPLEMENTARY MATERIALS

Recording Packages

The recordings that accompany the book come in two packages:

1. Four compact discs containing 49 important works discussed in the text.
2. Two cassette tapes containing 36 of the 49 works present in the four CD set

A complete list of music selections can be found inside the book's covers, along with the location of the piece (CD versus cassette), running time, and the text page number where the piece is discussed.

Instructor's Manual with Tests

The Instructor's Manual with Tests contains:

- A detailed outline for a typical 14- to 15-week course
- Chapter-by-chapter teaching opportunities
- Audio-visual resources for class use
- Forms for research reports and concert reports
- An extensive bank of test questions divided by chapter
- Suggestions for maximizing use of the Listening to Music Companion Website

Prentice Hall Custom Tests

This computerized test item file allows you to create your own personalized exams using your own computer. Available for Windows or Macintosh.

Critical Review Guide

This student resource, written by Professor Don Meyer of Lake Forest College, is designed to help students confirm their understanding of text material through handy chapter summaries, and expand their understanding of the music through multiple critical thinking exercises. Best of all, this valuable study aid is free when purchased in a package with *Listening to Music,* **Third Edition**.

Music on the Internet

This 80-page booklet is an invaluable introduction to the ever-expanding Internet universe. In addition to a brief history of the World Wide Web and the mechanics of its use, *Music on the Internet* offers over a dozen pages of exciting music-related websites around the world. Prentice Hall offers this free when purchased in a package with our textbook.

VALUE PACKAGES

The **Third Edition** of *Listening to Music* can be purchased in a package with any of the accompanying ancillary material at a reduced cost to the student. Your campus bookstore can order any of the following shrink-wrapped packages directly from Prentice Hall:

Listening to Music, 4 CD's, Critical Review Guide*
ISBN: 0-13-016081-4

Listening to Music, Critical Review Guide*
ISBN: 0-13-016082-2

Listening to Music, 2 Cassettes, Critical Review Guide*
ISBN: 0-13-016083-0

Listening to Music, 4 CD's, Critical Review Guide*, *Music on the Internet* '99–'00*
ISBN: 0-13-016084-9

Listening to Music, 2 Cassettes, Critical Review Guide*, *Music on the Internet* '99–'00*
ISBN: 0-13-016085-7

*Free item in a package with the textbook.

ACKNOWLEDGMENTS

The production of such a complex project as *Listening to Music, Third Edition* requires the contribution of many talents. I would like to thank the following: special thanks to distinguished announcer Martin Bookspan whose musical expertise, dedication, and love of music permeates this project; James Wayne of Silverdisc Productions and his staff for their assistance in locating and producing the superior recordings; June August, President of Writing That Works, and her staff for editing and suggestions: Bud Therien, Prentice Hall publisher, whose vision guided this innovative project; Christopher T. Johnson, Senior Acquisitions Editor; Jean Lapidus, Prentice Hall production editor, who managed the production; Anne Bonanno Nieglos, Prentice Hall, who designed my manuscript into a beautiful book; Leonard Stein, former Director of the Arnold Schoenberg Institute, for his judicious advice and editing of the chapter on Expressionism; Frederick Lesemann of the University of Southern California, Thornton School of Music, for his editing the chapter on Experimental and Technological Music.

I especially acknowledge my colleague, Professor Karl Swearingen of the University of Southern California, Thornton School of Music, for his innovative state-of-the-art development and construction of the www.prenhall/zorn *Companion Website.*™

I also acknowledge my talented teaching assistants—nearly 100 of them over the past twenty-seven years. With their collaboration I have had the pleasure of presenting the material in this text to thousands of music appreciation students—all of whom helped to shape the project.

Finally, I thank the following colleagues for their suggestions and input for the project: Eleanor Hammer, Los Angeles Valley College; Giulio Ongaro, University of Southern California; Raymond A. Barr, University of Miami; Thomas L. Riis, University of Georgia; Dan Schulz, Walla Walla College; Elaine Morgan, City College of San Francisco; Edward Szabo, East Michigan University; Marc Peretz, Ball State University; Dan Dunavan, Southeast Missouri State University; James Klein, California State University, Stanislaus; Diane Touliatos, University of Missouri, St. Louis; Christine Smith, Middlebury College; K. Marie Stolba, Indiana University, Purdue Campus; Nelson Tandoc, De Anza College; Leo Kreter, California State University, Fullerton; Earl L. Clemens, Northern Illinois University.

Jay Zorn
University of Southern California
Thornton School of Music
Los Angeles

THE NEW YORK TIMES SUPPLEMENTS PROGRAM

THE NEW YORK TIMES and PRENTICE HALL are cosponsoring a Themes of the Times: a program designed to enhance student access to current information of relevance in the classroom.

Through the program, the core subject matter provided in the text is supplemented by a collection of time-sensitive articles from one of the world's most distinguished newspapers, THE NEW YORK TIMES. These articles demonstrate the vital, ongoing connection between what is learned and what is happening in the world around us.

To enjoy the wealth of information of THE NEW YORK TIMES daily, a reduced subscription rate is available in deliverable areas. For information, call toll-free: 1-800-631-1222.

PRENTICE HALL and the NEW YORK TIMES are proud to cosponsor Themes of the Times. We hope it will make the reading of both textbooks and newspapers a more dynamic, involving process.

Unique online study resource . . . the
Companion Website™
www.prenhall.com/zorn

Prentice Hall's exclusive *Companion Website*™ that accompanies *Listening to Music, Third Edition,* offers unique tools and support that make it easy for students and instructors to integrate this online study guide with the text. The site is a comprehensive resource that is organized according to the chapters within the text and features a variety of learning and teaching modules:

FOR STUDENTS:

- **Study Guide Modules** that contain a variety of exercises and features designed to help students with self-study. These modules include:
  - chapter objectives that help students organize key concepts to be learned
  - essay questions that help strengthen critical thinking skills
  - quizzes with multiple-choice, true/false, and fill-in questions that supply instant scoring and feedback on student mastery of core material
  - built-in e-mail routing option that gives students the ability to forward essay responses and graded quizzes to their instructors.
  - many of these activities are enhanced by the use of RealAudio™ to deliver sound and music over the web.

- **Reference Modules** contain Web Destinations and Net Search options that provide the opportunity to expand upon the information presented in the text. Whether through a directory of websites relevant to the subject matter of a chapter or by simplifying key-term searching by automatically inserting terms from the chapter into major search engines, these reference features enable students to quickly reach related information on the web.

- **Communication Modules** include tools such as Live Chat and Message Boards to facilitate online collaboration and communication.

- **Personalization Modules** include our enhanced Help feature that contains a test page for browsers and plug-ins.

FOR INSTRUCTORS:

- **Syllabus Manager**™ tool provides an easy-to-follow process for creating, posting, and revising a syllabus online that is accessible from any point within the companion website. This resource allows instructors and students to communicate both inside and outside of the classroom at the click of a button.

The Companion Website™ makes integrating the Internet into your course exciting and easy. Join us online at the address above and enter a new world of teaching and learning possibilities and opportunities.

COMPANION WEBSITE™

Music Belongs To Everyone

Congratulations for enrolling in this course and for accepting the challenge of sampling more than 400 years of music in a short time. We could not possibly sample all of it during this course because there is so much to listen to, so much to choose from.

You have made yourself part of a powerful audience. As a member of that audience, your choices will have a far-reaching effect on the music of tomorrow, just as yesterday's audiences have influenced the music of today.

The focus of this book is fivefold:

- to give you the tools and experience to build your knowledge of music
- to take that knowledge confidently into any concert hall, auditorium, theater, or opera house throughout the world
- to use your expertise when others ask you questions or seek your insights about particular types of music
- to encourage your active participation in supporting the arts and arts education
- to help you become an intelligent consumer of music and to have a voice in the types of music available to the public.

1

This book is about listening, but the listening experience itself is indescribable—and irreplaceable. Throughout this course, you will have repeated opportunities to listen to music, to develop your personal taste, and to explore your values, which will enable you to make informed choices.

This is only a beginning. Learning about music is a lifetime journey of growth and enjoyment.

Music belongs to everyone—and it will be available to us *for as long as we want it to be.*

Chapter 1

From the Creator to the Listener

Let's begin your musical journey with one of the most important links in the musical process—you. Composers create their music not for other musicians, music critics, or historians, but for you, the listener. Without the listener, music has no audience—the performers play to an empty house.

The musical process originates with the *composer's ideas* and experiences, influenced by the era in which he or she lives. By manipulating the materials of music—*rhythm, melody, texture,* and *expression*—into a coherent *form,* the composer constructs a framework to support his or her creative ideas.

Then, using *music notation,* composers put their ideas on paper. Notation is a system of visual symbols that represent sounds and sound qualities. Performers can then read and interpret these symbols and re-create the composer's ideas through the *performance medium*—the voices or instruments. Transformed into sound, music communicates to you, the *listener.*

THE MUSICAL PROCESS

CREATION
COMPOSER
(creator)

RECREATION
PERFORMER
(recreator)

RESPONSE
PERCEIVER
(listener)

Creation

musical ideas
forms (framework)
musical notation

Recreation

medium

Response

listener-audience

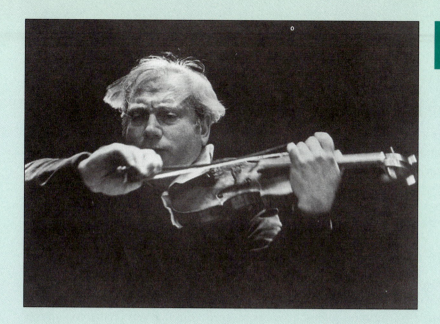

Chapter 2

How to Listen to Music

Looking at a panoramic landscape from a mountain, you have many possible vistas: close, distant, left, right. What you see results from the way you focus your attention. Similarly, the way you listen to music depends on how you focus. As you take in more and more of what you hear, that focus keeps changing.

If you are tired—perhaps after a busy day—you may have less energy with which to follow an intricate piece of music. But during those times when you feel relaxed or adventurous, you may be more willing to accept this challenge.

Music, like all the arts, can accommodate all viewpoints. Each of us perceives music differently. Your listening experience is your private world. There are no restrictions, no "correct" approaches to listening.

Here are the ways in which many concertgoers listen to music:

THE SENSORY LEVEL

Some listeners prefer to let the music wash over them, without giving it much thought. This passive rather than active listening approach can be relaxing—like basking on a beach on a sunny day with the surf rushing back and forth over you. Because the *sensory*

5

level is effortless and soothing, you can allow your brain to idle in neutral and your spine to tingle.

THE EMOTIONAL LEVEL

Music can speak directly to your emotions. If you have ever listened to music and found yourself daydreaming or reminiscing, you were listening on an *emotional level.* On this level, your emotions became part of the listening experience. In your private world, that beautiful melody by Chopin stirred your deepest feelings—the ones that rarely rise to the surface, the ones seldom verbalized.

THE CONTEXTUAL LEVEL

Some music supplies a background for a familiar event, an activity, or an environment. When you hear it, you immediately associate it with some context—a football game, a circus, a graduation. Even "patriotic" music falls into this category. With *contextual listening,* the association may become more important than the music itself.

THE SCRIPT LEVEL

Most music has no specific story for you to follow—although opera, ballet, and film music certainly do. But if you find yourself making up a story or unraveling a plot, you may be listening to music at the *script level.*

Metropolitan Opera star,
Marilyn Horne, mezzo-soprano

THE MUSICALLY ACTIVE LEVEL

Great music has layers of subtleties that invite your involvement. Here, at the *musically active level,* the excitement begins. You may still enjoy the sensory, emotional, and script levels, but as you become more aware, the music engages your heightened understanding, and you are able to enjoy it for its own sake.

Reaching the Musically Active Level

You do not have to be a trained musician to reach this level. Without any extra-musical guidance, pictures, or stories, you can develop the ability to focus on the music itself, understanding and experiencing the composer's creative choices.

When you achieve this awareness, you can follow the musical lines and patterns that the sounds create. You'll notice which instruments are performing, how the musical ideas are passed from instrument to instrument, the type of ornamentation in the melody, the texture or layers of parts, the quality of the harmony, and the forms the composer used to organize the music. The performer's tone quality, phrasing, consistency of style, and faithfulness to the composer's intentions will become clearer to you.

Chapter 4, "How the Basic Musical Elements Interact, and Chapter 5, "Performing Media: Instruments, Voices, and Ensembles" prepare you to reach the musically active level. Then, each piece of music and its background information, discussed in the remaining chapters, will contribute to your experience and enjoyment.

Chapter 3

Becoming a Musically Active Concertgoer

LISTENING ACTIVITY

ATTENDING CONCERTS: MARTIN BOOKSPAN, HOST

| Compact Disc 1, Track 1
| Cassette Tape, Side A, Example 1
| Running Time: 6:00

Your host and coach is Martin Bookspan, noted author, commentator, and announcer for the "Live at Lincoln Center" telecasts from New York City.

WHAT ARE THE DIFFERENT TYPES OF CONCERTS?

Symphony Orchestra

Symphony orchestra concerts are popular throughout the world. The rich variety of sounds emanating from a large orchestra is a marvel of civilized life and culture. With so many different instruments, the combinations of orchestral colors are vast. Talented and disciplined musicians, who have devoted a lifetime to perfecting their skills and intensely competing for positions, perform on instruments crafted by the greatest artisans. Regular concertgoers return year after year to enjoy the broad repertoire that spans nearly 300 years.

Vienna Chamber Orchestra

Chamber Music Ensemble

Two to six musicians generally perform at chamber music concerts. Although a chamber music ensemble may comprise any combination of two to twenty instrumental performers, string quartets and trios and brass and woodwind quintets predominate.

Chamber music was performed in chambers or rooms of the courts and palaces of Europe. Chamber music ensembles have been popular since antiquity.

Chamber Orchestra

The popularity of chamber orchestras has grown rapidly in recent years, especially in cities that already support several symphony orchestras. Music lovers are discovering that bigger is not necessarily better. To hear a chamber music orchestra in the ideal setting, attend a performance in a small-to-medium-sized hall. Much of the great music composed for chamber orchestra loses its original intimacy and clarity when performed by a large symphony orchestra in a hall with 3,000 or more seats. Like speech, musical ideas make more sense when you can hear them distinctly.

Samuel Ramey, bass-baritone

Recital

A recital features one or two musicians. Solo recitals are most commonly performed by singers, pianists, or violinists. The entire setting motivates artists to perform at their best, and they carefully choose music that displays their entire range of musicianship and vocal or instrumental mastery.

Vocal Ensemble

Concerts by vocal or choral ensembles are both vast and rich—a reflection of the long history of group singing. What follows is typical of the concerts you are likely to hear.

Vienna Boy's Choir

Secular Vocal Ensemble

LARGE CHOIRS Varying in size and known by different names, large choirs include *chorales, choral societies, women's choruses, men's choruses, collegiate choirs,* and *gospel choirs.* These ensembles are accompanied by pianos or by instrumental ensembles such as large orchestras, small orchestras, or various combinations of instruments.

SMALL CHOIRS Small vocal ensembles include *a cappella choirs, chamber singers, madrigal choirs, jazz choirs,* or the smaller versions of the large choirs listed above.

Religious Choir

Hearing music in a great church or a cathedral is like traveling back in a time machine. Surrounded by stained-glass windows and elaborate, ornate architecture, you can imagine how it sounded when Johann Sebastian Bach played the organ and conducted the choir in Leipzig, Germany, 275 years ago. Churches and cathedrals have unique acoustics. The music resonates and reverberates in every nook.

Many performances of sacred music still take place in churches, presented as concerts to the general public rather than as religious services. Since an organ is required as the main keyboard instrument, church settings facilitate its use to accompany the singers or the instrument in an instrumental ensemble.

Opera

Perhaps the reason for opera's lasting popularity is the integration of singing, instrumental music, poetry, drama, scenic design, costumes, and dance. The famous opera composer Giuseppe Verdi said, "Opera is passion before everything."

As we will examine later, especially in Baroque Style Music (Chapter 9), Classical Style Music (Chapter 11), and Romantic Style Opera (Chapter 15), the opera tradition goes back about 400 years, with the first productions occurring around 1600.

Broadway, New York City

Broadway Musical Theater

Interest in and attendance at Broadway musical theater productions have soared in recent years. Recent productions such as *Les Misérables, Phantom of the Opera, Miss Saigon, Rent,* and *The Lion King,* using the latest stagecraft and sound technology, have attracted young audiences. New audiences are discovering opera as the disparity decreases between opera and the Broadway musical (see Chapter 26, Broadway Musical Theater).

BALLET   Ballet also creates its effects through a wonderful blending of the arts: dance, drama, set design, costume design, and especially music. The music provides the catalyst for the choreography—specifically designed dance steps and movement. Many great masters have composed explicitly for ballet: Ludwig van Beethoven, Hector Berlioz, Peter Ilyich Tchaikovsky, Maurice Ravel, Igor Stravinsky, Sergei Prokofiev, Aaron Copland, and Leonard Bernstein.

Ballet orchestras usually perform in a pit in front of the stage. The number of players varies according to the music.

HOW CAN I FIND OUT ABOUT CONCERTS AND TICKET SALES

Newspapers

Most concerts are advertised in the entertainment or arts section of newspapers. Look for phone numbers, box-office location, dates and times, performers, and programs.

If you rely solely on newspaper advertisements for concert information, you may not get the best seats. By the time the advertisement appears, the house may have already been sold out.

Mailing Lists

For earliest notification, ask (by phone or a short note) that the concert hall or series management put your name on the mailing list so that you will

Winnipeg Ballet

John Williams

receive advance brochures and order forms. This will enable you to buy tickets by mail before an event and obtain the price and the seats you want.

Season Subscriptions

Once you are on a mailing list, you will receive an invitation to become a season subscriber. Subscribers are offered the best seats. After you determine the series of programs and seats you prefer, you can reserve them for the entire season. Subscribers receive notification of the upcoming concert season before those on the general mailing list.

Box Office

If seats for a particular performance are available, you can always purchase tickets at the box office. Arrive as early as possible. The first time you go to a concert or to a concert hall you are not familiar with, ask box-office personnel to show you a detailed seating plan and to advise you about the best seats.

Student-Rush Seats

Students often may have a considerable advantage over other concertgoers by arriving at the box office within an hour of the concert. Most orchestra concerts, operas, and ballets offer reduced-price, "student-rush" tickets. You must show current student identification, which usually entitles you to purchase only one ticket.

Attending Open Rehearsals

Many opera companies and symphony orchestras have regularly scheduled rehearsals that are open to the public for a small fee. Ask about this at the box office. Observing what goes on in preparation for a performance is fascinating. It is in the rehearsal that conductors and performers do their main work — unifying the interpretation and polishing the performance.

HOW CAN I PREPARE FOR A CONCERT?

Become Acquainted with the Music

As often as possible, listen to recordings of the music that will be featured on the program so you will become familiar with the music. We tend to enjoy the music we know best. Besides preparing for the concert, purchasing the recordings is an excellent way to build your personal record collection.

Municipal and university libraries also can be excellent resources. You can listen to recordings at the library or check them out for a few days. Also, pre-set your radio to your classical music stations (usually FM stations), and you will become familiar with many styles of music.

In addition to the music, get to know the composer, artists, and background of the music. You might find some of this information on the printed inserts that accompany recordings. Composers' biographies are fascinating. Many of the greatest geniuses made human errors in their everyday lives. Their stories are very moving, and you will gain new insight into their compositions.

WHAT DO I NEED TO KNOW BEFORE THE CONCERT BEGINS?

- Allow enough time to arrive at the concert hall early enough to pick up your program, find your seat, and examine the printed program. Some programs are free; others are available for purchase.
- Turn off a phone, a pager, or a watch that beeps. And unless you have permission from the concert management, you may not record, photograph, or videotape the performance.

WHAT CONCERT TRADITIONS DO I NEED TO KNOW ABOUT?

Like every activity that brings people together, music has developed formalities and traditions over hundreds of years. Similar traditions exist in other areas, such as sports. In golf and tennis, for example, the crowd is quiet while a player addresses the ball or prepares to serve. And in football, soccer, and boxing, the fans cheer whenever they feel like it.

Symphony and Chamber Orchestra Procedures

WARM UP   Before the concert, performers randomly enter and take their seats. Players warm up individually, checking the condition of their instruments and adjusting reeds, mouthpieces, bows, strings, and drumheads.

CONCERTMASTER   The concertmaster usually is the last orchestra member to enter the stage. As the conductor's assistant, especially in musical matters, the concertmaster sits at the front of the violin section closest to the conductor.

TUNING   Before the conductor enters, the concertmaster signals the oboe to sound the traditional tuning pitch "A." The placement of the oboe in the center of the orchestra and its unique tone make it especially effective as a tuning instrument. If a work is a piano solo, the instrument is moved out to the center of the stage between the audience and the conductor, and the concertmaster sounds the tuning "A" on the piano.

ENTRANCES AND EXITS OF THE CONDUCTOR AND SOLOISTS   Featured soloists usually enter and exit the stage just ahead of the conductor. If a piece of music does not call for a soloist, then the conductor enters the stage when the players are ready, greets the performers and the audience, mounts a podium, faces the orchestra, raises his or her arms (with or without a baton), and signals the down beat for the start of the music.

WHEN SHOULD I APPLAUD?

Here is the basic guideline:

When in doubt, wait until most of the audience applauds.

Unless you know the music well, avoid rushing to applaud, no matter how moved you are. You will find differences in when to applaud with each type of music.

During an opera, the audience usually applauds after an aria. However, during an instrumental performance a few people are likely to applaud at inappropriate times. For example, applauding during movements of a symphony breaks the continuity of the entire piece. Save yourself embarrassment by checking the printed program for the number of movements. A brief summary of appropriate times to applaud follows:

**Symphony Orchestra, Chamber Orchestra,
and Chamber Ensemble Concerts**
- the concertmaster (first violinist) enters the stage from the wings
- the conductor enters from the wings
- a soloist or soloists enter from the wings
- the orchestra concludes an *entire* piece—symphony, concerto, overture, and so on
- the conductor acknowledges key players, who usually stand
- the conductor signals the orchestra to stand at any time
- the conductor or soloist returns to the stage

**Large, Mixed-Media Productions—Opera,
Broadway Musicals, Ballets, Oratorios**
- the conductor enters the stage or orchestra pit
- the curtain rises on the stage and set (except for very serious works—use previous guideline)
- the star or stars enter
- a powerful song, aria, or ballet display concludes (use previous guideline)
- the curtain comes down
- the soloist, conductor, stage manager, or composer returns to the stage following a performance

WHAT IS THE CONDUCTOR'S ROLE?

As you watch a conductor during a performance, you might get the impression that setting the tempo and beating time are the conductor's main functions. They are not. Almost any member of the orchestra can do those things. As important as beating time is, interpreting the music is more important.

Coordinating the ensemble's performance and *interpreting* the music are the conductor's most important responsibilities. The conductor's downbeat coordinates the start of the performance and sets the tempo, with the orchestra or chorus following and watching for changes.

To understand how conductors convey interpretation, you would have to attend a rehearsal or be on stage and watch how they use their hands, face, and body to urge musicians to play louder or softer, more forcefully or heroically, more smoothly or tenderly. Public television stations regularly broadcast symphony orchestra concerts. Camera close-ups of the conductor's face help reveal the interpretative process.

A soloist adds another dimension to the conductor's work, because the orchestra accompaniment must be coordinated with the soloist's part. If, for instance, the soloist drags the tempo in a certain passage and speeds up in another, the conductor must inspire the entire orchestra to follow. Maintaining the balance between soloist and ensemble ensures that the soloist will be heard above the other instruments.

THE CONDUCTOR AS MUSIC SCHOLAR   It takes a lifetime of study for a conductor to learn the great body of music for symphony orchestra, chorus, ballet, or opera. Guiding an ensemble is demanding: a conductor must research various resources and examine writings about the music. Even a composer's note to a colleague can be informative.

Riccardo Muti

Why Do Some Conductors Use a Baton or Stick?

If you think of the baton as an extension of the conductor's arm, you will understand why the conductor uses one. Players in all parts of the ensemble can see the conductor's beats more clearly. Using the baton to execute patterns maximizes visibility and reduces exertion.

In the past, conductors used other objects—rolled-up music, a violin bow, a cane—but none was as effective as the white baton. In the seventeenth century, the composer and conductor Jean-Baptiste Lully pounded beats on the floor with a wooden staff. During one performance, the story goes he smashed the staff into his foot, which became infected. Lully died of complications, a victim of his own enthusiasm.

How Do Conductors Communicate?

Most conductors use standard conducting patterns that are universally recognized by classically trained musicians and even by many folk and popular music performers. This communication is one example of how music performance can transcend geographic boundaries.

GETTING READY TO PLAY   The conductor mounts the podium, waits until everyone in the orchestra is ready to perform, then raises his or her arms in the "ready" position.

DOWNBEAT   The downbeat is the first beat of any pattern. The conductor moves the baton down from the ready position to somewhere near the front of the waist. When the baton reaches bottom and begins to move upward, the downbeat is complete, and the performers begin to play.

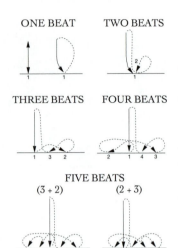

Drawing of standard conducting patterns

Standard Conducting Patterns

The standard conducting patterns are illustrated at left. The *meter,* or grouping of beats in the music, determines the pattern. Most music is grouped in recurring patterns—usually two, three, or four. Used less frequently are patterns of five and six beats.

Conducting Activity

Practice the standard conducting patterns for two, three, and four beats as shown. Then conduct the music on the recording accompanying this text. Here are some suggested selections:

The Two Pattern

CD Disc 1, Track 12	Bach, Brandenburg Concerto No. 2,
Tape: Side B, Ex. 3	Third Movement: moderately fast tempo
CD Disc 1, Track 15	Mozart, Horn concerto No. 2, Third
Tape: Side B, Ex. 6	Movement: fast tempo
CD Disc 3, Track 15	Copland, "Hoe Down" from Rodeo:
Tape: Side D, Ex. 9	very fast

The Three Pattern

CD Disc 1, Track 7	Bach, Cantata No. 140, opening chorus:
Tape: Side B, Ex. 1	moderate tempo
CD Disc 2, Track 1	Haydn, Symphony No. 94, Third
Tape: Side B, Ex. 8	Movement: moderate tempo
CD Disc 1, Track 6	Handel, "For Unto Us a Child Is Born"
Tape: Side A, Ex. 6	from Messiah: moderate tempo

The Four Pattern

CD Disc 1, Track 9	Vivaldi: The Four Seasons, Op. 8, No. 1,
Tape, Side B, Ex. 2	"Spring," first movement

Conductor's Left Hand Indications

EXPRESSION   The conductor's left hand indicates expression. For example, if the trumpets enter too loudly, the conductor, often looking like a police officer halting traffic, motions them to play more softly. Urging the violins to play louder, the conductor might use another left-hand signal.

CUEING   The left hand also signals a performer or section to play. Imagine a cymbal player who has been following the music for fifteen minutes, waiting for his or her part. The conductor's cue increases the player's confidence that the crash of the cymbals will occur at the right moment—and will avoid an embarrassing situation!

WHAT ARE THE TERMS COMMONLY USED IN PERFORMANCE?

On concert programs and throughout this text, you will encounter many commonly used musical terms. Explanations for some of these terms appear in later chapters. Table 3.1 lists the most commonly used terms. (See Glossary for additional terms.)

Left-hand expression: quiet—John Williams, conductor

Challenge Your Expertise

During the performance of a symphony, what should you do if most of the audience begins to applaud at the "wrong" time?

Table 3.1	Common Tempo Terms and Descriptions

From Slow to Fast

grave	extremely slowly and solemnly
largo	very slowly, broadly
lento	slow
adagio	slowly, leisurely
andante	slow to moderate walking pace
moderato	moderate
allegretto	moderately fast
allegro	fast, lively
vivace	very fast
presto	very fast
prestissimo	as fast as possible

Left-hand cue — Neville Marriner

Descriptions Often Used With Tempos

agitato	agitated
animato	animated
cantabile	singing style
con brio	with spirit
con fuoco	with fire
con moto	with movement
e or ed.	and
espressivo	expressively
grazioso	gracefully
ma	but
ma non troppo	but not too much
maestoso	majestically
meno	less
molto	very, much
piu	more
poco	little
poco a poco	little by little, gradually
sostenuto	sustained

Terms Indicating Tempo Changes

accelerando	quickening
ritardando	slowing
rallentando	gradual slowing
rubato	deliberate unsteady tempo

Terms for Loudness Levels From Soft to Loud

Abbreviation	Italian Term	English Meaning
pp or **ppp**	*pianissimo*	very soft
p	*piano*	soft
mp	*mezzopiano*	moderately soft
mf	*mezzoforte*	moderately loud
f	*forte*	loud
ff or **fff**	*fortissimo*	very loud

Terms and Symbols for Changes in Loudness

crescendo	becoming louder
decrescendo	becoming softer
or	
diminuendo	becoming softer

Other Performance Terms

a cappella	choir or voices without accompaniment
glissando	slide from pitch to pitch
legato	connected, smoothly
pizzicato	plucked strings, usually done with player's finger
staccato	detached, separated tones
tremolo	rapid repetitions of a tone or chord
vibrato	pulsating tones for expressiveness

WHAT IS IN THE PRINTED CONCERT PROGRAM?

Tempo indications in the printed program help you keep your place in the music because they show the speed of the movements. For instance, in the program on page 20, notice the indications for Gershwin's Concerto in F Major for Piano and Orchestra. *Allegro* means fast. *Andante con moto*—a moderate walking pace—is much slower. *Allegro con brio,* the third movement, means fast, with spirit. Using Table 3.1, try to figure out what each of the other tempo indications on the London Symphony program means.

Challenge Your Expertise

When is a piano instead of an oboe used to "tune" an orchestra?

WHAT ARE THE CATALOG SYSTEMS FOR COMPOSERS' WORKS?

The designation "Op. 68" after the title of a Beethoven symphony refers to the sequence among his compositions in which he wrote that work—*opus*, meaning "work," in Latin. In this case, Beethoven indicated that Symphony No. 5 was approximately his sixty-eighth work. Most composers were not as consistent as Beethoven in cataloguing their music; therefore, the opus numbers or other designations are rarely precise.

Instead of opus numbers, some composers' works bear other designations assigned much later by the person who catalogued the music. For instance, Ludwig von Köchel (1800–1877) catalogued Mozart's numerous works. Instead of an opus number in the London Symphony Orchestra's program featuring the Mozart Clarinet Concerto, the designation is K. 622. Written only months before Mozart's untimely death in 1791, this concerto was one of Mozart's last works.

Table 3.2 lists some of the most commonly used designations.

Table 3.2	Common Music Catalog Designations	
Composer	**Designation**	**Cataloguer**
Bach, J.S.	BWV (for "Bach-Werke Verzeichnis")	Wolfgang Schmieder: Thematischsystematisches Verzeichnis der musikalischen Werke von Johann Sebastian Bach
Haydn	H. or Hob.	A. von Hoboken
Mozart	K.	Ludwig von Köchel
Schubert	D.	O. E. Deutsch
Vivaldi	R. or P.	Peter Ryom

LONDON SYMPHONY ORCHESTRA
MICHAEL TILSON THOMAS, Conductor

LUDWIG VAN BEETHOVEN

Symphony No. 5 in c minor, Op. 68 (1808)

> Allegro con brio
> Andante con moto
> Allegro, *leading into*
> Allegro

WOLFGANG AMADEUS MOZART

Concerto in A Major for Clarinet and Orchestra, K. 622 (1791)

> Allegro
> Adagio
> Rondo: Allegro

Franz Hoeprich, Clarinet Soloist

Intermission

PETER ILYICH TCHAIKOVSKY

Symphony No. 4 in f minor, Op. 36 (1877)

> Andante sostenuto; Moderato con anima
> Andantino in modo di canzona
> Scherzo: Pizzicato ostinato
> Allegro con fuoco

GEORGE GERSHWIN

Concerto in F Major for Piano and Orchestra (1925)

> Allegro
> Andante con moto
> Allegro con brio

Michael Tilson Thomas, Piano Soloist/Conductor

How the Basic Musical Elements Interact

MULTIMEDIA PRESENTATION

The basic elements and the media through which they are performed make up the materials of music. To help you understand the basic elements, this chapter is coordinated with a compact disc that contains both music and visuals. The printed part of this chapter is a summary of the materials to assist you after you have worked through the disc.

SUGGESTED SEQUENCE   First, navigate through the recording while looking at the text. When you are comfortable with that presentation, close your text and try to understand the presentation only through the audio. Your goal is to understand music through its sounds.

Chapter 4

LISTENING GUIDE

ELEMENTS OF MUSIC:
MARTIN BOOKSPAN, HOST

Compact Disc 1, Track 2
Cassette Tape, Side A, Example 2
Running Time: 30:06

MUSIC
Leonard Bernstein,
Candide Overture

Composers use an assortment of sound materials—*the elements of music*—to organize their ideas. Just as painters use colors, shapes, light, and textures to create their works, composers use *rhythms, scales, melodies, harmonies,* and *textures* to create theirs.

RHYTHM (DURATION OF SOUND)

Music is a temporal art, existing in time. Sounds occur and continue for a certain duration, flowing at specific rates of speed, or tempos. You may have referred to this as *rhythm.* While listening, we flow along in time with the music, as though on a journey, for as long as it lasts.

Beat

MUSIC
Recurring drumbeat

MUSIC
Scott Joplin, "The Entertainer"

MUSIC
Claude Debussy,
Afternoon of a Faun

PROMINENT BEAT   When the beat is *prominent,* responding to it is easy. Even babies and animals react to a recurring, thumping beat. The beat motivates us to move—to snap our fingers, tap our feet, sway, dance, march, or exercise. An example of a prominent beat is Scott Joplin's rag, "The Entertainer."

WEAK BEAT   Some music has a *weak beat,* creating a feeling of floating, drifting, or gliding, as in Claude Debussy's *Afternoon of a Faun.*

Tempo

The speed, or *tempo,* of the music also affects us. A slow tempo may evoke a mood of reflection or may help us relax. A brisk tempo can lift our spirits. You won't find soldiers marching or aerobics classes exercising to music with a slow tempo. Both activities depend on the uplift that a fast tempo creates.

Metronome

Metronome Markings

MUSIC
Metronome ticking at 84 beats per minute

We can measure the speed or tempo of the beat with a device called a *metronome,* invented in 1816 by Johann Maelzel (1772–1838).

Composers usually indicate the tempos for playing their works by notating the metronome setting at the beginning of the music. A tempo indication of 84 in the music means that the basic beats should proceed at 84 beats per minute, which is a good tempo for a graduation march, for example, Edward Elgar's march *Pomp and Circumstance.*

Without a metronome, you can measure tempo the same way you measure your pulse. First, find your pulse on the inside of your wrist, below your thumb. Turn off the recording and count the number of pulse beats in 20 seconds, using a timer or the second hand of a watch. Then turn the tape on again. Do that now.

In 20 seconds, you probably counted 22 to 30 beats. Multiply the *number* you counted by three, and you'll have your pulse rate.

Now try to measure the tempo of "Hoe Down" from Aaron Copland's ballet *Rodeo*. Using a second hand or a stopwatch, count the number of beats you hear in 20 seconds.

PERCEPTION OF TEMPO   Our perception of whether a tempo is fast or slow tends to correspond to our individual pulse rate. We perceive a tempo as moderate (*moderato* in Italian) when it is close to our own pulse, usually between 65 and 90 beats per minute.

Listen to George Gershwin's "Prelude II," which runs about 84 beats per minute. How did you react to a tempo close to your own pulse?

STEADY TEMPO   The tempo in most music usually remains steady—especially if dancers or marchers are trying to move with the music.

FLEXIBLE TEMPO (RUBATO)   Did you notice that the tempo of the Gershwin piece was not entirely steady? In highly personal and emotional music, the performer often uses a flexible approach to the beat. The musical term for this is *rubato,* meaning "robbed" in Italian. To execute rubato, performers vary the pace of the music slightly by increasing the speed for some beats and slowing it down for others.

Listen again to Gershwin's "Prelude" and notice how the performer conveys the emotional quality of the music through rubato.

Meter (Groupings of Beats)

Rhythmic groupings in most concert music are predictable. Created by stressed and unstressed beats, the recurring group is called a *meter.* Two, three, and four beats are the most common meters.

TRIPLE METER   Waltzes, for instance, use recurring rhythmic patterns of three beats, usually with the first beat of the pattern accented. A three-beat pattern is called a *triple meter.*

/		/		/		/		/		/
ONE	-	two	-	three	-	ONE	-	two	-	three
STRONG	-	weak	-	weak	-	STRONG	-	weak	-	weak
BEAT	-	beat	-	beat	-	BEAT	-	beat	-	beat

Measuring Tempos

MUSIC
Edward Elgar, *Pomp and Circumstance,* March No. 1

MUSIC
Aaron Copland, "Hoe Down" from *Rodeo*

MUSIC
George Gershwin, Prelude II (tempo: 84 beats per minute)

MUSIC
George Gershwin, Prelude II, *Andante con moto e poco rubato* (walking tempo with movement and a little rubato)

Listen to the triple meter in this waltz.

MUSIC
Johann Strauss
(the Younger)
Blue Danube Waltz

DUPLE METER   Because marches are intended for marchers with *two* feet, recurring groups of two, or *duple meter*, are standard:

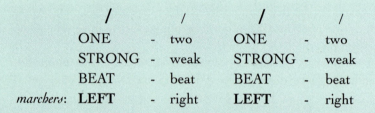

/		/		/		/	
ONE	-	two	ONE	-	two		
STRONG	-	weak	STRONG	-	weak		
BEAT	-	beat	BEAT	-	beat		
marchers: LEFT	-	right	LEFT	-	right		

MUSIC
John Philip Sousa's
march *The Stars and
Stripes Forever*, trio section

DETERMINING THE METER   Here is how to determine the meter of the music: Listen for the recurring pattern of strong, accented beats and weak, unaccented beats. Mark the beats on a piece of paper. Indicate an accented beat with a long line and an unaccented beat with a shorter line.

Examples:
Duple

Triple

Quadruple

You will now hear the opening section of the overture to the opera *Die Meistersinger* by Richard Wagner. Determine the meter by marking on your paper the accented and unaccented beats.

Did you hear the four pattern, or *quadruple meter*?

Listen to this next example and figure out the meter by marking the beats.

The music is a *minuet* by Joseph Haydn. The minuet was a popular *triple-meter* dance in the eighteenth century.

LESS COMMON METERS   If you cannot fit two, three, or four beats in a pattern, chances are you are listening to music with a less common meter, such as five, seven, or eleven.

Listen to "Take Five" by jazz composer Paul Desmond of the Dave Brubeck Quartet. Can you hear the five-beat meter?

MULTIPLE OF TWO (DUPLE METER)   You may perceive meters such as four and eight as *duple meter*. Meters that are multiples of two tend to sound like a duple meter. Without looking at the printed notation, you will often not recognize the difference.

MULTIPLES OF THREE (TRIPLE METER)   The same holds true for some multiples of three, such as six, nine, and twelve. A listener may hear them as *triple meter*.

SIX BEATS   Six is a multiple both of two and three. Depending on the tempo, you may hear six beats as either duple or triple meter.

SYNCOPATION   Some music, especially jazz, uses rhythm patterns with unexpected accents. Or, there may be silence where you would anticipate an accent. This type of rhythm is called *syncopation*.

Listen again to Scott Joplin's ragtime piece "The Entertainer." Joplin used syncopated rhythms throughout.

MUSIC

Richard Wagner, Overture to *Die Meistersinger von Nürnberg*, opening section

Minuet

MUSIC

Joseph Haydn, Symphony No. 94, third movement

MUSIC

Paul Desmond, "Take Five"

Ahmad Jamal Trio

Jazz rhythms

MUSIC

Scott Joplin, "The Entertainer"

MUSIC
Igor Stravinsky, *The Rite of Spring*, "Sacrificial Dance"

MUSIC
Ludwig van Beethoven, Piano Sonata No. 8, Op. 13, first movement

Printed Notes

MUSIC
Felix Mendelssohn, Violin Concerto, first movement

MUSIC
Arnold Schoenberg, *Suite for Piano*, "Praeludium"

MUSIC
Ludwig van Beethoven, Symphony No. 5, first movement

RHYTHMIC OSTINATO   Twentieth-century composers are especially fond of using a repetitive pattern called *rhythmic ostinato*. Jazz, rock, and dance music often depend on ostinato for the driving rhythm that motivates movement. Listen for the ostinato in the next piece by Igor Stravinsky.

SILENCE   Silence also is an important part of music. Listen to the opening of this piano sonata by Ludwig van Beethoven. Notice how the moments of silence create a dramatic effect.

PITCH (MELODY AND HARMONY)

Pitches or tones are the materials of *melodies* and *harmonies*. Pitches appear on paper as *notes*. Performers read the notes and play or sing the corresponding pitches.

Melody

A melody is a succession of individual pitches that makes sense when you perceive them as a group. This is similar to perceiving a complete sentence from a group of individual words. Listen to this section from Felix Mendelssohn's Violin Concerto. Notice how the succession of pitches creates a coherent melody.

Describing Melodies

As listeners, we can describe melodies and pitches in a number of ways.

PROMINENT OR NOT PROMINENT   Is the melody *prominent* or *not prominent*? A prominent melody forms a coherent whole. You can often hum or remember a prominent melody after you've heard it a few times. You can even follow it the first time you hear it. A melody is *not prominent* if you have trouble following it. When a succession of pitches sounds fragmented or aimless, you can describe the melody as *not prominent*.
   Listen to this twentieth-century piece by Arnold Schoenberg. Because the melody sounds fragmented, you may find it a challenge to remember or to hum it. For this reason, you probably would describe it as *not prominent*.

LENGTH OF PHRASE   Another aspect of a melody is its length of *phrase*, or melodic idea. Is the melodic idea *short* or *long*?

SHORT MELODIC IDEA   What we notice immediately about Beethoven's Symphony No. 5 is the unusual shortness of the opening phrase. Beethoven uses this short statement as a structural element throughout the first movement. A melodic idea used in this manner is called a *melodic motive*.

Listen again as the orchestra plays this section of Beethoven's Symphony No. 5. Notice how the rhythmic idea (short, short, short, long) persists, even when the melody changes. Therefore, the opening motive is also a *rhythmic motive*.

LONG MELODIC IDEA   Contrast Beethoven's short idea to the longer idea in Wagner's Overture to *Die Meistersinger*.

CADENCES   Notice how the melody keeps moving forward until it seems to arrive at a resting place. In music, we call these arrivals *cadences*.

ORNAMENTED MELODIES   Some melodies are plain, for example, the opening of Beethoven's Symphony No. 5. Others are ornamented with trills and embellishments. The type of *ornamentation* used is often a matter of the prevailing taste and fashion of the composer's time.

Listen to this section of Wolfgang Amadeus Mozart's variations of the French folk song "Ah, vous dirai-je maman." We know it as "Twinkle, Twinkle, Little Star." First, the plain, unornamented melody:

TRILLS.   Now listen to the variations. Mozart ornaments the melody with *trills*—a rapid alternation of two pitches.

Repetition, Imitation, and Sequence

Composers want you to become familiar with their melodic ideas. To help you, they may use musical devices such as *repetition, imitation,* and *sequence*.

REPETITION   Hearing a phrase or a melody again enables you to recognize it quickly. Repetition is like bringing a character from a play back on stage.

Listen to the catchy "Turkish March" by Mozart. You may be able to memorize it the first time you hear it, but Mozart eases the job by repeating it for you.

MUSIC
Richard Wagner, Overture to *Die Meistersinger von Nürnberg*, opening section

MUSIC
Wolfgang Amadeus Mozart, main theme. Variations "Ah, vous dirai-je maman," K. 265.

MUSIC
Wolfgang Amadeus Mozart, K. 265, Variation No. 12

MUSIC
Wolfgang Amadeus Mozart, "Turkish March" from Sonata in A Major, K. 331

IMITATION   *Imitation* is a form of repetition. We hear a motive or a melody. Shortly thereafter, we hear it played again, either by another voice or instrument or by the same voice or instrument in a higher or lower range. That restatement is called *imitation.*

MUSIC
Johann Sebastian Bach, *Brandenburg Concerto No. 2,* third movement.

Listen to this section from Johann Sebastian Bach's *Brandenburg Concerto No. 2.* Notice how the melody, stated first by the trumpet, is imitated by the oboe, then by the violin, and finally by the flute.

Canons and rounds. A *canon* is an imitation that continues throughout an entire work. Examples are "Row, Row, Row Your Boat" and "Frère Jacques." We sometimes refer to these songs as *rounds* or *circle canons*: different voices keep coming around to the same melody.

SEQUENCE   *Sequences* are another form of repetition: the same instrument repeats the melodic idea, using slightly different pitches.

MUSIC
Ludwig van Beethoven, Piano Sonata No. 8, Op. 13, opening

MUSIC
Ludwig van Beethoven, Symphony No. 5, first movement

Listen again to the opening of the Beethoven piano sonata. Beethoven takes the opening motive through a series of sequences.

Listen for *repetition, imitation,* and *sequences* in the opening section of the first movement of Beethoven's Symphony No. 5. Notice how Beethoven manipulates the melodic motive using different pitches. This is called a *sequence.* Then the motive is passed around the orchestra. This is called *imitation.*

Notice which instruments imitate the motive until that section comes to a cadence. First you will hear the violins in a low range. Then the violas imitate the melody. Next the violins continue the imitation in a higher range. Then the full orchestra repeats the opening statement, followed by *imitation* and *sequences,* until the next cadence.

Scales

Scales consist of ascending or descending pitches arranged in specified patterns. Most melodies in Western concert music are based on one of two common scales: *major* and *minor.*

MAJOR SCALE   In general, the major scale has a bright, happy quality.

MUSIC
C major scale and chord

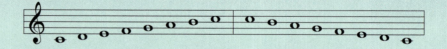

MINOR SCALE   The minor scale has a more plaintive quality.

MUSIC
c minor scale and chord

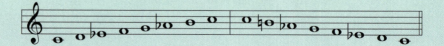

While you listen to concert music, try to discern the major or minor quality of the music you hear. The way the music makes you feel can sometimes be a clue.

OTHER SCALES To add freshness to their music, many twentieth-century composers have organized pitches in scale patterns other than major and minor. These innovations will be discussed in later chapters.

Harmony

Combinations of pitches sounded simultaneously create harmony. You will now hear three pitches. First they are sounded individually, as they would be in a melody. Then they are sounded together to form harmony.

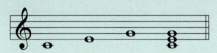

CHORD When those three pitches were sounded simultaneously, they become a *chord*—a major chord.

CONSONANT CHORDS The chord you just heard evokes a feeling of stability and *balance*. This type of chord is *consonant*. Listen to it again.

DISSONANT CHORDS In some chords, the pitches within the chord seem to clash with one another. They may even sound unpleasant or disagreeable to you. These types of chords are *dissonant*.

Listen to these three chords. You'll have no trouble picking out the one dissonant chord from the two consonant chords.

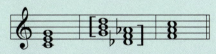

Did you recognize the second chord as the dissonant one? If not, listen again.

MAJOR AND MINOR CHORDS We also describe chords by their quality, referring to them as *major chords* or *minor chords*.

Listen now to five chords that alternate between major and minor chords, starting and ending with major.

TEXTURES

With these musical threads—*rhythms, scales, melodies,* and *harmonies*—composers weave their ideas into *textures.* Using layers of sounds, they create a musical fabric. Most concert music employs three types of texture: *monophonic, homophonic,* and *polyphonic.*

James Galway, flutist

MUSIC
Pitches C, E, and G individually, then together

MUSIC
C major chord

MUSIC
consonant and dissonant chords

MUSIC
C major, f minor, E-flat major, a minor, and D-flat major

MUSIC

Ludwig van Beethoven, Piano Sonata No. 8, Op. 13, second movement (melody only)

MUSIC

Ludwig van Beethoven, Piano Sonata No. 8, Op. 13, second movement (original form)

MUSIC

George Frideric Handel, *Messiah,* Chorus: "For Unto Us a Child Is Born"

MONOPHONIC TEXTURE   A *monophonic texture* is a melody without harmony, other melodic lines, or accompaniment.

HOMOPHONIC TEXTURE   Seldom does music use monophonic texture. The most common texture is a melody with a harmonic accompaniment of some sort. This combination of melody and chordal accompaniment is called *homophonic texture.* An example of this texture would be produced by a singer with guitar accompaniment.

Here is the same Beethoven melody supported by a harmonic accompaniment. Notice the *homophonic texture.*

POLYPHONIC TEXTURE   *Polyphonic texture* is more complicated. In polyphonic texture, you hear several independent, overlapping melodic lines.

Listen to this opening section of "For Unto Us a Child Is Born" from George Frideric Handel's *Messiah.* The constant overlapping of melodic lines is an example of *polyphonic texture.*

CONCLUSION   You have just heard some of the basic materials used in music—*rhythms, scales, melodies, harmonies,* and *textures.* As you listen to the remaining recorded music with this book, you will become more familiar with the works.

Itzhak Perlman

Challenge Your Expertise

- What two things do a waltz and a minuet have in common?
- What term describes a melody or a section of the music that comes to a conclusion?

Table 4.1	Summary of Basic Musical Elements*

Rhythm (Duration of Sound)

beat prominence: strong, weak	rubato
tempo: slow, medium, fast	ostinato
meter: duple, triple, quadruple, other	rhythmic motive
less frequently used groupings	silence
	syncopation

Melody

prominent	imitation
not prominent	sequences
short phrase	repetition
long phrase	scales: major, minor
cadence	other scales: chromatic,
ornamented	pentatonic, whole-tone,
plain	gapped, tone-row

Harmony

mostly consonant	major and minor chords
mostly dissonant	

Texture

monophonic
polyphonic
homophonic

*See Appendix D for a more complete summary of the Basic Musical Elements.

Chapter 5

Performing Media:
Instruments, Voices,
and Ensembles

Performers bring music to life. By singing or playing instruments, performers achieve the second step in the musical process: delivering composers' ideas to you, the listener.

Dedicated to giving the best possible performances, musicians not only spend a lifetime perfecting their skills but also constantly search for better and more interesting instruments. To meet these demands, manufacturers continually improve their traditional instruments and occasionally introduce new ones, most recently, electronic and computer-generated instruments.

ACOUSTICS OF VOCAL
AND INSTRUMENTAL SOUND

All voices and musical instruments need three basic components to function: an *energy source,* a *vibrating element,* and a *resonating chamber.* An energy source (air, bow, mallets) sets a vibrating element (strings, lips, vocal cords) into motion. For the sound to be audible, a resonating chamber (tube, drum, wooden box) must amplify it. Air waves then carry the sound to the listener.

Try it yourself. Put your fingers on your larynx. Take a breath and exhale, saying "ah." Your exhaled breath is the energy source that makes your vocal cords vibrate. Your mouth and head cavities serve as resonating chambers that shape and amplify the sound.

Notice the difference between the sounds you produce when your mouth is closed and when it is open. Also notice that the more energy you exert, the louder the sound you produce.

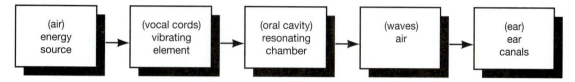

| (air) energy source | → | (vocal cords) vibrating element | → | (oral cavity) resonating chamber | → | (waves) air | → | (ear) ear canals |

Instrumental Performing Media

Instruments fall into at least one of six categories:

- string
- woodwind
- brass
- percussion
- keyboard
- electronic

How Instruments Produce Sound

Many variables contribute to an instrument's tone and sound production. Differences in size, shape, and construction materials alter *timbre*—the quality of the tone. Table 5.1 presents an overview of the acoustical components of the most common musical instruments.

Timbre
(*tam*-ber)

The Juilliard String Quartet

Table 5.1		Acoustics of Commonly Used Instruments		
	Instrument	**Energy**	**Vibrator**	**Resonator**
woodwind	flute/piccolo	air	air over mouth hole	metal tube
	oboe	air	double reed	wood tube
	English horn	air	double reed	wood tube
	clarinet	air	single reed	wood tube
	bassoon	air	double reed	wood tube
	saxophone	air	single reed	metal tube
brass	trumpet	air	player's lips	brass tube
	French horn	air	player's lips	brass tube
	trombone	air	player's lips	brass tube
	baritone horn	air	player's lips	brass tube
	tuba	air	player's lips	brass tube
string	violin	bow	string	wood box
	viola	bow	string	wood box
	cello	bow	string	wood box
	string bass	bow	string	wood box
	harp	finger	string	wood box
	guitar	finger or pick	string	wood box
	mandolin	finger or pick	string	wood box
	banjo	finger or pick	string	wood box
percussion	cymbals	hands/arms	cymbals	metal disks
	snare drum	hands/arms w/sticks	drumhead (plastic or skin)	metal or wood cylinder
	bass drum	w/mallet	drumhead	wood cylinder
	timpani	w/mallets	timpani heads	metal bowls
keyboard	piano	fingers/hammers	strings	wood box
	harpsichord	fingers/plectrum	strings	wood box
	organ	fingers/air	air columns	metal and wood pipes
	celesta	fingers/hammers	steel bars	wood box
electronic	synthesizer	fingers/electricity	transistors	loudspeaker

PERFORMING MEDIA AND PERFORMANCES: SOLO INSTRUMENTS AND ENSEMBLES

Solo Recitals

A recital can feature almost any instrument. Except for keyboard performances, recitals most typically present a soloist with an accompanist. For example, a violinist or cellist usually has a piano accompanist.

Ensembles

Although any combination of instrumentalists can play together in an *ensemble,* here are the most common:

SMALL ENSEMBLES   Combinations of only a few instruments are called *chamber ensembles.*

> **String trio:** one violin, one viola, one cello
> **String quartet:** two violins, one viola, one cello
> **Woodwind quintet:** one flute, one oboe, one clarinet, one French horn, and one bassoon
> **Brass quintet:** two trumpets, one French horn, one trombone, and one tuba

LARGE ENSEMBLES   The *symphony orchestra* and the *wind ensemble* are the most common large instrumental ensembles. Both ensembles may vary in size and instrumentation, according to the demands of the music. For special works, unusual instruments may be brought in. Our discussion of these ensembles begins with the symphony orchestra.

THE ORCHESTRA AND ITS INSTRUMENTS

Classical music concerts by symphony orchestras are by far the most popular and well attended. Concertgoers love the rich variety of tone colors emanating from the individual instruments as well as from the ensemble as a whole. Artistic directors of orchestras have an extensive body of works to choose from. Many of the large orchestral works have maintained a broad appeal from one generation to the next.

New York Woodwind Quintet

Chamber ensembles

Canadian Brass Quintet

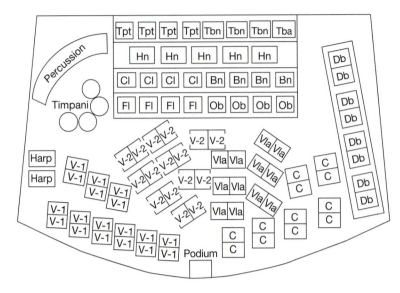

Typical Large Symphony Orchestra Seating Arrangement

Table 5.2	Number of Performers in Typical Orchestra		
Section	**Instrument**	**Abbreviation**	**Number in Orchestra**
String	first violins	V-1	18
	second violins	V-2	16
	violas	Vla	12
	cellos	C	12
	double basses	Db	8
Woodwind	flutes (including piccolo)	Fl	4
	oboes (including English horn)	Ob	4
	clarinets	Cl	2–4
	bassoons (including contrabassoon)	Bn	2–4
Brass	trumpets	Tpt	4
	French horns	Hn	4–6
	trombones (including bass trombone)	Tbn	3–4
	tuba	Tba	1
Percussion	cymbals		1
	snare drum		1
	bass drum		1
	timpani		2–6
	chimes, marimba, bells, xylophone, triangle, miscellaneous		1
	harp		1–2

Sections of the Orchestra

Modern orchestras use similar seating arrangements for the four main sections: *string, woodwind, brass,* and *percussion.* A conductor may vary the seating somewhat at his or her discretion. The figure on page 36 shows the approximate placement of the instruments, and Table 5.2 shows the typical number of instruments used in today's major orchestras.

STRING SECTION   With more than half of the musicians playing *violins, violas, cellos* (short for *violoncellos*), and *string basses,* the string section is the foundation of the orchestra.

The violins, the smallest of the string family, have the highest pitch range. Divided into two subsections—first and second violins—all the violinists sit together next to the conductor (see figure on page 36). Much of the time, you will hear the first violins carry the melody or theme in an orchestral piece. Sometimes the second violins play the same melody as the first violins; at other times, they play a harmony part.

Similar in appearance to a violin, the viola is slightly larger and plays in a lower range. Violas are usually placed next to the violins, as shown in the chart.

Although similar in shape to both the violin and the viola, the cello (or violoncello) is much larger. Cellists, who place their heavy instruments between their legs, often use a special forward-tilting chair for balance. A long pin supports the bottom of the instrument on the floor. Because of its larger size and longer strings, the cello produces pitches in a range lower than those of either the violin or the viola. You will most often find the cellos to the right of the conductor, toward the front of the stage.

The bass, the largest string instrument, is also known by several other names: double bass, contrabass, bass viol, standing bass, string bass. A bass player may perform standing up or partially sitting or leaning on a tall stool, usually behind the cellos on the outer edge of the orchestra.

String players produce sounds by drawing a *bow* across the strings. For a special effect, strings may be plucked (*pizzicato,* in Italian). To soften and change the timbre, string players can use a device called a *mute* on their instruments.

WOODWIND SECTION   Usually seated directly in front of the conductor behind the strings, the woodwinds make up the second most important section of the orchestra. The full section consists of *piccolo, flutes, oboes, English horn, clarinets, bassoons,* and *contrabassoon. Saxophones* may occasionally join the woodwind section for modern or jazz-influenced music.

Originally, all woodwind instruments were made of wood. Now, flutes and piccolos are nearly always metal. Whether wood or metal, all modern woodwinds have elaborate keying mechanisms that facilitate rapid playing.

Playing in the highest range of the flute section and the entire orchestra is the piccolo (Italian for "small"), the smallest woodwind. The flute is

Orchestra violin section

Violin
(vy-uh-*lin*)

Viola
(vee-*oh*-luh)

Cello
(*chel*-oh)

Violoncello
(*vee*-uh-lun-*chel*-oh)

String bass
(bayse)

Bow
(bo)

Pizzicato
(pits-ih-*kah*-toh)

Mute

Flute

Piccolo
(*pik*-uh-loh)

Members of an orchestra's woodwind section (left to right: flute, oboe, bassoon, clarinet)

English horn

Oboe

Clarinet

Saxophone

Bassoon

Contrabassoon

next in range and size. A flutist or piccolo player produces tones by blowing across a hole at the head of the instrument.

Placed next to each other, the oboe and the English horn both have a set of double reeds. The oboe has a highly audible, "reedy" sound. Its pitches are consistent and easily heard. For this reason, the first oboist usually sounds the "A" for the orchestra to tune by.

Slightly larger than the oboe, the English horn is distinguished by the curved pipe between its reeds and the body of the instrument. Neither English nor a horn, the instrument probably received its name because someone noticed that it resembled an angled hunting horn. In the early nineteenth century, when the instrument was introduced, "cor anglé" ("angled horn" in French) sounded similar to "cor anglais" ("English horn"). The name stuck.

Clarinets use a single reed. Capable of a wide range of pitches and timbres, these instruments vary in size from smaller, high-pitched soprano clarinets to large, deep-pitched bass clarinets. The instrument's upper register, higher than an oboe's, can be heard above the orchestra. The middle register can sound mellow, and the lower register, rich and "woody."

Saxophones also use a single reed. Although they have always been made of brass, saxophones are included in the woodwind category. The instruments range in size from the high soprano saxophones to the low baritones and basses.

With its double reeds, the bassoon is closely related to the oboe. Both the bassoon and its larger version, the contrabassoon, are made of large wooden tubes, with long pipes connecting their reeds to the body of the instrument.

BRASS SECTION   The brass section, named for the construction material of its instruments, includes *trumpets, French horns, trombones,* and *tubas.* Because the brass instruments are powerful enough to produce the loudest sounds in the orchestra, they usually are placed behind the woodwinds, or in the outer ring of the orchestra.

All brass players produce sounds by forcing air through their lips, which creates a buzzing or vibration that is funneled into the instrument through a mouthpiece. Then, the unique construction of the individual instrument shapes and resonates these initial sounds differently.

Smallest of the section, the trumpets produce the highest tones. Depending on the requirements of a particular piece, players use trumpets of different sizes and pitches.

Distinguished from the other brasses by its mellower tones, the French horn can produce a wide range of pitches. This versatile instrument can easily blend with either the woodwinds or the brass section. Though not visible in the photo on page 39, the horn player's right hand is partially inside the bell.

Playing in the middle and lower ranges of the brass section, the trombone is the only brass instrument without valves. Instead, the instrument

Trumpet

French Horn

Trombone

has a telescoping slide that changes the length of its tubing, and therefore its pitch.

Music often calls for the addition of a bass trombone. Its larger tubing and slightly larger bell make it capable of playing low and loudly.   **Bass trombone**

The tuba, easily recognized by its size, is the largest brass instrument and is capable of playing the lowest tones in the section. To prevent the tuba from overpowering other instruments in the orchestra, its bell is pointed toward the ceiling.   **Tuba**

The sousaphone, a popular marching band instrument (not an orchestra brass), is similar to a tuba. Named for "the March King," John Philip Sousa (1854–1932), the sousaphone is shaped so a player can carry it while marching.

Placing various mutes into the bell of a brass instrument will change its sound. The cone-shaped "straight" mute makes any of the brass instruments sound more like a woodwind instrument. The "cup" mute mellows sounds, and the "wa-wa" mute often is used in jazz pieces.   **Brass mutes**

PERCUSSION SECTION   Percussionists usually are placed at the outer perimeter of the ensemble. Members of this section strike, rub, shake, jiggle, pound, beat, or crash their instruments to produce a host of specialized sounds.

Challenge Your Expertise

- In terms of creating sound, what does a violin bow have in common with a pair of drumsticks?
- Which instrument is the smallest of the woodwinds?

Members of an orchestra's brass section (front, left to right: French horn, trumpet; rear: trombones)

Orchestra percussion section (left to right): bass drum, tom tom, timbale, marimba, snare drums, conga drum, timpani, bass drum. Photo: Robert Millard ©

Drums

Some percussion instruments—chimes, glockenspiel, celesta, bells, xylophone, and marimba—play defined pitches. Others do not, including drums of various sizes and shapes. Snare and field drums are played with sticks. Others, such as the bass drum, are played with padded mallets. Still others, such as the bongos and conga drums, are played with the hands.

Timpani
(*tim*-pa-nee)

The timpani, or kettledrums, deserve special mention for two reasons. First, they were the first percussion instruments to join the symphony orchestra. They made their debut in an opera orchestra around 1670. Later, Johann Sebastian Bach used them in some of his larger works. Two timpani were standard in Mozart's and Haydn's orchestras. In the nineteenth century, a third, fourth, and even more timpani joined the symphony orchestra when needed for particular works.

Second, they are the only drums tuned to specific pitches. Consisting of large, shiny copper bowls, timpani are impressive. Each bowl is topped with a stretched skin or a plastic head. The player uses an assortment of padded mallets to produce the desired effects. A pedal mechanism on today's timpani facilitates changing pitches and retuning during performances.

Exotic Instruments

Various cultures have contributed to the percussion section:

Africa: drums, wood blocks, gourds, xylophone
Islamic North Africa and Turkey: various cymbals, triangle, bass drum
Asia: Korean temple blocks, Chinese gongs, Indonesian finger cymbals

South and Central America: maracas, timbales, bongos, conga drum, claves, cowbell

Europe: castanets, tambourine

For a more detailed discussion of the contributions of world cultures to Western concert music, see Chapter 28.

The Turkish cymbals in the orchestra are either crashed together or hit with a stick or a mallet. Since a player may have to wait through pages of music for a brief cymbal part, a percussionist often plays other instruments in the section.

Almost any sound can be included in the percussion section: whips, thunder, bird calls, breaking glass, crashing cars, blasting cannons, firing rifles, roaring aircraft, and an infinite variety of electronically produced effects. George Gershwin called for taxi horns to add realistic street sounds in his orchestral piece *An American in Paris*. Ottorino Respighi enhanced the atmosphere of *The Pines of Rome* by adding recordings of genuine bird calls.

Sound effects

Note: All the recordings in this chapter will be discussed in more detail later in the text. In most cases, the text also contains a detailed listening guide for each work.

HOW DO I BECOME FAMILIAR WITH THE INSTRUMENTS?

Associating the sounds you hear with the instruments you see at concerts or on television is the best way to become familiar with them. Use the next listening activity to become acquainted with the instruments.

Zubin Mehta conducting the New York Philharmonic

LISTENING ACTIVITY

THE YOUNG PERSON'S GUIDE TO THE ORCHESTRA (1946), OPUS 34, BENJAMIN BRITTEN

Form: Theme, Variations, and Fugue
Performing Medium: Symphony Orchestra with Narrator

Compact Disc 4, Track 23
Running Time: 18:07

As you listen to *The Young Person's Guide to the Orchestra* by Benjamin Britten, follow along with the Listening Guide. Narrator Will Geer introduces the sections and individual instruments of the orchestra using a narration written by Benjamin Britten. As each instrument is introduced, notice its sound when it performs with its section and then later as a solo instrument.

Written to introduce concertgoers to orchestral instruments, *The Young Person's Guide to the Orchestra* is a set of variations and a fugue based on a theme by the seventeenth-century English composer Henry Purcell (*Pur*-sl, 1659–1695).

The work is in three sections, with a coda:

Main Theme	13 Variations	Fugue	Coda

Part one is a statement of Purcell's theme. The entire orchestra plays the theme. Next, each section plays it in turn—starting with the woodwinds, the brasses, the strings, and finally the percussion section.

Part two is a set of thirteen variations on Purcell's theme. Britten uses this part to introduce the individual instruments.

Part three is a fugue (see Glossary). The main melody or melody fragment is called a *subject*. Again, each of the main instruments of the orchestra plays the fugue subject.

The coda or conclusion of the piece starts with the percussion section and is answered by the full orchestra. The entire work ends with a loud held chord.

Variations

Fugue
(fyoog)

LISTENING GUIDE

*THE YOUNG PERSON'S GUIDE
TO THE ORCHESTRA* (1946), OPUS 34,
BENJAMIN BRITTEN

**Form: Theme, Variations, and Fugue
Performing Medium: Symphony Orchestra with Narrator**

Compact Disc 4, Track 23
Running Time: 18:07

THEME

23   0.00   THEME   played by the entire orchestra; *f*, triple meter

24   0:28   THEME   played by the *woodwind* section
25   0:54   THEME   played by the *brass* section
26   1:17   THEME   played by the *string* section
27   1:38   THEME   played by the *percussion* section, featuring timpani
28   1:57   THEME   played again by the entire orchestra

VARIATIONS

29   2:20   VARIATION 1   *flutes* and *piccolo;* fast passages of music; duple meter; *p*
30   2:53   VARIATION 2   *oboes:* smooth, plaintive melody
31   3:50   VARIATION 3   *clarinets:* broken chords and fast scale passages
32   4:30   VARIATION 4   *bassoons:* marchlike melody
33   5:24   VARIATION 5   *violins:* dancelike melody
34   5:59   VARIATION 6   *violas:* songlike melody, covering a wide range
35   7:01   VARIATION 7   *cellos:* rich, flowing melody
36   8:14   VARIATION 8   *string basses:* melody mainly based on sequences
37   9:13   VARIATION 9   *harp:* an inversion (upside down) statement of the theme
38   10:00   VARIATION 10   *French horns:* variation, using chords
39   10:53   VARIATION 11   *trumpets:* marchlike passage
40   11:23   VARIATION 12   *trombones* and *tuba:* heavy and majestic

| 41 | 12:40 | VARIATION 13 | *percussion:* starts with *timpani;* followed by *bass drum* and *cymbals, tambourine, triangle, snare drum, Chinese wood blocks, xylophone, castanets, gong;* concludes with the *whip* |

FUGUE

| 42 | 14:32 | SUBJECT (melody) | played by piccolo; fast tempo; duple meter |

Very Fast

p

	14:38	SUBJECT	played by *flutes;* piccolo in counterpoint (counter melody)
	14:47	SUBJECT	played by *oboes;* other woodwinds in counterpoint
	14:52	SUBJECT	played by *clarinets;* other woodwinds in counterpoint
	15:03	SUBJECT	played by *bassoons;* other woodwinds in counterpoint
	15:13	SUBJECT	played by *first violins;* other instruments in counterpoint
	15:15	SUBJECT	played by *second violins;* other instruments in counterpoint
	15:23	SUBJECT	played by *violas;* other instruments in counterpoint
	15:29	SUBJECT	played by *cellos;* other instruments in counterpoint
	15:33	SUBJECT	played by *string basses;* other instruments in counterpoint
	15:45	SUBJECT	played by *harp;* other instruments in counterpoint
	15:57	SUBJECT	played by *French horns;* other instruments in counterpoint
	16:03	SUBJECT	played by *trumpets;* other instruments in counterpoint
	16:11	SUBJECT	played by *trombones* and *tuba;* other instruments in counterpoint
43	16:17	SUBJECT/ MAIN THEME	played by upper *strings* and *woodwinds;* counterpoint of MAIN THEME played in long tones by *brasses;* tempo slows

CODA

| 44 | 16:57 | | Percussion enters forte; back to the fast tempo; full orchestra answers |
| | 17:16 | | Ending chord played by the entire orchestra |

HOW THE ORCHESTRA DEVELOPED

Toward the end of the eighteenth century, Joseph Haydn's thirty-piece court orchestra consisted of part-time musicians who had to double as servants, cooks, and stable hands to make a living. A generation later, Ludwig van Beethoven was limited to forty or fifty poorly trained instrumentalists, many of whom had difficulty reading his demanding music.

Today's symphony orchestra, with its highly skilled, professional performers playing the assortment of instruments we have come to know, developed during the latter part of the nineteenth century. Among the factors influencing this development were the emergence of both new and improved instruments, the growing popularity of public concerts in larger halls, and the establishment of funding sources to support expanded orchestras.

Before the Seventeenth Century

CHAMBER ENSEMBLES   Chamber ensembles were the main instrumental groups before the seventeenth century. Two to eight musicians performed on an as-needed basis to entertain in the chambers or rooms of a palace or manor house. Composers did not specify the instruments because they did not know which ones would be available. So it was possible to hear a piece played on a different combination of instruments from one performance to the next.

The Roman Catholic Church, the leading employer of musicians before that time, was more interested in vocal music. Although an ensemble of instruments was occasionally featured in the church service, the instrumentalist's primary role was to accompany the singers.

The Beginnings of Instrumentation

In Venice, around 1600, Giovanni Gabrieli (c.1555–1612) surveyed the possibilities offered by the huge interior of St. Mark's Basilica, where he was first organist and composer. He realized that instruments playing in different locations of the church could produce very rich sound effects. So he experimented with different combinations of instruments until he was satisfied with the results.

Gabrieli
(gah-bree-*ay*-lee)

To ensure the balance and quality of that sound, Gabrieli specified which instruments should play. Thus, we had the beginning of standardized *instrumentation,* which made it possible for a complex instrumental composition to be performed with the same instrumentation at each performance.

Another great Italian composer, Claudio Monteverdi, built on Gabrieli's ideas to set up the first orchestra with stable instrumentation. In 1607, he hired forty musicians to accompany his opera *Orfeo* (*or*-fay-oh).

Monteverdi
(mohn-teh-*vehr*-dee)

2	flutes (one high and one low)
2	oboes
1	very high trumpet (clarino)
3	high trumpets

4	medium trumpets
2	cornets (looking and sounding different from the modern cornet, and made either of wood or ivory)
2	small violins
2	violins (regular size)
10	viole da braccia (similar to the modern violin)
3	viole da gamba (similar to the modern cello)
2	double-bass viols (string bass)
2	deep-tone lutes (a cross between a guitar and a mandolin)
5	assorted keyboard instruments, including harpsichords

The String Instruments Achieve Perfection

Amati
(ah-*mah*-tee)

Stradivari
(strah-deh-*vahr*-ee)

Guarneri
(gwahr-*nayr*-ee)

Between 1650 and 1700, a breakthrough occurred in the construction of string instruments. This breakthrough was the next important step in the development of the orchestra. In the northern Italian town of Cremona, a few generations of craftsmen achieved near-perfection in creating their string instruments. Nicolò Amati (1596–1684), Antonio Stradivari (1644–1737), and Giuseppe Bartolomeo Guarneri (1698–1744) crafted priceless instruments cherished and played today by such soloists as Itzhak Perlman, Midori, Nigel Kennedy, Nadja Salerno-Sonnenberg, Yo-Yo Ma, and Lynn Harrell.

HISTORICAL PERSPECTIVE

What Is the Secret of the Cremona Instruments?

Modern technology has not yet been able to replicate the quality of string instruments created by the Cremona craftsmen. What makes those instruments so great? Not only are their tones beautiful, but their sounds resonate over the symphony orchestra.

Theories abound about the secrets of these instruments, but all remain unproven: the secrets died with the craftsmen.

Some have conjectured that the varnish and the glue had special qualities. Perhaps. Some suggest that the instruments were crafted from wood soaked in the polluted waters in the canals of Venice. What "magical" powers this particular water may have

transferred, no one knows. But recent analyses indicate that the soaking seems to have created a specially porous wood, which may indeed amplify sound.

Challenge Your Expertise

What do the tuba, contrabassoon, and bass viol have in common?

LISTENING ACTIVITY

THE FOUR SEASONS, OP. 8, ANTONIO VIVALDI

Concerto for Violin and Strings in E Major: "Spring"
First Movement: Allegro
Form: Violin Concerto
Performing Medium: Chamber Orchestra

Compact Disc: 1, Track 9
Cassette Tape, Side B, Example 2
Running Time: 3:10

Listen to the first movement of this famous Vivaldi violin concerto, which features a violinist with a chamber orchestra. A more detailed discussion and Listening Guide appears in Chapter 9.

SOLO PERFORMERS   Around 1700, several composers, Antonio Vivaldi in particular, were inspired by the improved string instruments. A violinist himself, Vivaldi grew up in Venice, about 100 miles east of Cremona, and he later taught at a girl's orphanage in Venice. Of his 500 concertos (music for one or several soloists with orchestra) featuring various instruments, he composed almost half for the violin.

VIRTUOSO PERFORMERS   Vivaldi's violin concertos were more technically demanding than earlier string music. With the availability of superior instruments, musicians aspired to become *virtuosos*—solo performers with exceptional technical ability.*

Virtuosos
(vur-choo-*oh*-sohs)

Highly proficient soloists could now earn more money—a fact that motivated other instrumentalists to attain virtuosity. After 1700, trumpeters, hornists, flutists, oboists, and bassoonists joined the ranks of virtuosos. A harpsichord or a chamber orchestra usually accompanied soloists.

Concertos
(con-*chayr*-tos)

*In music, we use either the Italian plural ending of words (concerti, virtuosi) or the English ending (concertos, virtuosos).

Chamber Orchestra

Because most performances took place in the court chambers, the larger Baroque instrumental ensemble is called a *chamber orchestra*. Not yet containing the variety of instruments associated with the modern symphony orchestra, the chamber orchestra consisted mainly of string instruments, a few winds, and harpsichord, often with the composer playing and conducting from the harpsichord, illustrated in the figure below.

Concerto Grosso

With more instrumentalists becoming virtuosos, composers of the early eighteenth century began to write concertos featuring several soloists in the same piece of music. To distinguish this work from a concerto for one or two instruments, composers called it *concerto grosso,* or "large concerto."

The Baroque Chamber Orchestra (10 to 20 players)

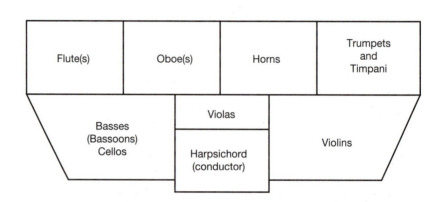

Haydn conducting a court chamber orchestra from the harpsichord

LISTENING ACTIVITY

BRANDENBURG CONCERTO NO. 2 (1721), JOHANN SEBASTIAN BACH

**Third Movement: Allegro Assai
Form: Concerto Grosso
Performing Medium: Violin, Flute, Oboe,
Trumpet, and Chamber Orchestra**

Compact Disc 1, Track 12
Cassette Tape, Side B, Example 3
Running Time: 3:01

Bach's six Brandenburg concertos are among the most exciting examples of the concerto grosso. Concerto No. 2 features four virtuoso performers—*trumpet, flute, oboe,* and *violin*—with a small string chamber orchestra and harpsichord. Listen to the third movement. Notice how each of the four soloists contributes to the entire work. In Chapter 9, we will return to this work and discuss it in detail.

The Court Orchestra Evolves

By the latter part of the eighteenth century, almost every European court of the ruling nobility had its small resident orchestra. The fifteen to thirty part-time players were on call to provide familiar entertainment for their employers and guests.

The words "familiar entertainment" are significant; aristocrats resisted surprises. Catering to this desire for predictability, court composers wrote music with standardized instrumentation for these small resident orchestras. Thus, members of the aristocratic leisure class could be assured of comparable entertainment, no matter where they traveled.

Challenge Your Expertise

Can you think of two reasons the brass section isn't in the front of the symphony orchestra?

Haydn's Contributions

Over a 30-year span of composing more than 100 symphonies for the classical orchestra, Joseph Haydn contributed significantly to the development of the orchestra. Adding a pair of timpani (kettledrums) to the standard orchestra and gradually phasing out the harpsichord, Haydn influenced Wolfgang Amadeus Mozart and other contemporaries to follow his lead. Haydn's refinements paved the way for the "modern" orchestra.

Beethoven's Expanded Orchestra

Beethoven, who often expressed his reluctance to appear in palaces, took his music to larger halls where the middle class could gather. Consequently, a larger orchestra evolved to produce enough sound to fill the available space and to be heard by larger audiences. As orchestras moved into larger halls, composers were free to explore the expressive potential of the orchestral sound.

For his Symphony No. 1, Beethoven used an orchestra similar in size to the ones Haydn and Mozart used (see Table 5.3). A few years later, for

The classical orchestra (18 to 30 players)

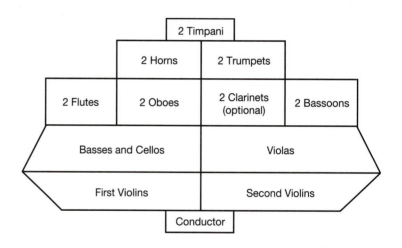

LISTENING ACTIVITY

SYMPHONY NO. 94 IN G (*SURPRISE*), JOSEPH HAYDN
LARGE FORM: SYMPHONY

Detailed Form: Minuet and Trio (Song Form and Trio)
Performing Medium: Chamber Orchestra

Compact Disc 2, Track 1
Cassette Tape: Side B, Example 8
Running Time: 5:32

Listen to the third movement from Haydn's Symphony No. 94 (*Surprise*). It is derived from an eighteenth-century dance (the minuet) in a triple meter. Note the sound of this small, or chamber, orchestra.

his Symphony No. 5, Beethoven added a piccolo, a contrabassoon, and three trombones, thus increasing the size and power of the orchestra.

By 1824, for his last symphony, the Ninth, Beethoven's orchestra had nearly doubled in size. Now it included new percussion instruments such as the triangle, bass drum, and cymbals (see Table 5.3). In the last movement of the Ninth Symphony, Beethoven calls for four soloist singers and a large chorus to perform with the orchestra.

Nineteenth-Century Expansion of the Orchestra

Inspired by Beethoven, other nineteenth-century composers continued to enlarge the orchestra. Berlioz added players in the wind and percussion sections. He also incorporated improved versions of existing instruments as well as newly invented instruments such as the tuba, English horn, saxophone, and contrabassoon. Berlioz was even adventurous enough to try several experimental instruments not usually found in orchestras (the ophicleide, basset horn, and Sax horn, for example). This last group of instruments was discontinued because of technical and tonal problems.

Table 5.3	Beethoven's Early, Middle, and Late Orchestras	
Symphony No. 1 (1800)	**Symphony No. 5 (1808)**	**Symphony No. 9 (1824)**
2 Flutes	1 Piccolo	1 Piccolo
2 Oboes	2 Flutes	2 Flutes
2 Clarinets	2 Oboes	2 Oboes
2 Bassoons	2 Clarinets	2 Clarinets
2 Horns	2 Bassoons	2 Bassoons
2 Trumpets	1 Contrabassoon	1 Contrabassoon
Timpani	2 Horns	4 Horns
First Violins	2 Trumpets	2 Trumpets
Second Violins	3 Trombones	3 Trombones
Violas	Timpani	Timpani
Cellos	First Violins	Triangle
Basses	Second Violins	Cymbals
	Violas	Bass Drum
	Cellos	First Violins
	Basses	Second Violins
		Violas
		Cellos
		Basses
		4 Vocal Soloists
		Large Chorus

LISTENING ACTIVITY

SYMPHONY NO. 5 IN C MINOR (1808)
LUDWIG VAN BEETHOVEN
OP. 67, FIRST MOVEMENT: ALLEGRO CON BRIO

Large Form: Symphony
Detailed Form: Sonata-allegro
Performing Medium: Medium-Sized Symphony Orchestra

Compact Disc 2, Track 10
Cassette Tape: Side C, Example 1
Running Time: 7:18

Listen to the first movement of Beethoven's Symphony No. 5, one of the most popular symphonies in the orchestra literature. Compare the sound of the orchestra with the recording of the third movement of Haydn's Symphony No. 94. You will notice that although the instrumentation is similar, Beethoven calls for a slightly larger, more forceful orchestra. A more detailed Listening Guide appears in Chapter 12.

BRASS VALVES AND WOODWIND KEYS   By the 1830s, many brass instruments had valves, enabling them to play in all keys. Formerly, brass instruments were largely limited to playing fanfares and bugle calls. Only a few early brass players could manage the instrument's extremely high register, where a few more pitches were available. Bach had a specific, talented trumpet player in mind when he wrote that demanding trumpet part in his *Brandenburg Concerto No. 2.*

The trombone, which uses a telescoping slide to produce pitches, retains its basic mechanism to this day.

A new system of keying, invented in 1832 by flutist Theobald Boehm, eventually allowed flutes, clarinets, oboes, and bassoons to be played faster and with greater ease. The woodwind keys, much like typewriter keys, allowed the players to open holes in the body of the instrument that were formerly beyond the reach of the player's fingers.

With the capabilities of both woodwind and brass instruments, composers began creating more important musical roles for them in the orchestra, as well as for concerto performance. Though not employed as frequently as the string section in the orchestra during the nineteenth century, the woodwind and brass sections were significantly elevated in importance.

Rising Standards of Performance

When composer Felix Mendelssohn accepted an appointment in 1835 as conductor of the Gewandhaus Orchestra in Leipzig, Germany, he began to transform the orchestra. He energetically recruited the best players in

Gewandhaus
(guh-*vahnd*-howse)

Europe, thus establishing the Gewandhaus Orchestra as the finest of its day. Living composers clamored to have the Gewandhaus Orchestra play their works, and audiences were able to hear superb performances of great masterpieces.

The Virtuoso Orchestra Emerges

To meet the performance demands of late-nineteenth-century composers—particularly Richard Wagner, Richard Strauss, Nikolai Rimsky-Korsakov, and Gustav Mahler—orchestras hired virtuoso performers for every section, giving us the orchestra we know today.

Then in 1913, Igor Stravinsky, for his ballet *The Rite of Spring* (*Le Sacre du printemps*), gave new prominence to the percussion section. Stravinsky calls for between 110 and 115 players for *The Rite of Spring*.

Strings (66 players)
   18 first violins
   16 second violins
   12 violas
   12 cellos
   8 string basses

Wagner
(*vahg*-ner)

Strauss
(shtrowss)

Rimsky-Korsakov
(*rim*-skee *kohr*-suh-koff)

Mahler
(*mah*-ler)

Sacre du printemps
(*sac*-ruh doo pran-*ton*)

LISTENING ACTIVITY

SYMPHONIE FANTASTIQUE (FANTASTIC SYMPHONY, 1830),
HECTOR BERLIOZ
FIFTH MOVEMENT: "DREAM OF A WITCHES' SABBATH"

Large Form: Symphony
Detailed Form: Sectional
Performing Medium: Large Symphony Orchestra

Compact Disc 2, Track 15
Cassette Tape: Side C, Example 2
Running Time: 10:20

Listen to the fifth movement of Hector Berlioz's *Symphonie Fantastique* and focus on the variety of instrumental timbres in the orchestra. In addition to the woodwinds and brass used by Beethoven, you will hear chimes and a high-pitched clarinet (soprano, E-flat). To create the atmosphere of a graveyard, complete with rattling bones, Berlioz requests that the string players turn their bows around and strike the strings with the wood side. This special effect is called *col legno* (Italian, for "with wood").

A more detailed discussion and Listening Activity appear in Chapter 14.

Col legno
(cohl *leyn*-yo)

Woodwinds (23 players)
    2 piccolos
    3 flutes (third doubling as second piccolo)
    1 alto flute in G
    4 oboes (fourth doubling as second English horn)
    2 English horns
    1 clarinet in D
    3 clarinets in A and B-flat
    2 bass clarinets
    3 bassoons
    2 contrabassoons

Brass (19 players)
    1 trumpet in D
    4 trumpets in C (fourth doubling as bass trumpet)
    1 bass trumpet in E-flat
    8 horns
    3 trombones
    2 tubas

*Percussion (4 to 7 players —some percussionists play more
  than one instrument)*
    5 timpani (played by two performers)
    1 bass drum
    1 pair of symbals
    1 set of tam tam (Chinese gong)
    1 set of antique cymbals (tiny, $2\frac{1}{2}$ to 3 inches)
    1 triangle
    1 guiro (a serrated African gourd, scraped with a stick)

LISTENING ACTIVITY

THE RITE OF SPRING, IGOR STRAVINSKY
"SACRIFICIAL DANCE" FROM *PART II: THE SACRIFICE*

Large Form: Excerpt from a Ballet
Detailed Form: Complex Rondo or Sectional

Compact Disc 2, Track 33
Cassette Tape: Side D, Example 2
Running Time: 4:33

Listen to the "Sacrificial Dance" from *The Rite of Spring* ballet by Stravinsky. Notice how the composer maintains a strong percussive drive throughout the entire piece. A more detailed discussion and Listening Guide appear in Chapter 20.

THE WIND ENSEMBLE

During the twentieth century, concert bands, symphonic bands, wind orchestras and wind bands became popular concert attractions. Consisting primarily of wind instruments and an occasional string bass, wind ensembles may vary in their size and instrumentation.

Since biblical times, outdoor music without string instruments has been associated with invading armies, powerful rulers, and successful conquests. Now wind ensembles are associated with pops concerts, summer outdoor concerts in park bandstands, and holiday celebrations. These ensembles bring music to masses of people who otherwise might never have the opportunity to enjoy a traditional symphony orchestra concert.

Around the turn of the twentieth century, the fine professional bands of John Philip Sousa, Arthur Pryor, and Patrick Conway spread the popularity of these ensembles throughout North America. During the World Wars, bands marched in parades, provided inspiration at patriotic rallies and War bond drives, and performed concerts throughout the world.

Today, with the abundance of fine performing ensembles in high schools, colleges, and the military, contemporary composers have found a new, profitable outlet—writing music for wind bands. Wind ensembles now have a wide variety of music from which to choose their concert programs.

KEYBOARD INSTRUMENTS

Keyboards of various sizes, sounds, and shapes have been popular since the Greeks invented a version of the organ, the water-powered *hydraulis*, sometime between 250 and 120 B.C. The *organ, harpsichord, piano,* and *electronic music synthesizer* now predominate at concert music performances.

Organ

Often called "the king of instruments," the organ is the largest and most powerful in the keyboard category. The sound from its hundreds of individual pipes fills churches such as St. Peter's in Rome, St. Mark's in Venice, St. Paul's in London, and the Washington Cathedral in Washington, D.C.

Early giant organs made great physical demands on the operators. For example, the organ installed in England's Winchester Cathedral in the tenth century required seventy energetic men to pump and jump and huff and puff to work the twenty-six bellows that provided air to its more than 400 pipes. The aerobics of these operators made it possible for the organist to produce music.

Today, most organs use electric energy to move the air through the pipes. Some pipes sound like woodwind instruments, others like brasses; still others produce sounds unique to the organ. The organist can select and combine any of the various pipes to create interesting timbres, similar to combining instruments in orchestration.

Most organs have at least two keyboards, and many have three or four, making it easier for the player to shift between the various combina-

LISTENING ACTIVITY

FUGUE IN G MINOR (*The Little*), BWV 578,
JOHANN SEBASTIAN BACH

Form: Fugue
Performing Medium: Organ

‖ **Compact Disc 1, Track 13**
‖ **Cassette Tape: Side B, Example 4**
‖ **Running Time: 3:44**

Listen to the Fugue in g minor (The Little) by Bach, composed in the early eighteenth century. Note the power and variety of sounds the organ produces. Try to imagine the famous organist Bach performing this work in one of the great cathedrals. A more detailed discussion and Listening Guide appear in Chapter 9.

tions of pipes and timbres. Organists can produce additional tones on a pedal board, playing with their toes and heels of both feet.

Harpsichord

Until the advent of the pianoforte in the eighteenth century, European music patrons favored the harpsichord for both solo and chamber ensem-

Mozart at the harpsichord

LISTENING ACTIVITY

VARIATIONS, "AH VOUS DIRAI-JE, MAMAN" K. 265,
WOLFGANG AMADEUS MOZART
("TWINKLE, TWINKLE, LITTLE STAR")

Large Form: Keyboard Piece
Detailed Form: Theme and Variations
Performing Medium: Harpsichord

‖ **Compact Disc 1, Track 14**
‖ **Cassette Tape: Side B, Example 5**
‖ **Running Time: 2:49**

Listen to the sound quality of the harpsichord in this excerpt from Wolfgang Amadeus Mozart's variations on the French folk song, "Ah vous dirai-je, maman." A more detailed discussion and Listening Guide appear in Chapter 11.

ble performance. Though similar in shape to a modern grand piano, the harpsichord produces its tone and sound quite differently.

When a harpsichordist strikes a key, a mechanism activates a plectrum, a picklike device made of bird quill or leather. This device plucks a string, resulting in a brittle twang. Hitting a piano key, in contrast, activates a felt-covered hammer that strikes the strings, producing full, more mellow tones.

An advantage of the harpsichord is that its lighter tone is useful for accompanying singers. A drawback to the harpsichord is that all tones have equal volume, no matter how hard the player hits the keys. To achieve a modest contrast in the volume, some harpsichordists have an additional keyboard that strikes louder-sounding strings.

Piano

Johann Sebastian Bach was not impressed by the piano collection of King Frederick the Great of Prussia. Although the monarch had specially invited Bach in 1747 to try out his array of newly invented instruments, the great master found them all in a rudimentary state of development.

Starting in 1770, however, twenty years after Bach's death, piano makers began significantly improving their instruments. In a 1777 letter to his father, Wolfgang Amadeus Mozart expressed his enthusiasm about the new instruments. Having them available, Mozart later added to the growing repertoire for the piano by composing twenty-seven concertos and twenty sonatas.

By 1800, piano makers had produced an instrument very similar to the modern piano—short for *fortepiano* (meaning "loud-soft" in Italian). For the first time, a keyboard instrument had been named for its capabilities. Keyboard artists could control dynamic shadings—very soft to very loud—with the touch of their hands.

Fortepiano
(*for*-tay-pee-*an*-oh)

LISTENING ACTIVITY

FANTAISIE IMPROMPTU, FRÉDÉRIC CHOPIN

Large Form: Short Recital Piece
Detailed Form: Three Part Form (A-B-A)
Performing Medium: Piano

Compact Disc 2, Track 22
Cassette Tape: Side C, Example 5
Running Time: 4:42

Listen to the *Fantaisie Impromptu* by Frédéric Chopin. Chopin's music allows pianists to display their technical brilliance and the instrument's expressiveness.

Championed by composer-performers such as Ludwig van Beethoven, Franz Schubert, Robert Schumann, Felix Mendelssohn, Frédéric Chopin, Johannes Brahms, and Franz Liszt, the piano enjoyed its golden era. With its greater expressive capabilities, it emerged as the preferred keyboard instrument of the nineteenth century, figuring prominently as a status symbol in the homes of prosperous and educated families.

ELECTRONIC INSTRUMENTS

Electronic Keyboards and Synthesizers

Electronic synthesizer keyboard

Recently, electronic keyboards and electronic music synthesizers have paralleled the piano's popularity. However, the term *synthesizer* does not adequately describe these instruments. Early synthesizers were designed to imitate the timbre of harpsichords, organs, violins, flutes, and other instruments. They still are able to produce these sounds, but they are also capable of much more. When combined with computers, synthesizers can create virtually unlimited varieties of sounds.

HUMAN VOICE

Many people consider the human voice, with its tremendous range of sound and emotion, to be the most expressive musical instrument. Think of the differences between the jazz "scat" singer, the crooner, the rapper, the gospel singer, the pop vocalist, and the opera singer.

There are several general voice classifications for classical music, as shown in Table 5.4.

Samuel Ramey as Atilla (bass-baritone)

Table 5.4		General Voice Classifications
female voices	soprano	the highest voice
	mezzo-soprano (*met*-soh)	the next highest, usually with a slightly darker timbre (*mezzo* is "middle" in Italian)
	contralto (alto)	lowest female voice, heavier and darker timbre than soprano
male voices	tenor	the highest male voice
	baritone	lower, with darker timbre than tenor
	bass (*basso*, It.)	the lowest and darkest timbre

Opera Singers

Additional subclassifications are used to describe the character, timbre, and type of roles, as shown in Table 5.5.

Table 5.5		Operatic Voice Classifications
sopranos	coloratura	usually high range with great vocal agility (Olympia in Offenbach's *Tales of Hoffmann*)
	dramatic	powerful, dramatic roles (Aida in Verdi's *Aida*)
	lyric	lighter timbre; sweeter roles, ingenue—young leading lady (Mimi in Puccini's *La Bohème*)
tenors	robusto	full, powerful voice roles (the Duke in Verdi's *Rigoletto*)
	lyric	lighter timbre; smooth, lyrical singing roles (Rodolfo in Puccini's *La Bohème*)
	heldentenor (heroic tenor)	powerful, expressive, agile (Walther in Wagner's *Die Meistersinger*)
baritone- basses	profondo	deep range; powerful, solemn roles (Commendatore in Mozart's *Don Giovanni*)
	cantante	smooth, lyrical singing roles (Don Giovanni in Mozart's *Don Giovanni*)
	buffo	agile, comic roles (Leporello in Mozart's *Don Giovanni*)

LISTENING ACTIVITY

"MADAMINA" ARIA FROM *DON GIOVANNI*, (1787)
WOLFGANG AMADEUS MOZART

Large Form: Opera
Detailed Form: Aria (Two-Part Song Form)
Performing Medium: Bass-Baritone
and Chamber Orchestra

Compact Disc 2, Track 8
Cassette Tape: Side B, Example 10
Running Time: 5:53

Listen to the famous "Madamina." The aria from Mozart's opera *Don Giovanni* features a *basso buffo* ("comic bass" in Italian) singing the role of Leporello. Pay special attention to the quality of the singer's voice.

LISTENING ACTIVITY

LA BOHÈME (THE BOHEMIAN LIFE, 1896), GIACOMO PUCCINI

Act I (excerpt)
Form: Romantic Opera, Recitatives and Arias
Performing Medium: Soprano, Tenor, and Orchestra

Compact Disc 3, Track 20
Running Time: 12:40

This scene from Act I features two singers: a lyric soprano and a lyric tenor. Chapter 15 discusses this opera in greater detail.

Summary of Terms

Boehm key system
bow
brass mutes
brass quintet
col legno
concerto
concerto grosso
contrabassoon
electronic keyboards
energy source
English horn
ensembles; chamber
   ensembles
instrumentation
keyboard instruments:
   electronic keyboards
   harpsichord
   organ

pianoforte
synthesizer
mute
orchestration
pizzicato
resonating chamber
saxophones
string quartet
string trio
symphony orchestra
synthesizer
timbre
vibrating element
virtuoso
virtuoso orchestra
voices:
   female voices:
      coloratura

contralto (alto)
dramatic soprano
lyric soprano
mezzo-soprano
soprano
male voices:
   baritone
   bass
   basso buffo
   basso cantante
   basso profondo
   heldentenor
   lyric tenor
   robusto tenor
   tenor
wind ensemble
woodwind quintet

Challenge Your Expertise

- The term "movement" on a concert program refers to which of the following?
  1. The orchestra enters and tunes.
  2. The conductor's arms are raised.
  3. A large section of a longer work is to be played.
  4. The soloist enters.

Chapter 6

An Introduction
to Musical Styles

WHY STUDY MUSICAL STYLES?

Musical styles reflect the tastes and cultural attitudes of the age in which they are created. People want their art to have certain characteristics, and artists usually give the people what they want—although this is less true in Twentieth Century music.

Artists also influence one another and tend to use similar vocabulary in creating their works. In music, composers of the same style period tend to reflect that style. We cannot study all the works of any style period, but we can come to know the representative ones. With that foundation, we can understand music we have not yet heard.

For example, the music of Haydn and of Mozart sound similar. The more familiar you become with the compositions of these two masters, the more you'll recognize their similarities in *style*.

Rather than presenting all style periods since the beginning of time, we have focused our listening upon the musical styles you are most likely to hear at concerts—mainly music composed after A.D. 1600—although we will take a brief look at the music that preceded it.

HISTORICAL PERSPECTIVE

Styles in the Arts

Stylistic similarities extend beyond music. Parallel trends have always existed among the other arts, philosophy, and even fashion. Artists and musicians seem to have an uncanny knack of anticipating these trends, often more accurately than business and governments do. Art not only reflects society and imitates life, but also *influences* society and changes life.

STYLISTIC EXCEPTIONS   Not all composers of a particular age compose in a similar style. Some resist falling into the general style of their contemporaries. Others may adhere to an earlier style. Composers may express their creativity through innovation: they strive to produce new forms of expression. For instance, Finnish composer Jan Sibelius (1865–1957), though creating most of his works in the twentieth century, chose a musical style more characteristic of the preceding century. When listening to his music, you would place it in an earlier style period.

George Gershwin's *Porgy and Bess,* featuring Priscilla Baskerville as Serena.

STYLISTIC GENERALIZATIONS   Effectively describing the vast variety of composers and their music requires some generalization. As we encounter exceptions, we will point out how their music deviates from others of their time.

The style periods of Western art music are usually divided into eras, as follows:

THE COMMON STYLE PERIODS OF CONCERT MUSIC

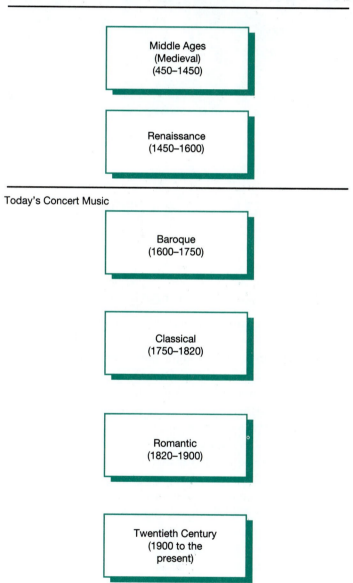

Middle Ages
(Medieval)
(450–1450)

Renaissance
(1450–1600)

Today's Concert Music

Baroque
(1600–1750)

Classical
(1750–1820)

Romantic
(1820–1900)

Twentieth Century
(1900 to the present)

Chapter 7

Music Before 1600

THE MIDDLE AGES (450–1450)

This 1,000-year span of European history begins with the decline of the Roman Empire and ends with the Renaissance. For centuries, the Roman legions had brought law, order, and stability to a vast region surrounding the Mediterranean Sea. With the gradual decline of the Roman Empire, Germanic nations captured these lands. The ensuing political and social chaos in many parts of Europe was relieved later by the growing influence of Christianity.

So dismal was the quality of life during the early Middle Ages that historians once labeled it the "Dark Ages." The late Medieval era, from A.D. 1000 onward, is sometimes called the "Age of Faith" because of the strength of the Church during those years.

During the Middle Ages, the Church became the center of learning in both secular and religious fields. By the eleventh century, the religious zeal of the Middle Ages reached its peak, as nobles who had once been enemies formed alliances to reclaim the Holy Land from the Moslems. Clad in armor and carrying colorful flags, European nobles led vast armies to Turkey, the Arabian Peninsula, and North Africa—on foot—in a series of bloody and costly Crusades.

Thirteenth-century Gothic cathedral in Burgos, Spain

As a "holy war," the Crusades failed. They were successful, however, in changing the socioeconomic structure of Europe by weakening feudalism and expanding the cultural perspective of the people.

Construction of the Gothic Cathedrals

An important development occurred in the twelfth and thirteenth centuries: construction began on many of the great Gothic cathedrals of Europe. Among the most notable are:

France	Notre Dame (Paris), 1163; Bourges, 1195; Chartres, 1194
Spain	Burgos, 1221; Toledo, 1227
England	Salisbury, 1220; Gloucester, 1332

Hierarchy of Common People, Church, and State

Reaching toward God and the heavens, the Gothic arches and spires of the great cathedrals, along with the castles of the nobility, symbolized the medieval view of society.

Notre Dame
(*noh*-truh *ðahm*)

Bourges
(*boorj*)

Chartres
(*shart*)

Burgos
(*boor*-gos)

Toledo
(toh-*lay*-do)

Salisbury
(*sahlz*-burry)

Gloucester
(*glos*-tur)

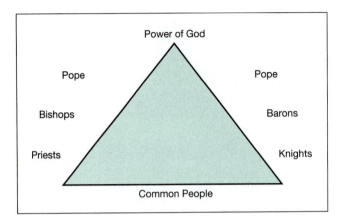

Music in the Church Service

Developing from Judaic roots, early Christian church liturgy borrowed much of its material from the Hebrew services: hymns praising God and asking for forgiveness, and psalms sung responsively between a soloist and the congregation.

Mass
Ordinary
Proper

THE MASS   Late in the sixth century, Pope Gregory standardized the rituals of the church service as part of his efforts to organize the liturgy. The most important of these liturgical celebrations is the *Mass,* consisting of two different kinds of texts. The *Ordinary* portions of the Mass are repeated in nearly every Mass, hence the name "ordinary." The *Proper* portions are specific to particular celebrations in the Church calendar; therefore, those sections change according to the day of the year. Here are the portions of the Mass most often set to music:

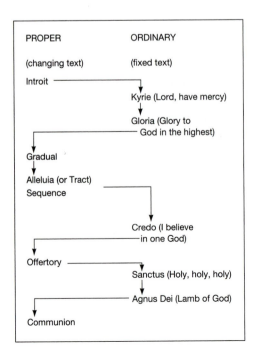

MUSIC OF THE MIDDLE AGES

Gregorian Chants

The largest body of music that has survived from before the year 1000 is *Gregorian chant,* also known as *Catholic liturgical chant, plainsong, plainchant,* or simply *chant.* Its identifiable characteristic is its *monophonic texture*—a melody without harmony or accompaniment. All singers perform the same melody in unison. The texts of Gregorian chants are in Latin. Many incorporated Hebrew and Roman melodies.

Monophonic Texture

Since the chants used in the Catholic service were passed on mainly through oral tradition, many were lost. Gregory I (The Great), Pope from A.D. 590 to 604, charged his monks with the task of organizing the remaining monophonic chants so that they would be better preserved.

Some two centuries later, a notation system was devised to further assist in their preservation. Since Gregory's reforms saved that literature, we tend to call medieval monophonic chants "Gregorian chants," even though most of the chants used in Catholic Church services today were composed after Pope Gregory's time.

Gregorian Notation

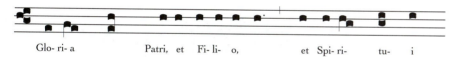

Glo- ri- a   Patri, et   Fi- li- o,   et Spi- ri-   tu-   i

Modern Notation (rhythm approximate)

Glo- ri-   a   Pa - tri, et Fi - li - o,   et Spi - ri -   tu –   i

LISTENING ACTIVITY

GREGORIAN CHANT: *ALLELUIA PASCHA NOSTRUM*

Large Form: Mass Section
Performing Medium: Men's Choir

Compact Disc 1, Track 3
Cassette Tape: Side A, Example 3
Running Time: 0:42

Listen to this Gregorian chant from an early Catholic Church Mass. Notice that all voices sing melody in unison—no harmony.

THE BEGINNINGS OF POLYPHONY

An important musical development began during the ninth century: a second musical line was performed with the monophonic chant. This created a texture called *polyphony,* meaning "many sounds."

One theory about the advent of polyphony is interesting, but unproven. The theory contends that men and boys were singing Gregorian chants together—the boys singing the same melody in a high range that the mature men were singing in a low range. When the soprano voices of some of the adolescent boys suddenly "cracked," this created an inner voice and a different pitch between the high part and the lower part. Church musicians called this early harmony *organum.*

organum
(*or*-guh-num)

Evidently, the monks liked the sound of organum. In addition to improvising this new line of music during performance, they began indicating it in the music written after about A.D. 1000.

Voice 1

Voice 2

Sit glo - ri - a Do - mi - ni in Sae - cu - la   lae - ta - bi - tur Do - mi - nus in o - pe - ri - bus su - is

Notre Dame, Paris, side view

Music in the Cathedral of Notre Dame

With the building of the great Gothic cathedrals in the Middle Ages came the need for larger choirs. This in turn created employment for resident cleric-composers, whose duties included composing and arranging music for church services.

Leonin
(lay-oh-*nan*)
Perotin
(pay-roh-*tan*)

THE SCHOOL OF NOTRE DAME   Until the construction of Notre Dame in Paris, composers had been mostly anonymous. Then, for the first time, two important music director-clerics of this new cathedral rose to prominence in the musical world—Leonin (1163–90) and Perotin (fl. 1200). Their works so influenced other church composers that they were referred to as the "School of Notre Dame."

Secular Music of the Middle Ages

Examining the body of extant music before the eleventh century, you might suppose that church music was practically the only type of music that existed. We will never know. Unfortunately, most of the nonreligious, or *secular,* music for dancing, singing, and general entertainment has been lost because performers did not know how to preserve it through music notation. We know from paintings and illuminated manuscripts, however, that music formed a part of many medieval events.

LISTENING ACTIVITY

ALLELUIA, DIES SANCTIFICATUS, LEONIN

Large Form: Mass Section
Performing Medium: Men's Choir

Compact Disc 1, Track 4
Cassette Tape: Side A, Example 4
Running Time: 0:53

Leonin used polyphonic texture, assigning the original Gregorian chant to the lower voice. This excerpt is from the Proper portion of the Mass.

Notice the use of organum. The lower voice (chant) holds unusually long tones. The upper voice moves faster and more freely, creating two independent musical lines, or polyphony.

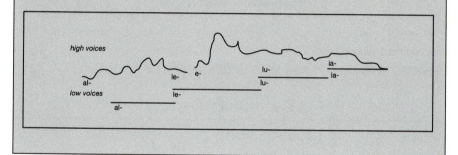

The Lute Player and the Harpist, engraved by Israhel van Meckenem

MINSTRELS   Beginning in the tenth century, small groups of professional poet-musicians wandered the French countryside performing in castles, palaces, taverns, and town squares. These common folk, called *minstrels,* were the newscasters of their day. Their songs reported folk legends, recent events, and local gossip.

Minstrels were also the original vaudevillians—performing magic tricks, telling jokes, juggling, doing acrobatics, and exhibiting trained animals. But society treated these itinerant strangers as outcasts. Perhaps minstrels did not take the time to document their songs because they were too busy struggling to make a living—and fleeing from officials.

TROUBADOURS   Beginning in the twelfth century, some secular songs composed by troubadours were notated. Troubadours were knights in the courts of Provence in southern France. In this age of chivalry, they rhapsodized about love, the beauty of women, honor, and the Crusades.

TROUVÈRES   Not to be outdone by their southern counterparts, noblemen in the courts of northern France composed songs in their own dialect.

trouvères
(tru-*vair*)

Known as *trouvères,* these musical poets of the twelfth and thirteenth centuries lyricized about the familiar topics of love and chivalry.

GERMAN MINNESINGERS Modeled after the troubadours, German knights-of-the-court developed their own music. Love (*minne,* in Old German) was also the main subject for the *minnesingers'* songs. Among these are watcher's songs, which warn lovers of the approach of dawn. Many others celebrated the beauty of women and of nature.

GERMAN MEISTERSINGERS Throughout the fourteenth, fifteenth, and sixteenth centuries, middle-class *Meistersingers* (mastersingers) built upon the minnesingers' tradition. Forming guilds, these Meistersingers established rigid rules for songwriting, just as the trade guilds had done. They even made aspiring songwriters take tests to demonstrate their adherence to "the rules."

Dances in the Middle Ages

Table 7.1	Important Composers of the Middle Ages
Troubadour Secular Songs	
Marcabru	(fl. 1128–50)
Bernart de Ventadorn	(died c. 1195)
Adam de la Halle	(c. 1250–c. 1290)
Church Music of Notre Dame	
Leonin	(c. 1163–90)
Perotin	(fl. 1200)
Church and Secular Music	
Philippe de Vitry	(1291–1361)
French prelate, composer, and theorist, known for his treatise *Ars nova* (new art), which explained early-fourteenth-century theory.	
Guillaume de Machaut	(c. 1300–77)
French court composer, cleric, and poet. Considered one of the greatest composers of the Middle Ages.	
Francesco Landini	(c. 1325–97)
One of the greatest Italian composers of the Middle Ages. Most of his compositions are *ballate,* a type of polyphonic song.	
Johannes Ciconia	(c. 1373–1412)
Born in France, Ciconia wrote church music and also secular madrigals, motets, and polyphonic vocal works.	
John Dunstable	(c. 1390–1443)
English composer who wrote mostly polyphonic music for the Mass and several secular songs.	

MONOPHONIC NOTATION   Although surviving medieval songs were notated in monophonic texture—melody only—literary descriptions and paintings suggest that the songs were accompanied by an instrument, usually a harp or a lute (a guitar-like instrument). Some harmony may have been used, but this is only conjecture.

Instrumental Music of the Middle Ages

Illustrations show medieval dancers accompanied by flutes, recorders, oboe-like instruments (shawms), and early violins of various sizes. Some pictures show trumpets and drums, although royalty usually reserved these instruments for ceremonial purposes.

Interior, Notre Dame, Paris

THE RENAISSANCE (1450–1600)

Rebounding from the cultural dormancy and devastation of the first wave of the Plague (Italy, 1348) and the Hundred Years' War (1337–1453) between England and France, the people turned away from the Church in favor of the secular world of art and science. Their quest for strength to cope with life led to a rebirth—the *Renaissance.*

As the Middle Ages drew to a close, interest revived in ancient Greek and Roman arts and philosophy. The Renaissance inspired exploration, practical inventions, and discovery. Christopher Columbus, Vasco da Gama, and Ferdinand Magellan discovered and explored new lands; Nicolai Copernicus and Galileo Galilei expanded our knowledge of the universe through astronomy.

Humanism

In contrast to the focus on the sacred in medieval thought, the Renaissance was an age of *humanism.* As individual achievement took on a new importance, artists proudly signed their works. The humanistic spirit awakened an optimism that all things were possible and knowable.

RENAISSANCE "MAN"   Artists, philosophers, inventors, and scientists enthusiastically crossed disciplines. Niccolò Machiavelli (1469–1527), for instance, was not only a political official but a political philosopher, a historian, an essayist, and an author of the famous treatise *The Prince.*

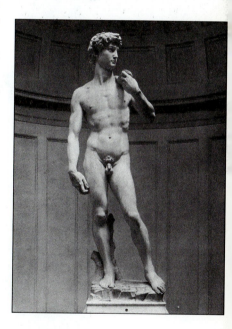

Statue of David by Michelangelo at the Galleria dell-Accademia, Florence, Italy

Challenge Your Expertise

What group could be considered one of the first musicians' unions?

Leonardo da Vinci
(dah-*veen*-chee)

Perhaps Leonardo da Vinci (1452–1519) epitomizes the Renaissance man. He is best remembered for his fresco *The Last Supper* and his painting *Mona Lisa*. His genius also provided the world with a legacy of inventions and knowledge in anatomy, architecture, hydraulics, hydrology, geology, meteorology, mechanics, machinery and gears, military weaponry and fortifications, human and avian flight, optics, mathematics, botany, and more.

Michelangelo
(mee-kehl-*ahn*-jeh-loh)

Leonardo's breadth of accomplishments is rivaled by that of Michelangelo Buonarroti (1475–1564), an Italian sculptor, painter, architect, and poet. His sculptures *David*, *Moses*, and the *Pietà*, and his paintings on the ceiling of the Sistine Chapel at the Vatican in Rome are among the greatest accomplishments in the history of Western art.

MUSIC IN THE RENAISSANCE

In contrast to the other arts, the music of the Renaissance had fewer significant innovations. As opportunities for performance increased, so did the number of composers, each contributing technical refinements.

Although religious music was still predominant, the demand for secular music increased. Court musicians were hired to entertain in the homes of the wealthy. Small instrumental groups performed in courtyards, on balconies, and in various rooms—thus, the term *chamber music*.

RESIDENT COURT COMPOSER   With their own chapels and resident clergy, the courts of the aristocracy were self-contained. The resident court composer was responsible for supplying all music—religious music for chapel,

Sketch of helicopter by Leonardo da Vinci

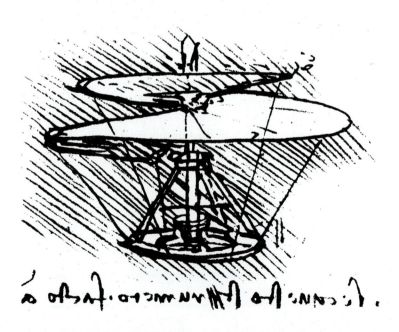

chamber music for instrumentalists, dance music and songs for solo entertainers, and choral music for the court choir.

THE MADRIGAL   Madrigals, still performed today by small groups of singers, were composed expressly for court entertainment. Originating in the Italian courts, the first madrigals were sung in Italian. Important Italian madrigal composers were Carlo Gesualdo (1560–1613), Luca Marenzio (1553–99), and Claudio Monteverdi (1567–1643).

As madrigals spread to other countries, they were written in the language of the court. English madrigals became extremely popular during Shakespeare's time and are still performed in concerts of choral groups. Some of the leading English madrigal composers were Thomas Morley (1557–1602), Thomas Weelkes (1575–1623), and John Wilbye (1574–1638).

Romantic love, sometimes erotic love, was high on the list of favorite madrigal subjects. But many madrigals reflected on nature, and some were settings of sonnets or pious devotions.

A close-up of Michelangelo's painting of Jeremiah the Prophet at the Sistine Chapel in Rome, commissioned by the Vatican as part of the counter-Reformation.

LISTENING INSIGHTS

How to Listen to Polyphonic Music

Polyphonic texture is sophisticated and somewhat complicated, often with four or five melodies sung or played simultaneously. During the Renaissance, one voice (or part) usually started the melody. Then a second voice picked up the melody, which was continually passed around through the several parts. As listeners, we tend to focus on the melody. In polyphonic music, that melody, or fragments of it, constantly shifts from part to part, requiring us to shift our attention with the music.

Counterpoint

In addition to the recognizable melody, composers use other connecting and supporting music—the glue that holds the work together—called *counterpoint*. Much of the beauty of Renaissance polyphony is its seamless interweaving of parts and the harmonies created both by the melody and by the connecting material—like a group of independent dancers, performing separate steps yet interacting with each other.

The following graphic representation of a section of four-part Renaissance polyphonic texture indicates both the imitative entrances of the melody and the connecting material:

Voice 1   MELODY — (counterpoint) — MELODIC IMITATION — (counterpoint) — etc.

Voice 2   MELODIC IMITATION — (counterpoint) — MELODIC IMITATION — (counterpoint) — etc.

Voice 3   MELODIC IMITATION — (counterpoint) — MELODIC IMITATION — (counterpoint) — etc.

Voice 4   MELODIC IMITATION — (counterpoint) — MELODIC IMITATION — (counterpoint) — etc.

POLYPHONY CONTINUES   Characterized by many independent musical lines, polyphony continued throughout the Renaissance to dominate the musical texture of secular as well as sacred music. Creating as many as five and six parts, composers usually separated or staggered the entrances of voices. In contrast to Middle Ages polyphony, Renaissance polyphony is mostly *imitative;* that is, the voices all sing the same or a similar melody, starting at different times. This note-against-note or melody-against-melody technique is also referred to as *counterpoint.*

Palestrina

Palestrina
(pah-leh-*stree*-nuh)

Of the many Renaissance composers, Giovanni da Palestrina stands out as one of the most respected by listeners and musicians. His seamless counterpoint is a mode of both the creativity and craftsmanship of the period.

Giovanni Pierluigi da Palestrina (c. 1525–94)

Giovanni Pierluigi da Palestrina was born in 1525 or 1526 in Palestrina, a small town near Rome. After receiving his musical education in Rome, young Palestrina returned to his native town in 1544. There, the Bishop of Palestrina appointed him organist and choirmaster at Sant Agapito.

When his patron was elevated to Pope Julius III in 1550, Palestrina returned to Rome as the music director and choirmaster of the Cappella Giulia (Sistine Chapel) at St. Peter's. The appointment irked Vatican officials, who objected to the fact that Palestrina was married, among other issues. Therefore, after Julius's death five years later, Palestrina found it difficult to stay at St. Peter's, although he remained in Rome.

For the next six years, he was choirmaster at St. John Lateran, then moving on to a similar but more prestigious position at Santa Maria Maggiore, where he once been a choirboy. In 1571, Palestrina returned to the Vatican, where he worked for the rest of his life.

Although Palestrina wrote secular madrigals, the great majority of his work is sacred. His compositions are considered perfectly representative of church style.

PRINCIPAL WORKS

Sacred Vocal Music: Over 100 Masses, including *Missa Papae Marcelli* and *Missa brevis;* 375 motets; 35 Magnificat settings; 68 offertories; lamentations, litanies, sacred madrigals, and hymns.

Secular Vocal Music: Over 140 madrigals.

LISTENING ACTIVITY

"Kyrie" from the Mass *De Beata Virgine,* Giovanni Pierluigi da Palestrina

Large Form: Ordinary Section of a Mass
Performing Medium: A Cappella Choir

Compact Disc 1, Track 5
Cassette Tape: Side A, Example 5
Running Time: 3:37

Listen to the recording of Palestrina's late-sixteenth-century polyphonic treatment of the "Kyrie" section from the Ordinary portion of the Mass *De Beata Virgine* (*To The Blessed Virgin*). Four separate voice parts weave in counterpoint. The melody (*cantus,* in Latin) of this Kyrie is an old Gregorian chant, around which Palestrina added other voice parts.

Notice that the sopranos begin, and the altos enter with counterpoint. Then the tenors and basses imitate the sopranos and altos. What you hear in this style is almost constant imitation, prompting you to shift your focus to whichever voice enters with the melody.

Important Composers of the Renaissance

Franco–Flemish Composers

Jacob Arcadelt (c. 1505–c. 1567)
  Wrote mainly *chansons* (songs) and madrigals

Gilles Binchois (c. 1400–60)
  Composed *chansons* for the court of Philip the Good of Burgundy

Jacobus Clemens (c. 1510–c. 1567)
  Composed mostly music for the church

Guillaume Dufay (c. 1400–74)
  The leading composer of his day in Burgundy, Dufay wrote Masses and motets for church services and *chansons* for the courts.

Heinrich Isaac (c. 1450–1517)
  Composed both church and secular music

Clement Jannequin (c. 1475–1560)
  Wrote mainly *chansons* for the French courts

Josquin des Prez (c. 1440–1521)
  One of the greatest composers of the Renaissance, Josquin was born in France but spent most of his productive life in Italy. He wrote both Masses and secular *chansons.*

Claude Le Jeune (1528–1600)
Composed motets and *chansons*

Orlando di Lasso (1532–1594)
Lasso, or Lassus, as he was known in Italy, was born in the Franco–Flemish north. One of the greatest composers of the period, Lasso worked in Milan, Naples, Rome, and Munich. He composed both sacred and secular vocal music.

Jacob Obrecht (c. 1452–1505)
Composed church music and *chansons*

Johannes Ockeghem (c. 1430–97)
Known for his canons and intricate counterpoint, Ockeghem wrote both church and secular music.

Claudin de Sermisy (c. 1490–1562)
Known mainly as a composer of *chansons*

Jan Sweelinck (1562–1621)
Mainly known for his keyboard music, Sweelinck also wrote *chansons*.

Adrian Willaert (c. 1480–1562)
Born in the Franco–Flemish north, Willaert made his way to St. Mark's in Venice, where he was renowned as a church composer and teacher. He also composed *chansons*.

Italian Composers

Costanzo Festa (c. 1490–1545)
Composed church music at the Papal Chapel in Rome, though he is best known for his Italian madrigals.

Andrea Gabrieli (c. 1533–85)
Andrea Gabrieli preceded his nephew Giovanni as first organist at St. Mark's in Venice. He composed both church music and madrigals.

Giovanni Gabrieli (c. 1555–1612)
Composed church music, concertos, instrumental music, and madrigals (More on Gabrieli in Chapter 9.)

Carlo Gesualdo (c. 1560–1613)
Mainly known for his innovative chromatic madrigals

Luca Marenzio (c. 1553–99)
Known mainly for his madrigals, Marenzio also composed many sacred motets.

Claudio Monteverdi (1567–1643)
Besides his late opera works in the Baroque period, he wrote many madrigals as a young composer. (More on Monteverdi in Chapter 9.)

Giovanni da Palestrina (c. 1525–94)
Considered one of the greatest Renaissance church composers (see biography)

Spanish Composers

Antonio de Cabezon (c. 1510–66)
  Wrote mainly keyboard compositions
Cristobal de Morales (c. 1500–53)
  An important church composer
Tomàs Luis de Victoria (c. 1549–1611)
  The most important Spanish church composer of the period

German Composers

Hans Leo Hassler (1564–1612)
  Wrote German polyphonic *lieder* (songs) as well as church music

English Composers

William Byrd (1543–1623)
  One of the best English composers prior to the Baroque era, he composed church music, keyboard music, and songs.
John Dowland (1562–1626)
  A prolific composer, Dowland wrote songs for several voices as well as music for the lute.
Thomas Morley (c. 1557–1602)
  Morley is known mainly for his popular English madrigals.
Thomas Tallis (c. 1505–85)
  Tallis wrote his most important works for the church.
John Taverner (c. 1490–1545)
  One of England's finest church-music composers
Thomas Weelkes (c. 1557–1623)
  Weelkes wrote some of the most popular English madrigals.

Summary of Terms

Age of Faith
cantus
chamber music
Chartres
counterpoint
Dark Ages
Gloucester
Gothic Cathedrals
Humanism

lute
madrigal
Mass
Meistersingers
minnesingers
minstrels
Notre Dame
Old Roman chants

Ordinary Mass
organum
plainchant
plainsong
Proper Mass
Salisbury Cathedral
troubadours
trouvères

Summary of Nonmusicians

Gregory I (Pope, called The Great) c. 540–604
Leonardo da Vinci (1452–1519)
Machiavelli (1469–1527)
Michelangelo (1475–1564)

Chapter 8

The Baroque Style Period (1600–1750)

PROTESTANT REFORMATION

When Martin Luther nailed a list of grievances on the door of Palast Church in Wittenburg, Germany, his protests included the widespread practice among Catholic clergy of selling indulgences to forgive sins and the lack of relevancy of the traditional church service. Thus, in 1517, during the Renaissance Period, the Protestant Reformation gradually challenged the omnipotence of the Church of Rome. By 1532, the Reformation had spread to Sweden, Scotland, and France, and soon after, across most of Europe.

CHANGING CHURCH SERVICE   Luther, a priest himself, doubted that his parishioners could derive full spiritual satisfaction by being merely passive observers of the traditional Latin service that the Roman Catholic Church offered. In his own services, Luther instituted two important changes to make the liturgy more accessible to his congregation:

- *Language change* Luther translated his services from Latin into German, the language of his congregants.

- *Congregational singing* In his desire to involve the entire congregation, Luther wrote easily learned, easily sung hymns

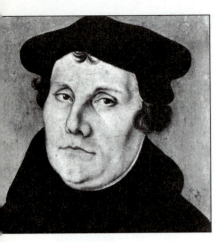

Portrait of Martin Luther, painted by Lukas Cranach

St. Peter's Basilica, Rome

Bernini
(bayr-*nee*-nee)

Bramante
(brah-*mahn*-tay)

The Cupola of St. Peter's in Rome

with a German text. Even those who could not read learned to sing them. (Today, most denominations throughout the world use books of hymns, or hymnals, for congregational singing.)

COUNTER-REFORMATION

Between 1545 and 1564, Roman Catholic church leaders met intermittently at the Council of Trent to devise strategies to deal with the Reformation. The result was the *Counter-Reformation,* which included a mandate for making the church more attractive—if not in substance, at least in image. Church leaders decided to implement this new image by enhancing eye appeal.

BAROQUE FACADES Highly ornate Baroque facades gave an architectural facelift to drab exteriors of older churches. Architects designed and built new, elaborate, Baroque-style churches.

One of the first projects became the showcase of the Vatican in Rome—St. Peter's Basilica (1546–1664). The exterior was completed in the early seventeenth century, with its rows of columns later designed by Gianlorenzo Bernini (1598–1680). Michelangelo, who simplified an earlier plan by Donato Bramante (1444–1514), is largely responsible for the dome and the present appearance of the church. *Gold leaf* and colorful brocaded *tapestries* adorn the altar. Bernini and other sculptors created statues of the Trinity, Holy Family, and important saints for the interior and exterior.

STAINED GLASS An important art form since the building of the great Gothic cathedrals in the Middle Ages, stained glass enjoyed a revival during this period. Baroque-style churches continued using stained-glass windows depicting scenes from the Bible. The colorful, cartoon-like scenes were useful instructional tools to help the mostly illiterate congregation understand church history and beliefs. (See Color Plate 4.)

Counter-Reformation Succeeds

The mission of the Counter-Reformation was accomplished by 1600, and the initial impact of Protestantism had waned. Having experienced self-renewal, the Catholic Church was to play a new role in the arts from 1600 to 1750.

Challenge Your Expertise

What were three purposes of stained-glass windows?

HISTORICAL PERSPECTIVE

Book and Music Printing

BOOKS   Until 1453, few people had access to books or could even read. That year, Johannes Gutenberg [*goot*-en-berg] (c. 1390–1468) of Mainz, Germany, printed the first book using movable type—a Bible. Printing remained a slowly developing art, so books were an expensive commodity for another 200 years. It is understandable that most people outside of the clergy or royalty had little access to the printed word.

MUSIC   The first music was printed in 1501 by Ottaviano Petrucci (peh-*troo*-chee) of Venice. Petrucci used Gutenberg's process of movable type.

Sixteenth-century facade of the Gothic Duomo in Mantua, Italy

Table 8.1	Overview of the Baroque Style Period (1600–1750)
Important Composers	Giovanni Gabrieli, Claudio Monteverdi, Heinrich Schütz, Jean-Baptiste Lully, Arcangelo Corelli, Henry Purcell, Alessandro Scarlatti, Domenico Scarlatti, Jean-Philippe Rameau, Antonio Vivaldi, Johann Sebastian Bach, George Frideric Handel
Artists	Gianlorenzo Bernini, Caravaggio, El Greco, Frans Hals, Rembrandt van Rijn, Peter Paul Rubens, Anthony Van Dyke
Writers	John Donne, John Milton, Alexander Pope, William Shakespeare, Jonathan Swift, Jean-Baptiste Molière
Philosophers	Francis Bacon, René Descartes, Thomas Hobbes, John Locke, Bernard Spinoza
Social, Political, and Cultural Events	First opera (c. 1600), Shakespeare's *Hamlet* (1600), King James version of the Bible (1611), Pilgrims land in America (1620), first opera house (1637), reign of Louis XIV (1643–1715), Newton's physical laws, beginning of Age of Enlightenment, expansion of colonialism

Characteristics of Baroque Style Music

General	Music often sounds heavy, grand, and expansive and often includes both singers and instruments
Performing Media	Chamber orchestras, chorus and chamber orchestra, soloist(s) and chamber orchestra, chamber ensembles, organ, harpsichord
Rhythm	Steady beats, running bass, complicated driving rhythms; meters: 2, 3, 4, 6; usually slowing of tempo at the end of the piece
Melody	Major and minor melodies; sequence, imitation, and elaborate ornamentation
Harmony	Strong harmonic movement; harmonic sequences and recurring cadences; major and minor tonalities
Expression	Contrasting layers of dynamics, echo imitation used; loud and soft juxtaposed—no crescendo or diminuendo

| Texture | Mainly polyphonic, thick texture; one or more melodies in high parts with countermelodies; harmonic filler parts and continuous bass line; occasional homophony (sounding together) |
| Forms | Concerto, concerto grosso, suite, oratorio, cantata, opera; trio sonata and other sonatas for instruments, keyboard prelude, fugue, toccata |

Summary of Nonmusicians

Bernini
Bramante
Gutenberg
Petrucci

Chapter 9

Baroque Style Music
(1600–1750)

During the Renaissance, the motivation that had generated cosmetic improvements in church buildings and paintings had not yet extended to church music. Even with the craftsmanship of Giovanni da Palestrina, its greatest master, Renaissance music, although beautiful, was still mostly austere, reserved, somewhat colorless, and usually performed *a cappella* —without accompaniment.

CHANGES OCCUR IN
THE NEW BAROQUE MUSIC

The Venice of 1600 was the commercial maritime center of the world, hosting visitors and merchants from many countries. It was also here that musical innovations in church services first appeared.

As you read in Chapter 5, Giovanni Gabrieli, music director of the Basilica of St. Mark in Venice, implemented the order of the Council of Trent to make church services more interesting. He experimented by placing singers in one alcove (balcony) of the nave, brass players in another, a boy's choir in another, and other vocalists and instrumentalists in other areas. Adding another dimension,

Gabrieli included the great organ of St. Mark. With music coming from several directions, the effect was stereophonic, or multiphonic, sound— also called *antiphonal* style.

What Is the Origin of the Word "Baroque"?

Although we now refer to the style period between 1600 and 1750 as Baroque, the actual term *Baroque* appeared in the late eighteenth century. Classical artists, looking back on the work of their predecessors, derived the term from a Portuguese word describing irregular pearls. These artists felt that the highly ornate Baroque architecture, statues, and music were not as orderly as their more controlled art.

Here is a simplified floor plan for a performance of Gabrieli's music in St. Mark's Basilica:

Simplified drawing of floor plan at the Basilica of St. Mark for the performance of *In ecclesiis*.

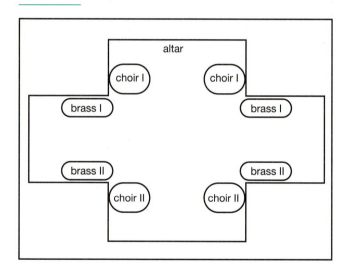

Antiphonal

Exterior of the Basilica of St. Mark in Venice

Interior of the Basilica of St. Mark in Venice

BAROQUE-STYLE VOCAL MUSIC

Concertato Style

Music combining vocal and instrumental ensembles was called *concertato style.* The words *concert* and *concerto* have the same root, and all three terms mean "bringing contrasting performing groups together." This type of music grew in popularity throughout the period in various genres: *opera, oratorio, cantata,* and the *Mass.* These genres are discussed later in this chapter, along with some of the great Baroque composers who championed them: Claudio Monteverdi, Heinrich Schütz, Georg Philip Telemann, George Frideric Handel, and Johann Sebastian Bach.

Concertato

Concert

Concerto

HISTORICAL PERSPECTIVE

The Sensory Appeal of the Catholic Church Service

During the Baroque period, hearing (music) joined the other senses in appealing to the congregation. All five senses were now involved:

sound   rich blends of voices, keyboards, and instruments; bells during the service

sight   elaborate statues; gold-leafed altar; stained-glass windows; ceiling and wall frescoes; ornate, brocaded, jeweled vestments; huge candles; choreographed movement of the priests, altar boys, and congregation

taste   the flavor of the wine and the wafer during Holy Communion

touch   the handling of the rosary beads; contact with holy water; the feel of the benches, floor, wine, and wafers

smell   the aroma of burning candles and incense

Baroque Opera

Opera was one of the most important innovations of the early Baroque era. The first full-length operas were staged around 1600 in northern Italy. Although drama with music existed in the Middle Ages and the Renaissance in the form of mystery plays and other liturgical dramas, nothing prepared audiences for the operas of the early 1600s. The spectacular combinations of dramatic solo singing, emotional choruses, orchestral music, scenery, and dance made opera attendance one of the most fashionable pastimes in Italy.

Venice and Florence hosted some of the earliest opera performances. Claudio Monteverdi, after the success of his *Orfeo* (1607), moved opera from elite court performances to increasingly larger public audiences. The first opera house, open to the general public as well as to the aristocracy, was built in Venice in 1637.

Characteristics of Early Opera

Perhaps Monteverdi's operas have timeless appeal because they contain most of the same characteristics found in more contemporary operas.

Libretto

LIBRETTO   The *libretto* ("little book" in Italian) is the story or play upon which the opera is based. Some of the earliest opera stories were adaptations of classic Greek dramas, such as *Orfeo* (Orpheus) and *The Return of Ulysses to His Country*. Since then, composers have used stories from later times, including their own.

Although opera quickly spread to England and France, the Italian language remained the favorite until the eighteenth century. Not only had the opera tradition developed in Italy, but for many years Italian was considered the most suitable language for singing. Today, an opera can be per-

Claudio Monteverdi (1567–1643)

The birthplace of Claudio Monteverdi (mohn-teh-*vehr*-dee) was Cremona, Italy, the famous violin-making center. Monteverdi began his music career as a string player, later becoming *maestro di cappella* (music director) at the court of Mantua. *Orfeo* (1607), Monteverdi's earliest opera, premiered in Mantua, then played in Venice.

Soon after Giovanni Gabrieli's death in 1612, Monteverdi replaced him at St. Mark's in Venice, the most prestigious appointment in Italy at that time. There, Monteverdi quickly established a reputation for his operas as well as for his religious music. Unfortunately, many of his operas have been lost.

During 1630 and 1631, Venice suffered heavy losses from the Plague. To give thanks for its passing, Monteverdi wrote a stirring *Gloria* in concertato style. Soon after, he took holy orders in the Church and spent approximately ten years concentrating primarily on sacred music.

In his later years, Monteverdi returned to opera. His last opera, *L'incoronazione di Poppea* (The Coronation of Poppea), which premiered in Venice in 1642, is still in the repertoire of today's opera companies.

PRINCIPAL WORKS

Operas: *Orfeo* (1607), *Arianna* (1608), *Il ritorno d'Ulisse in patria* (The Return of Ulysses to His Country, 1640), *L'incoronazione di Poppea* (The Coronation of Poppea, 1642)

Secular Vocal Music: Nine books of madrigals for five to eight voices and instruments, twenty-five Scherzi Musicali for voices and instruments, canzonettas

Sacred Vocal Music: *Vespers* (1610), *Gloria* (1631) for voices and instruments, Masses, and psalms

formed in any language. In fact, as a result of the unusual popularity of opera, some are translated from the original into the language of the country where the performance takes place.

SOLOISTS   Rarely are lines spoken in opera; therefore, principal characters must be trained singers. The variety of voices—sopranos, altos, tenors, and basses—adds interest to the production.

Early opera, however, occasionally used male voices in female roles. Only in the more enlightened and principal operatic centers, such as Venice, were women allowed on stage. (In England, this was also the custom for plays by William Shakespeare [1564–1616], Monteverdi's contemporary.)

Several of the male protagonists' roles—heroes, generals, and so on—called for an extremely high range. Often, a *castrato* would sing this type of   **Castrato** role. To ensure a supply of virtuoso singers, opera producers in the seventeenth and eighteenth centuries arranged for the castration of boys before their voices changed. Apparently, a boy who was a candidate for castrato had to have an unusual timbre: the upper range of a woman and the voice and power of a boy.

You may wonder why anyone would subject himself to castration, or how a boy's parents could consent to such an operation. To understand this practice, keep in mind that opera singers were major celebrities, with all the advantages that come with stardom. Therefore, many families, foreseeing a financially secure future for their children, agreed to the uncomfortable operation.

By the late eighteenth century, when women were permitted on stage to sing the female roles, the castrato gradually became a rarity. (Moreschi, the last of the castrati, died in 1922.)

Bel Canto

BEL CANTO   Operatic *Bel Canto* ("beautiful singing" in Italian) represents the lilting flow of the melody, often containing elaborate embellishments improvised at the time of performance. To perform *bel canto,* a singer must be capable of a highly expressive delivery, which requires extensive training. Thus, when *bel canto* emerged in seventeenth-century Venice, so did employment opportunities for teachers of vocal technique. Venice became the European center for the training of singers.

Recitativo
(reh-chee-tah-*tee*-voh)

RECITATIVO   To advance the story of the opera more quickly, opera composers used the technique of *recitativo* (recitative), a speechlike style of singing. Because singing takes more time than dialogue, the recitative offers an effective compromise between talking and singing. The accompanying orchestra or keyboard instruments usually are lighter than for arias because the text or story is most important in the recitative.

Aria

ARIA   The solo song, or *aria,* began to dominate opera soon after its inception. In the aria, the vocal power, virtuosity, and expressiveness of the singer can be given free reign. Even today, the prospect of hearing a great performer deliver a magnificent solo draws enthusiastic audiences to opera productions. In some cases, a few good arias have made the difference between an opera's success or failure.

ARIA FORM   By the early thirteenth century, operas often contained a series of arias, connected by recitative. These arias usually have a three-part form:

A	B	A

| **A Section:** highly melodic, minimum of ornamentation | **B Section:** contrasts of mood, tonality, or change of tempo | **A Section:** repeat of the first section. Singer is free to improvise, ornament, or embellish the original melody. |

ENSEMBLES (DUETS, TRIOS, QUARTETS)   *Duets, trios,* and *quartets* are songs for two, three, and four singers. Often using the same three-part form (A-B-A) as arias, these multivoice songs add dramatic interest and musical variety to the opera.

CHORUSES   Even in the earliest Greek plays, *choruses* of singers or choral speakers added depth to the drama by providing commentary on the action. In opera, the chorus adds realism and drama to the plot. Chorus members play the parts of soldiers, peasants, courtiers, onlookers, and others. The music provides balance and contrast to the solo singing.

OVERTURE   Monteverdi pioneered the use of the orchestra to provide an overture or introduction to the opera and to play musical interludes during the performance. To establish a mood, he introduced evocative sounds in the orchestra, such as *tremolo* and *pizzicato* (see Glossary).

Overture

Tremolo
(*treh*-mo-loh)

As accompaniment for recitatives and arias, Monteverdi and his contemporaries preferred only a few instruments, or just a lute or a harpsichord. Because the earliest operas were performed in rooms without an orchestra pit, a full ensemble probably would have overpowered the singers, and the audience would have had difficulty understanding the text. By Handel's time, singers performed on elevated stages, making it possible for an orchestra and a harpsichord to accompany recitatives, arias, and choruses.

Baroque Oratorio

Another popular vocal form, the *oratorio,* developed during the late Renaissance. The name derives from the small prayer chapel, or oratorio, within the church where these works were first performed.

Oratorio

Two outstanding composers of oratorios were Heinrich Schütz and George Frideric Handel. They set Bible stories to music in response to the Protestant movement's goal to reach parishioners.

HISTORICAL PERSPECTIVE

Use of Italian Terms in Music

You may wonder why music uses so many Italian terms, especially for expression and tempo indications. some examples are *piano, allegro,* and *rallantando* (see Glossary). After Gabrieli introduced these terms, European composers who had come to Venice to study with him brought the new terms back to their native countries. Italian soon became the international language of music.

Since Gabrieli's time, the vocabulary has greatly expanded. In addition to Italian, composers occasionally use their native languages. This, of course, makes the description less universal than Italian and may pose interpretation problems to performers who are not conversant in a particular language.

Heinrich Schütz (1585–1672)

From early childhood in his native Saxony, Germany, Heinrich Schütz (*shoots*) exhibited talent as a singer. When Prince Moritz, ruler of Hesse-Kassel, stayed overnight at the Schütz family inn, thirteen-year-old Heinrich sang for him. As a result, the prince invited the boy to live at the Kassel court and to sing in the choir.

Heinrich did well at court, and Prince Moritz, a composer himself, later subsidized Heinrich's traveling to Italy to study with Giovanni Gabrieli. Once in Venice, Schütz became one of Gabrieli's favorite pupils. After Gabrieli's death in 1612, Schütz returned to Germany to become *Kapellmeister,* music director, at the Lutheran court of Dresden. There, Schütz carried on the polychoral work of his Venetian master, working Gabrieli's style into the Lutheran service.

Unfortunately for Schütz, the Dresden court was constantly over-burdened with debts. He was poorly paid and miserable because he was never allowed to change positions. Finally, after fifty-five years of servitude, Schütz was released from his Dresden position. He continued composing until his death two years later at 70.

PRINCIPAL WORKS

Oratorios: *Christmas Oratorio* (1664), *The Seven Last Words of Christ on the Cross* (1657)

Passions: *St. Matthew* (1666), *St. Luke* (1666), *St. John* (1666)

Secular Vocal Music: *Italian madrigals* (1611)

Handel's Oratorios

Handel earned his reputation as a German composer of Italian-style operas for English audiences, but he owed the success of his later career to the oratorio. In 1728, after John Gay's *The Beggar's Opera* in English, London audiences began to lose interest in Italian-language opera. Handel maintained his stature as the most popular composer in London by switching to composing oratorios with English text.

A financial consideration also motivated him. The Church of England banned all stage productions during the pre-Easter season of Lent. Oratorios, however, fit into a loophole. They had religious subject matter; they contained no acting, costumes, or staging; they were usually performed in churches. Therefore, oratorios were permitted.

Immediately acclaimed, Handel's oratorios played throughout Lent, indulging London audiences in their desire to be entertained. Handel's appeal also extended to London's large Jewish population, which enjoyed his Old Testament oratorio subjects: *Solomon, Judas Macabbaeus, Israel in Egypt,* and others.

George Frideric Handel (1685–1759)

George Frideric Handel was born in Halle, Germany, near Berlin, into a family of clergy and doctors who concentrated their efforts on financial security rather than on the arts. His father, who died a week before George's twelfth birthday, had encouraged his son to study law. But an event two years earlier had influenced Handel profoundly.

Hearing that his father planned a short trip to visit his older son Karl, valet to Duke Johann Adolf, 10-year-old George wanted to go along. When his father left without him, a disappointed but determined young Handel followed after his father's carriage on foot until he caught up with him. During the visit, George stayed in the palace chapel. Although he had studied music for only two years, Handel sat down at the organ and began to play. The duke heard his playing and was sufficiently impressed to present the boy with a gift of money. The elder Handel allowed his son to use the gift for music lessons.

At eighteen, Handel entered the University of Halle, and within a few weeks, he accepted a one-year contract to be church organist of the Domkirche—a position that provided a salary, lodging, and prestige. Money was not an issue for Handel: he had an income from his father's estate. So when his contract expired, he left Halle for Hamburg, a lively, sophisticated, wealthy commercial center. In addition to church-supported music, Hamburg had a magnificent opera house with 1,675 seats. Handel worked as a violinist in the opera orchestra. His first opera, *Almira,* was a success when it premiered there in January 1705.

In 1706, after his fourth opera, Handel left Hamburg to study composition with Italian opera composers. He arrived in Florence, but because it was not a center of music, Handel went on to Rome. There he met the violinist and conductor Arcangelo Corelli, whose techniques for bowing and for managing an orchestra impressed Handel. Corelli insisted on the highest professional standards: an orchestra must behave and perform as an ensemble, with accuracy and consistency.

Venice, the opera center of the world, completely charmed Handel. He remained there until early 1708. Then he returned to Palazzo Bonelli in Rome, the home of Marchese Ruspoli, who became his patron. Ruspoli commissioned Handel to compose an oratorio for Easter, which was six weeks away. The two performances of *The Resurrection* were well received.

Handel returned to Germany with a pocketful of letters of recommendation. In June 1710, George the Elector of Hannover appointed him *Kapellmeister* (music director). But Handel needed more activity than Hannover could offer, so he obtained a one-year leave of absence to go to London. There, his music had its first local performance in early December at the famous Haymarket Theatre. In February 1711, his opera *Rinaldo* had its successful premiere at the Queen's Theatre.

Handel reluctantly returned to Hannover, using his time there to learn English. In the autumn of 1712, the Elector again granted Handel permission to return to London on the condition that he return promptly. Once back in London, Handel ignored his promise, remaining there for two years.

Then, a coincidence caused an embarrassing predicament between 32-year-old Handel and his employer. Following the death of Queen Anne in 1714, King George I ascended to the throne—the same George who had been Elector of Hannover. Rather than create an unpleasant confrontation, George accepted Handel's apology and, to show there were no hard feelings, doubled his salary.

In 1720, Handel became the director of the newly opened Royal Academy of Music. In addition to composing, his responsibilities took him all over Europe to audition opera singers. His operas, including *Giulio Cesare* and *Rodelinda,* premiered at the Academy.

After a long career that brought wealth and fame, mainly as an opera and oratorio composer, Handel's health declined. Although losing his eyesight, he continued to conduct and to perform at the keyboard but composed very few works during his last years. Handel remained in London until his death at 74.

PRINCIPAL WORKS

Operas: Over forty operas in Italian. *Rinaldo* (1711), *Giulio Cesare* (1724), *Rodelinda* (1725), *Alcina* (1735), and *Serse* (1738)

Oratorios: Over thirty oratorios. *Athalia* (1733), *Alexander's Feast* (1736), *Saul* (1739), *Israel in Egypt* (1739), *Messiah* (1742), *Samson* (1743), *Judas Maccabaeus* (1747), and *Solomon* (1749)

Secular Vocal Music: Over 100 Italian cantatas; trios, duets, and songs

Instrumental Music: *Water Music* (1717) and *Music for Royal Fireworks* (1749), six concerti grossos, Op. 3 (1734), twelve grand concertos, Op. 6 (1740), and organ concertos

Chamber Music: Trio sonatas for recorder, flute, oboe, and violin

Keyboard Music: Harpsichord suites, chaconnes, airs, preludes, and fugues

English Baroque Soloists and Monteverdi Choir, John Eliot Gardiner, Conductor

BAROQUE CANTATA

The cantata, another popular vocal form during the Baroque period, features soloists, chorus, and orchestra. Although similar to the oratorio both in style and general format (see comparison, summarized in Table 9.1), the cantata is much shorter than the oratorio.

Cantata
(can-*tah*-tuh)

Table 9.1	Baroque Opera, Oratorio, and Cantata Compared		
	Opera	**Oratorios**	**Cantata**
text or plot	usually secular	religious, Old and New Testament	religious and secular
language	Italian	local language	local language
staging	yes	no	no
scenery	yes	no	no
costumes	yes	no	no
characters	yes	yes	yes
acting	yes	no	no
soloists	yes	yes	yes
overture	yes	yes	yes
recitatives	yes	yes	yes
arias	yes	yes	yes
duets, trios	yes	yes	yes
chorus	yes	yes	yes
orchestra	yes	yes	yes
keyboard	harpsichord	organ/ harpsichord	organ/ harpsichord

LISTENING ACTIVITY

"FOR UNTO US A CHILD IS BORN,"
GEORGE FRIDERIC HANDEL
CHORUS FROM *MESSIAH* (1741)

Large Form: Oratorio
Detailed Form: Sectional
Performing Medium: Chorus and Chamber Orchestra

Compact Disc 1, Track 6
Cassette Tape: Side A, Example 6
Running Time: 4:16

The sectional form can be charted as follows:

Orchestra Introduction	A B C	A B C	A B C	A B C	Orchestra Coda

Messiah, the oratorio Handel wrote more than 250 years ago, gives us a glimpse of his genius for writing exhilarating choral music. Note the extensive use of imitation and sequences in the vocal parts. Notice also how Handel's music reflects the text. For the opening text, "For unto us, . . ." the music is more aggressive.

The climax of the chorus comes with the musical fanfare, "And the government shall be called Wonderful, Counsellor, the mighty God, the everlasting Father, the Prince of Peace."

LISTENING GUIDE

"FOR UNTO US A CHILD IS BORN,"
GEORGE FRIDERIC HANDEL
CHORUS FROM *MESSIAH* (1741)

INSTRUMENTAL INTRODUCTION

6   0:00   MAIN MELODY A   violin section of the orchestra; moderate tempo; 4 meter; *f*; major tonality; basso continuo

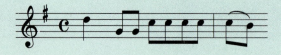

0:14   MAIN MELODY A   sopranos enter, *p*; accompanied by orchestra, moves with sequences, "For unto us . . ."

SOPRANOS

0:28   MAIN MELODY A   imitated by tenors, *p*; "For unto us . . ."

TENORS

0:31   MAIN MELODY A   imitated by sopranos, then running sixteenth-note counterpoint, "For unto us a Child is Born . . ."
0:44   MAIN MELODY A   imitation by altos, *p*; imitated by basses, running sixteenth-note counterpoint in basses, "For unto us . . ."
1:04   SECOND MELODY B   stated by tenors, *mf*; imitated by sopranos, then altos and basses together

TENORS

1:21   FANFARE THEME C   chorus and orchestra together, homophonic texture, *ff*; violins with steady sixteenth notes.
1:34   MAIN MELODY A   stated by altos, *p*; imitated by altos and tenors *f*; then running sixteenth-note counterpoint in tenors, "For unto us . . ."
1:48   SECOND MELODY B   stated by altos, *mf*; imitated by basses, "And the government . . ."
2:03   FANFARE THEME C   all voices and orchestra homophonically, *ff*; violins steady sixteenth notes, "Wonderful, Counsellor . . ."

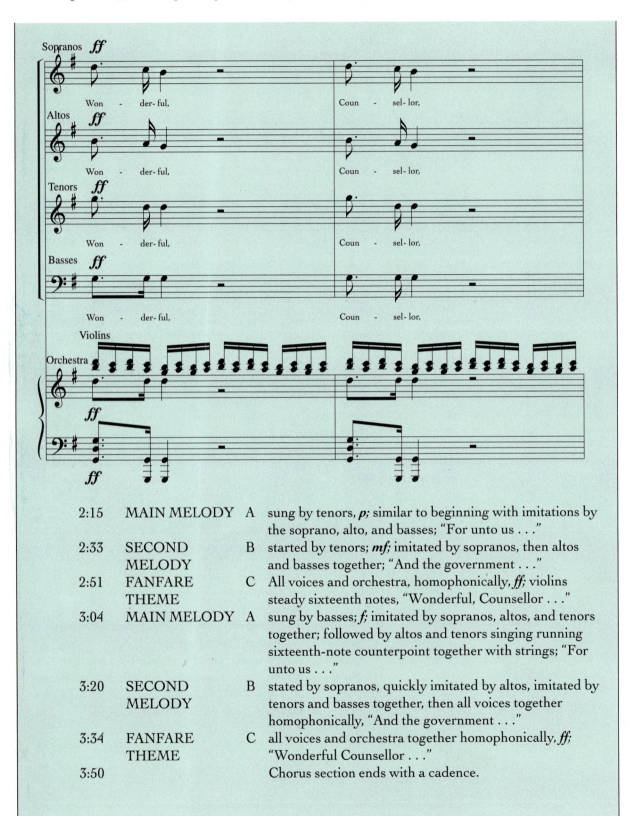

2:15	MAIN MELODY	A	sung by tenors, *p*; similar to beginning with imitations by the soprano, alto, and basses; "For unto us . . ."
2:33	SECOND MELODY	B	started by tenors; *mf*; imitated by sopranos, then altos and basses together; "And the government . . ."
2:51	FANFARE THEME	C	All voices and orchestra, homophonically, *ff*; violins steady sixteenth notes, "Wonderful, Counsellor . . ."
3:04	MAIN MELODY	A	sung by basses; *f*; imitated by sopranos, altos, and tenors together; followed by altos and tenors singing running sixteenth-note counterpoint together with strings; "For unto us . . ."
3:20	SECOND MELODY	B	stated by sopranos, quickly imitated by altos, imitated by tenors and basses together, then all voices together homophonically, "And the government . . ."
3:34	FANFARE THEME	C	all voices and orchestra together homophonically, *ff*; "Wonderful Counsellor . . ."
3:50			Chorus section ends with a cadence.

CODA

    3:54   MAIN MELODY A   orchestral restatement, *ff;* cadence with ritardando (slowing down)

    4:11   Final chord held.

HISTORICAL PERSPECTIVE

Handel's MESSIAH

Handel composed *Messiah* in only twenty-four days—an amazing feat for a three-hour work containing some of the grandest music ever written. Waving off food and often sleep, Handel worked feverishly to complete the monumental work.

In April 1742, the public first heard the work in Ireland at Dublin's Music Hall. Handel had staged a special preview there during an open rehearsal to build the public's anticipation for a formal premiere a few days later. His strategy worked. So great was the clamor for tickets after the preview that hundreds of people had to be turned away.

Dublin's Music Hall had no seats. Those attending *Messiah* had to stand for hours. In the interest of space, comfort, and additional sales, ticket holders were alerted in advance: women were not to wear their customary hoops; men had to forgo their swords. Despite these minor inconveniences, *Messiah* was a huge success. In fact, a special charity performance of the oratorio at the Dublin Cathedral raised enough money to free 142 people from debtors' prison.

Today, at concert performances of *Messiah*, audiences often stand during the "Hallelujah" chorus. This practice goes back to Handel's day when King George II, inspired by that section, rose to his feet. His subjects dutifully followed, thus inaugurating the tradition.

Messiah was first performed in New York in 1770. Since then, cities in North America have joined those throughout the world in presenting it during the holiday season. Fans of *Messiah* can participate in sing-along performances with professional choruses and orchestra. Watch your local newspapers for this opportunity.

SECULAR CANTATA   Cantatas performed as part of the Lutheran Church service usually glorified New Testament subjects. Secular cantatas, however, used popular themes. Bach's charming "Coffee Cantata" is an example of a secular cantata. He wrote this work for a Collegium Musicum student choir that assembled regularly at Zimmermann's Coffee House in Leipzig. The text, a comedy by the poet Picander, expresses women's desire to partake in the pleasure of drinking coffee and their objections to being excluded from the cafés.

Performance of a Lutheran cantata

USE OF CHORALES IN THE BAROQUE LUTHERAN CANTATA   Simple hymns or chorales, an important part of the Lutheran Church service during the Baroque period, were usually incorporated into the cantata. Martin Luther himself had been a lover of music, a singer, and a composer. He felt strongly that the congregation should take part in the musical portion of the service. To that end, Luther composed many chorales for his own services.

Luther's original chorales included only a text and melody—no harmony—and were intended for the congregation to sing in unison. Subsequent Lutheran Church composers harmonized the original chorales. Of all these, Bach's harmonizations are the most famous.

LISTENING INSIGHTS

How to Listen to Baroque Music

To get the most out of listening to Baroque music, try to follow its use of basic elements and its grand sweep. Much of the music combines soloists, choirs, and instruments, producing a large, colorful sound. Like the highly ornamented palaces and churches of its time, Baroque music is busy—there are many things going on at the same time. The characteristic overlapping lines of music—polyphonic texture—require the listener to follow the many entrances of ideas. It is similar to a play, with many actors on stage all speaking at once. Each comes forward with an idea, then steps out of the way to let the next one move forward, usually expressing the same idea.

The melodic movement relies heavily on three ingredients: repetition, imitation, and sequences. Try listening for these elements and you'll notice how frequently all three are used: long passages of sequences and imitations, and sections repeated exactly.

In addition to the polyphonic texture, the music often has an instrumental background support, consisting of a plodding or continuous bass line and harmonic fill lines in other parts.

Listen also for the rhythmic drive, making Baroque music lively and appealing.

Johann Sebastian Bach (1685–1750)

Born in Eisenach, Germany, into a distinguished family of professional musicians, Johann Sebastian Bach (*bahk*) lived and worked throughout his life within a 100-mile radius of his birthplace. The Bach family took great pride in having been elevated to the middle class, a status that included the opportunity to attend university. They also took seriously the responsibility of preparing each new generation of the family for a career in music. Bach received most of his musical training from his oldest brother, Johann Christoph, an organist, with whom Bach lived after he was orphaned at age 10.

At 18, Bach secured his first appointment—violinist in the small, private orchestra of Duke Johann Ernst of Saxe-Weimar. But the assignment also relegated him to a variety of menial, subservient tasks unrelated to music. Realizing that quitting the post could damage his reputation, Bach instead resisted those tasks until, less than a year later, the court dismissed him. However, he was to return to Weimar five years later.

During the interval, Bach served four years as church organist in Arnstadt and one year at St. Blasius in Muhlhausen. It was in Arnstadt that Bach and a cousin from his father's side, Maria Barbara, caused a stir. Maria Barbara, a singer, appeared as soloist for vocal pieces Bach had composed for the church service. Church officials objected: there had been no precedent in Arnstadt for a woman to be a soloist. Bach was able to withstand the criticism, and later, he and Maria Barbara were married.

Under Duke Wilhelm Ernst, the arts thrived in Weimar. The new duke appreciated and encouraged his organist, and Bach composed hundreds of organ works to play for him. The duke also acquired Italian musical works for his court orchestra, including compositions by Antonio Vivaldi, whose concerto structure greatly impressed Bach.

In 1717, when Bach did not receive a promotion to *Kapellmeister*, the top post for a musician at court, he indignantly requested his release. Angered by this request, the duke sent Bach to prison, where he remained for four weeks until the duke dismissed him.

Soon afterward, Prince Leopold of Cöthen hired Bach as his court *Kapellmeister*. Bach was very productive, composing *The Well-Tempered Clavier* for harpsichord, secular cantatas, orchestral music for chamber ensembles, concertos, and duo and trio sonatas. On a trip to Berlin to find a new harpsichord, Bach gave a command performance at the palace of Christian Ludwig of Brandenburg. Two years later (1721), Bach sent Ludwig six concertos for the court orchestra—the famous *Brandenburg* Concertos.

After the death of Maria Barbara, Bach remarried in 1721. He dedicated a book of clavier works to his new wife, Anna Magdalena. From these two marriages, Bach fathered many children, several of whom pursued a career in music.

In May 1723, Bach and his family arrived in Leipzig, where he assumed the prestigious post of Kantor of St. Thomas School. The post included music directorship for the city of Leipzig and its four principal churches. Bach also was director of the Collegium Musicum, which gave weekly performances throughout the year.

It was in Leipzig that Bach composed some of his greatest works, including *St. Matthew Passion* (1727). He began his *Mass in b minor* and, in 1733, he submitted the "Kyrie" and "Gloria" as part of his application for the post of court composer for the King of Poland. Bach received that appointment, which he maintained in addition to his post in Leipzig. Under the patronage of Poland's Roman Catholic king, Bach was able to complete the *Mass* in 1749.

Bach remained in Leipzig until his death at age 65. Although blind (like Handel) in his last years, Bach remained an active composer and performer.

Principal Works

Sacred Choral Music: *St. John Passion* (1724), *St. Matthew Passion* (1727), *Christmas Oratorio* (1734), *Mass in b minor* (1749), *Magnificat in D* (1723), nearly 300 church cantatas: No. 4 "Christ lag in Totesbanden" (Christ lay in the bonds of death, 1724), No. 80 "Ein feste Burg" (A mighty fortress, 1730), No. 140 "Wachet auf" (Sleepers, wake!, 1731), motets, chorales, sacred songs, arias

Secular Vocal Music: Over thirty cantatas: No. 211 "Coffee Cantata" (1732), No. 212 "Peasant Cantata" (1742)

Orchestral Music: *Brandenburg* Concertos 1–6 (1721), four orchestral suites (1725, 1731), harpsichord concertos, sinfonias

Chamber Music: six sonatas and partitas for solo violin (1720), six sonatas for violin and harpsichord (1723), six suites for solo cello (1720), *Musikalisches Opfer* (*Musical Offering*, 1747), flute sonatas, trio sonatas

Keyboard Music: Chromatic fantasia and fugue (1720), "The Well-Tempered Clavier" (1722, 1742), "Goldberg Variations" (1741), six English Suites (1724), six French Suites (1724), six partitas (1731), Italian Concerto (1734), French Overture (1735), *The Art of Fugue* (1745), 600 chorale preludes, hundreds of preludes and fugues, inventions, suites, concertos, dances, toccatas, fantasias, and sonatas

LISTENING ACTIVITY

CANTATA NO. 140, "WACHET AUF" (1731, WAKE UP!)
"OPENING CHORUS," JOHANN SEBASTIAN BACH

Large Form: Cantata
Detailed Form: Sectional
Performing Medium: Chorus and Chamber Orchestra

Compact Disc 1, Track 7
Cassette Tape: Side B, Example 1
Running Time: 6:06

In an elaborate, lively setting, Bach employs the Lutheran *chorale melody* written by Philip Nicolai in 1597. Notice the use of the animated polyphonic texture combined with instrumental accompaniment. After an instrumental introduction, the sopranos sing Nicolai's chorale melody. Then, different sections of the choir imitate the melody.

Notice how Bach's music emphasizes the action words employed in the text: *wake up! where? cheer up! stand up! prepare yourselves! go forth!*

Wachet auf, ruft uns die stimme	Wake up! Call to us the voices
Der Wächter sehr hoch auf der zinne,	Of watchmen high on the tower,
Wach' auf, du Stadt Jerusalem!	Wake up, thou town Jerusalem!
Mitternacht heisst diese Stunde;	It is now the hour of midnight;
Sie rufen uns mit hellem Munde:	They call us with shining faces;
Wo seid ihr klugen Jungfrauen?	Where are you now, clever maidens?
Wohl auf, der Bräut'gam kommt,	Cheer up! The Bridegroom [Jesus] comes,
Steht auf, die Lampen nehmt! Alleluja!	Stand up, and take your lamps! Hallelujah!
Macht eich tereit zu de Hochzeit,	Prepare yourselves, the wedding nears,
Ihr musset ihm ensprungen gehn.	You must go forth to welcome Him.

LISTENING GUIDE

CANTATA No. 140, "WACHET AUF" (1731, WAKE UP!)
"OPENING CHORUS," JOHANN SEBASTIAN BACH

INTRODUCTION

7   0:00   INTRODUCTION THEME   orchestra; *mf*; triple meter; moderate tempo; dotted-rhythm ("long, short"); major tonality; alternating rhythms; polyphonic texture; basso continuo

0:07   INSTRUMENTAL COUNTERMELODY   alternating imitations between violin and oboe

Chorus

0:28   CHORALE MELODY   sung by sopranos; "Wachet auf" (Wake up!); polyphonic texture; counterpoint imitations by altos, then tenors, then basses

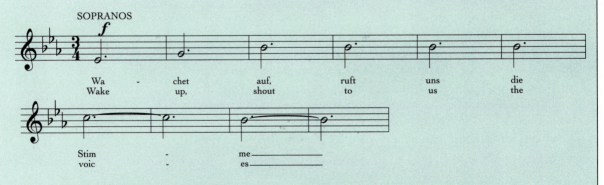

0:43   INTRODUCTION THEME   alternating imitations between oboe and strings

0:46   INSTRUMENTAL COUNTERMELODY   alternating imitations between violins and oboe

	0:49	CHORALE MELODY	long note values; new text; "der Wachter" (the watchmen), sung by sopranos, other voices in counterpoint
	1:05	INSTRUMENTAL COUNTERMELODY	instrumental interlude, alternating imitations between violin and oboe
	1:15	CHORALE MELODY	sung by sopranos, "Wach' auf" (Wake up!), other voices in counterpoint
	1:31	INTRODUCTION THEME	instrumental interlude, similar to opening
	1:59	CHORALE MELODY	sung by sopranos, "Mitternacht" (Middle of the night), other voices in counterpoint
	2:36	INSTRUMENTAL COUNTERMELODY	alternating imitations by violin and oboe
	2:45	CHORALE MELODY	sung by sopranos, "wo, wo" (where? where?), other voices in counterpoint
	3:04	INSTRUMENTAL COUNTERMELODY	alternating between violin and oboe
	3:23	CHORALE MELODY	sung by sopranos, "Wohl auf" (Cheer up!), other voices in counterpoint
	3:41	CHORALE MELODY	sung by sopranos, "Steht auf" (Stand up!)
8	3:57	ALLELUJA	sung by altos; imitated by tenors, then basses, then sopranos

ALTOS

Al - - - - le - lu - ja,——— al - le - lu -

ja,————————————————————————

Coda (A)

4:33	INTRODUCTION THEME AND ORCHESTRAL INTERLUDE	
4:41	CHORALE MELODY	sung by sopranos, "Macht euch" (Prepare yourselves!), other voices in counterpoint, chorus section, ends with cadence
5:33	INTRODUCTION THEME WITH INSTRUMENTAL COUNTERMELODY	exactly like opening, slowing tempo for the final cadence
6:02	FINAL CHORD	*f;* major tonality

BAROQUE INSTRUMENTAL MUSIC

The Baroque Concerto

Developed during the Baroque period, the concerto quickly became the principal instrumental form. At that time, a harpsichord and a chamber orchestra of mostly string instruments accompanied the soloist. As a form, the concerto continued its popularity into the nineteenth and twentieth centuries, and today's audiences can hear renowned soloists perform concertos with symphony orchestras.

HISTORICAL PERSPECTIVE

Evolution of Public Concerts: The Baroque Period

Today, we use the term *concert* for all kinds of public music performance: anyone can buy a ticket and attend. However, before the Baroque period, attendance at concerts—presented in academic settings or in private residences—was restricted to a privileged few. Public concert halls were virtually unheard of. Only in church could common people hear performances of fine music.

VENICE: THE FIRST OPERA HOUSE Opera marked the first important breakthrough in offering music performances to the general public. The milestone was the opening of Teatro San Cassiano in 1637 in Venice. As a major commercial trading center, Venice attracted merchants from all over the world. Its lively economy helped create a thriving middle-class population, eager and able to pay for entertainment and exposure to the arts. By 1700, with its seventeen opera houses, Venice had become the opera capital of the world.

LONDON Starting in 1672 and continuing for six years, the public could attend the first nonopera performances in London's Whitefriars. Building on the popularity of those afternoon concerts, a London coal merchant named Thomas Britton sponsored weekly performances in his storehouse loft. These "Coal-House Concerts" began in 1678 and continued for thirty-six years.

Other Early Opera Houses

1652	Vienna
1656	London
1671	Paris (Academie de Royale Musique)
1678	Hamburg Staatsoper—1,675 seats!
1705	Haymarket Theatre, London
1725	Prague
1731	Covent Garden, London

Dates of Interest

1725	First public concert in Paris
1731	First public concerts in Boston, Massachusetts, and Charleston, South Carolina
1735	First performance of ballade opera (*Flora*), Charleston

CONCERTO FORM   With few exceptions, the concerto has retained the same overall three-movement form that had developed during the Baroque period:

The Concerto Plan	
First Movement	*Fast* (Allegro)
Second Movement	*Slow* (Adagio, Andante, or similar tempo)
Third Movement	*Fast* (Allegro)

Antonio Vivaldi (1678–1741)

A Venetian by birth, Vivaldi (vee-*vahl*-dee) began studying music at an early age with his father, a leading violinist at the Basilica of St. Mark. The young Vivaldi also became a violinist and performed in the same orchestra as his father.

Although music was his first love, Vivaldi studied for the priesthood and was ordained in 1703, when he was 25. That same year he was appointed teacher of violin and orchestra at Pio Ospedale della Pietà, a girl's orphanage in Venice. He was called *il prete rosso* (the red-headed priest) because of his bright red hair. Because the school specialized in music, Vivaldi discovered that he was working with an exceptional orchestra and outstanding students, many of whom were fine soloists.

With the immense popularity of the concerto at court and in public concerts, almost every eighteenth-century composer wrote in this genre. Vivaldi, however, had the distinction of being the most prolific. Some of his compositions have been lost. Of his more than 700 existing numbered works, he wrote, approximately, 450 concertos, 70 sonatas, 45 operas, 35 cantatas, numerous chamber pieces, and sacred vocal music.

Given the title maestro de' concerti in 1716, Vivaldi wrote many of his concertos for his students—works for violin, cello, oboe, flute, piccolo, bassoon, trumpet, guitar, mandolin, or whatever instruments the girls played. His most famous concerto is the programmatic work known as *The Four Seasons*—four violin concertos, each depicting a different season of the year, from a larger work titled *Il cemento dell'armonia e dell'inventione* (1725).

At age 49, Vivaldi left his homeland to accept the position of court composer to Emperor Charles VI of Vienna, where he remained until his death.

Today, many consider Antonio Vivaldi the most original, influential Italian composer of his day. He is recognized as an innovator in form, orchestration, and technique.

PRINCIPAL WORKS

Many of Vivaldi's nearly 800 works have been lost.

Concertos: About 500—including 344 solo concertos (about 230 violin concertos, 81 concertos for two or more soloists), *The Four Seasons*

Chamber Music: Over ninety sonatas and trios for instruments

Operas: Over forty-five operas: *Giustino* (1724), *Griselda* (1735)

Sacred Choral Music: Three oratorios, psalm settings, motets

Secular Cantatas: About forty cantatas

LISTENING ACTIVITY

THE FOUR SEASONS, OP. 8, ANTONIO VIVALDI
CONCERTO FOR VIOLIN AND STRINGS IN E MAJOR: "SPRING"

First Movement: Allegro
Large Form: Violin Concerto
Detailed Form: Rondo or Ritornello
Performing Medium: Violin and Chamber Orchestra

Compact Disc 1, Track 9
Cassette Tape: Side B, Example 2
Running Time: 3:10

You may recognize Vivaldi's popular *The Four Seasons* as background music in film and television productions. The entire work consists of four violin concertos, each based on a descriptive sonnet and focused on a different season of the year.

Previously, we discussed how other Baroque composers, specifically Handel and Bach, derived musical inspiration from the texts they used. Vivaldi chose to depict the seasons instrumentally. To assist with the interpretation, Vivaldi had sonnets printed in each player's musical score. Many scholars believe that Vivaldi also wrote the sonnets. The following is a translation of the sonnet for the first movement of the "Spring" concerto:

> Spring has arrived, and festively,
> The birds greet it with cheerful song
> And the brooks, caressed by soft breezes
> Murmur sweetly as they flow.
>
> The sky is covered with a black mantel
> Lightning and thunder announce a storm
> When the storm dies away to silence, the birds
> Return with their melodious songs.

LISTENING GUIDE

THE FOUR SEASONS, OP. 8, ANTONIO VIVALDI
CONCERTO FOR VIOLIN AND STRINGS IN E MAJOR:
"SPRING"

9	0:00	INTRODUCTION THEME	*"Spring has arrived . . ."* violin soloist accompanied by a string orchestra; allegro; *f*; quadruple meter; E major; theme repeats *p*
	0:13	RITORNELLO THEME	violin solo and orchestra; *f*; syncopated melody, theme repeats *p*
10	0:28	BIRD CALLS	*"and festively, the birds greet it with cheerful song"* soloist and other violins answer each other with trills and scale runs
	1:00	RITORNELLO THEME	returns in violins, accompanied by other strings and continuo; *f*
	1:07	MURMURING BROOK	*"And the brooks . . ."* smoothly, alternating pitches; *p*
	1:29	RITORNELLO THEME	returns in violins, accompanied by other strings and continuo
11	1:36	STORM SECTION	*"The sky is covered with a black mantel . . ."* quick scale runs (lightning); arpeggios (fury of the storm)
	2:02	RITORNELLO THEME	solo violin; all strings and continuo; *f*
	2:09	BIRD CALLS	*". . . and the birds return . . ."* violin trills and scales
	2:26	INTRODUCTION THEME	like introduction: violin soloist and full group
	2:51	RITORNELLO THEME	*f*; repeated *p*; cadence

CONCERTO GROSSO   Composers realized that they could add even more interest to the already popular concerto by featuring more than one or two soloists. They called this "large concerto" a *concerto grosso*.

While Bach was employed as music director at the court of Cöthen, one of his duties was to supply music for court entertainment. It was here that he composed his six famous *Brandenburg* Concertos. Numbers one, two, four, and five are concerto grossos.

BAROQUE KEYBOARD MUSIC

The two most famous Baroque composers, Bach and Handel, were also virtuoso keyboard artists. Both played organ and harpsichord, the popular keyboards of the day. Other composers who wrote extensively for the key-

Challenge Your Expertise

- What was Antonio Vivaldi's distinctive physical feature?
- Which two Baroque-style period composers continued working after becoming blind?

Buxtehude
(*books*-tih-*boo*-duh)
Couperin
(koo-*pran*)
Rameau
(rah-*moh*)
Scarlatti
(skahr-*lah*-tee)
Telemann
(*tay*-lih-mahn)

board include Dietrich Buxtehude (c. 1637–1707), François Couperin (1668–1733), Jean-Philippe Rameau (1683–1764), Alessandro Scarlatti (1660–1725), Domenico Scarlatti (Alessandro's son, 1685–1757), and Georg Philipp Telemann (1681–1767).

The Fugue

A complex polyphonic instrumental composition, the fugue was brought to its highest level of perfection by Johann Sebastian Bach. Even though the fugue is basically an instrumental composition, usually for three or four instruments, the parts are called *voices*—reminiscent of voice parts from an earlier time of *a cappella* compositions. The composer's skill is displayed as the three or four voices interweave without stepping on each other—like three or four dancers moving on a small stage.

LISTENING ACTIVITY

BRANDENBURG CONCERTO No. 2 (1721), JOHANN SEBASTIAN BACH

Third Movement: Allegro
Detailed Form: Concerto Grosso
Performing Medium: Violin, Flute, Oboe, Trumpet, and Chamber Orchestra

Compact Disc 1, Track 12
Cassette Tape: Side B, Example 3
Running Time: 3:01

As discussed in Chapter 5, the *concerto grosso* (large concerto) features several soloists in the same piece of music. This concerto grosso example features four soloists with chamber orchestra: violin, flute, oboe, and trumpet. The tempo is marked *Allegro assai* (quite fast).

LISTENING GUIDE

BRANDENBURG CONCERTO No. 2 (1721),
JOHANN SEBASTIAN BACH

| 12 | 0:00 | MAIN MELODY | stated by the solo *trumpet, f;* with cello and harpsichord (basso continuo) accompaniment, allegro, duple meter (2), F major tonality |

	0:08	MAIN MELODY	imitated by the *oboe, trumpet* in counterpoint
	0:25	MAIN MELODY	imitated by the *violin, trumpet,* and *oboe* in counterpoint
	0:33	MAIN MELODY	imitated by the *flute, oboe,* and *violin* in counterpoint
	0:59		Orchestra strings enter with short accompaniment and counterpoint melodies in solo parts
	1:11	MAIN MELODY	stated by *violin, flute* in counterpoint, with cello and harpsichord continuo
	1:23	MAIN MELODY	imitated by *oboe, flute,* and violin in counterpoint
	1:30	MAIN MELODY	imitated by both cello and harpsichord in orchestra, other instruments in counterpoint
	1:40	MELODIC FRAGMENT	imitated by *trumpet* and *flute*
	1:47	MELODIC FRAGMENT	stated by *oboe,* imitated by *violin,* later by *flute, violin,* then *trumpet,* back to *oboe,* then *flute* playing running sixteenth notes
	2:16	MAIN MELODY	stated in *oboe,* imitations by *flute,* cello, and harpsichord in orchestra, *trumpet* then *flute* running sixteenth notes
	2:52	MAIN MELODY	final statement by *trumpet,* accompanied by all soloists and orchestra, sudden slowing of tempo on last few beats
	2:57	FINAL CHORD	F major tonality

SUBJECT (the point)   As used by Baroque composers, the fugue is based on a short melody called a *subject,* the main point of the work, which is **Subject** introduced at the beginning in a single voice, unaccompanied.

Counterpoint

COUNTERPOINT (against the point)   A second voice enters with the same subject, while the first voice moves into the background (counterpoint). Each time a voice enters with the subject, the other parts move in counterpoint in the background.

Form of the Fugue (A B A)

Exposition

[A] EXPOSITION (exposing the subject)   When all the voices have entered with the subject, the exposition is completed. The following is a simplified graphic representation of the exposition:

```
┌─────────────────────────────────────────────────────────────┐
│         GRAPHIC REPRESENTATION OF FUGUE EXPOSITION           │
│                                                    cadence   │
│  Voice 1   SUBJECT ──────── (counterpoint) ──────┤           │
│  Voice 2      SUBJECT ──────── (counterpoint) ──────┤        │
│  Voice 3         SUBJECT ──── (counterpoint) ──────┤         │
│  Voice 4            SUBJECT ── (counterpoint) ──┤            │
└─────────────────────────────────────────────────────────────┘
```

Episodes

[B] DEVELOPMENT (episodes or events)   The second section of the fugue tests the composer's inventiveness in manipulating fragments of the subject, mainly by using sequences, imitations, and changes of tonality.

[A] RECAPITULATION (restatement of the subject)   Often, the main subject returns briefly just before the conclusion of the fugue.

Coda

Stretto

CODA   A short *coda* usually ends the fugue. *Coda,* the Italian word for "tail," means an ending section. The fugal coda occasionally contains a short section called a *stretto.* Here the subject is imitated by the voices in close succession.

PERFORMING FUGUES   The challenge in performing a fugue on an organ is to keep each voice a distinctly independent melodic line. To sound all the parts, an organist must play more than one melody with each hand and use both feet on the pedal board.

Table 9.2	Overall Form of the Fugue
Exposition (A)	exposing of subject by all parts
Development (B)	free, fantasy section, containing imitation, sequences, and modulations of key
Recapitulation (A)	restatement of subject, similar to exposition
Coda	concluding section (may include a stretto)

🙣 **PLATE 1**
Le Concert champêtre: la musique (The Musicians of a Country Concert).
A chamber music ensemble including (left to right) a harpsichord, lute, recorder,
and a bass viol. (See Chapters 5 and 7)
SOURCE: Giraudon/Art Resource, New York

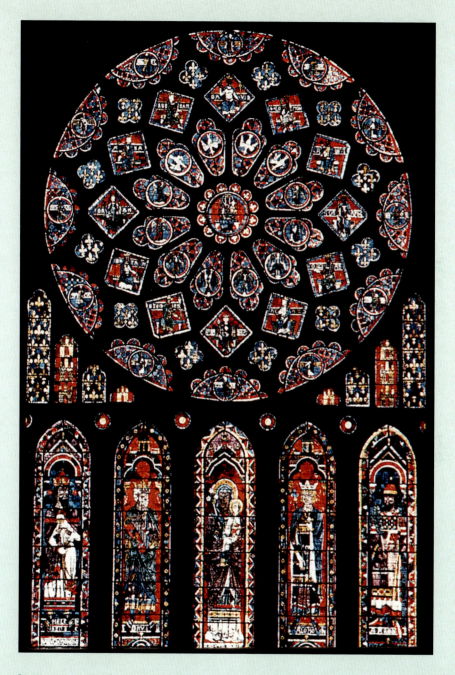

❦ **Plate 4**

The stained glass rose window of Chartres Cathedral in France. The great Gothic cathedral contains some of the best original stained glass windows that date back to the thirteenth century. (See Chapters 7 and 8).

PLATE 5
*Frederick the Great (1712-86),
King of Prussia, performing
by candlelight as soloist with his
court chamber orchestra. (See
Chapter 9)*
SOURCE: Archiv für Kunst und
Geschichte, Berlin

PLATE 6 *(above)*
*18th-century drawing room in the Schönbrunn Palace in Vienna.
Photograph by the author.*
SOURCE: Zorn/August slide collection

PLATE 7 *(right)*
*Seven-year-old Wolfgang Amadeus Mozart at the piano, with his sister
Nannerl singing, and his father, Leopold, playing the violin. Note the
many pillows the tiny Wolfgang had to use to reach the keyboard.
(See Chapter 11)*
SOURCE: Giraudon/Art Resource, New York

Bach at keyboard with his family in a nineteenth-century etching

LISTENING ACTIVITY

FUGUE IN G MINOR (LITTLE), BWV 578, JOHANN SEBASTIAN BACH

Form: Organ Fugue
Detailed Form: Fugue
Performing Medium: Organ

Compact Disc 1, Track 13
Cassette Tape: Side B, Example 4
Running Time: 3:52

This fugue is known also as "The Little" to distinguish it from other fugues Bach composed in the g-minor key. It is a four-voice fugue, meaning that it contains four different parts (voices). Because the main subject (melody) is stated at the beginning, try to remember and then follow it as it is imitated by other parts and as it goes through transformations.

LISTENING GUIDE

FUGUE IN G MINOR (LITTLE), BWV 578, JOHANN SEBASTIAN BACH

EXPOSITION (A)

13   0:00   **SUBJECT (VOICE 1)**   played in the middle register of the organ; moderate tempo; quadruple meter (multiple of two); g-minor tonality

0:17   **SUBJECT (VOICE 2)**   played in lower-middle register, a fourth lower than original, voice 1 plays counterpoint, creating a polyphonic texture

0:37   **SUBJECT (VOICE 3)**   played in low register in the original key of g minor, other voices in counterpoint

0:53   **SUBJECT (VOICE 4)**   played in lowest voice in key of d minor, other voices in counterpoint

DEVELOPMENT (B)

1:08   **SUBJECT FRAGMENTS**   in middle register, imitated in high register, then other registers, sequences, changes of keys

RECAPITULATION (A)

2:06   **SUBJECT (VOICE 4)**   in bass, counterpoint in other parts, original key of B-flat major

2:36   **SUBJECT (VOICE 1)**   in high register, counterpoint in other parts

3:14   **SUBJECT (VOICE 3)**   in middle-low part, counterpoint in other parts

CODA

3:28   **FINAL CHORD**   short coda, sudden slowing, cadencing on a held chord of G major

Challenge Your Expertise

- Why is Bach's Fugue in g minor known as the "Little"?
- What two developments resulted in the concerto grosso?

Summary of Terms

antiphonal	counterpoint	motet
aria	development	multiple soloists
aria form	duet	opera
Baroque	exposition	oratorio
Beggar's Opera	expression indications	overture
bel canto	fugue	pizzicato
cantata	imitative counterpoint	recapitulation
castrato	instrumentation	recitativo
chorales	Kapellmeister	secular cantata
choruses	libretto	stretto
coda	Lutheran cantata	subject
concertato	maestro di cappella	tremolo
concerto grosso	Mass	trio

Chapter 10

The Classical Style Period (1750–1820)

POLITICAL AND SOCIAL BACKGROUND

Two contrasting moods characterized the Classical period. Inside the castles and palaces, the complacent aristocracy settled into a predictable life of manners, morals, and music. Outside the walls, the frenzied people began rising in revolt. The result was a tug-of-war between guardians of the status quo and insurgents who wanted control of their own destinies.

- 1776—The United States sheds its domination by the British Monarchy.
- 1789—Parisian citizens storm the Bastille.
- 1790—Hapsburg troops suppress a revolution for independence in Brussels, Belgium.
- 1792—Angry French mobs take over the Tuileries Palace.
- 1793—Louis XVI, Marie Antoinette, their children, and scores of aristocrats are guillotined.
- 1795—Angry French citizens stage the Bread Riots and White Terror against the aristocracy.

As the eighteenth century drew to a close, Europe was a crazy quilt of wars. Spain declared war on a Britain weakened from its loss to the United States. Napoleon's armies invaded Germany, Italy, and Austria and defeated the Turks in Cairo, Egypt.

To drown out the cries of the mobs, the aristocracy demanded more music. Avoiding the reality of change, royalty retreated into greater self-indulgence, dependent for their comfort on the toil of the lower classes. Legions of servants served dinner on gold plates. Other hirelings, including musicians such as Haydn and Mozart, were meagerly paid to entertain their employers and guests.

Dancing the popular minuet at court

COURT FUNCTIONS   Once a court function was scheduled, servants delivered ornate invitations and returned with acceptances. On the appointed day, guests arrived in the afternoon for drinks, snacks, and chit-chat. Later, they retired to the guest rooms for a nap before changing their clothes for dinner.

COURT CONCERTS AND BALLS   After overindulging in food and drink, the entourage strolled into the music room. During the short concert, several guests would talk incessantly, others would doze noisily, and the rest would listen intermittently. With the concert over, guests would again nap and change their clothes for the ball, where they would dance into the morning hours.

THE MUSICIAN'S LIFE   Most French, German, and Austro-Hungarian courts maintained a staff of resident musicians who could become a small orchestra for concerts, operas, and dances. Considered servants, the musicians often had to put down a serving tray to pick up a violin bow.

The discovery of Pompeii's ruins in 1748 renewed interest in Greek and Roman art.

CLASSICAL ORIGINS

Buried since A.D. 79 in the volcanic ash from Mt. Vesuvius were the cities of Pompeii and Herculaneum. Archeologists excavated these ruins in 1748, uncovering Greek and Roman art, architecture, and artifacts. Their discoveries helped promote a renewed interest in classical art. Symmetry and simple, classical proportions became fashionable in the arts throughout the eighteenth century.

As applied to the music of this era, the concept of *classical* is appropriate because of its emphasis on clarity of sound and symmetry of form. This application certainly describes the music of the great classical composers — Haydn, Mozart, and early Beethoven.

Focus on Form and Symmetry   In court manners and daily life, as well as in the arts, form and symmetry were held in high regard. Notice in the photograph of the eighteenth-century mansion how the architectural design of the building consists of three parts:

As we discuss the music of the Classical period in the next chapter, you will discover how often the A B A form is used. Its balance and symmetry pervade classical forms.

A	B	A
First Section	Contrasting Section	Repetition of First Section

An eighteenth-century aristocratic mansion in Munich, Germany

Table 10.1	Overview of the Classical Period (1750–1820)
Composers	Joseph Haydn, Wolfgang Amadeus Mozart, young Ludwig van Beethoven
Writers	Robert Burns, Johann Wolfgang Goethe, Samuel Johnson, Alexander Pope, Johann Schiller
Artists	Jacques-Louis David, Jean-August Ingres
Philosophers	Denis Diderot, David Hume, Immanuel Kant, Jean-Jacques Rousseau, Voltaire (François-Marie Arouet)
Social, Political, and Cultural Events	Factory system spreads in England; James Watt invents steam engine; American and French Revolutions; Napoléon in power; Catherine the Great rules Russia; Hapsburgs rule Austria, Hungary, Italy, Spain, and the Netherlands; the American Constitution is written; the Age of Reason begins

Characteristics of Classical Music

General	Elegant, restrained, stable, balanced, mostly predictable, with clear musical ideas: you seem to know the music, even upon first hearing it
Performing Medium	Symphony orchestra, chamber orchestra and ensembles, soloists with orchestra, piano, opera companies
Rhythm	Simple, regular rhythms with steady beat; steady tempos with little change; meters mostly 2, 3, 4, 6
Melody	Lightly ornamented melodies; running scale patterns and broken chords; imitation and sequences; symmetrical phrases
Harmony	Chords by thirds, mostly built on scale tones; strong tonal center (key); major and minor tonalities
Expression	Moderate use of crescendo, diminuendo; neither very soft nor very loud (mostly *p, mf, f*)
Texture	Basically homophonic — melody (usually on top) with chordal accompaniment; some less formal polyphony, mainly in development sections
Forms	Clear-cut, easy-to-follow sections set off by obvious cadences and stops; exact repetition of sections; detailed forms: two- and three-part forms; sonata, rondo, minuet and trio; theme and variations; large forms; symphony, concerto, sonata, string trio and quartet; opera; some oratorios and masses

Chapter 11

Music of
the Classical Period

MOZART

Why would some biographers characterize Wolfgang Amadeus Mozart as an intractable genius, quarrelsome with and rebellious toward his patrons? What experiences had molded the young, undisciplined Wolfgang?

Raised in the luxury of the Hapsburg palaces, the infant prodigy was caressed and spoiled by Empress Maria Theresa. How surprising—even demeaning—it must have been to the adolescent Mozart when he realized that a composer was little more than a hired hand! No special station accompanied his employment in the court of the Prince-Bishop of Salzburg. His employer praised him extravagantly, but he paid him relatively poorly.

HAYDN

Financially, as his spacious homes seem to attest, Joseph Haydn fared well. Employed by the Esterházy family for more than thirty years, Haydn led a considerably more stable life than Mozart.

Haydn also grumbled about his employer's treating him as a servant. Having to live in a tiny apartment over the kitchen at the

Esterházy Palace was offensive to him. But Haydn was not as openly rebellious as Mozart, preferring instead to take little jabs at the aristocrats through his music.

YOUNG BEETHOVEN

About the same time Mozart was in Vienna writing some of his greatest works, Ludwig van Beethoven (*bay*-toh-ven, 1770–1827) was growing up in Bonn, Germany. Beethoven had always idolized Mozart, yearning for the day that he could study with him (see the boxed text in Chapter 12: "Beethoven Meets Mozart"). But when Beethoven finally settled in Vienna in 1792, Mozart was dead; thus, Beethoven studied with Haydn and other composers.

In 1778, Ludwig's father had heard about the success Leopold Mozart had with young Wolfgang, so he dressed his eight-year-old son in short pants and tried to foist him off as an infant piano prodigy. Beethoven will be discussed in greater detail in the next chapter.

Young Beethoven. Engraving by Johann Neidl after a drawing by Stainhauser.

Wolfgang Amadeus Mozart (1756–1791)

One of music's greatest child prodigies was born in Salzburg, Austria. Wolfgang Amadeus Mozart displayed his extraordinary musical ability at the age of four by performing in public on both the violin and piano. At age five, Mozart started composing music, and by the time he was eight, he had composed his first symphony. Mozart completed his first oratorio at age eleven and his first opera at age twelve.

When he was six years old, Wolfgang toured the great courts of Europe with his sister Maria Anna (Nannerl), playing the violin and piano to the amazement of his aristocratic audiences. Their tours were supervised by their nurturing father, Leopold (1719–87). To promote his talented children, he had curtailed his own musical career as a violinist and court composer in Salzburg.

For all his prodigious beginnings and genius, Mozart never had the benefit of a stable patron, though recent evidence reveals that his financial situation was considerably better than previously thought (see Historical Perspective: "Mozart Myths Revealed," in this chapter). In 1781, after resigning from his position as concertmaster (principal violinist) in the court orchestra of the Archbishop of Salzburg, Mozart went to Vienna to make his way as a freelance musician.

Soon after his arrival in Vienna, he met and married Constanze Weber. They had six children, only two of whom survived into adulthood—the average survival rate in the eighteenth century.

It was in Vienna that both Mozart and his public realized his greatest talents in opera. His German singspiels (comic opera with spoken dialogue) *Die Entführung aus dem Serail* (The Abduction from the Harem, 1782) and *Die Zauberflöte* (The Magic Flute, 1791) were successes and major departures from the traditional Italian-language opera that had dominated opera since its inception.

Mozart's taste for expensive clothes, entertainment, and travel led him to outspend his income and prompted him to borrow heavily from his father and friends. After he died, some of his creditors went after his estate.

At 35, Mozart died prematurely (see Historical Perspective: "Mozart Myths Revealed"), leaving a legacy of more than 600 compositions in almost every form.

PRINCIPAL WORKS

Symphonies: fifty symphonies: No. 35 (*Haffner*, 1782); No. 36 (*Linz*, 1783); No. 38 (*Prague*, 1786); No. 39 (1788); No. 40 (g minor, 1788); No. 41 (*Jupiter*, 1788)

Concertos: twenty-three piano concertos: No. 15, *K. 450 (1784); No. 17 K. 453 (1784); No. 18, K. 456 (1784); No. 19, K. 459 (1784); No. 20, K. 466 (1785); No. 21, K. 467 (1785); No. 23, K. 488 (1786); No. 25, K. 503 (1786). Five violin concertos; concertos for flute, flute and harp, oboe, clarinet, bassoon, horn; Sinfonia Concertante for oboe, clarinet, bassoon, and horn, K. 279b

Other Orchestral Music: serenades: Serenata notturna, K. 239 (1776); *Eine kleine Nachtmusik*, K. 535 (1787); divertimentos; cassations; dances

Chamber Music: twenty-six quartets; six string quintets; clarinet quintet; flute quartets; piano quartets; piano trios, one string trio; violin sonatas (with piano)

Piano Music: seventeen sonatas; rondos; variations; fantasias; piano duets

Operas: twenty operas: *Idomeneo* (1781); *Die Entführung aus dem Serail* (the Abduction from the Harem, original in German, 1782); *Le nozze di Figaro* (The Marriage of Figaro, 1786); *Don Giovanni* (1787); *Così fan tutte* (Women Are Like That, 1789); *Die Zauberflöte* (The Magic Flute, original in German, 1791)

Choral Music: eighteen masses: No. 16 (Coronation, 1779); Requiem (1791, unfinished); Exultate jubilate (1773); oratorios; sacred music

*K. refers to Ludwig Köchel (*ker*-shul, 1800–77) an attorney and amateur musician who catalogued most of Mozart's works according to their composition dates. Because of Mozart's pressing need to make money with his compositions, he rarely had time to catalogue his extensive output.

HISTORICAL PERSPECTIVE

Mozart Myths Revealed

Over the more than 200 years since Mozart's death, many myths have developed about his life. Recent investigations by physicians, economists, and historians seem to dispel some of these myths.

LIVED IN POVERTY?   The story that Mozart earned very little money, eked out a meager living, and died impoverished is not true. Mozart was too busy composing to keep accurate records of his finances, and his own accounting omitted major opera and other commissions, as well as many performances. A reasonable estimate of Mozart's earnings would certainly place him in an upper-middle-class category. How much did he earn? Responsible economists have given up on their efforts to convert the value of florins in the 1780s to that of today's dollars. The bottom line is that Mozart was no pauper, but rather a moderately affluent composer who chose to live beyond his means. As a young composer who was in demand, he apparently did not anticipate such an early death.

MURDERED BY A RIVAL?   Mozart's premature death has stirred controversy over the years. Rumors have persisted that he was poisoned by the jealous Antonio Salieri (1750–1825), featured in the play and movie *Amadeus*. However, more recent theories suggest that the cause of his death was kidney failure.

DUMPED INTO A COMMUNAL GRAVE?   It is true that after his death Mozart was unceremoniously dumped into a common grave at the Central Cemetery of Vienna. However, according to historian Volkmar Braunbehrens (*Mozart in Vienna, 1781–1791*), Emperor Joseph II decreed in 1784 that all bodies were to be buried as follows:

- put in a communal grave far removed from the city
- covered in a linen sack without a coffin
- sprinkled with lime
- left unmarked with no headstones at the grave site

Sanitary and practical reasons governed the emperor's decree. He wanted to avoid the spread of disease and drinking-water contamination, and to help the bereaved conserve their financial resources. Mozart was treated the same as all other citizens of Vienna during this period.

Challenge Your Expertise

Which is the higher number—Mozart's age at his death or the number of symphonies he composed?

Joseph Haydn (1732–1809)

Born in Rohrau, a small town in eastern Austria near the Hungarian border, Joseph Haydn began his music studies at an early age. At eight, he received a scholarship to study in Vienna, where he became a member of the Vienna Boy's Choir. Later, he held several court posts as a violinist, composer, and music director.

In 1761, Haydn was engaged as court composer and music director in the courts of the Esterházy family. Powerful and wealthy, this Hungarian family had palaces in both Hungary and Austria. During his thirty-year tenure there, Haydn traveled between the two palaces providing weekly operatic performances and orchestral concerts.

After the death of Haydn's Esterházy patron, the concert impresario Johann Peter Salomon made a special trip from London to offer Haydn a commission. Now in his sixties, Haydn found this period of his career fruitful. He wrote his twelve famous "London" symphonies — Nos. 93–104 — for the concerts in that city.

Having become a famous and wealthy artist, Haydn spent his remaining years comfortably in Vienna. There he composed his last works, which included the two great oratorios inspired by his London visits — *The Creation* and *The Seasons.*

Among his great contributions, Haydn helped establish the symphony and the string quartet as major instrumental forms. He was a mentor and friend of Mozart and a teacher of young Beethoven.

PRINCIPAL WORKS

Symphonies: one hundred six symphonies: No. 45 (*Farewell,* 1772); Nos. 82–87, Paris Symphonies; No. 92 (*Oxford,* 1789); No. 94 (*Surprise,* 1791); No. 100 (*Military,* 1794); No. 101 (*Clock,* 1794); No. 103 (*Drum Roll,* 1795); No. 104 (*London,* 1795)

Concertos: numerous concertos for piano, harpsichord, organ, violin, cello, horn, oboe, trumpet

Chamber Music: More than seventy string quartets; thirty-two piano trios; string trios

Piano Music: fifty-four piano sonatas

Operas: Six German operas for marionettes, at least fifteen operas in Italian (many were lost)

Choral Music: fourteen masses; oratorios: *The Seven Last Words of Christ* (1796); *The Creation* (1798); *The Seasons* (1801)

Esterházy Palace, called the "Hungarian Versailles"

HISTORICAL PERSPECTIVE

Haydn's Labor Protest: The "Farewell" Symphony

Haydn's Symphony No. 45 ("Farewell") is an example of his efforts on behalf of musicians. He composed it to protest the fact that members of his orchestra were not permitted to bring their wives and families to the Esterházy's palace in Eisenstadt, about thirty miles south of Vienna. Being away from their families for long periods and having to live in crowded and uncomfortable servant's quarters made life difficult for the musicians.

Haydn composed this clever symphony for one evening's court concert. The first three movements of the symphony were uneventful. In the middle of the fourth movement, according to Haydn's instructions, the second horn player and the first oboist packed up their instruments, blew out their reading candles, and walked out of the hall. Soon, others followed—the bassoonist, the second oboist, cellists and bassists, then the viola and violin players. All departing musicians blew out their candles and made a quiet exit. Finally, with only one candle burning, two violinists finished the symphony.

Haydn's labor protest produced the desired result: Prince Esterházy took the hint and declared an extended leave for the performers to visit their families.

Classical Music Forms

Catering to their patrons' wishes for predictability, composers wrote their works in recognizable forms. So fond were audiences of these familiar forms that composers used them repeatedly. The challenge for composers was to create fresh, interesting works while using this symphonic plan.

HISTORICAL PERSPECTIVE

Evolution of Public Concerts: Classical Period

Court and Subscription Concerts

Orchestra and chamber music concerts took place mostly at court and at the stately homes of the aristocracy. However, with growing frequency during this time, subscription performances were offered in town to the general public. Because few public concert halls existed, many of the early sites were town meeting halls.

With their guarantee of prepaid ticket sales, composers began regarding subscription concerts as an important source of income. Mozart wrote many of his orchestral works for public subscription concerts during his time in Vienna. In Haydn's later years, he traveled throughout Europe and England to perform his music at various subscription concerts.

Concert Programs

Eighteenth-century concerts consisted mainly of new music or music by living composers. The composer was usually present, often participating as a conductor, or a soloist, or both. Motivated by the need to create their personal performing repertories, composers had little interest in performing music by other composers.

With music publishing still inefficient, composers such as Mozart and Haydn had to carry their original, handwritten copies to concerts. Printed music by other composers was hard to come by. By 1800, deceased composers, no longer around to promote their works, were gradually forgotten. Therefore, works by Bach, Handel, and others were rarely performed.

MULTIMOVEMENT PLANS (LARGE FORM) In addition to the symphony, most multimovement works, such as *string quartets, sonatas,* and *concertos,* used the same forms. That is why, if you have heard one symphony by Haydn, another might sound familiar to you the first time you hear it, and also why music by Haydn may sound similar to music by Mozart.

Typical Multimovement Instrumental Forms
- Concerto (three movements)
- Symphony (four movements)
- String trio and quartet (three or four movements)
- Sonata for solo instrument and piano (three or four movements)

THE CONCERTO (THREE MOVEMENTS) Since its development during the Baroque period, the concerto form continued to be an audience favorite in the Classical period. Featuring a soloist and an orchestra, the concerto allowed great pianists such as Mozart and Beethoven to display their virtuosity. The first and last movements typically included a *cadenza,* a highly virtuosic solo passage.

Cadenza

The Concerto Plan	
First Movement	*Fast* (allegro). Usually the most involved and serious movement. Often *sonata form* used as detailed form, with the orchestra playing the exposition and the soloist entering on the repeat of the exposition. One or two cadenzas for the soloist in the movement.
Second Movement	*Slow* (adagio, andante, or similar tempo). Usually a songlike movement, with prominent melody. Many detailed forms used such as sonata, rondo, and theme and variations.
Third Movement	*Fast* (allegro). Usually having the fastest tempo, with a light and witty style. Often, *rondo* form is used with another cadenza for the soloist.

THE CLASSICAL-PERIOD SYMPHONY (FOUR MOVEMENTS)   Most Classical-period symphonies contain *four* movements. The overall form is similar to the concerto, with the addition of a dance movement as the third movement. Occasionally, composers omitted the dance movement, producing a three-movement symphony with an overall form similar to the concerto—*fast–slow–fast*.

Typically, the tempo and mood of each movement of the four-movement symphony follows this plan:

The Symphony Plan	
First Movement	*Fast* (allegro). This is usually the most involved and serious movement. Occasionally a slow introduction opens the work. Most often the *sonata* form is used.
Second Movement	*Slow* (adagio, andante, or similar tempo). Usually a songlike movement, with prominent melody. Using many forms: *sonata, theme and variations, rondo*.
Third Movement	*Moderately fast* (allegretto or menuetto). The popular dance of the period, the minuet, was used most often for this movement. The form is *minuet and trio* (song form and trio).
Fourth Movement	*Fast* (allegro). Usually having the fastest tempo, this movement ends the symphony with a light and happy mood. *Sonata* or *rondo* forms are the most common ones.

First performance of Haydn's
Creation

LISTENING INSIGHTS

How to Listen to Classical Music

The key to enjoying Classical-period music is recognizing and following its *forms*. In no other style period is the understanding of form
so important.

Mozart's and Haydn's audiences knew these forms well. Most of
them played instruments and had studied music as part of their court
education. Knowing the rules of the game, they followed the form with
its themes (melody or melodic fragment). They enjoyed noticing the
subtle deviations that composers used with a particular form.

You can easily follow the overall form (symphony, concerto,
sonata) because there usually are pauses between movements. Once
you understand the typical plan for these works, you know which
movement you are hearing.

Within each movement, the detailed forms are often built
around one or two clearly stated themes or melodies that are
repeated several times. As you listen to them, try to remember the
themes so you will recognize them when they return or are modified
later in the work.

Detailed Forms

The four movements of the symphony or the three movements of the concerto are the overall plan or form. Movements are the outer structure,
much like the structure of a building. Within each movement, composers
organize their music in more specific forms. These forms, then, would be
similar to the detailed infrastructure of a building.

Musical forms are guidelines; a composer may modify them to suit the needs of a particular work. Therefore, from work to work, slight differences may occur within the same form. The most commonly used classical forms used for movements in instrumental music follow:

- Theme and variations
- Rondo
- Minuet and trio (song form and trio)
- Sonata

The young prodigy Mozart being introduced to Maria Theresa at the Schönbrunn Palace, seat of the Hapsburg empire

THEME AND VARIATIONS FORM   A *theme and variations* uses one main theme throughout the movement, usually stated at the beginning of the piece. Then each succeeding section presents a variation or modification. Because the theme is usually recognizable throughout its transformations, this form is easy to follow.

THEME AND VARIATIONS FORM

A main theme	A^1 variation 1	A^2 variation 2	A^3 variation 3	A^4 variation 4

LISTENING ACTIVITY

VARIATIONS, "AH VOUS DIRAI-JE, MAMAN" K. 265 (ALSO KNOWN AS "TWINKLE, TWINKLE, LITTLE STAR"), WOLFGANG AMADEUS MOZART

Large Form: Keyboard Piece
Detailed Form: Theme and Variations
Performing Medium: Harpsichord

Compact Disc 1, Track 14
Cassette Tape: Side B, Example 5
Running Time: 2:49

Listen to this abridged version of Mozart's set of variations on a popular French children's tune of his day, "Ah vous dirai-je, maman" (Oh, what do you want me to tell you, mama?). You may know it in English as "Twinkle, Twinkle, Little Star." In 1778, while performing in Paris, Mozart heard the tune and wrote twelve variations to it. Two variations are performed here.

Since you probably know the theme, you will be able to recognize it throughout its variations. Mozart clearly states the main theme at the beginning with repetitions.

LISTENING GUIDE

VARIATIONS, "AH VOUS DIRAI-JE, MAMAN" K. 265 (ALSO KNOWN AS "TWINKLE, TWINKLE, LITTLE STAR"), WOLFGANG AMADEUS MOZART

14   0:00   MAIN THEME   moderately fast tempo, duple meter; C major tonality
[MAIN THEME] and sections repeated exactly

0:56   VARIATION 1   same tempo, running sixteenth notes (four to a beat) in the upper register incorporate pitches of the main theme; all sections repeated; clear cadence

1:53   VARIATION 2   same tempo and key; modified main theme in the upper register while bass plays running sixteenth notes

Mozart's apartment in a fashionable section of Vienna

RONDO FORM   *Rondo* was one of the favorite forms for the last movement of a concerto or sonata. Catchy, identifiable rondo themes also were used occasionally in symphonies and in string quartets. As you listen to a rondo in a fast movement, you will immediately notice its light, humorous style. Though there are many plans for a rondo, its principal ingredients are a recurring main theme, contrasted with several shorter, less important themes. The following are the most typical plans:

RONDO FORMS

THEME 1 (A)	THEME 2 (B)	THEME 1 (A)	THEME 3 (C)	THEME 1 (A)		

Rondo Form 1

1 (A)	2 (B)	1 (A)	3 (C)	1 (A)	2 (B)	1 (A)

Rondo Form 2

1 (A)	2 (B)	1 (A)	3 (C)	1 (A)	4 (D)	1 (A)

Rondo Form 3

Challenge Your Expertise

How long did Beethoven study with Mozart?

Mozart, age twenty-one, four years before his departure to Vienna

LISTENING ACTIVITY

HORN CONCERTO NO. 2 IN E-FLAT MAJOR, K. 417, WOLFGANG AMADEUS MOZART

Third Movement: Allegro
Large Form: Concerto
Detailed Form: Rondo
Performing Medium: French Horn and Chamber Orchestra

Compact Disc 1, Track 15
Cassette Tape: Side B, Example 6
Running Time: 3:24

This playful rondo movement is from one of Mozart's four concertos for horn soloist and chamber orchestra, written in his later years in Vienna. Mozart composed these concertos for his friend, hornist Joseph Leutgeb, with whom he had performed in the Salzburg court orchestra.

Since the rondo (theme 1 or A) is presented at the beginning, be prepared to become familiar with it so you can recognize it when it returns.

The form of this rondo may be charted as follows:

| THEME 1 (A) | THEME 2 (B) with cadenza | THEME 1 (A) | THEME 3 (C) |
| THEME 1 (A) | THEME 4 (D) | THEME 1 (A) | CODA |

LISTENING GUIDE

HORN CONCERTO NO. 2 IN E-FLAT MAJOR, K. 417,
WOLFGANG AMADEUS MOZART

15	0:00	THEME 1 (A)	horn solo with orchestra accompaniment, rondo theme; E-flat major key; homophonic texture; fast, duple-compound meter; orchestra imitates without soloist and repeats rondo theme, *f*
16	0:18	THEME 2 (B)	lighter; arpeggios in theme; same key; horn questions; strings answer
	0:33	TRANSITION	fanfare-like transition; horn imitated by strings; to cadence, B-flat major key
	0:42	CADENZA	solo horn featuring trills, arpeggios, and scales; transitions back to main theme
	1:00	THEME 1 (A)	exact repeat of opening main rondo theme, horn then orchestra without soloist; E-flat major key
	1:18	TRANSITION	fanfare-like transition; horn imitated by strings
17	1:25	THEME 3 (C)	legato (smooth) melody; c-minor key; horn solos; strings answer with playful ornaments
	1:51	TRANSITION	fanfare-like transition; horn imitated by strings
	1:55	THEME 1 (A)	similar to opening section; horn solo, then orchestra imitation; *f*; E-flat major
18	2:11	THEME 4 (D)	legato melody first in solo horn, then imitated by orchestra; *p*;
	2:28	TRANSITION	similar fanfare-like transition; trills in horn
	2:50	THEME 1 (A)	fragments of main theme, with pauses
	3:02	THEME 1 (A)	faster tempo; horn with main theme
		CODA	horn with fragments from transition fanfare; orchestra imitates; *f*; final cadence in original key of E-flat major

LISTENING ACTIVITY

PIANO SONATA NO. 8 IN C MINOR, OPUS 13 (PATHÉTIQUE),
LUDWIG VAN BEETHOVEN

Large Form: Piano Sonata
Detailed Form: Rondo
Performing Medium: Piano

Compact Disc 1, Track 19
Cassette Tape: Side B, Example 7
Running Time: 4:16

Beethoven's rondo is in typical form, with three different themes and transition material between some of the themes:

THEME 1 (A) with transition	THEME 2 (B) with transition	THEME 1 (A)	THEME 3 (C) with transition
THEME 1 (A) with transition	THEME 2 (B)	THEME 1 (A)	CODA

Listen especially to the opening main theme because it returns throughout the work. After you hear it several times, you should be able to become familiar with the other themes as well; then you will grasp the entire form.

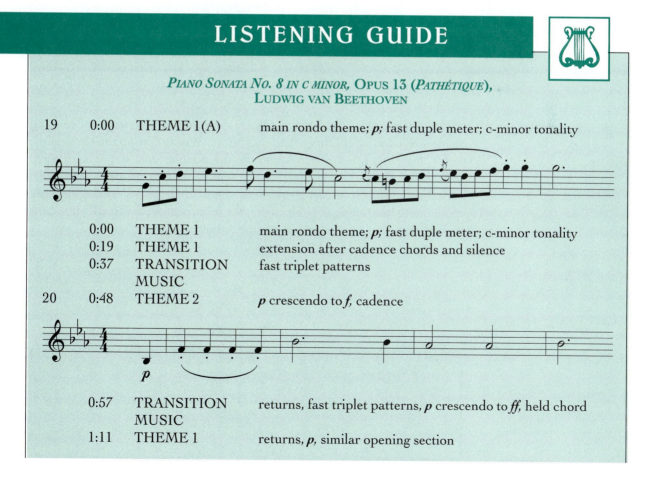

LISTENING GUIDE

PIANO SONATA No. 8 IN C MINOR, OPUS 13 (PATHÉTIQUE), LUDWIG VAN BEETHOVEN

19   0:00   THEME 1(A)   main rondo theme; *p;* fast duple meter; c-minor tonality

0:00   THEME 1   main rondo theme; *p;* fast duple meter; c-minor tonality
0:19   THEME 1   extension after cadence chords and silence
0:37   TRANSITION MUSIC   fast triplet patterns
20   0:48   THEME 2   *p* crescendo to *f,* cadence

0:57   TRANSITION MUSIC   returns, fast triplet patterns, *p* crescendo to *ff,* held chord
1:11   THEME 1   returns, *p,* similar opening section

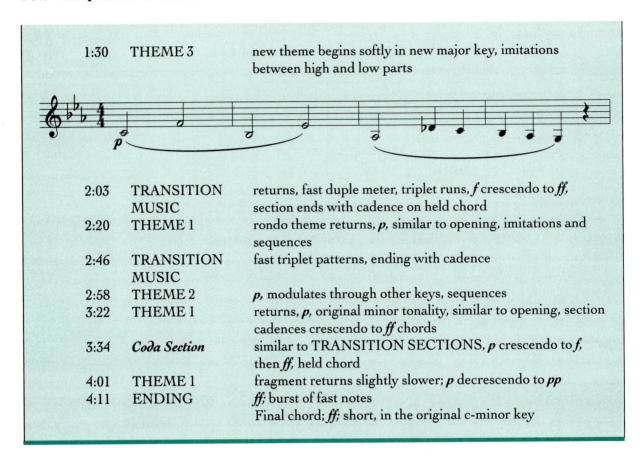

1:30	THEME 3	new theme begins softly in new major key, imitations between high and low parts
2:03	TRANSITION MUSIC	returns, fast duple meter, triplet runs, *f* crescendo to *ff*, section ends with cadence on held chord
2:20	THEME 1	rondo theme returns, *p*, similar to opening, imitations and sequences
2:46	TRANSITION MUSIC	fast triplet patterns, ending with cadence
2:58	THEME 2	*p*, modulates through other keys, sequences
3:22	THEME 1	returns, *p*, original minor tonality, similar to opening, section cadences crescendo to *ff* chords
3:34	*Coda Section*	similar to TRANSITION SECTIONS, *p* crescendo to *f*, then *ff*, held chord
4:01	THEME 1	fragment returns slightly slower; *p* decrescendo to *pp*
4:11	ENDING	*ff*; burst of fast notes Final chord; *ff*; short, in the original c-minor key

Minuet

Minuet and Trio   Mozart and Haydn realized the advantages of keeping the interest and attention of their audiences. Wisely catering to these audiences' fondness for dancing, especially the popular *minuet,* the composers included a minuet as the third movement of many of their symphonies, chamber music pieces, and even in some of their piano music. With its moderately fast tempo in triple meter, the minuet provides an effective contrast to the other movements in multimovement plans.

Challenge Your Expertise

How did archeological discoveries in 1748 promote a renewed interest in classical art and music?

The basic minuet and trio form has three parts: **Trio**

MINUET AND TRIO FORM

Minuet Section (A)–strongly rhythmic, triple meter, dance-style

Theme 1	Theme 1–modified	Theme 2	Theme 2–modified

each section repeats once

Trio Section (B)–lighter, smoother style

Theme 3	Theme 3–modified	Theme 4	Theme 4–modified

each section repeats once

Minuet Section (A)–(same as the first section)

Theme 1	Theme 1–modified	Theme 2	Theme 2–modified

usually no repeated sections

LISTENING ACTIVITY

SYMPHONY NO. 94 (SURPRISE, 1791), JOSEPH HAYDN

Large Form: Symphony
Detailed Form: Minuet and Trio (Song Form and Trio)
Performing Medium: Chamber Orchestra

Compact Disc 2, Track 1
Cassette Tape: Side B, Example 8
Running Time: 5:32

Listen to the third movement from Haydn's Symphony No. 94 (*Surprise*). The movement is a typical Classical-period minuet and trio. Although tempo indications in minuets of the day are usually marked *allegro* or *allegretto*. Because of the restrictive women's hoop skirts of Haydn's day, this favorite dance could not be performed *too* fast!

In this minuet as in most, the strong, three-beat meter is obvious. Repetitions of each section also are typical.

The trio section offers a lighter, more lyrical contrast to the heavier and louder minuet section.

LISTENING GUIDE

SYMPHONY No. 94 (SURPRISE, 1791), JOSEPH HAYDN

MINUET

1	0:00	THEME 1	played by violins and bassoons, full orchestra, *f*; then contrasting quieter sections, fast, triple meter, strongly rhythmic dance style, major key (G major), homophonic texture, sequences

	0:11	THEME 1 — modified	flutes and violins, *p*; then *f*
	0:25		opening section repeats identically
	0:48	THEME 2	modification of Theme 1 played by violins, *f*

	1:00	THEME 2 — modified	in violins, *f*; sequences, chords in winds, sudden *p*; imitation in woodwinds
	1:17	THEME 1	brief return, held chord
	1:30	THEME 1 — modified	*p*, ending section, *f*

TRIO (B)

	2:52	THEME 3	(trio theme) in violin and bassoons, same tempo and meter, *p*; softer and smoother than minuet, change of key to the dominant (D major)

	3:03	THEME 3	repeats exactly
	3:14	THEME 4	modification of Theme 3 in strings, still *p*

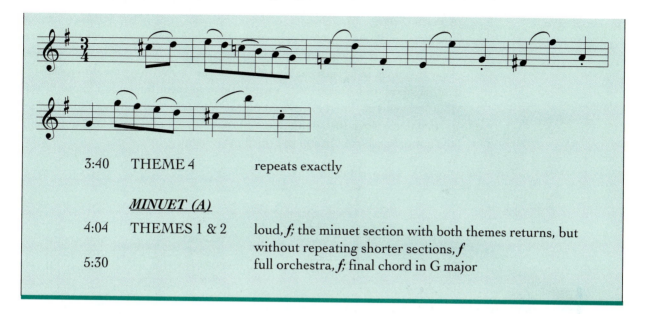

| 3:40 | THEME 4 | repeats exactly |

MINUET (A)

| 4:04 | THEMES 1 & 2 | loud, *f*; the minuet section with both themes returns, but without repeating shorter sections, *f* |
| 5:30 | | full orchestra, *f*; final chord in G major |

The Schönbrunn Palace in Vienna

HISTORICAL PERSPECTIVE

What Was Haydn's Surprise?

Haydn did not name his Symphony No. 94 "Surprise". Audiences named it because of one loud, unexpected chord (*ff*) in the second movement, following a simple, quiet *andante* theme. In 1791, during the symphony's first performance in London at one of the famous "Salomon" concerts, this surprising chord startled the audience. Haydn later denied having planned the effect "to make the ladies scream."

Sonata-allegro

SONATA FORM Movements of symphonies, concertos, sonatas, string quartets, and many other works of the Classical period often use the sonata form. In a fast movement, this is called *sonata-allegro*. Typically you will hear this form in at least the first movement of a multimovement work.

Haydn and Mozart often used a sonata form for two or three of the four movements in their symphonies. Mozart's Symphony No. 40, for instance, employs the sonata form in movements one, two, and four, with the minuet and trio form in the third movement.

Sonata-Allegro Form

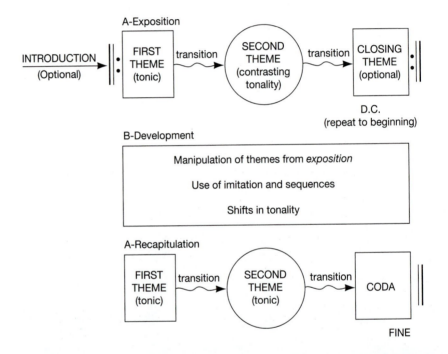

LISTENING ACTIVITY

SYMPHONY NO. 40 (1788, g minor), K. 550,
WOLFGANG AMADEUS MOZART

First Movement: Molto Allegro
Large Form: Symphony
Detailed Form: Sonata-Allegro
Performing Medium: Chamber or Symphony Orchestra

Compact Disc 2, Track 4
Cassette Tape: Side B, Example 9
Running Time: 8:02

Listen a few times to the first movement—Molto Allegro—of Mozart's Symphony No. 40 in g minor. First become acquainted with the overall progress of the work. Subsequent hearings will increase your familiarity with the themes or melodies Mozart has used to take you on a symphonic journey through the form.

The entire movement is constructed from two main themes: THEME 1 is a rapid theme that uses sequences and running notes.

To help you find your way, Mozart presents a clear cadence (stopping point) and then introduces THEME 2.

After a few listening experiences, you are ready to focus on the detailed form of the movement. Because it is in traditional sonata form, you should be able to follow its progress using both the Listening Guide and the Sonata Form Chart.

LISTENING GUIDE

SYMPHONY No. 40 (1788, g minor), K. 550,
WOLFGANG AMADEUS MOZART

EXPOSITION

4   0:00   THEME 1   played by violins, full orchestra, *p*; duple meter (4), g minor
     (2:01)   key, homophonic texture

0:32   TRANSITION   in violins, *f*; complete cadence and pause
(2:33) THEME

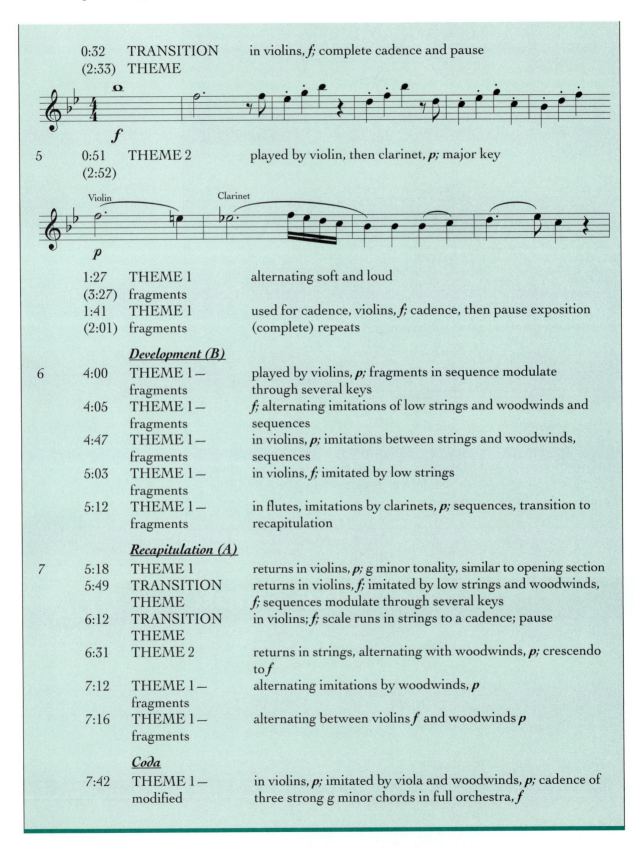

f

5   0:51   THEME 2   played by violin, then clarinet, *p*; major key
    (2:52)

p

	1:27 (3:27)	THEME 1 fragments	alternating soft and loud
	1:41 (2:01)	THEME 1 fragments	used for cadence, violins, *f*; cadence, then pause exposition (complete) repeats

Development (B)

6	4:00	THEME 1 — fragments	played by violins, *p*; fragments in sequence modulate through several keys
	4:05	THEME 1 — fragments	*f*; alternating imitations of low strings and woodwinds and sequences
	4:47	THEME 1 — fragments	in violins, *p*; imitations between strings and woodwinds, sequences
	5:03	THEME 1 — fragments	in violins, *f*; imitated by low strings
	5:12	THEME 1 — fragments	in flutes, imitations by clarinets, *p*; sequences, transition to recapitulation

Recapitulation (A)

7	5:18	THEME 1	returns in violins, *p*; g minor tonality, similar to opening section
	5:49	TRANSITION THEME	returns in violins, *f*; imitated by low strings and woodwinds, *f*; sequences modulate through several keys
	6:12	TRANSITION THEME	in violins; *f*; scale runs in strings to a cadence; pause
	6:31	THEME 2	returns in strings, alternating with woodwinds, *p*; crescendo to *f*
	7:12	THEME 1 — fragments	alternating imitations by woodwinds, *p*
	7:16	THEME 1 — fragments	alternating between violins *f* and woodwinds *p*

Coda

	7:42	THEME 1 — modified	in violins, *p*; imitated by viola and woodwinds, *p*; cadence of three strong g minor chords in full orchestra, *f*

Soprano Sheri Greenawald, as Donna Elvira, and baritone Timothy Noble, as Leporello, performing "Madamina" from Mozart's *Don Giovanni*

CLASSICAL-PERIOD OPERA

Opera—the musical theater of the Classical period—was the favorite entertainment of both the middle class and the aristocracy. From its debut in Italy around 1600, opera grew in popularity throughout Europe.

Although most concertgoers today know Haydn and Mozart chiefly through their symphonic, piano, and chamber music, both composers depended heavily on their operas for a living and reputation. Haydn composed more than twenty-five operas, some of which were lost. Of those that remain, six are in German, written for marionette theater, and nineteen are in Italian. Of Mozart's twelve major operas, nine are in Italian and three are in German.

Today, Haydn's operas are seldom produced, but several of Mozart's are part of the standard repertory for most professional companies: *Don Giovanni, Così fan tutte, The Magic Flute, The Marriage of Figaro,* and *Abduction from the Harem.*

Opera Language

Why were most of Haydn's and Mozart's operas in Italian, even though they were written for German-speaking audiences? Because opera first appeared in Italy, the Italian language was considered traditional. Even the German-born Handel, composing operas for his English audiences, preferred an Italian libretto.

Mozart was the first important composer to break this tradition, in his *The Abduction from the Harem* and *The Magic Flute.* Written in German, both operas were first performed in the *singspiel,* or folk theater, rather than

Singspiel
(*Zing*-shpeel)

in the traditional opera house. The predominantly middle-class audiences spoke only German, and they had no interest in Italian opera. To them, opera was a show, and they wanted the show in their native language.

Many have come to know Mozart best through his operas. They demonstrate his genius, wit, and uncanny sense of drama. No other composer of his day so keenly understood the qualities of good theater.

Mozart raised opera to new standards. Many of the plots for his operas were daring attacks on the decadence of the aristocracy. *The Marriage of Figaro,* for instance, exposes the aristocracy's frivolous court antics. His *Abduction from the Harem,* with its dancing, choruses of sailors, and light-hearted entertainment, directly influenced nineteenth-century operetta and modern Broadway musical theater.

LISTENING ACTIVITY

"MADAMINA" ARIA FROM *DON GIOVANNI* (1787), WOLFGANG AMADEUS MOZART

Large Form: Opera
Detailed Form: Aria (Two-Part Song Form)
Performing Medium: Bass-Baritone and Chamber Orchestra

Compact Disc 2, Track 8
Cassette Tape: Side B, Example 10
Running Time: 5:53

Before you listen to "Madamina" ("dear lady"), also known as the "Catalog" aria, here is some information to help place this charming aria in context.

BACKGROUND Don Giovanni is the Italian name of Don Juan, the legendary Spanish philanderer. Completely disregarding the feelings and ethics of his victims, he seduced his way through Europe with ladies of every class, compulsively gratifying his own pleasures.

Convention-driven audiences of the late 1700s may not have sympathized with this unscrupulous cad, but they were fascinated by his ability to overthrow restrictions in order to follow his heart — or at least his hormones.

Mozart wrote this opera in 1787, eleven years after the American Revolution and two years before the French Revolution. Daringly, Mozart and his librettist, Lorenzo da Ponte (1749–1838), reworked the Don Juan legend to fit contemporary Seville — though any European court would have served as well — and poked fun at the excesses of court life.

PLOT   As the curtain rises, Don Giovanni's servant Leporello is nervously guarding the courtyard, grumbling about having to work so late at night. His unappreciative master has sneaked into young Donna Anna's room to seduce her. With Donna Anna struggling to fight off her attacker, she and Don Giovanni noisily stumble down the palace stairs. Her father, the commandant, comes to her rescue with drawn sword, challenging Don Giovanni to a duel. In the skirmish, Don Giovanni kills the commandant and then flees.

In the second scene, Leporello mockingly consoles Donna Elvira after she complains that Don Giovanni had seduced and destroyed her. In one of the opera's comic moments, Leporello sings the "Madamina" aria. He pulls out a huge scroll, rolls it open across the stage, and summarizes his master's numerous affairs with women: 640 in Italy, 231 in Germany, 100 in France, 91 in Turkey, and 1,003 in Spain. Despite Don Giovanni's immorality and unscrupulous behavior, the opera has many comedic moments.

LISTENING GUIDE

"MADAMINA" ARIA FROM *DON GIOVANNI* (1787), WOLFGANG AMADEUS MOZART

Compact Disc 2, Track 8
Cassette Tape: Side B, Example 10
Running Time: 5:53

8	0:00	ORCHESTRAL INTRODUCTION	*allegro; duple meter (4); **p**; major key (D Major)*
	0:02	ARIA *Leporello* Madamina, il catalogo è questo Delle belle, che amo il padron mio, Un catalogo egli è, che ho fatt'io. Osservate, leggete con me.	*Leporello* My dear lady, this is a list Of the beauties my master has loved, A list which I have compiled. Observe, read along with me.
	0:23	ORCHESTRAL INTERLUDE	***f**; continuous downward scales, staccato, like laughter*
	0:27	*softly* In Italia seicento e quaranta, In Alamagna dueccento e trentuna	 In Italy, six hundred and forty, In Germany, two hundred and thirty-one

| Cento in Francia, in Turchia, novatuna, | One hundred in France, in Turkey, ninety-one. |

0:42   *tempo slows and style becomes more lyrical*

| Ma in Ispagna son già mille e tre! | But in Spain, already one thousand and three! |

1:02   *gradual crescendo to* **f**

V'han fra queste contadine,	Among these are peasant girls,
Cameriere, cittadine,	Servant girls, city girls
V'han contesse, baronesse,	Countesses, baronesses
Marchesane, principesse,	Marchionesses, princesses,
E v'han donne d'ogni	And women of every rank,
grado, d'ogni forma, d'ogni età!	every shape, every age!

1:22   *repetition of previous melodies,* **p**

In Italia seicento e quaranta,	In Italy, six hundred and forty
In Alamagna duecento e trentuna,	In Germany, two hundred and thirty-one,
Cento in Francia, in Turchia, novatuna.	One hundred in France, in Turkey, ninety-one.
Ma in Ispagna son gia mille e tre!	But in Spain, already one thousand and three!
V'han fra queste contadine,	Among these are peasant girls,
Camerierei, Cittadine,	Servant girls, city girls.
V'han contesse, baronesse,	Countesses, baronesses,
Marchesine, principesse,	Marchionesses, princesses,
E v'han donne d'ogni	And women of every rank,
grado, d'ogni forma, d'ogni età!	every shape, every age!

The entire opening section comes to a clear cadence.

9   2:23   MINUET STYLE   *slower tempo; triple meter;* **p**

Nel - la   bion - da   e - gli ha l'u - san - za

Nella bionda egli ha I'usanza	With a blonde it is his habit
Di lodar la gentilezza;	to praise her kindness;
Nella bruna, la costanza;	In a brunette, her faithfulness;

2:51   *music oozes sweetness*

Nella bianca la dolcezza.	In the light blond, her sweetness.
Vuol d'inverno la grassotta,	In winter he likes fat ones
Vuol d'estate la magrotta.	In summer he likes thin ones.

3:12   *crescendo, tempo slows to a held tone*

| E la grande maestosa, | He calls the tall ones majestic. |

3:35   *staccato tones, poking fun*

| La piccina è ognor vezzosa; | The little ones are always charming. |

Delle vecchie fa conquista	He seduces the old ones
Pel piacer di porle in lista.	For the pleasure of adding to the list.

3:57 *softly, almost spoken*

Sua passion predominante	His main passion
È la giovin principiante.	Is the young beginner.
Non si picca se sia ricca,	It doesn't matter if she's rich,
Se sia brutta, se sia bella,	Ugly or beautiful
Se sia ricca, brutta, se sia bella	If she is rich, ugly or beautiful.
Purchè porti la gonnella,	As long as she wears a skirt,

Coda

4:50 *slower and slower*

Voi sapete quel che fa	You know what happens.
Purchè porti la gonnella, ecc.	As long as she wears a skirt, etc.

fa,_____ quel   che   fa,_____

5:23 *vocalizing on* fa *and humming*

quel che fa!	You know what happens!
quel che fa!	You know what happens!

5:38 *cadences and running tones in the orchestra*
5:46 *final cadence in D major*

Challenge Your Expertise

- Which Classical-period symphony ends with fewer players onstage than it begins with?
- Why did Haydn use mostly Italian librettos, even though his audiences spoke German?

Summary of Terms

cadence	recapitulation	string quartet
concerto	rondo form	subscription
development	singspiel	performances
exposition	sonata-allegro	symphony
minuet and trio form	sonata form	theme and variation
opera	song form and trio	form

Chapter 12

Beethoven: Bridge to Romanticism

The first association that springs to anyone's mind when serious music is mentioned is "Beethoven." . . . What is the meat-and-potatoes of every piano recital? A Beethoven sonata. . . . What did we play in our symphony concerts when we wanted to honor the fallen in war? The Eroica. . . . What is every United Nations concert? The Ninth.

—Leonard Bernstein*

One of the most troubled yet greatest geniuses in music, Beethoven changed the course of music and influenced all composers who succeeded him. Not only did his music become the exemplar for the nineteenth century, his independence became an inspiration for all musicians.

Beethoven led the way for freelance composers to shed their dependence on noble patrons and to achieve financial security as freelance professionals.

Composing was a struggle for Beethoven because of his obsession with writing and rewriting his music. Several existing but dis-

*Leonard Bernstein, The Joy of Music. New York: Simon & Schuster, 1967.

carded versions of many of his most famous themes attest to this, yet his output was considerable, and his influence on future composers and audiences was enormous.

Ludwig van Beethoven (1770–1827)

From his early years in his native Bonn, Germany, Ludwig van Beethoven (*bay*-toh-ven) showed extraordinary talent at the piano, performing his first public concert at age eight. His father, a musician at the court in Bonn, had Ludwig study composition, organ, and violin, as well as piano.

Beethoven was only eighteen years old on July 14, 1789, when Parisians stormed the Bastille and Napoleon Bonaparte was just beginning his military career. Having grown up in a highly formalistic society dominated by the aristocracy, Beethoven witnessed the social changes that ultimately resulted in new forms of government. Through his music, he articulated the transition from classicism to the freer forms of the Romantic period.

At age thirteen, Beethoven was hired as assistant organist at the court in Bonn. In 1790 and again in 1792, Haydn made special trips to see Beethoven on his way from Vienna to London. Haydn encouraged Beethoven's patrons to send young Ludwig to Vienna for more intensive studies. They were convinced, and later, in 1792, the twenty-one-year-old Beethoven was off to Vienna, the center of musical life. His music was well received there.

Despite his success, Beethoven was moody and withdrawn. At age twenty-six, he began to lose his hearing, and in 1802 he considered suicide, as documented in his *Heiligenstadt Testament* (see Historical Perspective, Beethoven's *Heiligenstadt Testament*).

Transcending his increasing deafness, Beethoven actively composed during his entire life. Within his lifetime, his music was performed extensively throughout continental Europe and the United Kingdom—although in his later years he was unable to hear it played. Beethoven was recognized by his contemporaries as the greatest living composer. He died a relatively wealthy man at age fifty-six.

PRINCIPAL WORKS

Symphonies: nine symphonies: No. 3 in E-flat Major (*Eroica*, 1803); No. 5 in c minor (1808); No. 6 in F Major (*Pastoral*, 1808); No. 7 in A Major (1812); No. 9 in d minor (*Choral*, 1824)

Concertos: five piano concertos: No. 5 (*Emperor*, 1809); Violin Concerto (1806); Triple Concerto for Piano, Violin and Cello (1804)

Overtures and incidental music: *Leonore* overtures Nos. 1, 2, and 3 (1805–06); *Coriolan* overture (1807); *Egmont* overture (1810)

Chamber Music: seventeen string quartets; five string trios; piano quintet; sonatas for piano and violin; octet for wind instruments (1793)

Piano Music: thirty-two sonatas: No. 8 (*Pathétique*), Op. 13; No. 14 (*Moonlight*); Op. 27; No. 2; No. 21 (*Waldstein*), Op. 53; No. 23 (*Appassionata*), Op. 57

Opera: *Fidelio* (1805)

Choral Music: Mass in D (*Missa solemnis*, 1819–23)

Songs: *An die ferne Geliebte* (*To the Distant Beloved*), song cycle for tenor and piano (1816)

HISTORICAL PERSPECTIVE

Beethoven's Deafness

Increasing deafness began plaguing Beethoven shortly after his arrival in Vienna in 1792. At thirty, he wrote to a boyhood friend, ". . . my ears continue to hum and buzz day and night. For almost two years I have stopped attending social functions, because I find it impossible to tell people: I am deaf!"

To find a cure, he went from one physician to another, each of whom subjected him to painful but useless treatments. One of his doctors suggested that he take thermal bath treatments in the small town of Heiligenstadt outside of Vienna. So during the summer of 1802, a desperate Beethoven rented rooms there and bathed at the local thermal baths.

When, by the end of the summer, he was no better, a deep depression overcame him. On October 6, contemplating suicide, Beethoven wrote a letter containing his will and testament to his brothers Carl and Johann. Written as a letter addressed to the world, to be opened only after his death, the Heiligenstadt Testament expresses his ambivalence about living or dying.

HISTORICAL PERSPECTIVE

Beethoven's Heiligenstadt Testament

For my brothers Carl and Johann Beethoven:

Oh my fellow men, who consider me or describe me as hostile, obstinate, or misanthropic, how greatly you do me wrong. You do not know the secret reason why I appear this way.

Since childhood I have been filled with love of humanity, and a desire to do good things. But for the last six years, I have been afflicted with an incurable complaint, made worse by incompetent doctors. From year to year my hopes for a cure have been gradually shattered. Finally, I must accept the prospect of *permanent deafness* (which may take years to cure, if at all possible).

Though born with a passionate and sociable temperament, I was soon obliged to seclude myself and live in solitude. When I tried to ignore my infirmity, it became worse. Yet I could not bring myself to say to people: Speak up, shout, for I am deaf! Alas! how could I possibly refer to the impairing of *a sense* which should be more perfectly developed in me than in others—a sense which once was perfect.

. . . Oh, I cannot do it: so forgive me, if I withdraw from you. My pain is double because it makes people misjudge me. But I cannot relax with others, nor even enjoy conversations or mutual confidences. I must live alone, coming out only when necessity demands. When I'm with others, I am filled with burning anxiety that they will notice my condition.

. . . How humiliating when someone standing beside me has heard a flute playing and *I heard nothing.*

. . . I have been considering suicide, but my *art* has held me back. For indeed how could I die before I have composed all the music I feel inside.

. . . Now I realize I must be patient.

. . . Oh my fellow men, when some day you read this, remember that you have done me wrong. Let me take comfort from the thought that there may be some other unfortunate person who has also risen above the obstacles imposed by nature, to be in the ranks of noble artists and human beings.

You, my brothers Carl and Johann, after my death, ask Professor Schmidt, if he is still living, to describe my disease and to attach this document to his record, so that the world and I may be reconciled as much as possible. I appoint you both heirs to my small property (if I may so describe it). Divide it honestly, live in harmony, and help one another. You know that you have long ago been forgiven for the harm you did me.

I again thank you, my brother Carl, in particular, for the affection you have shown me recently. I hope your life is better and more carefree than mine. Urge your children to be *virtuous*, for only virtue can make a person happy. Money can't. I speak from experience. Only my virtue and my art have kept me from killing myself until now.

Farewell and love one another. I thank all my friends, and especially *Prince Lichnowsky* and *Professor Schmidt.* I would like one of you to take care of Prince [Lichnowsky]'s instruments, provided you do not quarrel over them. If you ever need money, sell them. I shall be glad, in my grave, if I can still do something for you both.

Well, that is all. Joyfully I go to meet Death. If it comes before I have developed all my artistic gifts, then in spite of my hard fate, I would like to postpone it. Even if I do die, I'll be content, for death will free me from this continual suffering. Come, whenever you like, with courage I will go to meet you.

Farewell. When I am dead, I deserve to be remembered by you, because I have often thought of you and tried to make you happy. Be happy.

Ludwig van Beethoven

Heiligenstadt
October 6th
1802

RENEWED CREATIVE MOOD   Emerging from this depression with new determination, Beethoven completed his Symphony No. 2. He went on to compose for another twenty-five years, producing his greatest music during the last years of his life.

Sketch of a Broadwood piano in one of Beethoven's many studios.

Keyboard Music

BEETHOVEN'S SEARCH FOR A MORE SUITABLE INSTRUMENT   As Beethoven's deafness intensified, so did his demand for more sound from his piano. The keyboards used by his contemporaries, Mozart and Haydn, did not satisfy him—they were not strongly built or versatile enough. Nor were they loud enough for the larger public concert halls that increasingly became the center of concert activity in the nineteenth century. So, in the early 1800s, Beethoven turned to John Broadwood, an Englishman who built both ships and pianos, and to Viennese piano builder Johann Streicher. He commissioned them to build larger, sturdier instruments similar to today's concert grands.

The new Broadwood and Streicher pianos were louder and more suitable for the large public concert halls than for the chambers at court or the rooms in Beethoven's own lodgings. His loud playing disturbed the neighbors, especially in the middle of the night. As a result, Beethoven was evicted from some eighty apartments in and around Vienna. Buildings throughout that city have plaques stating "Beethoven Lived Here."

LISTENING ACTIVITY

PIANO SONATA NO. 8 IN C MINOR, OPUS 13 (*PATHÉTIQUE*),
LUDWIG VAN BEETHOVEN

Large Form: Piano Sonata
Detailed Form: Rondo

Compact Disc 1, Track 19
Cassette Tape: Side B, Example 7
Running Time: 4:16

Listen again to the rondo from Beethoven's *Piano Sonata No. 8*. In the previous chapter, you followed the same work using the Listening Guide. For this hearing, try to follow the form and the musical events without the Listening Guide, as you normally would at a concert.

Beethoven composed this sonata in 1799 during his early years in Vienna. We are not sure why he titled the work *Pathétique*. We do know that he composed it during the onset of his hearing problems, only three years before writing his Heiligenstadt Testament.

The rondo in *Pathétique* shows a tinge of sadness. Classical rondos are usually extremely jolly, so this minor-keyed rondo tends toward the more melancholy moods of Romanticism. Following a basic rondo form, its main theme keeps returning, alternating with contrasting themes.

The form for this Beethoven rondo follows:

THEME 1 (A) with transition	THEME 2 (B) with transition	THEME 1 (A)	THEME 3 (C) with transition
THEME 1 (A) with transition	THEME 2 (B)	THEME 1 (A)	CODA

Beethoven's Orchestral Music

Because of the new avenues of emotional expression that Beethoven was exploring in his music, he began writing for more instruments and increasing the size of the orchestra. He also composed longer and structurally more complex symphonies than Haydn's and Mozart's twenty-minute works. Beethoven's Ninth Symphony, for example, takes about one hour and ten minutes to perform.

Beethoven used traditional Classical-period forms, expanding them to fit his Romantic-period viewpoint. Here are noticeable characteristics of Beethoven's symphonic works:

- The loudness of the orchestra increases along with the number of instruments.
- Developmental sections (free sections or side journeys) occur within almost all sections of the form (exposition, coda, etc.).
- Traditional forms are freer. He treated these forms with great originality in his later works.
- Music occasionally moves from one movement to the next without the usual breaks.
- Themes from one movement are occasionally restated in another.
- Changes in tempo within a movement are more frequent than in previous Classical-period works.
- Coda or finale sections are usually longer, more elaborate, and triumphant than those of Haydn and Mozart. They usually conclude with repeated, powerful chords.

Concert Hall in the Streicher Piano Factory in Vienna. Beethoven performed on Streicher pianos in concerts in Vienna.

HISTORICAL PERSPECTIVE

Beethoven Meets Mozart

When Beethoven was a young child, his father pressured him to emulate Mozart, first as a keyboard *wunderkind*, and then as a composer. Beethoven might have grown up resenting Mozart, yet he idolized him. It was Beethoven's dream to study composition with the great master, only fourteen years his senior.

In 1787, at age seventeen, Beethoven journeyed from his native Bonn to the great cultural center of Vienna. Historical documentation is missing for much of this short trip; however, several accounts indicate that Beethoven actually met with Mozart briefly and performed for him at his studio.

According to these accounts, Beethoven's first selection was a piano piece he had been practicing. Apparently, Mozart was only mildly impressed with young Beethoven's keyboard ability — Vienna had many gifted young pianists. Sensing this, Beethoven asked Mozart to supply him with a melody upon which he could improvise. Mozart did so, and Beethoven proceeded to dazzle Mozart and his friends with a stirring improvisation. Turning to his friends Mozart declared, "Keep an eye on this man. Someday he will give the world something to talk about."

After only two weeks in Vienna, Beethoven had to rush to the bedside of his gravely ill mother in Bonn. She died a few days later. Not until 1792 did Beethoven return to Vienna. Mozart had died only months before his arrival.

LISTENING ACTIVITY

SYMPHONY NO. 5 IN C MINOR (1808), LUDWIG VAN BEETHOVEN OP. 67, FIRST MOVEMENT: ALLEGRO CON BRIO

Large Form: Symphony
Detailed Form: Sonata-allegro
Performing Medium: Medium-Sized Symphony Orchestra

Compact Disc 2, Track 10
Cassette Tape: Side C, Example 1
Running Time: 7:18

Following along with the Listening Guide, listen to the first movement of this popular symphony. Notice how Beethoven builds a monumental structure from a simple idea. The approach is similar to that of an architect who uses a geometric shape such as a rectangle or triangle as the fundamental building shape throughout a structure. Buckminster Fuller's geodesic domes of interlocking polygons are architectural examples.

Beethoven's building idea is the famous theme that he later uses both as a melodic motive and as a rhythmic motive.

The overall form of the first movement is traditional classical sonata form. Notice, however, that Beethoven extends the coda to last as long as each of the other sections.

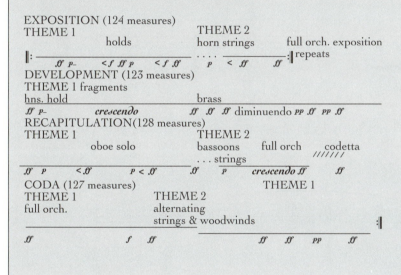

EXPOSITION (124 measures)
THEME 1

DEVELOPMENT (123 measures)
THEME 1 fragments

RECAPITULATION (128 measures)
THEME 1

CODA (127 measures)
THEME 1

LISTENING GUIDE

SYMPHONY NO. 5 (1808), LUDWIG VAN BEETHOVEN
FIRST MOVEMENT: ALLEGRO CON BRIO

EXPOSITION

| 10 | 0:00 (1:25) | THEME 1 | played by unison strings and clarinet; *ff*; duple meter, fourth tone held, same idea repeated as a sequence in the key of c minor |

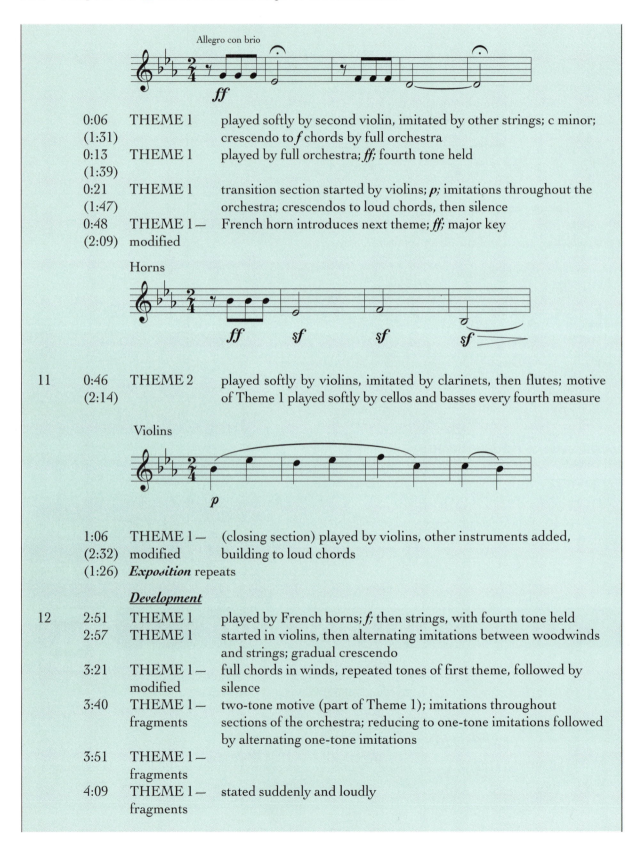

Allegro con brio

ff

	0:06 (1:31)	THEME 1	played softly by second violin, imitated by other strings; c minor; crescendo to *f* chords by full orchestra
	0:13 (1:39)	THEME 1	played by full orchestra; *ff*; fourth tone held
	0:21 (1:47)	THEME 1	transition section started by violins; *p*; imitations throughout the orchestra; crescendos to loud chords, then silence
	0:48 (2:09)	THEME 1 — modified	French horn introduces next theme; *ff*; major key

Horns

ff   *sf*   *sf*   *sf*

11	0:46 (2:14)	THEME 2	played softly by violins, imitated by clarinets, then flutes; motive of Theme 1 played softly by cellos and basses every fourth measure

Violins

p

	1:06 (2:32)	THEME 1 — modified	(closing section) played by violins, other instruments added, building to loud chords
	(1:26)	*Exposition* repeats	

Development

12	2:51	THEME 1	played by French horns; *f*; then strings, with fourth tone held
	2:57	THEME 1	started in violins, then alternating imitations between woodwinds and strings; gradual crescendo
	3:21	THEME 1 — modified	full chords in winds, repeated tones of first theme, followed by silence
	3:40	THEME 1 — fragments	two-tone motive (part of Theme 1); imitations throughout sections of the orchestra; reducing to one-tone imitations followed by alternating one-tone imitations
	3:51	THEME 1 — fragments	
	4:09	THEME 1 — fragments	stated suddenly and loudly

Recapitulation

13	4:14	THEME 1	played by full orchestra; _ff;_ fourth tone held
	4:32		short oboe cadenza, ending on held tone
	4:44	THEME 1— modified	acts as transition section, starting softly then getting louder as it is imitated by different instruments
	5:04	THEME 1— modified	played by bassoons
	5:08	THEME 2	started by violins; _p;_ then alternating imitations; gradual crescendo; C major

Coda

14	5:43	THEME 1	rhythmic pattern; alternating imitations between winds and strings containing many repeated tones
	5:52	THEME 1— modified	imitations, then two-tone motive developed
	6:05	THEME 2— modified	four-tone pattern; ascending sequences played by strings, then alternating imitations between woodwinds and strings, reducing to two-tone patterns
	6:55	THEME 1	full orchestra; _ff;_ played twice with fourth tone held
	7:04	THEME 1	softly in strings, then suddenly loud by entire orchestra;
	7:10		series of loud chords
	7:17	FINAL CHORD	in c minor

HISTORICAL PERSPECTIVE

Beethoven and the Changing Status of Composers

Before Beethoven, composers were almost totally dependent on either the church or the courts for employment. Mozart, for example, who lost his post with the Archbishop of Salzburg, struggled as a freelance musician. He was just beginning to achieve financial independence when his career ended with his untimely death.

Beethoven succeeded as a freelance musician. When he first arrived in the great musical city of Vienna, he accepted employment from the aristocracy. He tried to fit in, outfitting himself in the newest fashions and even taking dance lessons. But the clothes made him uncomfortable, and he claimed that he had difficulty moving in time to the music.

Beethoven felt out of place among some of his frivolous and snobbish patrons. First, he resented having to occasionally use the servants' entrance when he arrived to perform. Furthermore, when members of his audience talked during his playing, he became angry and often walked out in the middle of a piece.

So Beethoven searched for a new audience. Influenced by the social and political changes around him, he took control of his life by organizing and performing in concerts for the middle class at the public concert hall or in public buildings—and he usually turned a profit.

Toward the end of the eighteenth century, public concerts had grown rapidly in importance. The famous Salomon Concerts from 1791 to 1795 in London enabled the aging Haydn to amass more money than he ever could have from his wages at the Esterházy court. Beethoven studied briefly with Haydn during some of those years. He must have been encouraged by Haydn's financial successes with the London audiences, because Beethoven began developing new public concerts in Vienna.

Music Publishing: A New Source of Income

Mozart had earned negligible royalties from his few published works—some of which were distributed without his knowledge. But Beethoven was a shrewder businessman and knew how to negotiate a profitable deal, often with a sizable advance. Stories have been told about his negotiating with two or more publishers at a time, playing them against each other until he won his price. Eventually, royalties were his main source of income. Beethoven's success in negotiating encouraged future composers to follow his example.

SYMPHONY NO. 6 (PASTORAL)   After the mighty Fifth Symphony, Beethoven began searching for new inspiration and direction for his music. Although not as schooled in the traditional forms as court audiences, his new audiences at public concerts enjoyed the power and emotionalism in his music.

Music notebooks in hand, Beethoven roamed both the Vienna Woods and the Grinzing Woods near Heilingenstadt, seeking inspiration. Caught up in the beauty of the countryside, he worked quickly on his new work. Beethoven was touched by the romantic feeling of the woods, the delicate settings, the rustic life of the peasants, and the wonders of nature.

Beethoven's Symphony No. 6 depicts the feelings that nature inspired in him. Evidence of that inspiration is in the title—"The Pastoral Symphony, more the expression of feeling than painting." Beethoven also affixed highly descriptive phrases to each of the five movements, with the intention of transporting the audience out of the concert hall and into the countryside.

Challenge Your Expertise

Why did Beethoven earn more royalty income than Bach?

Beethoven's Symphony No. 6 (Pastoral), Opus 68		
Movement	Tempo Indication	Beethoven's Movement Titles
First Movement:	Allegro ma non troppo	"The awakening of joyful feelings upon arriving in the country"
Second Movement:	Andante molto mosso	"Scene by the brook"
Third Movement: *(into next movement without a break)*	Allegro	"Merry gathering of country folk"
Fourth Movement: *(into next movement without a break)*	Allegro	"Thunderstorm"
Fifth Movement:	Allegretto	"Happy, thankful feelings after the storm: shepherd's song"

THE GREAT NINTH SYMPHONY (CHORAL)

Beethoven composed his first eight symphonies over a twelve-year span, between 1800 and 1812, yet it would be another twelve years before he would release his tradition-shattering Ninth Symphony for its first performance. With the Ninth Symphony, Beethoven completely crossed the bridge into romanticism.

Beethoven attended the premiere performance of this work in Vienna on May 7, 1824, on a program featuring only his music. Word had spread of this premiere, and a large and distinguished audience streamed into the concert hall for the performance. Throughout the concert, they saw the composer himself standing at the podium, next to the conductor.

After the finale, the audience spontaneously rose for a standing ovation—cheering, applauding, and waving handkerchiefs. Beethoven heard none of this adulation. Finally, one of the soloists tugged on his sleeve to signal the composer to turn around and acknowledge the applause.

For the first time in a symphony, a chorus and vocal soloists performed with the orchestra. Beethoven set to music a poem that seemed to have meant a great deal to him throughout his life: Friedrich Schiller's "Ode to Joy." Its main idea embraced the spirit of emerging romanticism—the joy of the universal brotherhood: "Alle Menchen werden Brüder" (All men become brothers).

Schiller
(*shill*-er, 1759–1805)

Inspired by the grandeur of the Ninth Symphony, Romantic-period composers began writing larger, more emotional works, many containing choruses and soloists delivering texts and stories.

Summary of Terms

Appassionata Sonata	Heiligenstadt Testament	*Pastoral* Symphony
Choral Symphony	*Moonlight* Sonata	*Pathétique* Sonata
Emperor Concerto	Ninth Symphony	rondo form
Eroica Symphony	"Ode to Joy"	sonata form

Chapter 13

The Romantic Style Period (1820–1900)

"The road of excess leads to the palace of wisdom."

—*William Blake, Proverbs of Hell*

After 1820 and throughout the nineteenth century, Romanticism became the predominant style, not only in music, but in all the arts—a style and an outlook that reflected a new concern with emotional expression.

Beholden to the Church and the aristocracy for financial support, artists had worked under tight constraints. Now, with other available sources of income, composers no longer had to defer to patrons. Thus liberated, artists could create art by their own standards and for art's sake. Throwing themselves into their work, many were victims of burnout, and many died young. Excess, exuberance, and optimism, often followed by pessimism and depression, characterized this creative mode.

Self-sustaining and self-reliant, the arts and artists gave impetus to the lively, great cultural centers—Paris, Vienna, Prague, Budapest, Leipzig, Dresden, Amsterdam, and London. Public concert associations, philharmonic orchestral societies, and opera and ballet companies were established throughout Europe and the United States.

At last, artists were celebrities—respected members of society. Suddenly they were invited to the homes of the wealthy, not just as entertainers but as honored guests.

ROMANTIC SUBJECTS

In art, literature, and music, the Romantic movement expressed intense introspection and a fascination with the supernatural and the exotic. Some of the more popular topics follow:

Delacroix's "Liberty Leading the People" (1830).

- nature
- beauty
- love
- death
- the supernatural
- the mystical, magical, and mysterious
- travel, distant lands, and exotic cultures
- adventure
- drug-induced states
- the brotherhood of man
- the individual and the common man
- the superman and hero

ROMANTICISM IN MUSIC

EVOCATIVE TITLES FOR MUSICAL WORKS   Romantic subjects inspired evocative titles: Beethoven's *Pastoral* Symphony, Mendelssohn's *Scottish* Symphony, Schumann's *Spring* Symphony, Brahms's *Tragic Overture*, and Dukas' *Sorceror's Apprentice*. When listening to these works, we can visualize the stories or images that the titles suggest.

PROGRAM MUSIC   Public support was at a new peak, challenging composers to find ways of communicating with audiences who were unfamiliar with the classical forms. New ideas in the titles and stories seduced audiences into becoming involved with the passion of the music.

To carry these ideas further, some composers provided a detailed scenario, or *program,* to follow along with the music. Examples are Berlioz's *Symphonie fantastique,* Liszt's *Faust* and *Dante* symphonies, and Strauss's tone poems, *Don Juan, Death and Transfiguration,* and *A Hero's Life.*

EMOTIONAL MUSIC   Romantic composers became fascinated with the possibilities of deep emotional expression offered by the expanded use of the musical elements and instrumental tone colors. Audiences were enthralled by these exotic, emotional works.

What about today's audiences? If you examine programs from any major orchestra or opera company, you will find that at least half the music is from the Romantic period. We still favor Romantic music. It gives us an opportunity to experience our feelings.

Overview of the Romantic Period (1820–1900)	
Important Composers	Ludwig van Beethoven, Hector Berlioz, Georges Bizet, Alexander Borodin, Johannes Brahms, Anton Bruckner, Frédéric Chopin, Claude Debussy, Henri Duparc, Antonín Dvořák, Edward Elgar, Gabriel Fauré, César Franck, Mikhail Glinka, Charles Gounod, Edvard Grieg, Franz Liszt, Gustav Mahler, Felix Mendelssohn, Modest Mussorgsky, Jacques Offenbach, Giacomo Puccini, Nicolai Rimsky-Korsakov, Camille Saint-Saëns, Franz Schubert, Robert Schumann, Jan Sibelius, Bedřich Smetana, Johann Strauss, Jr. and Sr., Richard Strauss, Peter Tchaikovsky, Giuseppe Verdi, Carl Maria von Weber, Richard Wagner
Visual Artists	William Blake, Paul Cézanne, Honoré Daumier, Edgar Degas, Eugene Delacroix, Paul Gauguin, Francisco Goya, Claude Monet, Pierre-Auguste Renoir, Auguste Rodin, Georges Seurat, Joseph Turner, Vincent van Gogh
Writers	Louisa May Alcott, Honoré de Balzac, Anne, Charlotte, and Emily Brontë, Elizabeth Browning, Robert Browning, George Gordon Lord Byron, Anton Chekhov, Samuel Coleridge, Charles Dickens, Emily Dickinson, Fyodor Dostoevski, Nathaniel Hawthorne, Heinrich Heine, Victor Hugo, Henrik Ibsen, Henry James, John Keats, Henry Wadsworth Longfellow, Edgar Allan Poe, Aleksandr Pushkin, George Sand, Percy Bysshe Shelley, Marie-Henri Stendhal, Robert Louis Stevenson, Harriet Beecher Stowe, Alfred Lord Tennyson, William Thackeray, Leo Tolstoy, Mark Twain, Walt Whitman, Oscar Wilde, William Wordsworth
Philosophers	Auguste Comte, Ralph Waldo Emerson, Friedrich Engels, Ernst Haeckel, Georg Hegel, Thomas Henry Huxley, Søren Kierkegaard, Karl Marx, John Stuart Mill, Friedrich Nietzsche, Arthur Schopenhauer, Herbert Spencer, Henry David Thoreau
Social, Political, and Cultural Events	Industrial revolution, steamboat, railroads, photography, telegraph, telephone, phonograph, Monroe Doctrine, California Gold Rush, unification of Germany and Italy, reign of Victoria, "Gay '90s," Darwin's *The Descent of Man*, American Civil War

Characteristics of Romantic Music

General	Music has an emotional, subjective quality with frequent mood changes; expansive sound with large ensembles; intimate music with small ensembles; literature or extra-musical ideas often serve as a basis for the music.
Performing Media	Large symphony orchestras, piano, chamber music ensembles, opera and ballet companies
Rhythm	Rubato used often; changing tempos within sections and movements; more complex rhythms than in previous periods

Melody	Long, flowing, emotion-laden melodies; also short themes representing ideas or people; major and minor melodies with chromatic alterations; instrumental melodies with wide leaps and range
Harmony	Tonal (key-centered), but with increasing use of modulations and chromatic tones; rich, complex harmonies
Expression	Full range of dynamics (extremely soft to extremely loud); extensive use of crescendo and diminuendo
Texture	Mainly homophonic (melody with accompaniment); occasional use of polyphony
Forms	Some continued use of Classical-period forms; symphony, often with titles; concerto; new, small piano forms (nocturne, ballade, étude, waltz, mazurka); opera, ballet, symphonic tone poem, concert overture; programmatic and descriptive works

Chapter 14

Early-Romantic Music

ORCHESTRAL MUSIC

Hector Berlioz's (*behr*-ly-ohz) life typifies the spirit of the Romantic period. Although he placated his father, a respected physician, by attending one semester of medical school in Paris, Berlioz had other plans. According to his own account, his first experience with a cadaver hastened his career change:

> *At the sight of that terrible charnel-house—the fragments of limbs, the grinning heads and gaping skulls, the bloody quagmire underfoot and the atrocious smell it gave off, the swarms of sparrows wrangling over scraps of lung, the rats in their corner gnawing the bleeding vertebrae—such a feeling of revulsion possessed me that I leapt through the window of the dissecting-room and fled for home. . . .**

Now he could pursue his real interest—music. Though Berlioz had learned to read music, had composed a few small works while a youngster, and could perform a few pieces on flute and guitar, he

*Hector Berlioz, *Memoirs*. New York: Alfred A. Knopf (Publisher of First American Edition), 1969.

was far from an accomplished musician. His father, fearing that his son's strong interest in music would interfere with his becoming a doctor, blocked his boyhood music studies. Specifically, his father prevented Hector from studying piano, the traditional instrument of composers. Yet at 19, Berlioz pursued his new career with enthusiasm. True to the Romantic spirit that *anything is possible if you really want to accomplish it,* Berlioz studied music in Paris, then in Italy, and eventually became one of the world's great composers.

Hector Berlioz (1803–1869)

Born in a little town near Lyon, France, Hector Berlioz (*behr*-ly-ohz) began studying music seriously at nineteen, taking lessons in composition and orchestral instruments in Paris. Because of his late start, he was not accepted as a music student at the Paris Conservatory. Ironically, later in his career he was hired to teach orchestration and composition at the Conservatory.

Objecting to his choice of music for a career, his parents cut off his allowance. To support his studies, Berlioz gave music lessons and held odd jobs in the theater. He struggled until 1830, when he won the prestigious Prix de Rome.

Now with funds, he continued his studies in Rome. When he returned to Paris, he threw himself into composition and was accepted into the Parisian artistic community, which included musicians Frédéric Chopin and Franz Liszt, artist Eugene Delacroix, and writers Victor Hugo and George Sand.

Berlioz, fascinated with instrumental effects and new instruments, employed his latest discoveries in his orchestral works. He wrote the first important orchestration textbook, *Treatise on Instrumentation.* Because Berlioz was interested in the dramatic quality of music, his works often contained detailed stories.

PRINCIPAL WORKS

Orchestral: *Symphonie fantastique* (1830); *Harold in Italy* (viola concerto, 1834); *Roméo et Juliette* (Romeo and Juliet, 1839); *Le Carnaval romain* (The Roman Carnival, 1844)

Wind Band: *Grande symphonie funèbre et triomphale* (Grand Funeral and Triumphant Symphonie, 1840)

Operas: *Benvenuto Cellini* (1838); *Les Troyens* (The Trojans, 1858); *Béatrice et Bénédict* (1862)

Choral: *Requiem* (1837); *Te Deum* (1849); *L'enfance du Christ* (The Childhood of Christ, 1854)

SYMPHONIE FANTASTIQUE   The events surrounding the creation of *Symphonie fantastique* exemplify Berlioz's Romantic spirit. In Paris, he attended an English-language performance of Shakespeare's *Hamlet* by a London company. Though he did not understand one word of English, Berlioz became instantly infatuated with the actress who played Ophelia, Harriet Constance Smithson (1800–54).

(sam-fo-*nee* fahn-tah-*steek*)

Vowing to marry her, he began writing letters to her. To further demonstrate his love, Berlioz dedicated his *Symphonie fantastique* to her. He even made Harriet the central character in the symphony by weaving a melody that represented her throughout the fabric of this five-movement, programmatic orchestral work. Berlioz called this type of central theme an *idée fixe*.

Idée fixe
(ee-*day feex*)

Recurrent themes and melodies

After Berlioz, many composers employed the technique of recurrent themes and melodies to represent characters, ideas, and locations. In the late nineteenth century, Richard Wagner, Franz Liszt, and Richard Strauss used the technique extensively in music dramas and tone poems. In today's films and Broadway musicals, a recurrent theme can serve as a unifying device to sustain suspense, heighten emotion, and define character.

HECTOR BERLIOZ AND HARRIET SMITHSON   Dedicating his *Symphonie fantastique* to Harriet Smithson was part of Berlioz's strategy. He invited her to a performance of the work, explaining that she had been the inspiration and was the central character. So impressed was Harriet that she consented to his courtship. Berlioz learned some English. Harriet learned some French. A few years later, they married.

In spite of its romantic beginnings, the marriage came to a stormy ending. With Harriet out of his life, Berlioz was forced to seek other inspirations for his passionate creative genius.

Hector Berlioz at age twenty-nine. Oil portrait by Signol (1832).

Harriet Smithson at age twenty-eight, after a portrait by Dubufe (1828).

HISTORICAL PERSPECTIVE

Berlioz's Innovative Orchestration

Most composers write at a keyboard because it enables them to work on a number of parts at once. Therefore, their notation of orchestral music usually resembles keyboard music, with occasional suggestions about which instruments might play which ideas. Later, they orchestrate the music—renotate it for full orchestra. The process is similar to that of many painters who first sketch their ideas on a piece of paper, and then transfer the idea to a large canvas and develop the painting in a full range of colors.

Since Berlioz could neither compose nor play his works at the piano, he started immediately to notate an entire orchestral score. What started as a handicap—his inability to play the piano—intensified his determination. Driven by his vision, he learned about each of the orchestral instruments until he was able not only to compose but to orchestrate brilliantly, setting a standard for those who followed.

Berlioz, the creative orchestrator, treats the listener to many interesting and unusual sounds, featuring unusual instruments and instrumental effects. In the "Witches' Sabbath," from the *Symphonie fantastique*, you will hear a high clarinet (E-flat clarinet) playing sounds that resemble squeaking laughter. Also featured are tubas and chimes, rare in orchestras at that time.

Occasionally Berlioz calls for the string performers to play with mutes attached to the bridges of their instruments—*con sordini* (con sor-*dee*-nee). He also calls for the players to run their bows very close to the bridges, producing eerie, glassy sounds—*sul ponticello* (sool pon-tee-*chell*-o). To simulate dancing skeletons—perhaps an image that remained from his disgust in the dissecting room—Berlioz requires the string players to turn their bows around and strike the strings with the wood portion to produce a sound like clattering bones—*col legno battuta* (cohl *len*-yoh bah-*too*-tah).

LISTENING ACTIVITY

SYMPHONIE FANTASTIQUE (FANTASTIC SYMPHONY, 1830),
HECTOR BERLIOZ
FIFTH MOVEMENT: "DREAM OF A WITCHES' SABBATH"

Large Form: Symphony
Detailed Form: Sectional
Performing Medium: Large Symphony Orchestra

Compact Disc 2, Track 15
Cassette Tape: Side C, Example 2
Running Time: 10:20

Before you listen to the music, read the program that Berlioz wrote for the fifth and last movement of his *Symphonie fantastique*. Because he wanted his audience to know the story that Harriet had inspired, Berlioz wrote it out in detail. The entire story is usually printed in the concert program and accompanies the recording.

INTRODUCTION

A young musician of morbid sensitivity and ardent imagination poisons himself with opium in a moment of amorous despair. The narcotic dose, while too weak to kill him, plunges him into deep hallucinations. His strange visions, sensations, feelings, and memories are translated in his brain into musical ideas and images. Even his beloved becomes a melody for him and his fixation with her (idée fixe) haunts him.

FIFTH PART "DREAM OF A WITCHES' SABBATH"

He sees himself at a Witches' Sabbath. Shadowy figures, sorcerers, and monsters of every kind have gathered for his burial. Strange noises, groans, bursts of laughter, and faraway cries seem to be answered by other cries. He hears the melody of his beloved again, but now lacking its noble and gentle quality, it is nothing more than a dance tune, mocking, trivial, and grotesque.

She (the beloved) arrives at the Sabbath, greeted by shouts of joy. She joins the diabolical orgy. . . . The funeral bell tolls, a burlesque parody of the Dies irae, dies illa *("Day of wrath, O judgment day"). While the day of wrath melody continues, the witches dance.*

The plan Berlioz uses for the last movement of his *Symphonie fantastique* is a *sectional form:*

Introduction
Theme 1—*idée fixe:* "Beloved Theme Modified"
Theme 2—*Dies irae, dies illa:* from the Gregorian chant, "Day of wrath, O judgment day"
Theme 3—"Witches' Round Dance," a loosely constructed fugue
Coda

Here is the original *idée fixe*, the "beloved" melody, introduced in the first movement:

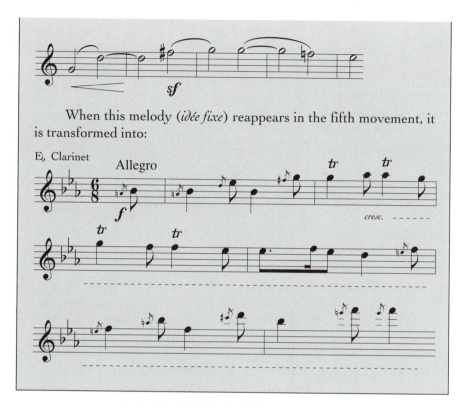

When this melody (*idée fixe*) reappears in the fifth movement, it is transformed into:

E♭ Clarinet

LISTENING GUIDE

Symphonie fantastique (1830), Hector Berlioz
Fifth Movement: "Dream of a Witches' Sabbath"

Introduction

| 15 | 0:00 | | violins and violas tremolo; ***pp***; cellos and basses upward swoop; ***p < mf***; three times capped off with soft thud on bass drum; duple meter (4), moderately slow |

	0:11		woodwind-held chords, over rapidly repeated figures in upper strings into pizzicato strings, answered by winds playing staccato (short tones); ***f*** in piccolo, flutes, and "squeaky" E-flat clarinet ending with downward glissando (smear), imitated by muted horn over bass drum roll; ***ppp***
	0:32	FANFARE MOTIVE	
	0:55		similar to opening with upward swoops

| | 1:20 | FANFARE MOTIVE | returns in the same instruments, but louder; **pppp**; muted horn imitates still softer; **mf**; over quiet bass drum roll |

Idée Fixe — "Beloved Melody"

16	1:37	THEME 1 — fragment "Beloved Melody"	clarinet plays mocking dance style; **ppp**; over percussion; duple meter (2) compound, allegro; homophonic texture

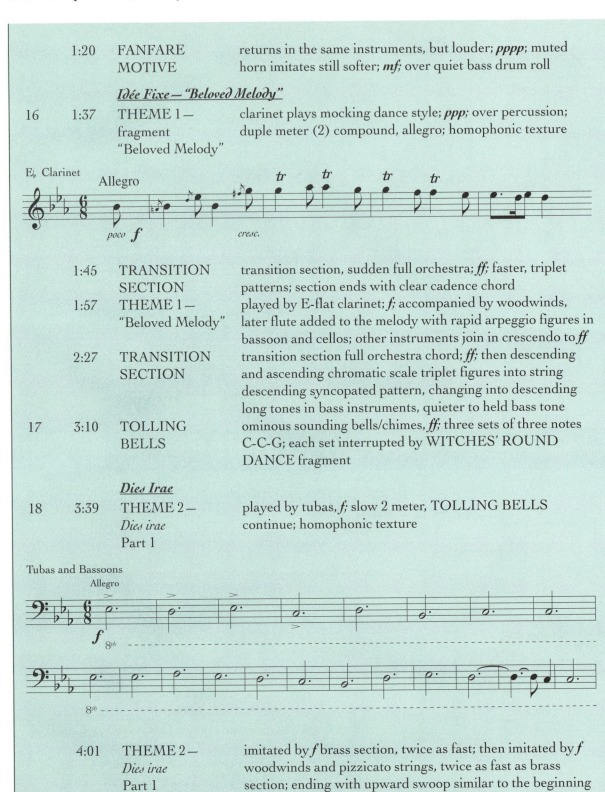

E♭ Clarinet — Allegro

poco **f**   *cresc.*

	1:45	TRANSITION SECTION	transition section, sudden full orchestra; **ff**; faster, triplet patterns; section ends with clear cadence chord
	1:57	THEME 1 — "Beloved Melody"	played by E-flat clarinet; **f**; accompanied by woodwinds, later flute added to the melody with rapid arpeggio figures in bassoon and cellos; other instruments join in crescendo to **ff**
	2:27	TRANSITION SECTION	transition section full orchestra chord; **ff**; then descending and ascending chromatic scale triplet figures into string descending syncopated pattern, changing into descending long tones in bass instruments, quieter to held bass tone
17	3:10	TOLLING BELLS	ominous sounding bells/chimes, **ff**; three sets of three notes C-C-G; each set interrupted by WITCHES' ROUND DANCE fragment

Dies Irae

18	3:39	THEME 2 — *Dies irae* Part 1	played by tubas, **f**; slow 2 meter, TOLLING BELLS continue; homophonic texture

Tubas and Bassoons — Allegro

f 8vb

| | 4:01 | THEME 2 — *Dies irae* Part 1 | imitated by **f** brass section, twice as fast; then imitated by **f** woodwinds and pizzicato strings, twice as fast as brass section; ending with upward swoop similar to the beginning |

	4:17	THEME 2 — *Dies irae* Part 2	tubas; *ff*; imitated by pizzicato basses and cellos; then imitated by brass section twice as fast; then woodwinds and pizzicato strings twice as fast as brass section; ending with upward swoop
	4:43	THEME 2 — *Dies irae* Part 1	returns in tubas and bassoons; *f*; syncopated low strings; brass section imitates twice as fast; then woodwinds and pizzicato strings twice as fast as brass section, ending with upward swoop; TOLLING BELLS continue
	5:20	THEME 3 — fragment Witches' Round Dance	transition section in strings, *mf*; several times, *crescendo* to cadence chord, *ff*

violins and violas

Witches' Round Dance (loosely constructed fugue)

19	5:38	THEME 3 — Witches Round Dance	duple meter compound, slower tempo; fugue started in low strings, imitated in upper strings; then woodwinds, punctuated by loud, syncopated brass figures; later section quiets down; polyphonic texture

	7:28	THEMES 2 AND 3 — fragments	horns; *f*; DIES IRAE, strings; *p*; WITCHES' ROUND DANCE; long transition over bass drum roll, gradual *crescendo* to loud syncopated figures; section ends with a cadence
	7:35	THEME 3 — Witches' Round Dance	returns, *ff*; in strings, original tempo, continue through brass entrances
	8:33	THEME 2 — *Dies irae*	returns in winds, *ff*; continues together with THEME 3 in strings, *ff*
	9:03	THEME 3 — fragments	transition section (resembling dancing ghosts and skeletons), trill ornaments in upper strings, *f*; rattling wood

		part of their bows (*col legno battuta*) over the strings, staccato woodwinds (laughingly), then brass chords, full orchestra-held chord
	CODA	
9:41	THEME 2— returns *Dies irae*	in tubas, *f*; twice as fast, then woodwinds twice as fast
9:42	CODA MATERIAL	full orchestra, *ff*; triplet figures dominate, then loud chords, descending chromatic scale in trombones
10:25	FINAL CHORD	held, *ff*

LISTENING INSIGHTS

What to Listen for in Romantic Music

To enjoy Romantic music more fully, look for extra-musical clues that have possibly contributed to the composer's inspiration for the music. The most obvious clues come from the title of the work—*Spring* Symphony, *Faust* Symphony, *Italian* Symphony, *1812 Overture*. Before you listen to the music, anticipate how the composer might convey the title's meaning through the music. While you listen, decide whether the music confirms your images.

Read the printed concert program or notes accompanying the recording for the title and other clues. You may also find background information about the music and the composer in the library.

THE ROMANTIC ART SONG

Lied (pl., Lieder)
(*leed, leed*-er)

The small, intimate *art song* (*Lied,* in German) epitomizes Romantic music. A composer of Romantic art songs would choose an existing poem—a work that stands on its own—and set it to music to heighten the drama of the text. Subjects include nature, beauty, love, death, and heroism.

When a group of songs was designed to be performed together, often around a common subject or musical idea, composers placed them in a *song cycle.*

Song Cycle

Art Song Performances

Performances of art songs became a favorite entertainment during the Romantic period. Originally held in the homes of the wealthy, these performances were part of an evening that typically included poetry readings and

Franz Schubert (1797–1828)

Showing early musical talent, Franz Schubert (*shoo*-bert) studied violin with his father and piano with his brother. He became a choirboy in the Imperial Chapel of his native Vienna (Vienna Boy's Choir) and, as one of the benefits, he was able to study music and other subjects at Vienna City School. At thirteen, Schubert studied composition with Salieri.

Schubert did well in school, and by eighteen, he had become a schoolmaster, like his father. But he was unhappy teaching young students and resented the rigidity of the teaching profession. Schubert's real interest was composing, which he was able to do full time when he left his teaching post at age twenty-one.

Schubert's meager income provided him a near-pauper's existence, occasionally alleviated by the help of his more fortunate friends.

His last five years were fraught with illness, but he kept composing until his death at age thirty-one. Like Mozart, he died young in Vienna, yet he left the world a wealth of beautiful music.

PRINCIPAL WORKS

Orchestral: nine symphonies: No. 5 in B-flat Major (1816); No. 8 (*Unfinished*, 1822), No. 9 (*Great*, 1825); Concert overtures; Incidental music: *Rosamunde* (1823)

Chamber Music: fifteen string quartets: *Death and the Maiden* (1824), String Quartet in C (1828); piano quintet: *The Trout* (1828)

Piano Music: twenty-one sonatas, six *Moments musicaux* (1828), impromptus, dances, fantasias, variations, marches

Songs: about 600: "An die Musik" (To Music), "Ave Maria," "Erlkönig" (The Erlking), "Der Wanderer" (The Wanderer), "Die Forelle" (The Trout); Song Cycles: *Die schöne Müllerin* (The Beautiful Maid of the Mill, 1823), *Winterreise* (Winter's Journey, 1827)

Operas: *Alfonso und Estrella* (1822), *Fierabras* (1823)

Choral Music: thirty choral works, including seven masses

philosophical discussions. Guests included an assortment of poets, novelists, painters, musicians, philosophers, and patrons of the arts. As the popularity of the art song spread, performances often moved to small concert halls and were open to the general public.

PIANIST'S ROLE IN ART SONGS   In performing art songs, the singer and the pianist have an equal role. Accompanist and vocalist share the melodic

A musical evening with Schubert at the piano and the singer Vogl at his right.

ideas, providing a context for the poetry. The musical dialogue and constant interaction between soloist and accompanist elevate both the poetry and the music to a high artistic plane.

German Art Song Composers

The most notable composers of German art songs were Franz Schubert, Robert Schumann, Felix Mendelssohn, Johannes Brahms, Franz Liszt, Hugo Wolf (1860–1903), Richard Strauss, and Gustav Mahler.

French Art Song Composers

Gabriel Fauré (1845–1924) and Henri Duparc (1848–1933) used poems in their native French, as did the twentieth-century composers Claude Debussy, Maurice Ravel, Francis Poulenc, and many others.

Scandinavian Art Song Composers

Of the Scandinavian composers, Edvard Grieg (1865–1931) wrote many of the most beautiful songs in the genre.

LISTENING ACTIVITY

ERLKING (ERLKÖNIG), FRANZ SCHUBERT

Large Form: Art Song
Detailed Form: Through-Composed
Performing Medium: Baritone and Piano

Compact Disc 2, Track 20
Cassette Tape: Side C, Example 3
Running Time: 4:14

Before following the Listening Guide and recording of Schubert's *Erlkönig* (Erlking), read the text. In this art song, Schubert chose a poem by one of the great German poets, Johann Wolfgang Goethe (1749–1832). Germanic legend describes the Erlking as a messenger of death who kills everyone he touches. The subjects, death and the supernatural, are typically Romantic.

Notice that there are four character roles in the poem, challenging the singer to distinguish among the characters by using distinctly different voice qualities for each portrayal:

- a narrator
- an ill child
- the child's father on horseback
- the beckoning Erlking

The form for the song is *through-composed*—the melodies keep changing with little or no return.

Through-Composed

Notice how the piano, playing its repeated triplet patterns, adds to the agitated mood, and how the accompaniment enhances the ideas in the text.

LISTENING GUIDE

ERLKING (ERLKÖNIG), FRANZ SCHUBERT

20   0:00   *triplet patterns in piano continue throughout, f, key of g minor, ominous sounding triplet runs in bass*

0:23 *Narrator*
Wer reitet so spät durch Nacht und
  Wind?
Es ist der Vater mit seinem Kind;
Er hat den Knaben wohl in dem Arm,
Er faßt ihn sicher, er hält ihn warm.

Who rides so late through the night and
  wind?
It is a father with his child.
He holds the young boy within his arm,
He clasps him tightly, he keeps him warm.

0:56 *The Father*
"Mein Sohn, was birgst du so bang
  dein Gesicht?"

"My son, why do you hide your face in
  fear?"

1:05 *The Child* (with fear)
"Siehst, Vater, du den Erlkönig nicht
Den Erlkönig mit Kron' und
  Schweif?"

"See, father, isn't that the Erlking?
The Erlking with crown and cape?"

1:22 *The Father* (calming his child)
"Mein Sohn, es ist ein Nebelstreif."

"My son, it's only a misty cloud."

1:32 *The Erlking* (sweetly)
"Du liebes Kind, komm, geh' mit mir!
Gar schöne Spiele spiel' ich mit dir;
Manch' bunte Blumen sind an dem
  Strand,
Meine Mutter hat manch' gülden
  Gewand."

"You lovely child, come, go with me!
Such pleasant games I'll play with thee!
The fields have bright flowers to behold,

My mother has many robes of gold."

1:54 *The Child*
"Mein Vater, mein Vater, und
  hörest du nicht,
Was Erlkönig mir leise verspricht?"

"My father, my father, now don't you
  hear
What the Erlking whispers in my ear?"

2:07 *The Father*
"Sei ruhig, bleibe ruhig, mein Kind;
In dürren Blättern säuselt der Wind."

"Be calm, stay calm, my child;
The dry leaves rustle when the wind
  blows wild."

2:18 *The Erlking* (beckoning)
"Willst, feiner Knabe, du mit
  mir geh'n?
Meine Töchter sollen dich warten
  schon;
Meine Töchter führen den nächtlichen
  Reih'n
Und wiegen und tanzen und singen
  dich ein.

"My fine boy, won't you go with me?

My daughters shall wait on thee,

My daughters nightly revels keep,

They'll sing and dance and rock you to
  sleep.

	Sie wiegen und tanzen und singen dich ein."	And sing and dance and rock you to sleep."
2:36	*The Child* "Mein Vater, mein Vater, und siehst du nicht dort Erlkönigs Töchter am düstern Ort?"	"My father, my father, can't you see him there The Erlking's daughters in that dark place?"
2:49	*The Father* "Mein Sohn, mein Sohn, ich seh' es genau, Es scheinen die alten Weiden so grau."	"My son, my son, all I can see, Is just the old gray willow trees."
3:00	triplet patterns in the piano	
3:07	*The Erlking* "Ich liebe dich, mich reizt deine schöne Gestalt, Und bist du nicht willig, so brauch' ich Gewalt."	"I love you, your form enflames my sense; Since you are not willing, I'll take you by force."
3:19	*The Child* "Mein Vater, mein Vater, jetzt faßt er mich an! Erlkönig hat mir ein Leid's getan!"	"My father, my father, he's now grabbing my arm, The Erlking wants to do me harm!"
3:34	*The Narrator* Dem Vater grauset's, er reitet geschwind, Er hält in Armen das ächzende Kind,	The father shudders, he speeds through the wind, He holds the moaning child in his arms,
4:00	*The Narrator* (**music slows**) Erreicht den Hof mit Müh und Not; In seinen Armen das Kind war tot!	He reaches home with pain and dread: In his arms, the child lay dead!
4:13	final chord in g minor	

Challenge Your Expertise

What was Johann Maelzel's invention, and how did it affect music performance?

Robert Schumann (1810–1856)

Robert Schumann (*shoo*-mahn) was born in Zwickau, Germany, near Leipzig. His father, a writer and publisher, sent Robert to Leipzig University to study law. But Robert's strong interests in music and literature distracted him, and he never attended classes.

At nineteen, he studied piano with Friedrich Wieck (*veek*). It was then that Robert met his teacher's nine-year-old daughter Clara, a piano prodigy. Robert moved into Wieck's home as a lodger the following year. In 1840, he married Clara Wieck, then age twenty-one. Clara became one of the nineteenth century's leading concert pianists and the greatest exponent of her husband's music. Their famous love affair was the subject of several Hollywood films.

As a result of syphilis, Schumann developed a lesion on his hand and began to have great difficulty with the flexibility of his fingers. Unsuccessful medical treatment probably aggravated the problem, which was devastating to his planned career as a performer.

Also contributing to Schumann's hand problems was his use of mechanical finger-strengthening devices, popular at that time, which may have damaged his flexibility. This, however, was a rumor.

Unable to perform in public, he followed his abiding interest in literature and journalism, founding the *Neue Zeitschrift für Musik* (The New Journal for Music), which is still in existence. As its editor and leading writer, Robert became one of the first and finest music critics, calling attention to such creative geniuses as Schubert, Berlioz, Mendelssohn, Chopin, and Brahms.

Toward the end of his life, Schumann was plagued by depression, hallucinations, and erratic behavior. He even attempted suicide by throwing himself into the icy winter waters of the Rhine River. In 1856, after being rescued from his suicide attempt, Schumann was taken to an asylum, where he died later that year at age forty-six.

Principal Works

Orchestral Music: four symphonies: No. 1 (*Spring*, 1841), No. 3 (*Rhenish*, 1850); Piano Concerto in a minor (1845)

Chamber Music: twenty-three works for various chamber music groups

Piano Music: "Abegg" Variations, Op. 1 (1830); *Papillons* (Butterflies), Op. 2 (1831); *Carnaval*, Op. 9 (1835); and *Kinderszenen* (Scenes from Childhood)

Songs: Over 275 songs, including several song cycles: *Frauenliebe und Leben* (A Woman's Love and Life, 1840), and *Dichterliebe* (A Poet's Love, 1840)

Early daguerreotype photograph of Clara and Robert Schumann

ROMANTIC PIANO MUSIC

Nineteenth-Century Piano

The piano of the nineteenth century was greatly superior to the earliest versions in Frederick the Great's collection that Bach had found wanting. Enlarged, with an improved mechanism and more keys, the piano was now capable of producing a full range of expression and level of dynamics. It became the perfect medium with which to display the virtuosity of the Romantic keyboard performer in public concert halls.

Salon concerts of piano music, art songs, or chamber music became the vogue among wealthy music enthusiasts. The hosts invited a select group of sophisticated guests to hear a recital by Chopin, Schubert, Mendelssohn, Liszt, Clara Schumann, and the influential piano teacher-composer Anton Rubinstein (1829–1894). Performances usually took place in a patron's home, or occasionally, for an audience larger than a residence could accommodate, in a public recital hall.

Salon concerts

Clara [Wieck] Schumann (1819–1896)

As early as age twenty-one, Clara Wieck Schumann had written in her diary, "I once thought that I possessed creative talent, but I have given up this idea; a woman must not desire to compose—not one has been able to do it, and why should I expect to?"

At age five, Clara began piano lessons with her father, Friedrich Wieck, a noted piano teacher in Leipzig, Germany. She progressed so rapidly that by age nine she performed a full piano recital in the famous Gewandhaus concert hall in Leipzig. The following year, her father organized a concert tour, and Clara performed throughout central Europe, traveling as far as Paris. Her fame quickly spread, and by sixteen, she was recognized as a highly talented child prodigy. Among her admirers were Felix Mendelssohn, Frédéric Chopin, and of course, Robert Schumann, her future husband. After hearing Clara perform, the great virtuoso-pianist Franz Liszt declared that she had "complete technical mastery, depth, and sincerity of feeling."

While still in her teens, Clara had several of her piano compositions published. Because of her widespread fame, she had an easier time at this age getting her works published than most of her women contemporaries. This would change later in her life.

Clara continued concertizing through her teen years with great acclaim. Her successes on the stage were dampened by conflicts in her personal life. Clara and Robert Schumann had fallen in love, much to the chagrin of her father, who felt that marriage to Robert would threaten her brilliant career. Robert had moved into the Wiecks' house as a twenty-year-old piano student and lodger when Clara was only ten years old. When Clara was eighteen, Robert asked Professor Wieck to give his permission for Clara to marry him. Friedrich refused, and a bitter legal as well as a personal battle began, which ended with the law court's ruling that the two lovers could marry. By then, the two were the talk of Europe's musical world.

Clara and Robert married in 1840. Much of her father's concern became a reality. Clara's performing and composing career waned for several years while she bore eight children, seven of whom lived beyond childhood. Clara tended to a very busy household, which later included a boarder and music student, Johannes Brahms.

After Robert's illnesses, attempted suicide, and eventual death in an asylum, Clara continued both composing and performing, though in a more limited way. She was no longer a child prodigy, and her composing was thwarted by nineteenth-century prejudice against women's asserting themselves in the arts and commerce.

Clara became a celebrated pianist, specializing in the music of both Schumann and Brahms. Clara and Brahms maintained a caring though mostly long-distance relationship that was rumored to have been quite serious. Mysteriously, they destroyed each other's correspondence. In addition to performing as she grew older, Clara became an influential teacher, working for some years at the Leipzig Conservatory of Music and later at the Hoch Conservatory in Frankfurt. She died at age seventy-six.

PRINCIPAL WORKS

Orchestral and Chamber Music: Concerto in a minor (1837); Three Romances for Violin and Piano (1853); Trio in g minor for Violin, Cello, Piano (1846)

Piano Music: Romance-Variations on a Theme of Robert Schumann (1853); Soirée musicales (1836); numerous works in many forms, such as variations, caprices, nocturnes, mazurkas, waltzes, and scherzos

Choral Music: Choral songs for a cappella mixed choir (1848)

Songs: numerous songs (*lieder*)

LISTENING ACTIVITY

Scherzo, Opus 10, Clara Wieck Schumann

Large Form: Short Piano Recital Piece
Detailed Form: Scherzo with Two Trios
Performing Medium: Piano

Compact Disc 2, Track 21
Cassette Tape: Side C, Example 4
Running Time: 4:59

One of the most brilliant virtuoso pianists of her time, Clara Schumann composed many piano pieces like this scherzo (meaning *joke,* in Italian) to display her own abilities. It was Beethoven who made the form popular when he began using the scherzo to replace the traditional minuet in multimovement works such as the symphony and string quartet. Slower and more stately, the minuet had been a favorite dance of the leisure-class aristocrats at the courts of Europe. Revolutions and uprisings had brought down many of the courts; therefore, the late eighteenth and early nineteenth centuries were a time when composers began disassociating themselves with the courts to bring more music to the growing middle-class audiences.

Faster and more lively than the minuet, the Romantic-period scherzo developed into an entertaining vehicle for a variety of solo instruments to display the performer's technical prowess. With its extremely fast tempo (*presto*), Clara Schumann's Opus 10 scherzo makes great demands on the pianist to maintain the furious pace set in the beginning.

LISTENING GUIDE

SCHERZO, OPUS 10, CLARA WIECK SCHUMANN

| 21 | 0:00 | INTRODUCTION THEME | Solo piano; very fast tempo (presto); triple meter; alternating pitches and sequences in the upper register; *p*; d-minor tonality; homophonic texture; expression indication "with passion" |

Presto.   Scherzo con passione.

| | 0:08 | SCHERZO THEME | Unison melody with accented chords, alternating with arpeggios; *p*; d-minor tonality |

| | 0:19 | INTRODUCTION THEME | Introduction Theme restated; g-minor tonality; *p* to *f* then diminuendo to *p* |
| | 0:36 | SCHERZO THEME | Scherzo Theme returns in d-minor tonality |

1:04	SCHERZO THEME (modified)	alternating pitch figures
1:30	TRIO 1 THEME	Slower tempo; smooth, expressive stepwise descending melody in upper voice with arpeggio chordal accompaniment creating a homophonic texture; followed by upward arpeggios and accents in lower part; crescendo, becoming more agitated

1:57	SCHERZO FRAGMENTS	in octaves in the bass, imitated in upper voice; *f*, A-Major tonality; original presto tempo; agitated; *ff*; gradually becoming smoother and calmer
2:12	SCHERZO THEME	restated f and rhythmically; gradually softer toward two pauses
2:41	TRIO 2 THEME	introduced; *p*; melody rising and falling, mostly stepwise; *p* bass chords on the second beat; E-flat Major tonality; section is repeated more accented; rubato; gradually slowing

3:28		Original presto tempo; SCHERZO FRAGMENTS in lower part, upper part continues TRIO 2 THEME; then fragments of INTRODUCTION THEME in lower part; transitions to full INTRODUCTION THEME
4:04:	INTRODUCTION THEME	returns with the same tempo and tonality as in the beginning
4:12	SCHERZO THEME	returns in original d-minor tonality; then imitated in bass part; crescendo and more furious; fragments of INTRODUCTION THEME heard, followed by a loud lower-voiced chordal final cadence

Frédéric Chopin (1810–1849)

Born near Warsaw, Poland, Frédéric Chopin (sho-*pan*) gave his first piano recital there when he was eight. Concentrating mainly on piano performance, he studied at the Warsaw Conservatory until he was nineteen.

Frédéric's father, a Frenchman, had left France to avoid serving in Napoleon's army. In Poland, the elder Chopin was a political activitist who vehemently opposed the czarist Russian occupation. Because the family lived in fear of reprisal, they thought Frédéric would be safer elsewhere so he could advance his career.

After Frédéric left Poland, he concertized first in Vienna, then throughout Germany. He finally settled in Paris, where the artistic community quickly accepted him. Among his friends were painter Delacroix, musicians Liszt and Berlioz, and writers Victor Hugo, Honoré de Balzac, Alexandre Dumas (père), Heinrich Heine, and George Sand.

Sand was actually a woman, Aurore Dudevant. To become published, she was forced to use a man's name and circumvent the prejudice against women writers. She and Chopin lived together for years, and she nursed him through his bouts with tuberculosis. He finally died from the disease at thirty-nine. True to the romantic and nationalistic spirit, his body was buried in Paris, but his heart was returned to Poland for burial.

Chopin left a legacy of piano compositions that are among the greatest ever written.

PRINCIPAL WORKS

Orchestral Music: two concertos for piano and orchestra, No. 1 in e minor (1830); No. 2 in f minor (1830)

Piano Music: hundreds of pieces in a variety of short forms: ballades, preludes, fantasies, impromptus, nocturnes, polonaises, scherzos, études (studies), variations, and waltzes

Published Piano Music

The popularity of both public and salon performances encouraged composers to create and publish an unsurpassed variety of piano music. Learning to play the piano was considered an essential element of a nineteenth-century education, particularly among middle-class and wealthy families. The demand for published music increased, and composers now had a lucrative outlet for their works.

Intimate Piano Music

To take full advantage of the instrument's expressive potential and to hold the interest of their audiences, Chopin, Liszt, Mendelssohn, Brahms, and other composers generally wrote fewer of the longer, more formal piano pieces, such as the sonata. Instead, they developed a variety of simple, intimate forms, generally lasting from two to five minutes.

- ballades
- capriccios
- consolations
- études (studies)
- fantasies
- impromptus
- mazurkas

- nocturnes
- polonaises
- preludes
- rhapsodies
- scherzos
- songs without words
- waltzes

LISTENING ACTIVITY

FANTAISIE IMPROMPTU, FRÉDÉRIC CHOPIN

Large Form: Short Piano Recital Piece
Detailed Form: Three Part Form (A-B-A)
Performing Medium: Piano

Compact Disc 2, Track 22
Cassette Tape: Side C, Example 5
Running Time: 4:42

Listen to the *Fantaisie-Impromptu* by Chopin. Lasting under five minutes, the piece covers a wide range of expression and allows the performer to dazzle the audience. Notice the slight deviations from steady tempo—*rubato*—which enhance the emotional mood of the piece.

The title, *Fantaisie-Impromptu,* gives two clues to the nature of the music. *Fantaisie,* or "fantasy," denotes whimsy, a fanciful vision, a pleasant daydream. *Impromptu* suggests extemporaneous or improvised music. Though Chopin notated the music on paper, he wanted the music to suggest a feeling of spontaneity.

Chopin's melody in the middle section (B) is so appealing that during the 1940s it was turned into a popular song called "I'm Always Chasing Rainbows."

The detailed form, A-B-A, which Chopin uses here, is one of the most popular in music. Often called a three-part song form because of its extensive use in songs, the first and last sections (A) are similar and bracket a contrasting middle section (B).

LISTENING GUIDE

FANTAISIE IMPROMPTU, FRÉDÉRIC CHOPIN

Section A

22	0:00	THEME 1	Allegro, duple meter, rubato throughout, sixteen-note patterns in upper voice and triplet patterns in the bass, c-sharp minor tonality, *f* diminuendo to *p*, then brief swells crescendo and diminuendo
	0:48		chromatic runs from high to low, slowing and modulating to D-flat major tonality

Section B

	1:03	THEME 2	moderate tempo, softer, homophonic texture—melody with ornaments in high voice, rolling triplet arpeggios in bass accompaniment

Section A

	3:03	THEME 1	presto (very fast) like the beginning, c-sharp minor tonality, crescendos and diminuendos
			chromatic runs from high to low, still c-sharp minor tonality

Coda

	3:57	THEME 2	*ff* gradual diminuendo and slowing of tempo, brief restatement of melody from section B in bass, ending with two rolling chords, very soft

Franz Liszt (1811–1886)

Franz Liszt (*list*) was born near Sopron in the Austro-Hungarian empire. Because Sopron was once predominantly Austrian, Liszt's native language was German. The town is forty miles south of Vienna and only twelve miles from the Esterházy's Austrian palace in Eisenstadt, where Haydn worked. During Haydn's time, Liszt's father was one of the managers of the Esterházy's summer palace in Hungary, which Haydn frequently visited.

Liszt exhibited enormous talent as a pianist and was sent to Vienna to study with Antonio Salieri and Karl Czerny (*chair*-nee) (1791–1857). Following his piano debut in London at age eleven, Liszt began touring the musical capitals of Europe and was soon considered the greatest piano virtuoso of the nineteenth century.

Settling in Paris at age sixteen, Liszt was quickly welcomed into the inner circles of great artists: Berlioz, Heine, Hugo, Sand, and later, Chopin. With Paris as his home base, Liszt toured extensively throughout central Europe, Russia, Turkey, the British Isles, Spain, and Portugal.

At age thirty-eight, he accepted the position of music director to the Grand Duke of Weimar (*vy*-mar), near Leipzig. There, Liszt devoted himself mainly to composing and conducting. He also introduced several works of his friend, Richard Wagner. That friendship became family when Liszt's daughter Cosima married Wagner.

At age fifty, Liszt moved to Rome and went through a religious stage there, taking minor orders in the Catholic Church. Later, he continued traveling and performing until his death at age seventy-four in Bayreuth (*by*-royt), Germany. Liszt's music is known for its extramusical associations, either through their titles, or from specific programs.

PRINCIPAL WORKS

Orchestral Music: *Faust Symphony* (1854); *Dante Symphony* (1856); Symphonic Poems: *Tasso* (1849); *Les Préludes* (1854); Piano Concertos No. 1 in E-flat (1849); No. 2 in A (1849); *Totentanz* for Piano and Orchestra (1849)

Piano Music: *Transcendental Studies* (1851); *Traveler's Album* (1836); *Six Consolations* (1850); Sonata in b minor (1853); Hungarian Rhapsodies, ballads, études (studies)

MENDLESSOHN'S CONCERTS   As the newly appointed conductor of the Leipzig Gewandhaus Orchestra, 26-year-old Felix Mendelssohn addressed his musicians, imploring them to make their orchestra the best in Europe. He was able to motivate them, and they worked harder than ever before. Finally, the orchestra did earn that distinction under Mendelssohn's direction.

To compensate them for their extra work, Felix used his own money to double the salaries of his players. He also established the first pension plan for orchestral musicians. Treated like professionals, they had greater feelings of self-esteem.

Mendelssohn created a new type of concert offering. Until his time, orchestras primarily played works by living composers, with rare performances of music by dead composers. Aware that a wealth of great orchestral music was being neglected, simply because the composer was no longer around to promote it, Mendelssohn assembled programs similar to what we find today—works by several composers, from several style periods. He staged concerts featuring Handel's oratorios, Bach's works for chorus and orchestra, and Mozart's and Beethoven's symphonies.

Mendelssohn showcased his contemporaries as well. Struggling composers could come to him for his generous financial help. By featuring their music in his Gewandhaus concerts, Mendelssohn enabled both audiences and publishers to become familiar with the works of Franz Schubert, Robert Schumann, Hector Berlioz, Luigi Cherubini, Franz Liszt, Gìacomo Meyerbeer, Johannes Brahms, and Frédéric Chopin.

Hundreds of musicians and composers were indebted to Mendelssohn for his nurturing. During his short life, he served as a catalyst for promoting music as a desirable profession.

Felix Mendelssohn (1809–1847)

Felix Mendelssohn was born in Hamburg, Germany, into one of Europe's wealthiest and most interesting families. His grandfather, the noted writer and philosopher Moses Mendelssohn (*men*-dl-sun), was a political and financial advisor to King Friedrich the Great of Prussia. (Moses was largely responsible for the assimilation of Jews into German society.) Felix's father, Abraham, started the banking business that influenced European affairs until the Nazi era.

When Felix was an infant, his family moved to Berlin. He began receiving a thorough education through tutors when he was very young. Many people—including Felix's teachers and Goethe, a frequent visitor at the Mendelssohn home—described the boy as "an exceptionally attractive, agreeable, and talented child."

His musical talents were often compared to Mozart's. Performing brilliantly on the piano at an early age, Felix displayed his genius by writing six symphonies by age twelve, seven more by fourteen, and *A Midsummer Night's Dream* Overture at seventeen.

The Mendelssohn's Berlin home was a meeting place for some of the most influential artists and thinkers of the world. Felix's father added the name "Bartholdy" to the family name because of the pressures of anti-Semitism. Although he tried to pass this name on to his children, they secretly rejected its use. Felix often signed letters to his sister Fanny as "Felix 'not-Bartholdy' Mendelssohn."

Traveling extensively throughout Germany, England, Scotland, and Italy, Felix incorporated his impressions into musical compositions. At age twenty-six, he became conductor and musical director of the Gewandhaus (guh-*vahnd*-house, "Cloth Hall") Orchestra in Leipzig, a post he held for the rest of his life.

Also in Leipzig, he founded one of Europe's great schools of music, the Leipzig Conservatory. After the death of his beloved sister Fanny, his health began to fail. Mendelssohn died several months later at age thirty-seven.

PRINCIPAL WORKS

Orchestral Music: twelve string symphonies; five full orchestra symphonies: No. 3 (*Scottish*, 1842), No. 4 (*Italian*, 1833), No. 5 (*Reformation*, 1832); Overtures: *A Midsummer Night's Dream* Overture (1826), *Calm Sea and Prosperous Voyage* (1828), *The Hebrides* (*Fingal's Cave*) *Overture* (1830), *Ruy Blas Overture* (1839), Piano Concertos: No. 1 in g minor (1831), No. 2 in d minor (1837); Violin concerto in e minor (1844)

Chamber Music: six string quartets, two string quintets

Piano Music: forty-eight Lieder ohne Worte (Songs without Words)

Choral Music: oratorios in the Handel tradition: *St. Paul* (1836), *Elijah* (1846)

Fanny Mendelssohn (1805–1847)

Four years older than her brother Felix, Fanny Mendelssohn was described as being equally talented. Like her brother, Fanny began piano lessons with her mother. She made such excellent progress in her piano studies that by age thirteen she could play from memory Bach's entire *Well-Tempered Clavier*. Foregoing a performing career for a husband and a family, Fanny married painter Wilhelm Hensel. However, she and her family did travel extensively throughout Europe, with extended stays in Milan, Venice, Naples, and Genoa.

Fanny remained an excellent pianist as well as a composer, though most of her compositions were unpublished during her lifetime. Because of the discrimination against women composers, she had to publish six of her songs, which were well received, under Felix's name.

Fanny and her brother Felix remained close throughout their short lives, consulting each other on personal as well as musical matters.

Like her brother, Fanny nurtured new composers at the Elternhaus in Berlin, where she, like Felix, produced performances of their works. Fanny's death at age forty-one was a dramatic, tragic event. It happened on stage during a rehearsal of Felix's *Walpurgisnacht* cantata at the Elternhaus. Felix was devastated by Fanny's untimely death and went into a deep depression and took ill. He too died a few months later.

PRINCIPAL WORKS (OVER 200, SOME PUBLISHED WORKS FOLLOW)

Chamber Music: Trio in d minor for Violin, Cello, and Piano (Op. 11)

Piano Music: Romances without Words (7) (Op. 2, 6, 8); *Der Jahr* (The Year) a suite of thirteen pieces, various sonatas

Challenge Your Expertise

- Which composer courted his loved one in a language she did not understand?
- Which of the following composers could have been a guest at Chopin's thirtieth birthday party—Mendelssohn, Schubert, Liszt, Beethoven?

LISTENING ACTIVITY

CONCERTO FOR VIOLIN AND ORCHESTRA (1844, OP. 64),
FELIX MENDELSSOHN

First Movement: Allegro Molto Appassionatto
Large Form: Violin Concerto
Detailed Form: Scherzo with Two Trios
Performing Medium: Piano

Compact Disc 3, Track 16
Running Time: 11:42

Mendelssohn's Violin Concerto in e minor is one of the most frequently played violin concertos today. He composed the work in 1844 for his friend Ferdinand David, a famous violinist. The concerto is in the typical concerto form of three movements: fast-slow-fast.

Traditionally, audiences would applaud the soloist after the first movement of a concerto, interrupting the mood of the music. Inspired by Beethoven's Piano Concerto No. 5 (*Emperor*), Mendelssohn indicates no stops between movements for the audience to applaud. Both composers wanted audiences to concentrate on the music rather than on the soloist.

Mendelssohn, like Beethoven, also wrote out the soloist's cadenzas, insisting that they be played as written. Thus Mendelssohn did not allow soloists to improvise or to insert their own cadenzas in his violin concerto.

The first movement is in classical sonata form. After only a three-beat, quiet orchestral introduction, the violin soloist enters with the main theme. This is a minor departure: most Classical-period concertos contain two expositions, one by the orchestra and one by the soloist.

One of the outstanding features of this movement is its lyricism. All three melodies—Theme 1, Transition Theme, and Theme 2—are warmly melodic, allowing the soloist to display his or her rich violin tone quality and expressiveness.

LISTENING GUIDE

CONCERTO FOR VIOLIN AND ORCHESTRA (1844, OP. 64),
FELIX MENDELSSOHN

EXPOSITION

| 16 | 0:00 | THEME 1 | in solo violin, *p;* after a three-beat orchestral introduction, song-like duple meter, e minor tonality; homophonic texture |

	0:29		solo violin passage, *f;* after short orchestral chords, *f;* repeated in sequence, violin continues with sequences accompanied by orchestra.
	0:57	THEME 1	full orchestra without soloist, *ff;* original tempo and key, section moves into new theme
	1:29	TRANSITION THEME	introduced by the orchestra, *p;* then played by solo violin, same key (e minor)

	2:07	TRANSITION	transition section, *p;* solo violin sequences
			transition section, *p;* solo violin slowly, calmly, and expressively to held high tone; then descending line
17	2:46	THEME 2	introduced by woodwinds, *pp;* slower tempo, G-Major tonality

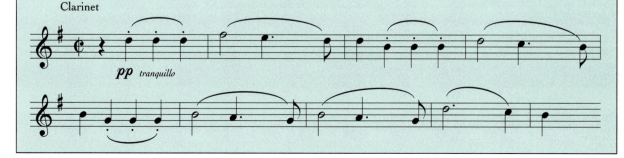

	2:58	THEME 2	played by solo violin, **pp**; calmly and expressively, imitations between soloist and orchestra move to held note and cadence
	3:48	THEME 1	returns in solo violin; **p**; original tempo and tonality (e minor); into brilliant solo passages, including sequences, with pizzicato string accompaniment
	4:37	THEME 1	solo violin and orchestra trills, **ff**; forcefully; section ends

DEVELOPMENT

18	4:58	TRANSITION THEME fragments THEME 1 — fragments	both used, rubato
	5:57	THEME 1 — fragments	in solo violin, **pp**; descending sequences; orchestra crescendos to held loud dominant chord
	6:22	CADENZA	unaccompanied solo violin; arpeggios, trills, fragments of THEME 1, rapid arpeggios, diminuendo; transition back to orchestra

RECAPITULATION

19	7:51	THEME 1	played softly by the orchestra, original tempo and key
	8:07	TRANSITION THEME— fragments	played first by orchestra, **ff**; then sequences, played by solo violin; becomes softer, slows down, modulates to new key
	8:37	THEME 2	returns first in woodwinds, then solo violin, E major tonality; section ends with held high note, and cadence
	9:48	THEME 1 — fragments	played softly by orchestra, followed by solo violin passages accompanied by pizzicato strings; orchestra crescendo
	10:28	TRANSITION	loud orchestra chords separate unaccompanied solo violin passage, similar to cadenza
	10:31	THEME 1 — fragments	solo violin, **ff**; separated by orchestra trills, **ff**; then diminuendo

CODA

	10:54	TRANSITION THEME— fragments	played softly by the solo violin; faster tempo, increasingly faster and louder until the end
	11:38		**ff**; e minor; orchestra stops, except solo bassoonist who holds one tone, softly as a transition to the second movement

Challenge Your Expertise

- Can you think of two composers who published their works under someone else's name?
- How did Mendelssohn effectively use a combination of affluence and influence in his work with other musicians?

Summary of Terms

art song	mazurkas	salon concerts
ballades	nocturnes	scherzos
consolations	orchestration	song cycle
études	polonaises	songs without words
fantasies	preludes	tone poems
idée fixe	recurrent melody	waltzes
impromptus	recurrent theme	
lieder	rhapsodies	

Chapter 15

Romantic Opera

Opera is dramatized music. With its sung dialogue, elaborate costumes and scenery, cast of characters, and dancing—all accompanied by an orchestra—opera naturally lends itself to romanticism.

Audiences have always been drawn to opera as a contrast to everyday realism. Though some operas are based on realistic plots, most operas transport you to another time and place, to idealized love, to magic and mystery. Operatic superheroes and superbeings can do what no mortal can. By its very nature, then, opera became a very popular medium for nineteenth-century Romantic composers and audiences.

Adding Dimension to Instrumental Music

With singers performing a text in his Ninth Symphony, Beethoven strove to say more than instrumental music alone could convey. With grand opera, all of the subjects, spirit, and extramusical ideas associated with romanticism materialized in the grandest manner—many within the same opera.

Here are a few examples:

- *Fidelio* (1805) by Ludwig van Beethoven
  heroism, love, death
- *Der Freischütz* (1821) by Carl Maria von Weber
  magic, mystery, the supernatural
- *La Traviata* (1853) by Giuseppe Verdi
  love, death, beauty
- *Die Walküre* (1870) by Richard Wagner
  hero, supernatural, love
- *Carmen* (1875) by Georges Bizet
  the common man, love, death, exotic cultures
- *Madama Butterfly* (1904) by Giacomo Puccini
  distant lands, travel, exotic cultures, love, death
- *Turandot* (posthumous, 1926) by Giacomo Puccini
  distant lands, travel, exotic cultures, love, death

Earlier Opera

Until the early nineteenth century, operas were primarily a series of songs (arias and duets). Adhering to tightly knit plots was of little importance to the early opera composers. Choruses and instrumental music served as introductions, interludes, or fillers between songs.

Often, when it was time for an aria, all action on stage stopped. The performers stood frozen in tableau, while the soloist crossed downstage and, with little regard for the dramatic situation, delivered his or her aria to the audience. Suddenly, the fair maiden, about to die in bed, would throw off her covers, stand up, and sing. Following the aria, the death scene continued. The hero, about to plunge his sword into the villain's chest, postponed the kill until after his aria.

HISTORICAL PERSPECTIVE

Opera in North America

Inaugurated in 1883, the Metropolitan Opera Company in New York City became the first major opera company in North America. Though many limited-season opera companies held occasional performances in various cities throughout North America after 1883, the next permanent opera company, the San Francisco Opera Company, did not start until fifty years later, in 1923.

Today, there are more than fifty major opera companies in North America, with productions rivaling those anywhere in the world.

Opera Stars

Since its beginning, opera has attracted loyal fans to hear their favorite singers. Just as they enjoy virtuoso concerto soloists, audiences marvel at a singer's range, special tone quality, and *bel canto* abilities.

Great opera stars are capable of far more than just the musical performance. They transform themselves into the characters they are playing: the resounding bass voice becomes a fierce villain; the ringing tenor with his high "C" becomes the handsome prince; the warm, lilting soprano becomes the fair young maiden.

Quality Plots

Romantic composers—Carl Maria von Weber, Richard Wagner, Giuseppe Verdi, Giacomo Puccini, Georges Bizet, Charles Gounod, and others—elevated the significance and quality of the stories and heightened the drama of their operas. Now, audiences began to come to the opera for its drama, not solely for the vocal abilities of the stars or for the grand spectacle of its production values.

ITALIAN ROMANTIC OPERA

Italian Language

Italian composers and the Italian language had dominated opera from its inception. Even Mozart used the Italian language. To continue that dominance into the Romantic period, early-nineteenth-century Italian composers such as Gioacchino Rossini (roh-*see*-nee, 1792–1868), Gaetano Donizetti (don-ih-*tzeh*-tee, 1797–1848), and Vincenzo Bellini (beh-*lee*-nee, 1801–1835) created a new round of exciting Italian operas.

Bel Canto Style of Singing

Romantic-period Italian composers perpetuated the *bel canto* style that characterized early Italian opera. Their aria melodies became elaborate vocal gymnastics, designed to astound audiences with the soloist's virtuosity.

Verdi's Opera Innovations

Both Verdi and Wagner are credited with developing opera into a fully integrated art form. Verdi's characters continued to sing appealing arias, but their songs grew out of the plot more convincingly than ever before. Though audiences still applaud at the end of his arias, Verdi tried to manipulate the action on stage and the orchestration to sustain the mood of the drama throughout the scene without applause.

Scene from Verdi's opera
Falstaff

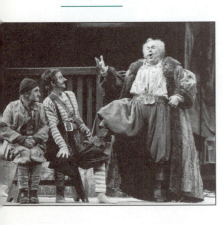

Summary of Verdi's Opera Innovations

- His libretto (book or story) for each opera was of high quality— adapted from stories by Shakespeare, Hugo, Dumas, and Schiller.
- His characters were believable and human.
- His arias blended into the action.
- His orchestral interludes and accompaniment were highly expressive and contributed substantially to the mood of the entire work.

Gaetano Donizetti (1797–1848)

Born in the northern lake district of Bergamo, Italy, Gaetano Donizetti (dohn-ih-*tzeh*-tee) later studied opera composition with the German composer Johann Simon Mayr (1763–1845). Some of his early operas were produced in northern Italy, but the later productions in Rome and Naples greatly advanced his popularity throughout the Italian peninsula.

His popularity then spread to France. For most of his later years, Donizetti lived in Paris, writing operas with French texts.

Donizetti was one of the most prolific of all the opera composers. He became famous for his dazzling arias, such as the "Mad Scene" from *Lucia di Lammermoor* (1835), which requires great vocal flexibility and extraordinary range.

PRINCIPAL WORKS

Operas: 75 operas, including *Anna Bolena* (Anne Boleyn, 1830), *L'elisir d'amore* (The Elixir of Love, 1832), *Lucrezia Borgia* (1833), *Lucia di Lammermoor* (1835), *La Fille du régiment* (The Daughter of the Regiment, 1840), *La Favorite* (1840), and *Don Pasquale* (1843)

Other Works: About 100 songs, several symphonies, concertos, oratorios, cantatas, chamber music, and church music

Vincenzo Bellini (1801–1835)

Vincenzo Bellini's (beh-*lee*-nee) ten operas brought him great success and fame before his death at age thirty-three. Like Donizetti, Bellini wrote in both Italian and French and was adored by opera audiences in both Italy and France. Most of his works are still produced regularly today by opera companies around the world.

PRINCIPAL WORKS

Operas: *La Sonnambula* (The Sleepwalker, 1831); *Norma* (1831); *I Puritani e i Cavalieri* (The Puritans and the Cavaliers, 1835)

Gioacchino Rossini (1792–1868)

Gioacchino Rossini (roh-*see*-nee) was one of the last masters of opera buffa. He was born in the Italian town of Pesaro on the Adriatic coast and studied music in Bologna. Following the 1810 premiere in Venice of his comic opera *La cambiale di matrimonio* (The Bill of Exchange for Marriage), his reputation spread quickly. Commissions poured in from across Europe. Soon he was composing for the most important opera houses in Italy, including La Scala in Milan.

By age 21, only three years after his debut in the genre, Rossini had composed ten operas. By the time he was 30, he had produced 32 operas. Perhaps the most famous of that prolific period was *Il barbiere di Siviglia* (The Barber of Seville). His combination of appealing, flowing melodies and wit, comedy, and brilliant staging made Rossini one of the most important opera composers of the early nineteenth century.

In 1823, Rossini settled in Paris where, for the next six years, he continued his considerable output. Then, at age 37, after a series of disappointing love affairs and bouts with ill health, Rossini suddenly turned away from opera. Using a libretto in French, he composed his 39th and last opera, *Guillaume Tell* (William Tell). In the twentieth century, the Overture to William Tell began to have a life of its own, attaining greater popularity than the original opera.

Although Rossini continued composing, he limited his works mostly to religious music and songs. Nevertheless, by his death at age 74, Rossini had achieved tremendous success and financial security. Many of his operas are regularly performed in the contemporary repertoire.

PRINCIPAL WORKS

Operas: *L'Italiana in Algeri* (The Italian Girl in Algiers, 1813), *Il barbiere di Siviglia* (The Barber of Seville, 1816), *La Cenerentola* (Cinderella, 1817), *Semiramide* (1823), *Guillaume Tell* (William Tell, 1829)

Sacred Choral Music: *Petite messe solennelle* (1864), *Stabat Mater* (1841), Masses

Secular Vocal Music: *Les Soirées musicales* (Musical Evenings, 1835), cantatas

Giuseppe Verdi (1813–1901)

Busseto, a small town in northern Italy, was Giuseppe Verdi's (*vehr-dee*) birthplace. And it was there that he studied music until age 18, when he applied for admission to the Milan Conservatory. But Verdi could not pass the entrance examinations because the administrators of the Conservatory claimed that his pianistic abilities were substandard. Instead, Verdi had to study with various private music teachers in Milan.

Between the ages of 26 and 80, Verdi composed more than twenty-five operas. His first, *Oberto,* premiered in 1839 at Milan's famous Teatro alla Scala (La Scala). What should have been a year of joy and triumph for the young man was overshadowed by the tragic, mysterious deaths of his wife and two children. Fifty-four years later, La Scala staged Verdi's last opera, *Falstaff.* Today, many of his works, including some of the obscure ones, are consistently produced throughout the world during every opera season.

For a time, Verdi became involved in Italian politics and Italy's struggle for independence from the Austro-Hungarian Empire. His name was used as a rallying acronym—*Vittore Emanuele Ré D'Italia* (Victor Emanuel, King of Italy). When Victor Emanuel became the first king of a united Italy, Verdi was appointed to the new parliament and was later elected to the senate. Among his accomplishments was the establishment of a home for retired opera singers and musicians. His death in Milan stirred Italy, and his funeral drew some of the largest crowds in that nation's history.

PRINCIPAL WORKS

Operas: *Nabucco* (1842), *Ernani* (1844), *Macbeth* (1847), *Rigoletto* (1851), *Il trovatore* (The Troubadour, 1853), *La traviata* (The Courtesan, 1853), *Un ballo in maschera* (A Masked Ball, 1859), *La forza del destino* (The Force of Destiny, 1862), *Don Carlos* (1867), *Aïda* (1871), *Otello* (1887), *Falstaff* (1893)

Sacred Music: *Requiem* (1874), *Quattro pezzi sacri* (Four Sacred Pieces, 1889–97)

LISTENING ACTIVITY

LA TRAVIATA (*THE COURTESAN*, 1853), GIUSEPPE VERDI

Act I: "É strano! É strano!" "Sempre libera"
Form: Romantic Opera, Recitatives and Arias
Performing Medium: Soprano and Orchestra

Compact Disc 2, Track 23
Cassette Tape: Side C, Example 6
Running Time: 8:07

The text, or *libretto*, for the opera was based on Alexandre Dumas' (the younger) popular French novel *The Lady of the Camellias* (*La Dame aux camélias*). Verdi, along with his librettist, Francesco Piave, changed the name of the title role from Camellia to Violetta. Violetta is a Parisian courtesan, a French word literally meaning "a court woman." In nineteenth-century Paris, it meant that she was mistress to a series of wealthy patrons who supported her lavishly.

Act 1

Having temporarily recovered from a bout with incurable tuberculosis, Violetta throws a party at her opulent apartment. She is introduced to Alfredo, a young man from a wealthy, respectable family. Alfredo tells her that during her illness, he called on her many times to inquire about her health, and that he has fallen in love with her. She is touched by his passionate admiration, and she agrees to meet him the next day.

The guests leave. Alone in her apartment, Violetta contemplates the possibility that Alfredo is her true love. She sings about this in the next recorded example. By the end of Act 1, both Violetta and Alfredo are unable to resist their strong passion for each other.

Act 2

The couple decide to live together away from Paris in an elegant country home. Only Violetta's recurrent coughing spells interrupt their bliss. To maintain their lifestyle, Violetta has secretly sold most of her possessions. But their debts mount, and Alfredo goes off to Paris seeking funds.

While he is away, his father calls on Violetta. He pleads with her to give up her relationship with Alfredo because her reputation is jeopardizing his daughter's pending marriage. Violetta reluctantly agrees to end the love affair. When Alfredo returns, Violetta pretends to have fallen out of love with him and returns alone to Paris.

Act 3

Back in Paris, Alfredo is a party guest at the home of Violetta's friend. When Violetta arrives on the arm of another man, Alfredo publicly expresses his contempt for her lack of devotion to their relationship. Unaware of his father's role in the breakup, Alfredo leaves the party—and Paris.

Act 4

Violetta, alone in her apartment, is on the verge of death. Delirious, she dreams of her lost relationship with Alfredo, regretting the sadness of their parting. Having learned the true story of Violetta's decision to end their affair, Alfredo quickly returns to Paris and Violetta—a moment before she dies.

LISTENING GUIDE

La Traviata (The Courtesan, 1853), Giuseppe Verdi

After a night of partying and meeting her new love Alfredo, Violetta enters a quiet room. Alfredo and all the guests have left: she is alone. (See Act 1, paragraph 2 for the context of this recording.)

RECITATIVE

23   0:00   *Soprano (Violetta) starts with a secco (dry) recitative without orchestra; allegro, rubato rhythm with pauses; then symphony orchestra enters filling in the pauses; **ff** then **pp**; homophonic texture*

Violetta	*Violetta*
È strano! È strano! In core	*How strange! How strange! His words*
Scolpiti ho quegli accenti!	*Are burned upon my heart!*
Saria per me sventura un serio amore?;	*Would a real love be a tragedy for me?*
Che risolvi, o turbata anima mia?	*What decision are you taking,*
	O my soul?
Null'uomo ancora t'accendeva—	*No man has ever made me fall in*
O gioia!	*love—O joy!*
Ch'io non conobbi, esser amata amando!	*Which I have never known, loving and*
	being loved!
E sdegnaria poss'io	*Could I coldly reject it*
Per l'aride follie del viver mio?	*For the shallow folly of my existence?*

ARIA

24   1:06   *Orchestral introduction; **p**, then **pp** when soprano enters; moderate tempo; steady rhythm in triple meter; homophonic texture; f-minor tonality; homophonic texture*

Violetta   **p**   dolciss.

Ah,   for - s'è   lui - che   l'a - ni - ma
[Ah,   per - haps   he is the one   whom   my soul.]

Ah, fors' è lui che l'anima   Ah, perhaps he is the one
Solinga ne' tumulti   Whom my soul
Godea sovente pingere   Lonely in the tumult, loved!
Dè suoi colori occulti!   To secretly imagine!
Lui che modesto e vigile   He who with modest vigilance;
All' egre soglie accese,   Came here while I lay ill,
E nuova febbre accese,   Awakening a new fever;
Destandomi all' amor.   The fever of love.

Momentarily forgetting her long struggle with illness, Violetta is hopeful and in love. The melody of her aria is a reprise of Alfredo's aria in which he professes his love for her.

        2:17   *Change to F-major tonality; soft arpeggios in the orchestra; soprano is louder and highly expressive; homophonic texture*

Violetta
f

A   quel - l'a - mor,   quel l'a - mor   ch'e   pal - pi - to
[Of   love,   of   love   which is   the breath]

A quell' amor, ch'è palpito   Of love which is the breath
Dell' universo intero,   Of the universe itself
Misterioso, altero,   Mysterious, noble,
Croce e delizia al cor.   Embracing the heart's sorrow and
                                       rapture.

RECITATIVE

25   3:28   *Soprano begins without accompaniment, then allegro; symphony orchestra enters with eighth-note and triplet figures accompanying the recitative; **p**; key of F major; homophonic texture*

Violetta suddenly wakes from her day-dreaming.

Follie! follie! Delirio vano è questo!	*Folly! Folly! This is mad delirium!*
Povera donna sola,	*A poor woman, alone,*
Abbandonata in questo Popoloso deserto	*Lost in this crowded desert*
Che appellano Parigi,	*Which is known as Paris.*
Che spero or più? Che far degg'op! Gloire,	*What can I hope for?*
	What should I do? Die,
Di voluttà ne' vortici perir.	*In the whirl of earthly pleasures!*

ARIA "SEMPRE LIBERA"

26   0:00   *Allegro; meter is duple-compound (fast 6/8); introduction played by full orchestra; f; melody in upper strings and woodwinds; A♭-major; after a short pause, soprano enters with same melody as the orchestral introduction.*

Sempre libera degg'io	*Forever free, I must pass*
Folleggiare di gioia.	*Madly from joy to joy.*
Vo' che scorra il viver mio	*My life's course shall be*
Pei sentieri del piacer.	*Forever in the paths of pleasure.*
Nasca il giorno, o il giorno muoia,	*Whether it be dawn or dusk,*
Sempre lieta ne' ritrovi.	*I must always live gaily*

0:35   *After the orchestra stops, soprano holds high C, then repeats the aria's opening melody; homophonic texture. From the distant garden, we hear the voice of Alfredo professing his love.*

A diletti sempre nuovi	*In the world's gay places*
Dee volare il mio pensier.	*Ever seeking newer joys.*

Last line of text is repeated several times; then aria cadences with a coloratura, cadenza-like sequence that moves up to a high D♭ above high C; aria ends in A♭ Major.

Giacomo Puccini (1858–1924)

Born in Lucca, Italy, into a family of church composers and musicians, Giacomo Puccini (poo-*tchee*-nee) early in life planned a career as a church composer. But at age seventeen, when he saw a production of Verdi's *Aïda*, he became hooked on opera. Changing his plans, Puccini enrolled at the Milan Conservatory to study opera composition.

After his studies, Puccini began composing, finishing his first opera, *Le villi*, when he was twenty-five. The famous music publisher Giulio Ricordi was in the audience at that first production in Teatro alla Scala in Milan. He commissioned Puccini to write more operas, and their association lasted throughout Puccini's life.

Giacomo Puccini became one of the most important Italian opera composers of the late nineteenth and early twentieth centuries. Many of Puccini's operas are tragic love stories set far from Italy: Japan (*Madama Butterfly*), China (*Turandot*), and even California (*The Girl of the Golden West*).

PRINCIPAL WORKS

Operas: *Manon Lescaut* (1893), *La bohème* (The Bohemian Life, 1896), *Tosca* (1900), *Madama Butterfly* (1904), *La fanciulla del west* (The Girl of the Golden West, 1910), *Turandot* (posthumous, 1926)

Scene from La Bohème, Act I, Metropolitan Opera Production, New York

LISTENING ACTIVITY

LA BOHÈME (*THE BOHEMIAN LIFE*, 1896), GIACOMO PUCCINI

Act 1 (excerpt)
Large Form: Romantic Opera, Recitatives and Arias
Performing Medium: Soprano, Tenor, and Orchestra

Compact Disc 3, Track 20
Running Time: 12:40

Few composers have had as great a gift as Puccini for composing operas with soaring, emotional melodies—one glorious aria after another. To the delight of singers, Puccini's arias display the singers' virtuosity without overtaxing their voices.

Based on a novel by H. Murger (1822–1861), *Scènes de la Vie de Bohème* (*Scenes from the Bohemian Life*), Puccini's *La bohème* (*The Bohemian Life*) uses the "realistic" *verismo* style of opera that became popular toward the end of the nineteenth century. Typical of this style, *La bohème* romantically depicts the borderline poverty of struggling Parisian artists and workers.

Although they were not necessarily connected with the country of Bohemia (the Czech Republic today), artists and artisans of the Left Bank were called *bohemians*—a term that was used to classify free-living artists who struggled to survive outside the establishment.

RENT: THE MUSICAL

Jonathan Larson's hit musical Rent *premiered on Broadway in 1996, exactly 100 years after the opening of Puccini's* La bohème. *Updated and set in New York City's East Village instead of Paris's Left Bank,* Rent *borrows heavily from* Bohème, *incorporating a story similar to the opera's libretto. For example, a song in the first act, sung at the Life Cafe, is called "La Vie de Bohème." In the* Rent *version, the heroine Mimi is dying from AIDS rather than tuberculosis. Rodolfo, the writer, becomes Roger, the ex-junkie songwriter, who is also HIV-positive.*

Larson's "candle" scene—the meeting of Roger and Mimi—is also similar to the Puccini opera. Alone in his loft apartment, Roger is composing what he hopes will be his one great song ("One Song Glory"), his last chance to redeem his empty, marginal life. Roger plays a short musical quote from La bohème— *several measures from "Musetta's Waltz." When the electricity goes out in the apartment building, Mimi knocks on Roger's door to ask whether he has a light for her candle ("Will You Light My Candle?"). The two are drawn to each other, but Roger, a recovering addict, resists when he realizes that Mimi is a junkie.*

SETTING Mid-nineteenth-century Paris. The curtain rises on a small, shabby loft apartment—the home of four young bohemian artists: the poet Rodolfo (tenor and leading man), the painter Marcello (baritone), the philosopher Colline (bass), and the musician Schaunard (baritone).

It is Christmas Eve. The apartment is cold because the impoverished artists cannot afford to buy wood for a fire. Rodolfo and Marcello are trying to work, but the cold distracts them, and their poverty depresses them. In disgust, Rodolfo tosses his manuscript into the fireplace for fuel.

The mood abruptly changes when Colline and Schaunard burst into the apartment, bringing money that Schaunard has earned. Their jubilance is interrupted by Benoit, their landlord, who has come to collect their past-due rent. Although they have a little money, they would rather use it to have fun. So the four young artists ply Benoit with wine, and when he is tipsy, they send him away without the rent. Marcello, Colline, and Schaunard want to celebrate at a local cafe, but Rodolfo chooses to stay in the apartment and work. He sends the others off, promising to join them as soon as he completes the article he has been writing.

After the others leave, Rodolfo tries in vain to write his article. There is a knock on the door. In the hall is Mimi—a frail, young seamstress—who explains that her candle blew out. She asks Rodolfo for a light so she can find her way back to her own apartment. The recorded excerpt enacts their first meeting and the blooming of their mutual love.

Noticing that Mimi is weak from climbing the stairs, Rodolfo offers her a chair and some wine. When her key falls to the floor, they both grope for it in the dark. Rodolfo finds it, but secretly slips it into his pocket. As they continue looking for it, their hands touch. Rodolfo is surprised that Mimi's hand is so cold and sings the famous aria, "Che gelida manina!" ("How cold your little hand is!"). Musically, we hear a mix of recitative and aria as Rodolfo and Mimi tell each other about their lives and begin falling in love.

LISTENING GUIDE

La bohème (*The Bohemian Life*, 1896), Giacomo Puccini

ORCHESTRA INTRODUCTION

20   0:00   *flute with trills, woodwinds, and strings; large orchestra; moderate tempo, softly, major tonality (B major); homophonic texture; tempo slows for recitatives*

Rodolfo tries to write, but he becomes impatient and tears up his work.

0:14   **RECITATIVES**

Rodolfo	***Rodolfo***
Non sono in vena	*I'm not inspired.*

0:16   *recitative over held chords; slower and softer; D-major tonality.*

There is a timid knock on the door.

Rodolfo	***Rodolfo***
Chi è là!	*Who's there?*
Mimi's Voice	***Mimi's Voice***
Scusi.	*Excuse me.*
Rodolfo	***Rodolfo***
Una donna!	*A woman!*

He opens the door.

Mimi's Voice	***Mimi's Voice***
Di grazia, mi s'è spento il lume.	*Forgive me. My candle has gone out.*
Rodolfo	***Rodolfo***
Ecco.	*Oh.*
Mimi	***Mimi***
Vorrebbe . . . ?	*Would you . . . ?*
Rodolfo	***Rodolfo***
S'accomodi un momento.	*Won't you stay a moment?*
Mimi	***Mimi***
Non occorre.	*Please don't bother.*
Rodolfo	***Rodolfo***
La prego, entri.	*Please come in.*

0:49   *tempo is faster, agitated with rubato; triple meter; louder*

Mimi enters, gasping for breath, coughing, and staggering.

Rodolfo	***Rodolfo***
Si sente male?	*Are you feeling ill?*
Mimi	***Mimi***
No . . . nulla.	*No . . . it's nothing.*
Rodolfo	***Rodolfo***
Impallidisce!	*But you are turning pale!*
Mimi	***Mimi***
Il respir . . . quelle scale . . .	*My breath . . . those stairs . . .*

Rodolfo helps her to a chair. The candlestick and her room key drop from her hands.

Rodolfo	***Rodolfo***
1:12 Ed ora come faccio?	*And now what can I do?*

Rodolfo brings some water and sprinkles it over her face.

Rodolfo	***Rodolfo***
Così!	*There!*
Che viso d'ammalata!	*How ill she looks!*

She revives.

21   1:29   *moderately slow, steady tempo in duple meter; recitatives over light staccato orchestra;* **pp**

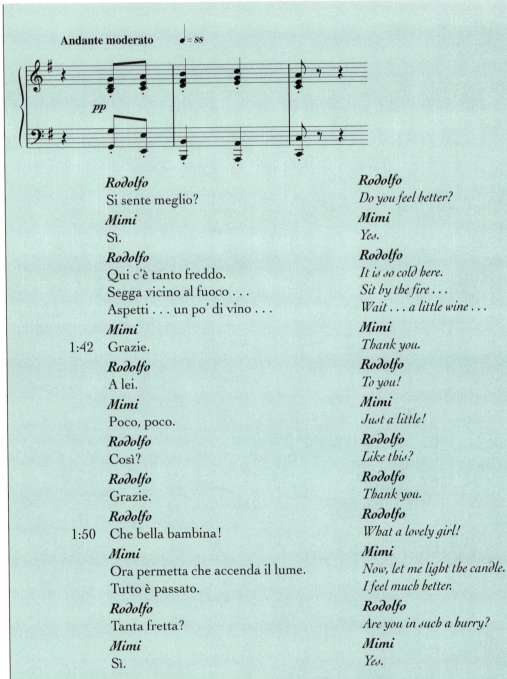

Andante moderato   ♩ = 88

pp

Rodolfo	**Rodolfo**
Si sente meglio?	*Do you feel better?*
Mimi	**Mimi**
Sì.	*Yes.*
Rodolfo	**Rodolfo**
Qui c'è tanto freddo.	*It is so cold here.*
Segga vicino al fuoco . . .	*Sit by the fire . . .*
Aspetti . . . un po' di vino . . .	*Wait . . . a little wine . . .*
Mimi	**Mimi**
1:42 Grazie.	*Thank you.*
Rodolfo	**Rodolfo**
A lei.	*To you!*
Mimi	**Mimi**
Poco, poco.	*Just a little!*
Rodolfo	**Rodolfo**
Così?	*Like this?*
Rodolfo	**Rodolfo**
Grazie.	*Thank you.*
Rodolfo	**Rodolfo**
1:50 Che bella bambina!	*What a lovely girl!*
Mimi	**Mimi**
Ora permetta che accenda il lume.	*Now, let me light the candle.*
Tutto è passato.	*I feel much better.*
Rodolfo	**Rodolfo**
Tanta fretta?	*Are you in such a hurry?*
Mimi	**Mimi**
Sì.	*Yes.*

2:04   *moderately slow, steady tempo in duple meter; staccato figures; pp*

Rodolfo picks up the candle, lights it, and gives it to Mimi. She starts out the door.

Mimi	**Mimi**
Grazie. Buona sera.	*Thank you. Good night.*
Rodolfo	**Rodolfo**
Buona sera.	*Good night.*

Mimi comes back to the doorway.

2:14   *Faster tempo; agitated; louder; key of B♭ major*

Mimi
Ah! Sventata, sventata!
La chiave della stanza
dove l'ho lasciata?

Rodolfo
Non stia sull'uscio;
il lume vacilla al vento

Mimi's candle blows out again

Mimi
Oh Dio! Torni ad accenderlo?

Running to the door, he blows out his candle.

Rodolfo
Oh Dio! Anche il mio s'è spento

Mimi
Ah!
E la chiave sarà . . .

Rodolfo
Buio pesto!

Mimi
Disgraziata!

Rodolfo
Ove sarà?

Mimi
Importuna è la vicina.

Rodolfo
Ma le pare!

Mimi
Importuna è la vicina.

Rodolfo
Cosa dice, ma le pare?

Mimi
Cerchi.

Rodolfo
Cerco.

Mimi
Oh! How careless, careless!
Where did I leave my room key?

Rodolfo
Don't stand in the doorway;
the wind is making the candle flicker.

Mimi
Oh Heavens! Would you light it again?

Rodolfo
Heavens, mine has also gone out!

Mimi
Oh!
And the key is . . .

Rodolfo
Pitch dark!

Mimi
How terrible!

Rodolfo
Where can it be?

Mimi
What trouble I'm causing!

Rodolfo
Not at all!

Mimi
What trouble I'm causing!

Rodolfo
What do you mean?

Mimi
Please look for it.

Rodolfo
I'm looking.

3:08   *short orchestral comment in woodwinds, while Rodolfo searches for the key on the floor*

Mimi
Ove sarà

Mimi
Where can it be?

He finds the key and quickly conceals it in his pocket.

Rodolfo	*Rodolfo*
Ah!	*Ah!*
Mimi	*Mimi*
L'ha trovata?	*Have you found it?*
Rodolfo	*Rodolfo*
No!	*No!*
Mimi	*Mimi*
Mi parve . . .	*I thought . . .*
Rodolfo	*Rodolfo*
In verità	*No really!*
Mimi	*Mimi*
Cerca?	*Are you looking?*
Rodolfo	*Rodolfo*
Cerco!	*I'm looking!*

3:30   *orchestral transition; expressively; gradually slowing and getting softer*

As they grope for the key, their hands touch.

Mimi	*Mimi*
Ah!	*Ah!*

RODOLFO'S ARIA

22   3:50   *slower, steady tempo in duple meter; key change to D♭ major*

Che gelida manina,	*What a frozen little hand!*
Se la lasci riscaldar.	*let me give it back its warmth.*
Cercar che giova?	*What's the use of looking?*
Al buio non si trova.	*We won't find it in the dark.*

4:13   *orchestra answers softly; melody in the harp; rubato tempo*

Ma per fortuna	*But fortunately*
è una notte di luna,	*it's a moonlit night,*
e qui la luna	*and here the moon*
l'abbiamo vicina.	*is very near us.*

Mimi tries to withdraw her hand.

Aspetti, signorina,	*Wait a moment,*
le dirò con due parole	*I'll tell you in a couple of words*
chi son, e che faccio	*so you may know what I do,*
come vivo. Vuole?	*how I live. May I?*

4:50   *moderately slow, steady tempo in triple meter; recitative*

Chi son? Sono un poeta.	*Who am I? I'm a poet.*
Che cosa faccio? Scrivo.	*What do I do? I write.*
E come vivo? Vivo.	*And how do I live? I live!*

5:18 *slow tempo in quadruple with some rubato; expressive*

In povertà, mia lieta	*In my light-hearted poverty*
scialo da gran signore	*I squander, like a great lord,*
rime ed inni d'amore.	*rhymes and love-songs.*
Per sogni e per chimere	*When it comes to dreams and visions*
e per castelli in aria,	*and castles in the air,*
l'anima ho milionaria.	*I've the soul of a millionaire.*
Talor dal mio forziere	*From time to time two thieves*
ruban tutti i gioelli	*steal all my jewels*
due ladri: gli occhi belli.	*out of the safe—two pretty eyes.*
V'entrâr con voi pur ora,	*They came in with you just now*
ed i miei sogni usati	*and all my usual dreams,*
e i bei sogni miei	*my beautiful dreams,*
tosto si dileguâr!	*at once melted into thin air.*
Ma il furto non m'accora,	*But the theft doesn't disturb me,*

6:42 *high strings take over the melody and are joined by the tenor soaring to a high B♭*

poichè, poichè v'ha preso stanza	*because hope has taken*
la speranza!	*their place!*

aria ends, followed by tenor recitative; transition to soprano aria; softly; rubato

Or che mi conoscete,	*Now that you know all about me,*
parlate voi, parlate. Chi siete?	*won't you tell me who you are?*
Via piaccia dir!	*Please won't you say?*
Mimi	**Mimi**
Sì.	*Yes.*

slow tempo; duple meter; soft and calm

MIMI'S ARIA

23 7:40

Mi chiamano Mimi,	*They call me Mimi,*
ma il mio nome è Lucia.	*but my name is Lucia.*
La storia mia	*My story*
è breve: a tela o a seta	*is a brief one: I embroider linen or silk*
ricamo in casa e fuori.	*at home or outside.*
Son tranquilla e lieta,	*I am contented and happy,*
ed è mio svago	*and it gives me pleasure*
far gigli e rose.	*making lilies and roses.*

a little faster; sweetly; quadruple meter; very soft; D major

Mi piaccion quelle cose	*I love those things*
che han si dolce malia,	*which possess such sweet enchantment,*
che parlano d'amor, di primavere;	*and which speak of love and springtime;*
che parlano di sogni e di chimere,	*which speak of dreams and visions,*
quelle cose che han nome poesia.	*all those things that are so poetic.*
Lei m' intende?	*Do you understand?*

| **Rodolfo** | **Rodolfo** |
| Sì. | Yes. |

9:24 *slower; expressively; pp*

Mimi	**Mimi**
Mi chiamano Mimi.	They call me Mimi.
Il perchè non so.	Why, I don't know.

9:39 *moderately fast with rubato; duple meter*

Sola mi fo	All on my own
il pranzo da me stessa.	I get my own supper.
Non vado sempre a messa,	I don't always go to Mass,
ma prego assai il Signor.	but I pray very hard to God.
Vivo sola, soletta,	I live all by myself,
là in una bianca cameretta;	there in a little white room;
guardo sui tetti e in cielo,	which looks out on the rooftops and the sky.

10:09 *slower, very sustained, with grand expression; gradual crescendo to ff; then slower and softer*

ma quando vien lo sgelo,	But when the snow thaws,
il primo sole è mio;	the first sunshine is mine,
il primo bacio dell'aprile è mio!	April's first kiss is mine!
Il primo sole è mio!	The first sunshine is mine!

11:03 *more slowly; pp; aria ends slowing down and with a cadence*

Germoglia	In a vase
in un vaso una rosa;	a rose blossoms:
foglia a foglia	leaf by leaf!
la spio! Così gentil	I watch it there! The perfume
il profumo d'un fior.	of a flower is so sweet.
Ma i fior ch'io faccio, ahimè! . . .	But the flowers which I make, alas,
i fior ch'io faccio, ahimè!	the flowers which I make, alas
non hanno odore!	have no scent!

RECITATIVE

11:53 *dry recitative over held D-major chord in the orchestra*

Mimi	**Mimi**
Altro di me non le saprei narrare:	There is nothing else to tell you:
sono la sua vicina	I am merely your neighbor
che la vein fuori d'ora	who came inopportunely
a importunare.	to bother you.

FRENCH ROMANTIC OPERA

During the first half of the nineteenth century, the aftershocks of the French Revolution, the turbulent Napoleonic Empire, and the rising middle class all contributed to making Paris an important European political and cultural center. Its elaborate opera productions made it the opera capital of the continent.

Composers of all nations flocked to Paris to have their new works performed—Luigi Cherubini (1760–1842), Gasparo Spontini (1774–1851), Gioacchino Rossini, Gaetano Donizetti, Vincenzo Bellini, and Giacomo Meyerbeer (1791–1864).

Cherubini
(keh-roo-*bee*-nee)

Spontini
(spohn-*tee*-nee)

Meyerbeer
(*my*-er-beer)

French Grand Opera

Designed mainly to appeal to the relatively unsophisticated middle class, nineteenth-century French opera became known as *grand opera*. As important as the music was, it was the spectacle that drew audiences. Elaborately costumed crowd scenes, large choruses, plenty of ballet, and lavish sets are the hallmark of French grand opera.

French Comic Opera

Also popular was the less pretentious *opéra comique* (comic opera). With fewer singers and extras and less elaborate staging, *opéra comique* emphasized wit and satire, both in the libretto and in the music.

Jacques Offenbach (1819–1880) was the first to write in the French comic-opera style. His operas *Orpheus in the Underworld* and *Tales of Hoffman* later influenced the operettas of the famous English team of William Gilbert (1836–1911) and Arthur Sullivan (1842–1900)—*The Mikado, H. M. S. Pinafore, Pirates of Penzance*—and those of Johann Strauss, Jr. (1825–1899) in Vienna (*Die Fledermaus* "The Bat," *Zigeunerbaron* "Gypsy Baron"), as well as the Broadway musical of the twentieth century.

Offenbach

Gilbert and Sullivan

Strauss

Jacques (Jacob) Offenbach (1819–1880)

Jacques Offenbach's father, originally named Isaac Judah Eberst, took the family name from the place of his birth, Offenbach-am-Main. In 1802, after years of wandering from town to town in anti-Semitic Germany, Isaac brought his family to Cologne, where Jacob, the seventh of ten children, was born on June 20, 1819.

By profession, Isaac was a cantor—a lead singer and sometimes conductor of a synagogue choir. Isaac also was sufficiently accomplished on the violin so that he could supplement his income by playing in local taverns and giving lessons. Among his most talented students

*Used with permission Jay Zorn and June August.

were his sons Julius and Jacob. Jacob revealed his prodigious musical talent very early in life. He was playing the violin by the age of six, composing by the age of eight, and mastering the cello by the age of nine.

Determined to have his sons study at the Paris Conservatory, Isaac scraped up the money to take them to France. The country was very attractive to oppressed Jews, not only because of France's liberal religious attitudes following the 1789 Revolution, but also because Paris was the cultural center of Europe. Isaac finally arranged an audition with the crotchety, 73-year-old director of the Conservatory, Cherubini, renowned for his reluctance to accept young students. He had even turned away the 12-year-old Liszt for that very reason. Isaac persisted, however, and as the story goes, Cherubini stopped 14-year-old Jacob halfway through his cello audition and told him that he was accepted.

By 1835, Jacob had changed his name to Jacques and had left the Conservatory to begin his performing and composing career by publishing a few symphonic waltzes using synagogue motifs or incorporating the Viennese waltz style. But Offenbach's real interest was theater. He regularly attended performances at the Opéra and the Opéra-Comique, where he was soon hired as a cellist in the orchestra. His virtuosity attracted the attention of English concert manager John Mitchell, who arranged a successful cello tour of England. Jacques fell in love with Mitchell's French stepdaughter, Herminie, whom he married in the summer of 1844.

Offenbach's first significant opportunity as a composer came in 1847 with the successful presentation of his one-act comic opera *L'Alcôve*. As a result, he was promised a commission to write a comic opera for the 1848 season of the Théâtre-Lyrique. Unfortunately, France's July Revolution broke out in July 1848, and Offenbach, not yet a French citizen, took his wife and daughter to the safety of Cologne. After almost two years of revolutionary disturbances had subsided, the Offenbachs returned to Paris. In 1850, Jacques became the conductor of the Comédie-Française, a position he held for six years. This gave him the opportunity to include his own compositions regularly on the program.

Off the Champs Élysées was a 50-seat wooden building called Théâtre Lacaze. Offenbach rounded up some wealthy backers, or "angels," leased and remodeled the building, and changed its name to Théâtre des Bouffes-Parisiens. The theater, a guaranteed outlet for his works, opened its doors to the public in July 1855. There was only one hitch: Offenbach was limited to short one-act operettas for that first season, all playing to full houses.

Although summer audiences were willing to sit on the steeply tiered seats, winter audiences were not. By November, the rickety little building was too drafty for comfort, so Offenbach moved his company to more appropriate winter quarters. In the summer of 1856, they returned to their summer home. Between seasons, Bouffes-Parisiens went on tour. The success of their tours greatly influenced operetta history by encouraging Viennese and London composers and librettists to pursue the short operetta form.

The lifting in 1858 of France's outdated licensing restrictions allowed Offenbach to incorporate a chorus and as many characters as he wanted in his productions. The following year, he presented his first full-scale work, *Orfée aux Enfers*, or in English, *Orpheus in the Underworld*. The two-act operetta created a sensation. By the 228th consecutive performance, the cast was so exhausted that Offenbach reluctantly retired the piece for a few weeks so the performers could rest.

With his fame spreading across Europe, Offenbach's music became as well known throughout the Continent as it was in Paris. In 1869, he wrote the highly successful comic operetta *The Brigands*, which he sent to W. S. Gilbert (of Gilbert and Sullivan). Coincidentally, a resemblance exists between *The Brigands* and Gilbert and Sullivan's *The Pirates of Penzance*.

At his death in 1880, Offenbach was still working on the last act of *The Tales of Hoffman*. Ernest Guirand, who completed the work, was able to maintain Offenbach's distinctive style. Besides his countless songs and orchestral works, Offenbach's legacy includes more than 100 operettas—many satirizing the social mores of the day, life at the royal court, and works of other composers. To this day, he is one of the most-performed composers who ever lived.

PRINCIPAL WORKS

Operas, Comic Operas, Operettas: *Orpheus in the Underworld* (1859), *Brigands* (1869), *Les contes d'Hoffmann* (Tales of Hoffman, 1881, posthumously)

Ballet: *Le papillon* (The Butterfly), *Gaité Parisienne*

Challenge Your Expertise

- Who composed the most operas—Puccini, Rossini, or Verdi?
- What is the difference between *castrato* and *concertato*?

Georges Bizet (1838–1875)

Georges Bizet was born in Paris, the son of professional musicians. His father was a singing teacher and composer; his mother was an excellent pianist. Georges was very young when he displayed his talents at the piano, and when he was nine, his parents enrolled him at the Paris Conservatory. There, at age fourteen, he won first prize in piano.

As part of his composition and orchestration studies at the Conservatory, Bizet wrote his now highly popular Symphony No. 1 in C. At age nineteen, he won the Offenbach Prize for a one-act opera, *Le Docteur miracle* (1857). That same year he won the coveted Grand Prix de Rome.

Now Bizet could study in Rome, but in exchange for tuition, the Grand Prix required the recipient to compose a Mass for the Church. The young Bizet accepted the prize money and fulfilled his obligation by writing his *Te Deum* (1858).

Returning to Paris, Bizet threw himself into opera composition. However, both audiences and critics received his operas coolly. Even his last and best-known opera, *Carmen,* performed thirty-seven times at the comic-opera theater during its first season, had mixed reviews.

At the end of that season, Bizet died. He was only 36 and he had never experienced the acclaim his works would ultimately receive—especially *Carmen,* which has become a staple of the contemporary repertory.

Principal Works

Operas: *Le Docteur miracle* (1857); *Les pêcheurs de perles* (The Pearl Fishers, 1863), *La jolie fille de Perth* (1867), *Djamileh* (1872), *Carmen* (1875)

Orchestral Music: Symphony No. 1 in C (1855), *Vasco da Gama* (1859), a symphonic ode with chorus; Souvenirs de Rome (1869), a symphonic suite; *L'Arlésienne* Suites 1 and 2 (1872)

Choral Music: Cantatas: *David* (1856), *Clovis et Clothilde* (1857), *Te Deum* (1858)

Piano Music: More than 150 piano pieces, including *Jeux d'enfants* (1872) for four hands

---

CARMEN   Georges Bizet's opera *Carmen,* which premiered in Paris in 1875, was a landmark in French opera. Although it was classified as an *opéra comique* because of the spoken dialogue in the original version, *Carmen* was hardly comic. Rather, it is a realistic drama focusing on the passion and infidelity of two doomed lovers in Seville, Spain.

Katherine Prinz, appearing in the role of Carmen, and Salvador Novoa, in the role of Don Jose, in Act IV of Bizet's Carmen

Bizet used melodic arias, brilliant orchestration, colorful dancing, exciting staging, and haunting rhythms to tell the story of a poignant, tragic romance. Despite these qualities, nineteenth-century audiences and critics were not as enthusiastic about the work as they are today. Perhaps it was too realistic for French audiences accustomed to more distant settings and otherworldly stories.

In contrast, *Carmen* draws us into the action until we are empathizing with the central characters: Carmen, the seductive cigar-factory girl, and Don Jose, the dashing bullfighter. What starts out as a playful flirtation quickly turns serious. Don Jose's immediate attraction for Carmen becomes almost an obsession. Tension mounts as he discovers that Carmen has been unfaithful. Don Jose cannot control his jealousy. Carmen continues to taunt him. When he threatens to kill her, we can sense the danger. Then we witness the stark reality as he carries out his threat—not behind a curtain, but right there, in the Seville plaza.

Carmen began a trend of operatic realism (*verismo*) that inspired, among others, *Cavalleria rusticana* (1890) by Pietro Mascagni (1863–1945), *I Pagliacci* (1892) by Ruggiero Leoncavallo (1858–1919), and Puccini's *La bohème* (1896) and *Tosca* (1900).

GERMAN ROMANTIC OPERA

Nowhere in Europe was the bonding between music and literature as strong as in Germany. With Mozart's singspiel *Die Zauberflöte* (The Magic Flute) and Carl Maria von Weber's mystical opera *Der Freischütz* (The

Der Freischütz
(der *fry*-shoots)

Gesamtkunstwerk
(guh-*zamt-koonst*-vehrk)

Freeshooter), German opera composers began using their native German instead of the traditional Italian language.

Imbued with the ideals of romanticism, German composers sought out librettos incorporating magic, mystery, the supernatural, the mystical, distant lands, exotic cultures, love, and heroes (see Chapter 13). Middle-class audiences were ready to embrace the new subjects and reject the typical court intrigues and farces that had been so popular with the mostly aristocratic audiences of the eighteenth century.

Carl Maria von Weber (1786–1826)

Carl Maria von Weber (*vay*-ber) was born in the north of Germany into a family of musicians—Constanze, Mozart's wife, was one of Weber's cousins. Weber's early musical studies were with Michael Haydn (1737–1806), Joseph's brother, in Salzburg. He wrote his first opera at age twelve and two more before he was fifteen.

As a pianist and composer, Weber traveled extensively throughout central Europe, finally settling in Prague as music director for the Prague Opera Company. Weber's most influential opera, *Der Freischütz*, premiered in Berlin. It was a huge success. Audiences were stunned by its special stage effects and mysticism, especially in the Wolf's Glen scene. Weber composed other operas, but none achieved the success of *Der Freischütz*.

Weber never reached his fortieth birthday. He died in London during a production of his opera *Oberon*.

PRINCIPAL WORKS

Operas: *Der Freischütz* (The Freeshooter, 1821), *Euryanthe* (1823); *Oberon* (1826)

Orchestral Music: two piano concertos; two clarinet concertos; one bassoon concerto; Konzertstuck for piano and orchestra (1821); opera overtures: *Der Freischütz, Euryanthe, Oberon*

Choral Music: two Masses; six cantatas

Piano Music: Invitation to the Dance (1819) [modern transcription for orchestra], four sonatas; miscellaneous pieces

Richard Wagner (1813–1883)

Richard Wagner grew up in Leipzig, Germany, his birthplace. Although Wagner (*vahg*-ner) claimed he was mostly self-taught in music, he did attend St. Thomas's School, where a century earlier Bach had been choirmaster. Later, Wagner continued his music studies at Leipzig University.

At age twenty, while employed as rehearsal director of the choir in a small opera house in Leipzig, he had a love affair with Minna, one of the sopranos in the chorus. Two years later they were married.

During the next ten years, Wagner and Minna lived in poverty while he was writing his first operas. Their restless, stormy marriage was plagued with infidelities on both sides. After *Rienzi* (1842) was produced, several other successes followed. Wagner's work caught the attention of the King of Saxony, who hired Wagner to be the Saxon State conductor.

In 1848, Wagner became a political activist and published articles calling for revolution. To avoid arrest, he fled to Switzerland. His marriage to Minna ended, and he became involved with a succession of married women.

When Ludwig II, also known as "Mad King Ludwig," was crowned king of Bavaria, one of his first acts was to summon Wagner to Munich to produce operas. There, Wagner married Franz Liszt's daughter, Cosima, with whom he had been having an extended affair.

Cosima, a shrewd businesswoman, used her wiles to inveigle financial backing out of the "mad" king. The Wagners used the money to build Festspielhaus at Bayreuth, devoted entirely to staging Wagnerian operas. Although artistically successful, the productions were far too costly, and the Bavarian treasury always had to subsidize Wagner heavily.

Exhausted after composing his last opera, *Parsifal,* Wagner went for a rest in Venice. He died there of heart failure at age seventy. Carried by gondola in an elaborate procession down the Grand Canal to the railway station, Wagner's body was transported to Bayreuth for burial.

PRINCIPAL WORKS

Operas: *Rienzi* (1842); *Der fliegende Holländer* (The Flying Dutchman, 1843); *Tannhäuser* (1845); *Lohengrin* (1850), *Tristan und Isolde* (1865), *Die Meistersinger von Nürnberg* (The Mastersingers of Nuremberg, 1868); *Der Ring des Nibelungen* (The Ring of the Nibelung); four operas, 1) *Das Rheingold* (The Rhine Gold, 1869), 2) *Die Walküre* (The Valkyrie, 1870), 3) *Siegfried* (1876), 4) *Götterdämmerung* (Twilight of the Gods, 1876); *Parsifal* (1882)

Orchestral Music: *Siegfried Idyll* (1870)

Songs: *Wesendonk-Lieder* (1858)

Wagner's Music Dramas

Richard Wagner carried Romantic opera to its extreme. His vision was to create a total art work (*Gesamtkunstwerk*), which he called *music drama*. Toward that goal, he exerted complete control: he wrote his own librettos; composed, orchestrated, and conducted the music; designed the sets; and directed the staging.

You might think all that involvement would have satisfied Wagner. Hardly. He persevered until he could design and build his own opera house—Bayreuth—a shrine to himself. Dedicated to performing only his music, exactly the way he envisioned it, the opera house continues that tradition today.

Wagner delighted in composing long works, some lasting as long as five hours. As a way of unifying the music and drama throughout these works and sustaining the interest of his audiences, he used specific melodies and harmonies to represent particular characters or ideas. He called this pervasive theme a *leitmotif* (leading motive). You may recall that Berlioz used this idea (called the *idée fixe*) throughout his *Symphonie fantastique* to represent his beloved Harriet.

LISTENING ACTIVITY

OVERTURE TO *DIE MEISTERSINGER VON NÜRNBERG* (1868),
RICHARD WAGNER

Large Form: Opera Overture
Detailed Form: Sectional
Performing Medium: Large Orchestra

‖ Compact Disc 3, Track 24
‖ Running Time: 8:39

DIE MEISTERSINGER *Die Meistersinger von Nürnberg* (The Mastersingers of Nuremberg) concerns the relationship between the creative artist and his critics, the conflict between tradition and innovation. The opera is set in sixteenth-century Nuremberg, Germany, when the craft guilds (professional unions) were at their zenith. Older members of these guilds represent the Establishment—reluctant to upset the status quo. Membership as mastersinger had elevated them to the middle class.

Wagner opens the opera with a scene in the local church in Nuremberg, where Walther, a young stranger, spies Eva, the goldsmith's beautiful daughter, seated near him. They are instantly attracted to each other.

After the church service, the town begins preparations for its annual singing contest. We soon learn that it is the contest that has brought Walther to town.

Seemingly insurmountable bureaucratic hurdles are thrown into Walther's way to prevent him from competing. Even Hans Sachs, a respected member of the Mastersinger's Guild, cannot successfully intercede in Walther's behalf.

The goldsmith has offered his daughter Eva and her dowry as the prize to the winner of the singing contest. Adding further interest to the plot, Walther does not yet know that Eva is one of the prizes.

On the day of the singing festival, all masters and apprentices of Nuremberg's trade guilds parade onstage. Clad in robes, ribbons, and insignias, they carry their guilds' banners.

Just before the contest, Hans Sachs, favoring Walther, deliberately skews the rules, declaring that audience response will be one of the criteria. Beckmesser, a petty local clerk who also serves as one of the judges, starts the contest with a bungled rendition of Walther's song. When the audience laughs at him, he is furious. Beckmesser's philosophies closely paralleled those of a music critic named Hanslick, who consistently attacked Wagner's music for departing from tradition.

Hans Sachs seizes the opportunity. He tells everyone that the song is really lovely and suggests that the composer should sing it himself. The mastersingers accede to Sach's suggestion. Up steps Walther, the composer, who wins the contest with his "Prize Song," gets his membership in the Mastersinger's Guild, and the hand of Eva in marriage.

Listen to the Overture to Wagner's opera *Die Meistersinger von Nürnberg.* An overture, or a prelude to an opera, has the same purpose as in a musical show: to acquaint the audience with the main melodies and to set the mood for the story.

In this overture, Wagner introduces four of the main recurrent melodies —*leitmotifs:*

LEITMOTIF 1   represents the Mastersingers and all that was dependable and noble in the medieval German burgher.

Leitmotif
(*lyt*-moh-*teef*)

25   LEITMOTIF 2   played first by the flute and then by the oboe, represents Walther's and Eva's love for each other.

espressivo

26   LEITMOTIF 3   introduced by the brass represents the banner and heritage of the Mastersinger's Guild.

27   LEITMOTIF 4   is the Prize Song, a love song in which Walther imagines Eva in Paradise.

The overture climaxes with the full orchestra playing three of the four leitmotifs—the Prize Song, the Banner, and the Mastersingers—simultaneously.

LISTENING GUIDE

OVERTURE TO *DIE MEISTERSINGER VON NÜRNBERG* (1868),
RICHARD WAGNER

24		***Exposition***	
	0:00	LEITMOTIF 1 — Mastersingers	full orchestra, *ff*; moderate march tempo; 4 meter, key of C major
26	0:52	LEITMOTIF 2 — Love of Walther and Eva	played by flute and clarinet, imitated by oboe, then flute, then clarinet; *f* with expression, *p* in the strings
	1:20	TRANSITION	transition section; *crescendo* to *f*; violins, starting high, descending in sequences
26	1:30	LEITMOTIF 3 — Mastersinger's Heritage	played by brass section, marchlike; strings with upward swoops; *f*

	2:08	LEITMOTIF 1— Mastersingers	played by violins, then joined by winds; *ff*; sequences
	3:07	TRANSITION	transition; agitated fragments in violins; dynamic swells, *f crescendo* to *ff* and back to *f*
27	3:28	LEITMOTIF 4— Walther's Prize Song	played by violins, *p* and expressively, change of key to E major

Development Section

	4:39	LEITMOTIF 1— Mastersingers	fragments played first by the oboe; *p*; melody is twice as fast as opening, though basic tempo is the same as the opening
	5:49	LEITMOTIF 1— Mastersingers	played by trombones, *f*, original style as opening

Polyphonic Section

		(Leitmotifs 1, 3, and 4 together)	
	6:05	LEITMOTIF 4— Walther's Prize Song	played by first clarinet, first horn, first violin, and cello; *p*; together
		LEITMOTIF 1— Mastersingers	played by bassoon, bass trombone, and string basses; *p*
		LEITMOTIF 3— Mastersinger's Heritage	twice as fast; played by flutes, oboes, horns, violins and violas; *p*

Recapitulation Section

	8:08	LEITMOTIF 1— Mastersingers	full orchestra, *f*

Wagner and Hitler

Richard Wagner was and still is a highly controversial figure. He was an artistic genius and wrote great music; however, many feel that as a person, Wagner was despicable. To achieve his ends, he lied, cheated, walked out on debts, exploited people, and had affairs with some of his friends' wives.

Born six years after the composer's death, Adolph Hitler embraced Wagner's anti-Semitism. He adored Wagner's music and played it constantly, even during war-strategy meetings. How much was Hitler influenced by Wagner? We will never really know. But there is an ironic similarity between the ending of the Third Reich and the ending of Wagner's opera *Götterdämmerung* (Twilight of the Gods).

During the finale of that opera, the great warrior, Siegfried, is killed. His body is then burned on a funeral pyre. But the flames get out of control, and Walhalla, the home of the dead battle heroes, goes up in flames and collapses in the conflagration. To end the opera, the Rhine River overflows, flooding the land and drowning the flames.

Walhalla
(vahl-*hah*-luh)

Hitler, too, staged his own dramatic finale by deliberately ignoring several opportunities to end World War II, particularly in the last few days when Berlin was surrounded by the Allies. Instead of surrendering, Hitler locked himself in a Berlin bunker, leaving the city and thousands of its residents to die in the firestorm following the bombing and shelling of the city. He himself was consumed in flames in his bunker after committing suicide.

Challenge Your Expertise

What are at least three ways in which Wagner exerted total control?

LISTENING INSIGHTS

Understanding Wagnerian Opera

One of the keys to following and understanding Wagner's operas is to associate the melodies or leitmotif, with the characters or ideas they represent. For instance, when the hero Parsifal silently contemplates his quest for the Holy Grail, the orchestra plays the Holy Grail leitmotif. Although Parsifal is not singing, and the action onstage is static, we know that he is thinking about the quest because we recognize the theme.

Summary of Terms

Bayreuth	Gesamtkunstwerk	lyric opera
comic opera	leitmotif	music drama
French Grand opera	libretto	singspiel

Late-Romantic Music

THE STATE OF MUSIC IN THE LATE-ROMANTIC PERIOD

In the second half of the nineteenth century, Beethoven's vision for musicians became a reality. As professional composers became highly respected and revered, they also attained financial security. No longer did they have to devote the major portion of their energies promoting and staging concerts of their own works. Throughout Europe, public concert societies had assumed that task.

ADVENT OF PHILHARMONIC AND SYMPHONY ORCHESTRA SOCIETIES Throughout the nineteenth century, most major cities in Europe and the United States were beginning to establish philharmonic and symphony orchestra societies.

DEMAND FOR NEW MUSIC As concert audiences expanded throughout the nineteenth century, so did the number of performances. Solo recitals, chamber music, ballet, and opera flourished, creating a constant demand for new music.

HISTORICAL PERSPECTIVE

Evolution of Public Concerts: The Late Romantic Period

Early Orchestral Societies in Europe and North America

Founded in 1781, the Gewandhaus Orchestra of Leipzig was one of the earliest permanent orchestras. It was not until 1835, when Felix Mendelssohn took over as conductor, that it became a full-time professional orchestra. Mendelssohn's Gewandhaus Orchestra inspired other orchestras to attain professional status. A brief list of some of the most important orchestras and their founding dates follows:

1781	Gewandhaus Orchestra, Leipzig	1891	Chicago Symphony Orchestra
1792	Paris Conservatory Orchestra	1882	Berlin Philharmonic Orchestra
1842	New York Philharmonic Orchestra	1883	Concertgebouw Orchestra, Amsterdam
1842	Vienna Philharmonic Orchestra	1895	Cincinnati Symphony Orchestra
1874	Cologne Orchestra, Germany	1895	Pittsburgh Symphony Orchestra
1880	St. Louis Symphony Orchestra	1900	Philadelphia Orchestra
1881	Boston Symphony Orchestra	1906	Toronto Symphony Orchestra

Radical versus the Traditional

Mainstream concert music began to branch into two movements in the mid-nineteenth century. Richard Wagner championed the radical movement; Johannes Brahms, the traditionalist movement. Suddenly, European composers, artists, and audiences took sides. The Schumanns and others sided with Brahms. Liszt and later Richard Strauss were in Wagner's camp.

WAGNERIANS   With formal control now subordinate to emotion, music took new directions. Wagner and his followers embraced a wandering tonality, conveying the feeling of an extended journey. They expanded harmonic movement away from its traditional tonic or home key rooting. Using loose and often vague forms, composers began to rely increasingly on extra-musical associations (stories, ideas, poems) for continuity. They built their symphonic poems, overtures, symphonies, and chamber music around programs or descriptive titles.

BRAHMSIANS   To those composers who aligned with Brahms, formal control still mattered. They adhered to the classical traditions of Haydn, Mozart, Schubert, and especially, Beethoven. Tonality and form, they believed, should remain recognizable, with minimal extramusical associations and overcharged emotionalism.

Continuing the classical tradition, both Schumann and Brahms focused their efforts on chamber music, three-movement concertos, and four-movement symphonies. Of the two, only Robert Schumann attempted to write an opera, though his *Genoveva* is rarely performed today.

Brahms's Orchestral Music

Brahms idolized Beethoven. He was so much in awe of Beethoven's nine symphonies that Brahms labored over his own First Symphony for twenty years, reworking it until he felt he had finally attained the Beethoven standard. He was right. Audiences hailed the first performance of Brahms's First Symphony as "Beethoven's Tenth."

Unlike Beethoven, Brahms was not an innovator. Proudly declaring himself a musical conservative, he avoided extreme changes in musical expression as proposed by the followers of Liszt and Wagner.

Brahms and Beethoven shared many characteristics. Both were born in Germany and composed their major works in Vienna. Both profited from freelance employment and publishing royalties. Both expressed their love of mankind, yet led reclusive lives, devoting their main creative energies to their art and never marrying.

Brahms's desire for personal freedom seems to have superseded his ability to develop close personal relationships. Although he had been in love with Clara Schumann for many years, he moved away from her after Robert Schumann's death. Possibly it was a conflict between his love for her and his devotion to his mentor that drove Brahms from Düsseldorf. Yet he remained close to Clara and loved her seven children throughout his life. Perhaps it was due to their age difference—Clara was fourteen years older than he. In Brahms's own family, though, his mother was seventeen years older than his father.

A mystery in Brahms's life was his deliberate avoidance of obligations that might restrict his freedom. A fine conductor, recognized as the foremost musician of his time, Brahms could have secured any post he wanted. Yet he accepted only minor positions—coaching women's choirs and directing minor orchestras. Throughout his life he remained a freelance musician, earning his living from private teaching, publishing royalties, occasional piano performances, and guest conducting appearances.

Johannes Brahms (1833–1897)

Johannes Brahms grew up in Hamburg, Germany. The family lived near the center of the city, not far from Alster Lake. Brahms's first piano teacher was his father, a bass player in a salon orchestra. As one story goes, Brahms's childhood was impoverished and, while still a teenager, he had to augment the family's income by playing piano in bars and brothels. Recent research, however, seems to contradict this long-accepted legend. Some agreement does exist that his early experiences indelibly marked his personality, making him seem aloof, misogynistic, and somewhat crude.

Nevertheless, Brahms's enormous talent brought him to the attention of prominent musicians, and by age 20, he was engaged in a concert tour with the Hungarian violinist Remenyi, considered one of the best European violinists of his time.

When Brahms decided to devote himself to composing serious music, he went to Düsseldorf to study with the highly respected Robert Schumann. Soon after their first meeting, Brahms was invited to remain in the Schumann home as a boarder. In an article in his influential publication *Neue Zeitschrift für Musik* (The New Magazine for Music), Robert described Brahms as the "new genius of music." But before long, Robert, who had grown progressively addled, entered an asylum for two years. During this period and after Schumann's death, a close and, some say, intimate relationship developed between Brahms and Clara Schumann.

Brahms eventually moved to Vienna where he maintained a permanent residence until his death at age 64. There, Brahms was employed as the director of a women's choir. He also performed regularly as a pianist and appeared as guest conductor of various orchestras throughout Europe. Although he was eventually celebrated as a leading composer, much of Brahms's life and work is surrounded by uncertainties and ambiguities because he deliberately covered his tracks. Not only did Brahms destroy what he considered to be his inferior compositions and early traces of his published works, but also many of his letters and other personal documents.

PRINCIPAL WORKS

Orchestral Music: four symphonies: No. 1 in c minor (1855–76), No. 2 in D Major (1877), No. 3 in F Major (1883), No. 4 in e minor (1885); two piano concertos: No. 1 in d minor (1858), No. 2 in B-flat Major (1881); other works: Violin Concerto (1878); *Academic Festival Overture* (1880); *Tragic Overture* (1881)

Chamber Music: two string sextets, two string quintets, three string quartets, Piano Quintet in f minor, three piano quartets, three piano trios; Clarinet Quintet; violin sonatas

Piano Music: sonatas, rhapsodies, intermezzos, ballades, capriccios, variations, *Liebeslieder Walzer, Hungarian Dances*

Choral Music: *A German Requiem* (1868), *Alto Rhapsody* (1869), and more than 180 songs

LISTENING ACTIVITY

ACADEMIC FESTIVAL OVERTURE, OP. 80, JOHANNES BRAHMS

Large Form: Concert Overture
Detailed Form: Sectional, Medley of Songs
Performing Medium: Large Symphony Orchestra

Compact Disc 2, Track 27
Cassette Tape: Side C, Example 7
Running Time: 10:22

The background of the *Academic Festival Overture* gives us a glimpse of Brahms's great prestige in the late nineteenth century. In 1880, the University of Breslau honored him with a Doctor of Philosophy degree for being "Germany's leading composer."

In appreciation, Brahms composed the *Academic Festival Overture*. Its form is that of a *concert overture*—an overture not associated with either a ballet or an opera. Nineteenth-century concert overtures are usually highly descriptive works.

Brahms described his overture as a "very boisterous *potpourri* of student songs." Most of them were actually drinking songs. The piece ends with the well-known "Gaudeamus igitur," a noble, anthem-like tune played by the full orchestra.

Hail to youth and hail to love! Hail to life so won-der-ful!

LISTENING GUIDE

ACADEMIC FESTIVAL OVERTURE, OP. 80, JOHANNES BRAHMS

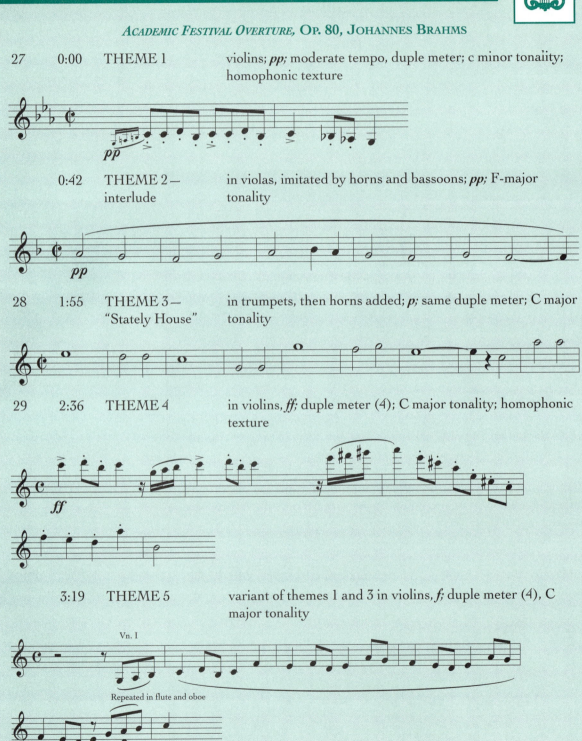

27   0:00   THEME 1   violins; *pp;* moderate tempo, duple meter; c minor tonaiity; homophonic texture

0:42   THEME 2 — interlude   in violas, imitated by horns and bassoons; *pp;* F-major tonality

28   1:55   THEME 3 — "Stately House"   in trumpets, then horns added; *p;* same duple meter; C major tonality

29   2:36   THEME 4   in violins, *ff;* duple meter (4); C major tonality; homophonic texture

3:19   THEME 5   variant of themes 1 and 3 in violins, *f;* duple meter (4), C major tonality

Vn. I

Repeated in flute and oboe

3:46   THEME 6 —   in first and second violins, *f*, same meter and tempo, E-major
          "The Fatherland"   tonality with shifts to G-major tonality

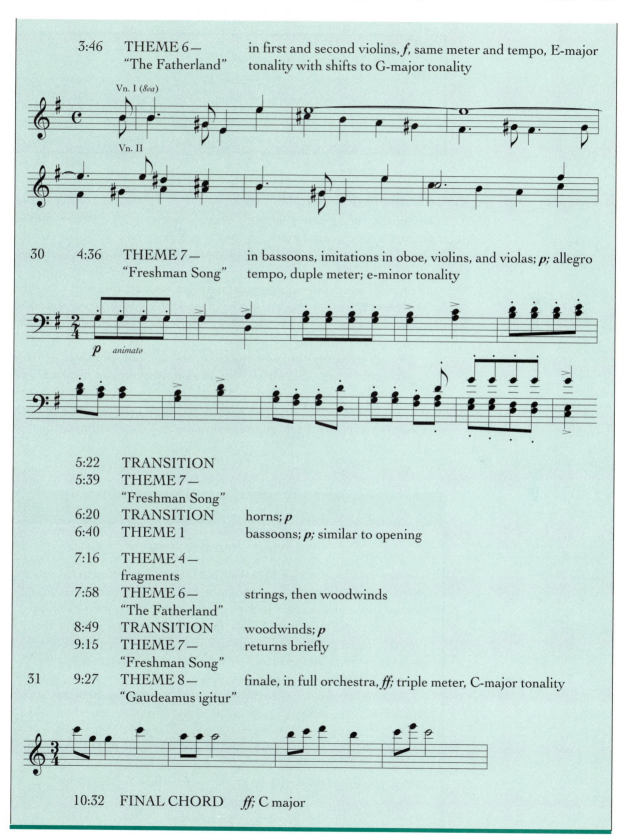

30   4:36   THEME 7 —   in bassoons, imitations in oboe, violins, and violas; *p*; allegro
                    "Freshman Song"   tempo, duple meter; e-minor tonality

5:22   TRANSITION
5:39   THEME 7 —
          "Freshman Song"
6:20   TRANSITION   horns; *p*
6:40   THEME 1   bassoons; *p*; similar to opening

7:16   THEME 4 —
          fragments
7:58   THEME 6 —   strings, then woodwinds
          "The Fatherland"
8:49   TRANSITION   woodwinds; *p*
9:15   THEME 7 —   returns briefly
          "Freshman Song"
31   9:27   THEME 8 —   finale, in full orchestra, *ff*; triple meter, C-major tonality
                    "Gaudeamus igitur"

10:32   FINAL CHORD   *ff*; C major

Challenge Your Expertise

- Can you name two symphonies that do not have four movements?
- How are Felix Mendelssohn's travels reflected in his works?

Romantic-Period Chamber Music

Increasingly during the nineteenth century, wealthy art patrons opened their homes for chamber music performances. Artists, writers, and friends gathered to hear the latest compositions of Mendelssohn, Schumann, Brahms, and others.

During the eighteenth century, string trios and quartets were the favorite chamber music groups. By the nineteenth century, string and wind chamber ensembles often added a piano. Works for these groups are *piano trios, piano quartets,* and *piano quintets.*

Though concertgoers know the Romantic composers mainly by their large orchestral works, Schubert, Mendelssohn, Schumann, Brahms, and others actually wrote more chamber music than orchestral pieces. Schumann and Brahms, for instance, each wrote four symphonies, yet each composed exactly twenty-three works for chamber music ensembles.

LISTENING INSIGHTS

Enjoying Chamber Music

The key to enjoying chamber music is to become involved in the intimacy of the performance. During a chamber music performance — usually in a small concert hall and close to the audience — chamber musicians communicate closely with one another. You'll notice that they sit close together, often in a semicircle facing the audience. As a member of the audience seated close to the stage, you can see as well as hear each player's performance.

Chamber music is usually woven like a conversation among friends. Players subtly pass musical ideas to one another and add gentle support when a background role is required. Since there is only one player on each part of music, all are equally important.

Because recordings cannot convey the intimacy of chamber music, you fully experience involvement only by attending a live performance.

Gustav Mahler (1860–1911)

When Bohemia was part of the Austro-Hungarian Empire, Gustav Mahler (*mah*-ler) was born into a family living next to a military barracks. As a boy, Mahler was fascinated by two kinds of music. One was military music, with its strong emphasis on brass. The other was folk music that he heard in his village and in the surrounding towns. He later incorporated both types into his symphonies.

At age 15, Mahler's parents sent him to Vienna to study at the Conservatory. After three years, he was awarded a diploma in composition. Mahler's career as a conductor now began. He gradually secured increasingly important conducting positions as he moved from Prague to Leipzig to Budapest to Hamburg and then to the Vienna State Opera. His last two conducting positions were in the United States with the Metropolitan Opera Company (1908) and the New York Philharmonic (1909–11). Ironically, although he spent most of his life conducting operas, Mahler never wrote one.

Mahler's demanding perfectionism earned him a reputation as a tyrant. Other problems plagued him too. Fighting against the tide of anti-Semitism developing in Austria, in 1897, at age 37, Mahler had to resort to trickery to secure his appointment at the Vienna State Opera. Because the management would not give the post to a Jew, Mahler promptly though reluctantly converted to Christianity. Unfortunately, once he was appointed, the anti-Semitic Viennese critics continued to hound him.

In 1902, he married Alma Schindler, a famous Viennese beauty. The death of their young daughter strongly affected Mahler.

Falling ill during his second season as conductor of the New York Philharmonic, Mahler returned to Vienna seeking medical help. He died there at age 50.

PRINCIPAL WORKS

Orchestral Music: 10 symphonies: No. 1 (*The Titan,* 1888); No. 2, with soprano (*Resurrection,* 1894); No. 4, with soprano (1900); No. 8, with soloists and choruses (*Symphony of a Thousand,* 1909)

Songs (with orchestra): Song cycles: *Lieder eines fahrenden Gesellen* (Songs of a Wayfarer, 1885); *Kindertotenlieder* (Songs on the Death of Children, 1904); *Des Knaben Wunderhorn* (Youth's Magic Horn, 1893–98); *Das Lied von der Erde* (The Song of the Earth, 1909)

Choral Music: *Das klagende Lied* (The Song of Sorrow, 1880)

LISTENING ACTIVITY

SONGS OF A WAYFARER (1885)
"GING HEUT MORGEN ÜBER FELD"
("I WALKED THIS MORNING OVER THE FIELDS"),
GUSTAV MAHLER

Large Form: Song Cycle
Detailed Form: Modified Song Form
**Performing Medium: Baritone and Large Symphony
Orchestra**

Compact Disc 2 Track 32
Cassette Tape: Side D, Example 1
Running Time: 4:37

Mahler's songs are quite different from the art songs (*leider*) of Schubert and Schumann that you heard earlier. Those composers and others wrote piano accompaniment for a singer performing in an intimate setting—a small hall or a private home. The music more or less "whispered" their innermost romantic feelings. On the other hand, Mahler "proclaimed" his feelings, bearing his soul for large audiences. For his songs, a full symphony orchestra accompanied a singer on a stage in a large concert hall.

Mahler's emotionalism exemplifies the wonderful excesses of the Romantic period: "You never know what is enough until you know what is too much." Mahler's detractors see his self-indulgent displays of emotionalism as excessive. Others consider them glorious expressions of true feeling.

Keep Mahler's wide range of emotionalism in mind when you listen to the second song in his *Songs of a Wayfarer* cycle, "Ging Heut morgen übers Feld" ("I Walked This Morning Over the Fields"). Mahler's highly personal lyrics are mostly autobiographical, written between 1883 and 1885, after singer-actress Johanna Richter spurned his love. The first of the four songs of the cycle, "Wenn mein Schatz Hochzeit macht" ("When My Love Has Her Wedding Day"), conveys Mahler's sadness over his rejection.

However, by the second song, "Ging Heut' morgen übers Feld," Mahler seems to have recovered as a new day dawns. On this beautiful day, the wanderer (Mahler) walks through sunlit fields, with birds chirping greetings to him as he rediscovers the wonder of nature. His exuberance is short lived as he plunges into sadness, asking, "When will my luck begin?" ("Wenn sind mein glück voll an?"). He answers himself, "No! No! I don't think it ever will" ("Nein, nein, das ich mein . . .").

Born a Jew in Bohemia, Mahler worked for most of his career in staunchly anti-Semitic Austria and Germany. Therefore, he considered himself an outsider and often commented that he thought of himself as a "wanderer," at home nowhere. His perfectionism and fiery temperament did not help his cause. Perhaps this inner turmoil contributed to his decision to move to the United States to conduct the Metropolitan Opera Orchestra and the New York Philharmonic.

LISTENING GUIDE

SONGS OF A WAYFARER (1885)
"GING HEUT MORGEN ÜBER FELD"
("I WALKED THIS MORNING OVER THE FIELDS"),
GUSTAV MAHLER

31   0:00   WALKING THEME   *flutes and piccolo staccato; duple meter;* **p***; D major; baritone soloist enters with "Walking Theme"; homophonic texture*

Ging heut' morgen übers Feld, | I walked this morning over the fields;
Tau noch auf den Gräsern hing; | Dew still hung on the grass;
Sprach zu mir der lust'ge Fink: | The merry finch spoke to me:
Ei du! Gelt? | Hey, you! Is that right?

0:19   WALKING THEME—SECOND PART   *mostly strings accompany singer;* **pp**

Guten Morgan! Ei gelt? | Good morning! Isn't it?
Du! Wird's nicht eine schöne Welt? | You there! Isn't it a lovely world?

0:33	*full orchestra, **ff**, then, **pp***	
	Zink! Zink! Schön und flink!	Sing! Sing! Pretty and quick!
	Wie mir doch die Welt gefällt"	How I love the world!"
0:45	*Short orchestral transition, loud diminishing to soft, "walking theme" returns*	

WALKING THEME—FIRST PART

	Auch die Gockenblum' am Feld	Also the bluebell in the meadow
	Hat mir lustig, guter Ding'	—cheerful, kind creature—
	Mit den Glöckchen, klinge, kling.	With its bells went ring-ring.
	Klinge, kling.	Ring, ring.

1:08	WALKING THEME—SECOND PART	
	Ihren Morgengruss geschellt:	And rang a morning greeting for me:
	Wird's nicht eine schöne Welt?	Isn't it a lovely world?
	Kling, kling! Kling, kling!	Ring-ring! Ring-ring!
	Schönes Ding!	Pretty thing!
	Wie mir doch die Welt gefällt!	How I love the world!
	Heia!"	Hey-ho!"
1:36	*orchestral interlude with soaring flutes and violins, modulating to key of B major;* **pp**	

1:55	WALKING THEME—FIRST PART	
	Und da fing im Sonnenschein	Then in the sunshine
	Gleich die Welt zu funkeln an:	The world suddenly began to glitter;

2:13	WALKING THEME—SECOND PART	
	Alles, alles Ton und Farbe gewann	All things took on sound and color
	Im Sonnenschein!	in the sunshine.
	Blum' und Vogel, gross and klein!	Flowers and birds, both large and small!
	Guten Tag, guten Tag!	"Good day, good day!
	Ist's nicht eine schöne Welt?"	Isn't it a lovely world?
	Ei, du, gelt? Ei, du, gelt?	Hey you, Is that right?
	Schöne Welt?	Lovely world?

2:56	WALKING THEME—FIRST PART	*tempo slows, orchestra very soft, tonality modulates to F-sharp major*
	Nun fängt auch mein Glück wohl an?	When will my luck begin?
	Nun fängt auch mein Glück wohl an?	When will my luck begin?
	Nein, nein, das, ich mein,"	No, no, I don't think
	Mir nimmer blühen kann!	it ever will!
4:15	*orchestra ends the song, fading softer and softer toward an F-sharp major chord*	

The Virtuoso Orchestra

Economics had a favorable influence on music, just as it did on other professions. After Mendelssohn elevated the performance standards and professional prestige of his Gewandhaus Orchestra, higher-paying positions attracted players. Two outstanding composer/conductors continued the Mendelssohn tradition: Gustav Mahler and Richard Strauss.

Knowing that jobs usually went to the best players, musicians strove to improve their abilities. Beginning in the late nineteenth century, each player in the major symphony orchestras was a virtuoso, capable of performing as a soloist.

Mahler's Symphonies

Although Mahler's symphonies abound with extra-musical references, including poetry and philosophy, he considered them evolutions of the classical tradition. Awash with intermingled extramusical ideas, his long symphonies contain some of the most highly charged, emotional music of the Romantic period. The music reflects the composer's own emotional swings, for which he sought therapy from Vienna's leading psychiatrist, Sigmund Freud (1856–1939).

Freud
(froid)

Mahler established two records in music: one in length and one in number of players. His Third Symphony lasts 1 hour and 35 minutes, longer than any other. His Eighth Symphony, "Symphony of a Thousand," the largest work ever written for a symphony orchestra, used more than 1,000 performers at its premiere: an orchestra of 171, 8 vocal soloists, a children's choir of 350, and two choruses of 250 each.

Longest Symphony

Largest Symphony

Early in the twentieth century, his music was somewhat neglected. While Mahler was composing his last works—from 1900 to 1911—modern musical trends had begun. Yet he was rooted in the past and did not follow the changing times. Many listeners began to regard Romantic music as outmoded and overly sentimental in contrast to the cerebral, more concise twentieth-century music.

After Mahler's death, his music was still considered old-fashioned. In the 1930s and 1940s, Hitler banned Mahler's music throughout Germany and Austria, along with the music of other Jewish composers.

Then, in the 1950s, as many listeners began moving away from the harsh dissonances of modern music, seeking more consonant and emotional music, they rediscovered Mahler. Since the 1960s, his music has been enjoying a popularity greater than any he knew in his lifetime.

Challenge Your Expertise

- Which opera is associated with "tobacco and bulls"?
- Which opera contains elephants and pyramids?

Symphony No. 1 (The Titan), Gustav Mahler
First Movement

Large Form: Symphony
Detailed Form: Sectional

❙❙ Compact Disc 4, Track 1
Running Time: 12:27

Mahler composed his First Symphony over a period of several years, mostly during summer breaks from his various conducting duties. After hearing Richard Strauss's tone poems, Mahler decided to write a symphonic poem as his first symphony, which he titled *The Titan*. His original plan was to produce a five-movement symphony with a program about nature—patterned after Beethoven's *Pastoral* Symphony. After reworking the music a number of times, he finally decided on four movements without a program.

Because Mahler had built his first movement on ideas of youth, flowers, early dawn, the forest, and endless spring. The Introduction may remind you of Beethoven's *Pastoral* Symphony, with its bird calls and the sounds of the forest and nature. This is no coincidence. Mahler even retraced Beethoven's steps through the Vienna Woods, trying to recapture the feeling and sounds that had inspired the *Pastoral*.

After the slow introduction, the first movement proceeds at a faster tempo into "Days of Youth." For its main theme, Mahler reuses a theme from his song cycle, *Songs of a Wayfarer*.

Note on Following the Listening Guide: Melodies and their fragments enter and leave and are commented upon by various instruments of the orchestra. Mahler uses a highly flexible and complex form, mainly relying on melodic ideas for continuity. So varied is the form that a listening guide noting every sound event would distract you from following the mood and the broad sweep of the music. Therefore, only major events are included here.

LISTENING GUIDE

SYMPHONY NO. 1 (THE TITAN), GUSTAV MAHLER
FIRST MOVEMENT

INTRODUCTION—marked: *Langsam, schleppend wie ein Naturlaut* (slowly and drawn out like a sound of nature)

1	0:00	FOREST SOUNDS	the pitch "A" high strings (harmonics); ***ppp;*** slow tempo, duple (4) meter
	0:31	FANFARE	in clarinets, ***pp***
	1:07	FANFARE	played by distant (off-stage) trumpets, ***ppp***
2	1:33	FOREST MELODY	played by horns; ***pp***

	1:48	FANFARE	played by trumpets, slightly faster tempo
	1:58	FOREST MELODY	in horns, ***pp***
	2:13	FANFARE	in trumpets
	2:20	TRANSITION SECTION	played by cellos and basses; ***p;*** faster tempo, horns and woodwinds in background
	2:58	BIRD CALL—cuckoo	played by clarinet, ***p***

MAIN SECTION

| 3 | 3:02 | TRANSITION | played by cellos; ***pp;*** imitated by bassoon, then solo trumpet; BIRD CALL in clarinets; then violins enter, completing |
| | | WALKING THEME— Days of Youth | the melody; extensions of the melody in violins and wood-winds; rubato tempo; D-major tonality |

| | 4:36 | WALKING THEME —Days of Youth | started again by horns, ***ff,*** continued by strings and woodwinds |

	5:00	FOREST SOUNDS	slower; introduction music returns—forest sounds; BIRD CALLS played by woodwinds
	7:32	HUNTING HORNS	played by horns; ***ppp***
	7:49	WALKING THEME— fragments	played by cellos; faster
4	9:09	WALKING THEME— Days of Youth	returns Long developmental section, using new themes and hints of all themes already played; changing tempos and styles cymbals crash, full orchestra, fanfares, *ff*
		FINALE SECTION	
5	10:41	HORN CALL	containing the interval of a fourth, similar to other melodies and earlier Forest Melody; *ff*
6	11:21	WALKING THEME— Days of Youth	returns in trumpet, *ff*; imitations by other instruments, tempo accelerates; pause; fast, agitated woodwinds; *ff*; pause; full orchestra cadence to final chord, *ff*

Challenge Your Expertise

- What sort of records did Mahler break?

Richard Strauss (1864–1949)

Richard Strauss (*shtrowss*—no relation to the waltz composers) was born in Munich, the son of the principal horn player in the Court Orchestra. (Notice how often Strauss favors the horn in his orchestral works; he also wrote two great concertos for that instrument.) Music was a large part of his family life, and Strauss began composing at age six. Soon he was studying composition and orchestration with members of his father's orchestra.

Strauss's earlier compositions were in the conservative tradition of Schumann and Brahms. After taking a series of conducting posts, he veered toward the more radical Wagner and Liszt camp.

In 1898, Strauss was appointed conductor of the Royal Court Opera in Berlin and soon after, devoted most of his remaining years to composing operas. In 1919, he was made director of the Vienna State

Opera, a post formerly held by his longtime friend Gustav Mahler. During World War II, Strauss chose to remain in Nazi Germany, spending most of the war in retirement in Bavaria. At 85, he died in the Bavarian town of Garmisch.

PRINCIPAL WORKS

Orchestral Music: Symphonic poems: *Aus Italien* (1886), *Don Juan* (1889), *Death and Transfiguration* (1889), *Till Eulenspiegels lustige Streiche* (Till Eulenspiegel's Merry Pranks, 1895), *Also sprach Zarathustra* (Thus Spake Zarathustra, 1896), *Don Quixote* (1897), *Ein Heldenleben* (A Hero's Life, 1898), *Symphonie Domestica* (1903); Horn Concertos: No. 1 in E-flat (1883), No. 2 in E-flat (1942); Oboe Concerto (1945)

Operas: *Salome* (1905), *Elektra* (1909), *Der Rosenkavalier* (The Cavalier of the Rose, 1911), *Ariadne auf Naxos* (1912), *Die Frau ohne Schatten* (The Woman without a Shadow, 1919), *Arabella* (1933)

Songs: *Four Last Songs* (with orchestra, 1948), about 200 with piano

Challenge Your Expertise

What incentives encouraged musicians to improve their skills?

Late-Romantic Period Program Music

Searching for new ways of expression, Romantic composers began to depict an entire "program," or story, through music. These stories are not the same as the "program" notes that provide background information about a composition, although the story or text may appear in the printed concert program.

Program

Music "programed" to follow a story or nonmusical ideas is not new. Songs, oratorios, cantatas, and operas usually translate textual ideas into musical ones. Handel's oratorios, such as *Messiah,* abound with such treatments. Other composers have written highly descriptive instrumental music. Based on a set of sonnets, Vivaldi created a musical description of each of *The Four Seasons:* bird calls in the *Spring,* thunderstorms in the *Summer,* harvesting in the *Fall,* shivering and ice in *Winter.*

In his *Pastoral* Symphony of 1808, Beethoven suggests the idea of program music by specifically titling each of the five movements. However, he cautioned that the titles suggest only "expression of feelings" (see Chapter 12). Later nineteenth-century composers carried these ideas further. Mendelssohn's *Hebrides* (*Fingal's Cave*) *Overture* describes his journey to the seascape and caves surrounding the islands off the western coast of Scotland.

Berlioz provides the listener with a blow-by-blow account of what is happening in his *Symphonie fantastique.* He specifically intended his story to be included in the printed concert program for the audience to follow. Franz Liszt used programs for several of his works. His *Dante* Symphony and *Faust* Symphony have particularly detailed programs.

Many pieces suggest that the composer did follow a detailed program, even though no story was written out. Several of Tchaikovsky's concert overtures and symphonic fantasies obviously follow a detailed story: *1812 Overture, Francesca da Rimini,* and *Romeo and Juliet.*

LISTENING INSIGHTS

Enjoying Programmatic and Highly Descriptive Music

You don't have to know its background in order to enjoy music. A fine orchestral work can stand on its own without associations to literature or any other art. Most music has no direct reference to a specific, extra-musical source.

When we encounter a work that openly calls attention to its source, we should look into that source—beyond the music alone—for greater understanding and enjoyment. A piece becomes more interesting after you have read the nonmusical ideas that inspired the composer.

If the story of a programmatic or descriptive work does not appear in your printed program or on the insert with a recording, a little detective work will pay off. Composers' biographies, histories of music, books, and magazine articles on specific composers or works can yield further insights into a composition. Often, the search for meanings and the concomitant pleasure provide some of the joys of music.

Tone Poems (Symphonic Poems)

Of all the programmatic music composers, Richard Strauss was the most successful in wedding a program with music. Calling his programmatic works *tone poems,* or *symphonic poems,* Strauss asks the listener to follow his orchestral accounts of detailed poems and stories.

In *Don Juan,* for instance, Strauss describes the infamous rake—the same character who inspired Mozart's *Don Giovanni.* Strauss's symphonic poem depicts Don Juan's searchings, seductions, flights from relationships, and emotional moods, ending in bitterness and despair.

Challenge Your Expertise

Who wrote the words for a tone poem?

Summary of Terms

chamber music	programmatic music	tone poem
descriptive music	symphonic poem	virtuoso orchestra
philharmonic societies	symphony orchestra	
program music	societies	
program notes		

Chapter 17

Nationalism

POLITICAL INFLUENCES

A spark of nationalism ignited Europe, Scandinavia, and Russia throughout the nineteenth century. Wars that followed, including the devastating World Wars I and II of the twentieth century, periodically rekindled the flames until the creation of the Common Market in 1957 (later becoming the European Economic Community).

As countries finally realized the value of pooling their resources, European nationalism subsided. Today, Eastern European countries, formerly cut off by political and economic differences, are rejoining the family of nations.

Historians are divided over the precise onset of nationalism, but it seems to have coincided with the American and French Revolutions toward the end of the eighteenth century. Weary of oppression, citizens began overthrowing monarchies and taking control of their own countries.

For centuries, without regard for the interests of citizens, rulers had been arranging marriages and royal successions in conquered lands intended to maintain family holdings. In fact, royalty often held their subjects in disdain. And since French or German was the language of the courts, most rulers in Russia, the Baltic states, Scandinavia, and the Slavic nations could not communicate with the people.

THE FORMATION OF NEW REPUBLICS   In response to the public outcry for a greater voice in their governments, clusters of independent cities and states consolidated into new republics:

- 1830   The Netherlands (Holland) and Belgium split off from the Grand Duchy of Luxembourg.
- 1861   The Italian Parliament created a unified kingdom from former city-states.
- 1871   Germany was unified into an empire.
- 1872   Portugal became a republic.
- 1917   The Russian people overthrew the Czar and began to establish the Soviet Union.

INDUSTRIAL AND TECHNOLOGICAL INFLUENCES   Contributing further to the growing nationalistic phenomenon was the industrialization of Europe. Farmers who flocked to the cities in search of a better life came into contact with people from all parts of their homeland. By discovering their shared values, these countrymen developed a sense of national pride and dared to become more politically active.

TRAVEL INFLUENCES   New, relatively inexpensive means of transportation encouraged *wanderlust.* More people could travel and become acquainted with other cultures. As early as 1828, tourists boarded France's new passenger trains. By accommodating more people with greater efficiency and in relative comfort, railways soon replaced stagecoach lines as the primary means of mass transportation. The steamship replaced the sailing ship, reducing Transatlantic crossings from three difficult, uncertain weeks to a safer, nine-and-a-half-day passage.

Wanderlust

Artists also explored the world, incorporating their discoveries into their works, such as Robert Browning's poem *Home Thoughts from Abroad,* Joseph Conrad's novel *Lord Jim,* Paul Gaugin's exotic paintings of Tahiti, and Felix Mendelssohn's *Scottish* Symphony and *Italian* Symphony.

NATIONALISM IN MUSIC

Since the time of Vivaldi and Bach, French, German, and Italian music and musicians had dominated almost every court, opera house, and concert hall from Moscow to Madrid. But as nationalism gained momentum, composers in Russia, Scandinavia, Spain, and other countries began examining their own cultures. Many realized that they could incorporate it into compositions indigenous to their countries. Thus, nationalistic music became the new fashion.

RUSSIAN NATIONALISM

The scene   St. Petersburg, Russia, on the Baltic Sea

The time   Latter half of the nineteenth century

The situation   Five Russian composers band together to create Russian nationalistic music.

Their training   Free from most of the Western European influences in music.

Their goal   To promote purely Russian music

Their approach   Incorporating situations from history, folklore, legends, and native instruments and music

Modest Mussorgsky (1839–1881)

A militant nationalist, Modest Mussorgsky was born in Pskof, Russia, into an aristocratic family. He studied at the Preobrazhensky Guard school in St. Petersburg and later spent three years on active duty with the Guard.

Although he was a fine pianist and had dabbled in composition, Mussorgsky had not considered music seriously until his later years. He resigned his commission in the Guard to earn his living as a clerk in the civil service—composing on the side.

His great difficulties with money and health were mainly due to his excessive drinking. Although his little formal musical training was primarily from Balakirev, he was one of the most original and influential Russian composers of his day. Searching for a new Russian musical language, Mussorgsky became fascinated with the Russian spoken language, incorporating its unique inflections into his songs and operas.

In spite of his older appearance in the 1881 portrait at left, Mussorgsky was only 42 years old when he died.

PRINCIPAL WORKS

Operas: *Boris Godunov* (1869), *Khovanshchina* (completed by Rimsky-Korsakov, 1886)

Songs: *The Nursery* (1870), *Sunless* (1874), *Songs and Dances of Death* (1877); more than fifty other songs

Orchestral Music: *A Night on Bald Mountain* (tone poem) (1867)

Piano Music: *Pictures at an Exhibition* (later orchestrated by Ravel); numerous songs and piano pieces

"The Mighty Five"

- Nikolai Rimsky-Korsakov (*rim*-skee *kor*-sa-kof, 1844–1908)
- Modest Mussorgsky (moo-*zorg*-skee, 1839–1881)
- Alexander Borodin (*bor*-uh-deen, 1833–1887)
- César Cui (*say*-zar *kwee*, 1835–1918)
- Mily Balakirev (*mee*-lee bah-*lah*-kih-ref, 1837–1910)

Peter Ilyich Tchaikovsky (1840–1893)

A favorite composer of audiences around the world, Peter Ilyich Tchaikovsky was born in Votinsk, Russia. After studying law in St. Petersburg, he grudgingly worked as a clerk in the Ministry of Justice.

Returning to school at age twenty-three at the newly founded St. Petersburg Conservatory of Music, Tchaikovsky studied composition with Anton Rubinstein (1829–1894). Three years later, he was hired to teach music at the new Moscow Conservatory, where he remained until his retirement at age thirty-seven. He was then able to devote himself full time to composing and conducting music.

As guest conductor with various orchestras, he toured Russia, London, and Europe extensively. In 1891, the New York Philharmonic invited Tchaikovsky to the United States as guest conductor for the opening of Carnegie Hall.

Hounded by bigots and disgraced in court because of his homosexuality, Tchaikovsky fell into a severe depression. The cause of death was listed as cholera, but there is little doubt that he committed suicide at age 53.

PRINCIPAL WORKS

Operas: *Eugene Onegin* (1865), *Mazeppa* (1884), *The Queen of Spades* (1880)

Orchestral Music: 6 symphonies: No. 2 (*Little Russian*, 1872), No. 3 (*Polish*, 1875), No. 4 (1878), No. 5 (1888), No. 6 (*Pathétique* 1893); Concertos: Violin Concerto (1878); 3 piano concertos, No. 1 (1875); Ballets: *Swan Lake* (1877), *Sleeping Beauty* (1889), *The Nutcracker* (1892); Fantasy Overtures: *Romeo and Juliet* (1869), *Francesca da Rimini* (1876), *Capriccio italien* (1880), *1812 Overture* (1882), *Marche slav*

Chamber Music: String sextet (1890), string quartets, piano trio

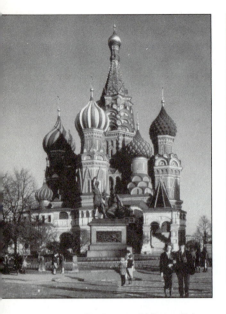

Kremlin Square in front of the Church of the Redeemer

LISTENING INSIGHTS

How to Listen to Nationalistic Music

Nationalist composers expected their listeners to focus on the native resources in their music. Listen for the folk and patriotic melodies and indigenous instruments, such as Russian balalaika and bells, and Spanish castanets, guitars, and tambourines.

The more rigid, intellectual forms that German composers favored held little interest for most nationalist composers. Their forms were loose, usually relying on forms suggested by descriptions, stories, and titles. You will generally hear many contrasting sections of music with only a smattering of repeated ideas and very little thematic development.

A New York Philharmonic performance of Tchaikovsky's *1812 Overture* in Central Park

TCHAIKOVSKY AS A NATIONALIST Although he was their contemporary, the so-called "Russian Five" excluded Tchaikovsky from their group. They considered him an outsider—too cosmopolitan, too influenced by the music of other nations through his frequent travels, especially to Germany, France, and Italy.

Despite his exclusion by "The Five," their music inspired Tchaikovsky to compose nationalistic music. However, he did not limit his nationalistic sources to Russia. His ballets *Swan Lake* and *Nutcracker* (see Plate 11) include folk dances of other countries. His six symphonies, *March Slav*, operas, and numerous other works contain Russian songs. However, his orchestral work *Capriccio italien* is not Russian. It is a musical diary of his travels to Italy. (Rimsky-Korsakov, a member of "The Five," similarly memorialized his travels to Spain in his work *Capriccio espagnol*.)

Perhaps "The Five" were right. Tchaikovsky did not consistently display the nationalistic fervor that they did. But the *1812 Overture* epitomized his passion as a Russian nationalist.

HISTORICAL PERSPECTIVE

The 1812 Overture: Spectacular Performances

Tchaikovsky's *1812 Overture* is one of the most bombastic and nationalistic works ever written. It was originally commissioned by the czarist government to celebrate the seventieth anniversary of Napoleon's devastating defeat by the Russian army in Moscow and Napoleon's subsequent retreat to Paris with only about 400,000 of his original 550,000 troops. Moscow Square was the original setting. The piece includes army rifle and cannon firing, augmented by the great bells of the colorful Church of the Redeemer. (The firing of cannons and rifles is not random. Tchaikovsky treated them as orchestra members by indicating their exact entrances in the score.)

Today, this highly programmatic piece has become a favorite at outdoor concerts throughout the world. In addition to the large symphony orchestra, today's performances often are further enhanced by adding military-style bands to its concluding section. The work is often capped by spectacular fireworks display.

Indoors and on recordings, the sounds of the church bells, rifles, and cannons often are replicated by prerecorded tapes. During the reign of the Communists, who overthrew the Czar in 1917, the playing of the "Czars Hymn" that Tchaikovsky used was forbidden. The Soviets substituted a new, considerably less exciting melody. With the breakup of the Soviet regime, however, the original "Czar's Hymn" was back in the *1812 Overture*, even in Russia.

LISTENING ACTIVITY

THE 1812 OVERTURE (1882), PETER ILYICH TCHAIKOVSKY

Large Form: Programmatic Concert Overture
Detailed Form: Sectional
Performing Medium: Large Symphony Orchestra with
Additional Brass Band

Compact Disc 3, Track 1
Cassette Tape: Side D, Example 3
Running Time: 14:34

NATIONALISTIC RESOURCES   With its rich setting and program focusing on a slice of Russian history, the *1812 Overture* exemplifies nationalism. It employs an abundance of resources associated with nationalities and cultures, including:

- Russian Orthodox Church hymns
- Russian folk songs and dances
- The French national anthem "La Marseillaise"
- Russian patriotic music: "Czar's Hymn"
- bells and chimes representing the great bells of the churches in Russia

THE PROGRAM The work opens with a Russian hymn, "God Preserve Thy People." In an agitated section, Napoleon's troops advance toward Moscow. The horns introduce a slow march as the Russian troops prepare for battle. The armies clash and fall back, as the orchestra plays fragments of the French national anthem, "La Marseillaise."

Freezing in the bitter winter's evening, the Russian troops think of their warm homes and families, as we hear a Russian lullaby and a playful Russian folk song.

Morning arrives, and the French troops advance with the "La Marseillaise." A minor battle ensues and both sides retreat to their camps for another cold night. We again hear the lullaby and the folk song.

Then a new, more furious battle begins—armies clash, cannons and rifles blast over the music. We hear the opening hymn again, this time with church bells and chimes signifying the Russian victory.

Triumphantly, the Russian troops march back to Moscow, greeted by the "Czar's Hymn." Bells toll. Rifle and cannon fire signal victory.

LISTENING GUIDE

THE 1812 OVERTURE **(1882),** PETER ILYICH TCHAIKOVSKY

1	0:00	THEME 1—Russian Orthodox Church hymn	Large orchestra, hymn begins in the strings; *p*; very slow (largo) tempo; triple meter; E-flat Major tonality; homophonic texture

	1:20	THEME 1—fragments	imitation and sequences between woodwinds and strings, crescendo to *fff*

| 2 | 2:00 | THEME 2—Russian folk song | played by the oboe, *p*; imitations by flutes and cellos; c minor tonality |

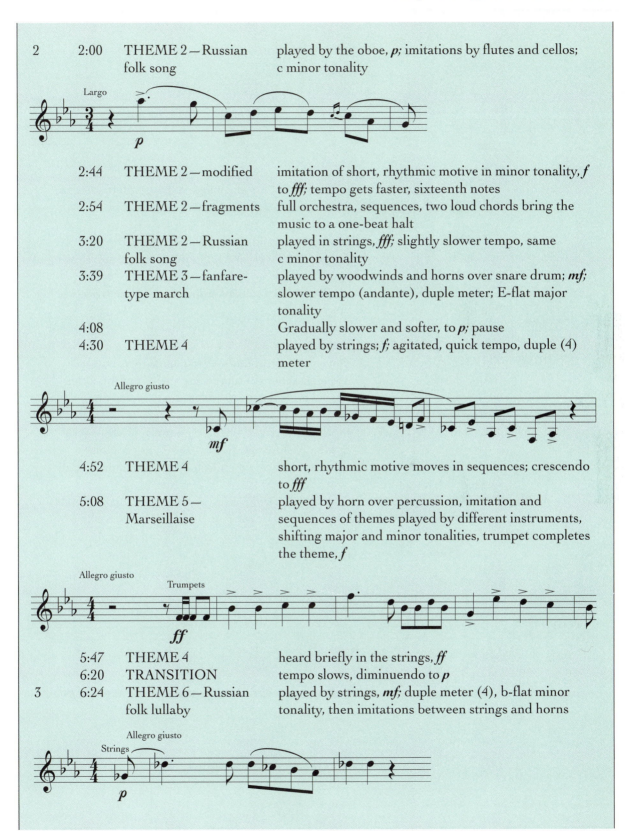

	2:44	THEME 2—modified	imitation of short, rhythmic motive in minor tonality, *f* to *fff*; tempo gets faster, sixteenth notes
	2:54	THEME 2—fragments	full orchestra, sequences, two loud chords bring the music to a one-beat halt
	3:20	THEME 2—Russian folk song	played in strings, *fff*; slightly slower tempo, same c minor tonality
	3:39	THEME 3—fanfare-type march	played by woodwinds and horns over snare drum; *mf*; slower tempo (andante), duple meter; E-flat major tonality
	4:08		Gradually slower and softer, to *p*; pause
	4:30	THEME 4	played by strings; *f*; agitated, quick tempo, duple (4) meter

| | 4:52 | THEME 4 | short, rhythmic motive moves in sequences; crescendo to *fff* |
| | 5:08 | THEME 5—Marseillaise | played by horn over percussion, imitation and sequences of themes played by different instruments, shifting major and minor tonalities, trumpet completes the theme, *f* |

	5:47	THEME 4	heard briefly in the strings, *ff*
	6:20	TRANSITION	tempo slows, diminuendo to *p*
3	6:24	THEME 6—Russian folk lullaby	played by strings, *mf*; duple meter (4), b-flat minor tonality, then imitations between strings and horns

| 7:49 | THEME 7 — Russian folk dance | played by flutes over tambourine, *p*; same tempo, e-flat minor tonality |

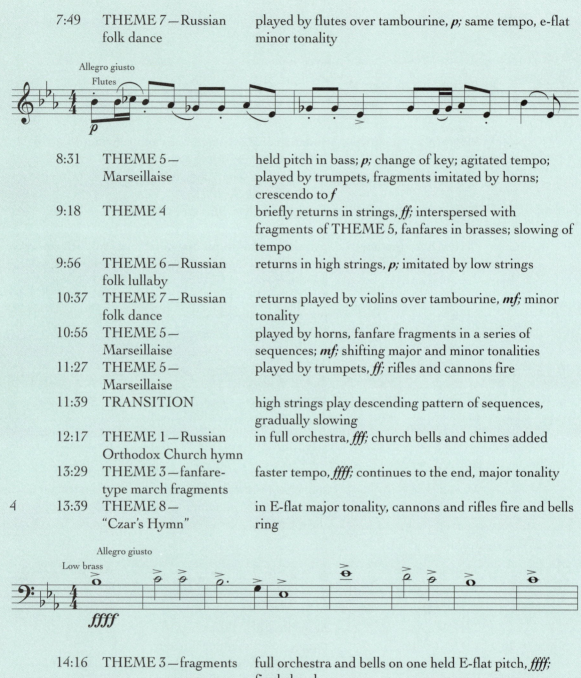

8:31	THEME 5 — Marseillaise	held pitch in bass; *p*; change of key; agitated tempo; played by trumpets, fragments imitated by horns; crescendo to *f*
9:18	THEME 4	briefly returns in strings, *ff*; interspersed with fragments of THEME 5, fanfares in brasses; slowing of tempo
9:56	THEME 6 — Russian folk lullaby	returns in high strings, *p*; imitated by low strings
10:37	THEME 7 — Russian folk dance	returns played by violins over tambourine, *mf*; minor tonality
10:55	THEME 5 — Marseillaise	played by horns, fanfare fragments in a series of sequences; *mf*; shifting major and minor tonalities
11:27	THEME 5 — Marseillaise	played by trumpets, *ff*; rifles and cannons fire
11:39	TRANSITION	high strings play descending pattern of sequences, gradually slowing
12:17	THEME 1 — Russian Orthodox Church hymn	in full orchestra, *fff*; church bells and chimes added
13:29	THEME 3 — fanfare-type march fragments	faster tempo, *ffff*; continues to the end, major tonality
4	13:39	THEME 8 — "Czar's Hymn"	in E-flat major tonality, cannons and rifles fire and bells ring

| 14:16 | THEME 3 — fragments | full orchestra and bells on one held E-flat pitch, *ffff*; final chord |

Nikolai Rimsky-Korsakov (1844–1908)

Born in Tikhvin, Russia, Nikolai Rimsky-Korsakov (*rim*-skee-*kors*-a-cuff) later served for eleven years as a naval officer with the title Inspector of Naval Bands.

But Rimsky-Korsakov's interest was in music—not in the military. Thus, he joined the faculty of the St. Petersburg Conservatory of Music to teach composition and orchestration. Like his colleagues in the "Mighty Five," Rimsky-Korsakov used native folk melodies in his compositions. He also arranged and edited collections of Russian folk music.

A highly renowned orchestrator and composer, Rimsky-Korsakov edited many of Mussorgsky's and Borodin's works to facilitate their performance. His most famous students were Igor Stravinsky and Sergei Prokofiev (discussed in Chapters 20 and 22). Although his compositions include symphonies, chamber music, choruses, and songs, his most well-known works are his symphonic poems and operas.

PRINCIPAL WORKS

Orchestra Music: Concerto for Trombone and Brass Band (1877); Symphonic suite *Scheherazade* (1888); *Capriccio espagnol* (1887); and the *Russian Easter Overture* (1888)

Operas: sixteen operas, *Sadko* (1898); *Snegurochka* (Snow Maiden, 1882); *Mozart and Salieri* (1897); *Skzka o Tsare Saltane* (Tale of Czar Saltan, which includes "The Flight of the Bumble Bee," 1900); *Le Coq d'or* (The Golden Cockerel, 1909)

Challenge Your Expertise

- To which professional association did Nikolai Rimsky-Korsakov, Alexander Borodin, Mily Balakirev, César Cui, and Modest Mussorgsky belong?
- Which popular Russian composer worked as a law clerk?

Twentieth-Century Russia

Many Communist-era composers retained a nationalistic approach in their music. The government not only encouraged them to do so but reprimanded them when their music became too "international." Most of these composers are discussed in Chapter 22: *Alexander Scriabin (1872–1915)*, *Sergei Rachmaninov* (rahk-*mah*-nih-nof, *1873–1943*), *Sergei Prokofiev (1891–1953)*, *Dmitri Shostakovitch* (shos-tah-*koh*-vich, *1906–1975*), *Aram Khachaturian* (kahtch-a-*tur*-ee-an, *1903–1978*), and *Dmitri Kabelevsky* (kab-a-*leff*-skee, *1904–1987*).

Sergei Rachmaninov (1873–1943)

Sergei Rachmaninov's (rahk-*mah*-nih-nof) early musical studies were at the St. Petersburg Conservatory. Later he studied at the Moscow Conservatory, graduating at age nineteen. A brilliant career as a pianist, conductor, and composer followed, affording him enough economic security to travel extensively.

When his First Symphony (1895) was not well received by the Moscow public, Rachmaninov withdrew from composing for a while. But with the completion and successful premiere of his Second Piano Concerto in 1901, Rachmaninov regained his stride and went on to compose some of his most popular works.

In 1917, fleeing the Russian Revolution, Rachmaninov and his family emigrated to the United States, where he was immediately acclaimed for his pianistic abilities. Subsequent concert tours and record contracts kept him extremely busy, yet he found time to compose, premiering several of his works with the Philadelphia Orchestra.

With his nineteenth-century Romantic style becoming increasingly anachronistic, Rachmaninov decided to abandon composition. He continued as a successful concert pianist until his death at his Beverly Hills home at the age of 69.

PRINCIPAL WORKS

Orchestral Works: Piano Concertos: No. 1 in f-sharp minor (1891); No. 2 in c minor (1901); No. 3 in a minor (1909); No. 4 in g minor (1926); Symphonies: No. 1 in d minor (1895); No. 2 in e minor (1907); No. 3 in a minor (1936); *The Isle of the Dead* (1909); *Rhapsody on a Theme by Paganini* for piano and orchestra (1934); *Symphonic Dances* (1940)

Piano Music: Preludes (23) (1904, 1910), sonatas, études, and variations

Choral Music: *Liturgy of St. John Chrysostom* (1910); *The Bells* (1913)

Opera: *Aleko* (1893)

Miscellaneous songs and chamber music

Béla Bartók (1881–1945)

Béla Bartók (*bahr*-tok) was born in Hungary during the last years of the Hapsburgs' reign. After early piano training with his mother, he studied at the Budapest Royal Academy of Music.

Following graduation, Bartók embarked on a successful career as a concert pianist, composing in his spare time. Throughout most of his life, Bartók's main source of income was from piano teaching—thirty years at the Budapest Academy.

Bartók's studies had been mainly in the Austro-German tradition until 1904, when he began discovering the vast resource of folk music. Along with Hungarian composer Zoltán Kodály, Bartók compiled and analyzed the folk music not only of his native Hungary but of other countries. Both men utilized their findings in composing nationalistic music.

In 1940, when Hungary entered into a collaboration with the Nazis, Bartók fled with his family to the United States. In their haste, they had to leave most of their possessions in Hungary, settling in New York City with meager resources.

Unable to find work immediately, Bartók used what was left of his money to support his family. Their financial difficulties were compounded by his bouts with leukemia.

Columbia University came to the family's rescue by appointing Bartók to a position as a folk music researcher at the university library. In addition, a few composing commissions helped ease Bartók's circumstances, especially the Boston Symphony's commission in 1943 for the *Concerto for Orchestra*. Bartók died at age 64 in a New York City hospital.

PRINCIPAL WORKS

Orchestral Music: *Kossuth* (1903); *Dance Suite* (1917); *Music for Strings, Percussion, and Celesta* (1936); *Concerto for Orchestra* (1943); three piano concertos; two violin concertos, Viola Concerto (1945)

Ballets: *The Wooden Prince* (1917); *The Miraculous Mandarin* (1926)

Opera: *Bluebeard's Castle* (1918)

Chamber Music: six string quartets; *Contrasts* for Violin, Clarinet and Piano (1938); Sonata for Solo Violin (1944); sonatas for violin and piano

Piano Music: *14 Bagatelles* (1908), *Allegro barbaro* (1911), *Suite* (1916), *Sonata* (1926), *Out of Doors* (1926), *Mikrokosmos* volumes 1–6 (1926–39)

Choral Music: *Cantata profana* (1930)

Miscellaneous choral works, songs, and folk song arrangements

Jean Sibelius at age twenty-three

Other Nationalist Composers

THE CZECH REPUBLIC   Until 1919, the country we know today as the Czech Republic was part of the Austro-Hungarian (Hapsburg) Empire. It was home to several outstanding nationalist composers. *Antonín Dvořák (1841–1904)* and *Bedřich Smetana (1824–1884)* are the most widely known.

Dvořák is particularly interesting to Americans. After having achieved fame as a composer in his native Bohemia, he moved to New York City to become director of the National Conservatory of Music (no longer in existence) from 1892 to 1895. During that time, he wrote his famous New World Symphony (Symphony No. 9).

HUNGARY   *Franz Liszt* (see biography in Chapter 14) and the twentieth-century composers *Zoltán Kodály (1882–1967)* and *Béla Bartók (1881–1945)* are the Hungarian composers whose music you are most likely to hear at concerts.

SCANDINAVIA   *Edvard Grieg (1843–1907)* of Norway wrote many Norwegian songs and is well known for his nationalistic *Peer Gynt Suites. Jean Sibelius* (yan sib-*bayl*-yus) *(1865–1957)* of Finland is best known for his *Finlandia* Violin Concerto, tone poems, *Valse triste,* and his symphonies, especially Symphony No. 2.

UNITED KINGDOM   *Edward Elgar (1857–1934)* was a distinctly English composer. His most famous works are the *Pomp and Circumstance* Marches and *Enigma* Variations.

Dvořák

Smetana
(*shmeh*-tuh-nuh)

Liszt

Kodály
(koh-*dye*)

Bartók

Grieg
(greeg)

Sibelius

Elgar

Ralph Vaughan Williams (1872–1958), another English nationalist composer, once wrote:

Vaughan Williams

> *Art, like charity, should begin at home. If it is to be of any value, it must grow out of the very life of himself (the composer), the community in which he lives, the nation to which he belongs.*

To accomplish this task, Vaughan Williams incorporated English folk songs into many of his works, notably his *English Folk Song Suite* and *Fantasia on "Greensleeves."*

Percy Grainger (1882–1961) is less easy to classify. Born in Australia and educated in London, he lived in the United States during the latter part of his life. For many years, Grainger wandered through the English and Irish countrysides with an Edison cylinder-recorder and music paper, recording and notating folk songs that he heard. He abundantly incorporated these songs into his music. He is best known for his many British folk song settings, such as *Irish Tune from County Derry, Country Gardens,* and his wind band work *Lincolnshire Posy.*

Grainger

ITALY Several famous opera composers are considered Italian nationalists. The greatest were *Giuseppe Verdi* and *Giacomo Puccini,* both discussed in Chapter 15.

Ottorino Respighi (1879–1936) is best known for his orchestral works: *Roman Festivals, The Pines of Rome, The Fountains of Rome,* and *The Birds.*

Respighi
(res-*pee*-ghee)

SPAIN *Isaac Albéniz (1860–1909), Enrique Granados (1867–1916),* and *Manuel de Falla (1876–1947)* incorporated lively flamenco and Andalusian dance rhythms into their colorful music. Also, because of the use of instruments indigenous to Spain, such as castanets, tambourine, and guitars, their music sounds distinctly Spanish.

Albéniz
(ahl-*bay*-neeth)

Granados
(grah-*nah*-dohs)

de Falla
(*fah*-yah)

NORTH AMERICAN Chapters 24 through 27 discuss composers in the United States.

Summary of Terms

Andalusian rhythms	Czar's Hymn	La Marseillaise
balalaika	flamenco dance rhythms	Russian Five
bells	folk song	tambourine
castanets	guitar	wanderlust

Chapter 18

Impressionism

IMPRESSIONISTIC POETRY AND PAINTING

A Claude Monet painting, *Impression — Soleil Levant* (*Impression: Sunrise;* see Plate 10), provided the inspiration for the name of a new movement in France. Alienated by German intellectualism and "oversentimentality," French artists of the late nineteenth century felt more spiritually attuned to quieter, more sensual expression. For example, the poet Mallarmé was more interested in beauty and in the sound of the French language than he was in the content.

French painters reflected their interest in the "impression" of a subject rather than in its detailed, specific content. The works of Monet, Manet, Renoir, and others epitomize the Impressionistic style—uncomplicated subject matter portrayed in the quiet of pastel colors, with vague definition.

New Inventions Influence Art

Two practical inventions boosted Impressionistic painting: the camera and the paint tube (similar to the toothpaste tube).

THE CAMERA   Until the invention of the camera, a painter's primary role was that of a "photographer"—to capture the moment for posterity. Notice how Hans Holbein's sixteenth-century portrait of Henry VIII looks more like a snapshot than a painting.

254

In 1827, Joseph Niépce produced the earliest photographs on a metal plate, encouraging painters to look at a subject with a fresh eye. Painters gathered in Parisian cafés, intently discussing new options for capturing the feelings and impressions of the moment. Although the details of their paintings may seem veiled, as though you were looking at them through a slight haze, the mood is always clear (see Monet's *Les Meules*).

THE PAINT TUBE   Before the invention of the lead tube of oil paint, artists rarely worked outdoors. When they did, they found it quite inconvenient. Oil paint thinned with alcohol dries in minutes in the open air. To avoid lugging containers of paints and alcohol everwhere, artists were limited to making pencil sketches of their outdoor subjects. Later, in their studios, they had to recreate the scene, mixing paint to match the colors that they could recall.

With the freedom of a tube, an artist could dab colors on a palette, cap the tube, and quickly paint a scene. And although artists still had to wait for sunlight and paint quickly, they could capture the spontaneity and mood of the moment. Impressionistic painting, with its sparse details, invites each perceiver to fill in the gaps with personal impressions.

Aided by the new paint tube, Claude Monet (1840–1926) painted the west facade of the Rouen Cathedral from the same location at various times of the day. Changes in light and shadow make each painting different (see Plate 10). Monet was also fascinated by the effect of changing lights, shadows, and colors on the lily pads in the pond on his estate in Giverny, France. He thus created a series of masterpieces—his impressions of these lily pads as the sun progressed through the day.

IMPRESSONISM IN MUSIC

Toward the end of the nineteenth century, French composers rejected the Germanic mainstream in favor of their own music. Championed by Claude Debussy, the new French music reflected some of the new trends in poetry and painting. It came to be known by the same name: Impressionism.

The painting *Henry VIII* (1540), by Hans Holbein the Younger

Les Meules (The Haystacks, 1891), by Monet

Claude Debussy (1862–1918)

Claude Debussy (de-byoo-*see*) was born in Saint-Germain-en-Laye, a small town near Paris. At age eleven, he entered the Paris Conservatory, studying piano and composition. After winning the prestigious Prix de Rome, he went to study in that great city.

At age 25, returning to Paris to compose and perform as a pianist, Debussy became part of a wide circle of artists, writers, and musicians who met often to discuss new directions for the arts. He became the main developer of Impressionistic music.

Toward the end of his career, Debussy became associated with the Ballets Russes, composing his last work, *Jeux,* for that ensemble. World War I had its effect on Debussy: he produced only a few minor works until his death in 1918 at age 55.

PRINCIPAL WORKS

Orchestral Music: *Prélude à l'après-midi d'un faune* (Prelude to The Afternoon of a Faun, 1894); *Nocturnes* (1899); *Danses sacrée et profane* (1904); *La mer* (The Sea, 1905); *Première Rapsodie for Clarinet and Piano* (1910); *Images* (1912)

Ballet: *Jeux* (Games, 1913)

Incidental Music: *Le Martyre de St. Sébastien* (1911)

Chamber Music: *String Quartet* (1893), *Petite Pièce for Clarinet and Piano* (1910), *Sonata for Cello and Piano* (1915), *Sonata for Flute, Viola, and Harp* (1915); *Sonata for Violin and Piano* (1917)

Piano Music: *Suite, pour le piano* (1901); *Suite bergamasque* (1909); *Estampes* (1903); *Images* (1905); *Children's Corner* (1908); Préludes, two books (1910, 1913); *Études* (1915)

Opera: *Pelléas et Mélisande* (1902)

Songs: *Fêtes galantes* (1881, 1904); *Chansons de Bilitis* (1898); more than sixty others

Choral Music: *La Demoiselle élue* (The Chosen Maid, 1888)

Paris World Exposition

The Paris World Expositions of 1878 and 1889 profoundly influenced Debussy, who was searching for new material at the time. Hearing the Indonesian *gamelan* ensemble use delicate finger cymbals, Debussy decided to incorporate the instrument into his orchestral works. Groups from Japan and China also attracted his interest, and soon thereafter, Debussy incorporated Asian scales into his music.

Characteristics of Impressionism

Creating a new world of sound was Debussy's challenge. To accomplish this, he developed techniques that contrasted with those of the late Romantic composers.

FORM: AVOIDING HARD OUTLINES Debussy avoided clear-cut cadences and resting points. Instead, his music has a feeling of wandering or floating. (Some have said that the undulating sounds of *La mer* [The Sea] make them feel "seasick.")

ORCHESTRAL COLORS: USING DELICATE TONE COLORS Debussy's instrumental effects were delicate, subtle, and full of color, bearing a similarity to Impressionistic painters' choices of delicate colors. He preferred the following instruments (in order of importance):

The painting *Rouen Cathedral, West Facade, Sunlight,* by Monet

flutes
oboes
clarinets
strings (often muted)
harp (sweeping arpeggios
   veil tonality)

brass (used sparingly, usually with
   mutes)
percussion (used sparingly, avoiding
   military instruments; employed
   antique cymbals and triangles)

RHYTHMS: DE-EMPHASIZING SOLID, SYMMETRICAL RHYTHMS To deviate from the predictability of typical rhythms (for example, those found in marches and waltzes), Debussy calls for vague beats and complex subdivisions (7, 11, 13). A run of seven tones to a beat may follow thirteen tones to a beat.

SCALES: INCORPORATING THE NONTRADITIONAL Rather than use diatonic scales (do, re, mi), which give the feeling of a solid base, Debussy incorporated three other scale types: *pentatonic, chromatic,* and *whole-tone.*

PENTATONIC SCALES. Debussy had heard Asian performers use a variety of five-tone scales at the Paris Fair. The following is only one of the many pentatonic scales:

Photograph of Rouen Cathedral, West Facade

GOODBYE, OLD PAINT

Good - by, old Paint, I'm a leav- ing Chey - enne.

The Pentatonic scales that Debussy incorporated were not completely new to Western music. Many concert pieces and folk songs use them—European folk songs, cowboy songs, and Native American songs.

CHROMATIC SCALES.   The chromatic scale, though sparingly used, has appeared in Western concert music since the music of Bach. In music, "chromatic" refers to all the black and white keys on a keyboard. Moving in half steps, these scales incorporate all the tones used in Western music.

Because each interval in the chromatic scale is of equal size—a half step—the scale seems to avoid a home base or tonal center.

ASCENDING CHROMATIC SCALE

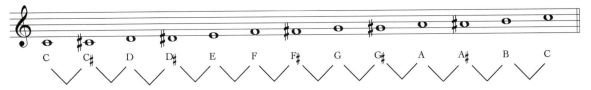

half steps

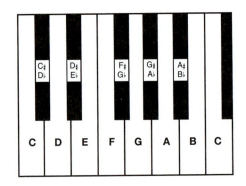

Traditional diatonic scales are constructed with a mixture of whole and half steps, giving the feeling of key-based stability.

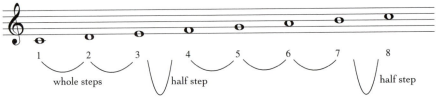

WHOLE-TONE SCALE.   In his search for music materials to convey the vagueness of Impressionism, Debussy used a *whole-tone scale.* A whole-tone scale consists of equal large steps (whole-step intervals). Similar to the chromatic scale, which consists of equal small steps (half-step intervals), the whole-tone scale seems to avoid a key centered on a specific pitch.

The Eiffel Tower in 1989, celebrating its centennial

HARMONY   Because it provided a feeling of solidity based in a certain key base, traditional harmony did not easily fit into Debussy's style. So he extended the traditional chords of three and four tones built on any degree of the diatonic scale. (See Appendix A, Music Notation).

Extended chords

9th chord   11th chord   13th chord

Notice that the 13th chord contains all of the pitches of the scale. Because all pitches are equal, the 13th chord has only a remote reference to the root tone or key centre.

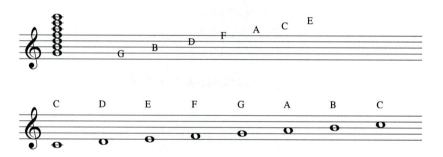

LISTENING INSIGHTS

How to Listen to Impressionistic Music

Debussy and the other Impressionist composers expected audiences to listen more sensually than intellectually, encouraging the listener to feel relaxed and unstressed. Imagine yourself at the seashore on a beautiful, sunny day watching the movement of the tide as sailboats glide by on the horizon and white, puffy clouds move lazily across a blue sky. Without following the music too intellectually, observe the interesting sound combinations and melodic movement.

LISTENING ACTIVITY

PRELUDE TO THE AFTERNOON OF A FAUN (1894), CLAUDE DEBUSSY

Large Form: Orchestral Tone Poem
Detailed Form: Modified Three-Part Form
Performing Medium: Large Symphony Orchestra

Compact Disc 4, Track 7
Running Time: 10:21

Stéphan Mallarmé inspired Debussy's tone poem *Prélude à L'aprés-midi d'un faune* (Prelude to The Afternoon of a Faun).

The poem concerns a mythical half-man, half-animal forest creature. Awakening from a dream of lovely nymphs, the creature is disoriented. Is he awake or still dreaming? Because the afternoon is warm and lazy, he decides to go back to sleep. Not much action, but the scenario is perfect for Impressionism.

A flute opens and closes the piece with a dreamy, chromatic melody. Fast runs in the orchestra make the middle section slightly more active. Notice that antique cymbals at the end, influenced by southeast Asian music that Debussy heard at the Paris World's Fair.

LISTENING GUIDE

PRELUDE TO THE AFTERNOON OF A FAUN (1894), CLAUDE DEBUSSY

SECTION A

| 7 | 0:00 | CHROMATIC MELODY | flute solo, unaccompanied at beginning; *p;* slow tempo, changing meters, rubato; chromatic and pentatonic scales; extended chords; harp glissandos blur tonality |

| | 0:56 | CHROMATIC MELODY | mainly in solo flute, tremolo strings; *pp* |

	2:01	CHROMATIC MELODY	flute solo expressively with harp arpeggios
	2:42	CHROMATIC MELODY	flute solo with harp arpeggios
	3:16	TRANSITION	cadence; clarinet
	3:35	WHOLE-TONE MELODY	solos by clarinet, then flute; faster tempo, changing meters; whole-tone scales

	4:21	TRANSITION	faster and animated; crescendo to *f*; gradual diminuendo and slowing; modulating and cadencing to A-flat tonality

SECTION B

8	4:49	TRANSITION	clarinet; descending string chords
	5:05	PENTATONIC MELODY	woodwinds; slower tempo, mostly triple meter; *p*; pentatonic scale used part of the section

	5:38	PENTATONIC MELODY	strings with pentatonic melody; harp arpeggios; full orchestra crescendo to *ff*
	6:26	PENTATONIC MELODY	violin solo accompanied by woodwinds; *p*

SECTION A

9	6:46		slower tempo; similar to the opening section; flute solo with harp arpeggios and long chords in strings
	7:21	CHROMATIC MELODY	flute solo with harp arpeggios and long chords in strings
	7:59	CHROMATIC MELODY	flute section; *p*; antique cymbals, shimmering strings with tremolos
	8:39	CHROMATIC MELODY	flute and viola; *pp*; antique cymbals; harp arpeggios
	9:43	CHROMATIC MELODY	muted horns; slow tempo, gradually slowing and diminuendo until the end; antique cymbals; *ppp*

Debussy was the most prominent of the Impressionist composers, but others such as Maurice Ravel, used the same techniques. Although Ravel composed in many styles, including jazz, several of his pieces were influenced by Impressionism—*Pavane pour une infante défunte* (Pavane for a Dead Princess) and the *Daphnis et Chloé* ballet.

Challenge Your Expertise

In addition to music, which creative art forms reflect Impressionism?

Maurice Ravel (1875–1937)

Maurice Ravel (rah-*vel*) was born in the Pyrenees in the south of France. Like Debussy, Ravel studied at the Paris Conservatory of Music. Though clearly the most outstanding student composer, Ravel was denied the prestigious Prix de Rome four times. So outraged were Ravel's teachers, friends, and the public about his not receiving the award that they forced the resignation of the conservatory director.

During World War I, Ravel drove an ambulance on the front lines. With the war over, Ravel resumed composing and was soon recognized as France's leading composer.

Early in 1928 when George Gershwin visited Paris, the two composers became friends. Gershwin had wanted to study European styles with Ravel. Instead, Ravel advised him to continue his unique style of incorporating jazz into his concert music. As a result of their discussions, Gershwin went home to compose the tone poem *An American in Paris*, and Ravel wrote his Piano Concerto in G, in which he used Gershwin-style jazz.

Ravel developed into a master of orchestration, as displayed in works such as *La valse, Daphnis et Chloé*, and his orchestration of Mussorgsky's *Pictures at an Exhibition* (1922). At age 60, Ravel contracted a brain disease and died two years later.

PRINCIPAL WORKS

Orchestral Music: *Alborada del gracioso* (1905); *Rapsodie espagnole* (1908); *La valse* (1920); *Bolero* (1928); *Piano Concerto in D Major for Left Hand* (1930); *Piano Concerto in G Major* (1931)

Chamber Music: *String Quartet* (1903); *Trio for Violin, Cello and Piano* (1914); violin sonatas

Ballets: *Ma Mère l'Oye* (Mother Goose, 1912); *Daphnis et Chloé* (1912)

Operas: *L'Enfant et les sortilèges* (The Child and the Spells, 1925), *L'Heure espagnole* (1909)

Piano Music: *Pavane pour une infante défunte* (Pavane for a Dead Princess, 1899, later orchestrated); *Jeux d'eau* (1901); *Sonatine* (1905); *Miroirs* (1905); *Valses nobles et sentimentales* (1911); *Le tombeau de Couperin* (1917)

Songs: *Shéhérazade* with orchestra (1903); *Histoires naturelles* (1906); *Chants populaires* (1910)

Summary of Terms

antique cymbals

Ballets Russes

chromatic scale

extended chords

gamelan

Paris World Exposition

pentatonic scales

Prix de Rome

13th chord

whole-tone scale

Chapter 19

The Twentieth-Century Style Period

INFLUENCE OF THE WORLD WARS

The fever of nationalism in Europe, so charmingly conveyed in the nineteenth century, veered out of control in 1914. As country after country entered the hostilities, Europe was swept into a world war.

When the war ended in 1918, many of Europe's prized libraries, theaters, concert halls, and museums were in ruins. Throughout the continent, economies were in shambles. The toll of World War I was staggering: 8.5 million killed, 21 million wounded, and 7.5 million prisoners and missing in action.

World War I also had a devastating effect on the European artistic community. Drafted into service to fight the war, many artists were killed. Some fled to the United States. Others sought refuge in neutral countries where they could continue working. The November 1918 armistice finally halted "the war to end all wars."

After only a brief period of recovery in the late 1920s, the Great Depression paralyzed Europe and North America. Playing on the panic of the people, the fascist governments of Adolf Hitler, Benito Mussolini, and Hideki Tojo laid the groundwork for World War II (1939–1945).

When peace finally returned in 1945, fifty-seven countries of the world were scarred by the greatest trauma in human history: an estimated 54.8 million people killed, most of them civilians. Millions more were left crippled and homeless. The extent of the war's cruelty brought civilization to its knees. Nazi genocide killed at least 14 million Jews, Poles, Slavs, gypsies, homosexuals, and political dissidents.

Devastated, the artistic community revived slowly. With the cost of war, and post–war rebuilding, resources allocated toward the funding of the arts were strained. For approximately fifty years (1914–1964), the arts in Europe struggled. Aided partly by the United States' Marshall Plan, most European nations gradually regained financial and artistic stability in the 1960s.

ART REDEFINED

Before the twentieth century, most art was defined by the adjective "beautiful." Music was beautiful, harmonious sound; painting was beautiful pictures; dance was beautiful movement, and so on.

Could music, painting, poetry, dance, and the theater seem "ugly," and still be "art"? Picasso's *Guernica* (see painting below) depicts a hideous scene: the result of Hitler's *Luftwaffe* testing their new weapons by bombing the peaceful Spanish town of Guernica in 1937. Twisted, wrenching victims expose the horror of this despicable act.

Igor Stravinsky and Pablo Picasso were friends and shared views on art. Adhering to an outlook similar to Picasso's, Stravinsky composed his ballet *Rite of Spring* (discussed in the next chapter). Subtitled "Scenes from Pagan Russia," the ballet is characterized by angular dancing, stark scenery, and dissonant music. Its infamous 1913 debut changed the direction of music for the rest of the twentieth century.

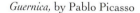

Guernica, by Pablo Picasso

Overview of the Twentieth-Century Period (1900 to Present)

Composers

Samuel Barber, Béla Bartók, Alban Berg, Leonard Bernstein, Ernest Bloch, Nadia Boulanger, Pierre Boulez, Benjamin Britten, Carlos Chávez, Aaron Copland, Edward Elgar, Edward Kennedy "Duke" Ellington, Manuel de Falla, Gabriel Fauré, George Gershwin, Edvard Grieg, Paul Hindemith, Gustav Holst, Arthur Honegger, Charles Ives, Leos Janácek, Jerome Kern, Zoltán Kodály, Franz Lehár, Witold Lutoslawski, Oliver Messiaen, Gian Carlo Menotti, Darius Milhaud, Francis Poulenc, Sergei Prokofiev, Sergei Rachmaninoff, Maurice Ravel, Ottorino Respighi, Richard Rodgers, Sigmund Romberg, Erik Satie, Arnold Schoenberg, William Schuman, Alexander Scriabin, Dmitri Shostakovich, Jean Sibelius, Karlheinz Stockhausen, Richard Strauss, Igor Stravinsky, Edgard Varèse, William Walton, Kurt Weill, Ralph Vaughan Williams, Anton Webern, Ellen Taaffe Zwilich

Visual Artists

Mateo Alonso, Max Beckmann, Georges Braque, Alexander Calder, Marc Chagall, Jean Cocteau, Salvador Dali, Willem De Kooning, Walt Disney, Marcel Duchamp, Max Ernst, Erte, Buckminster Fuller, Juan Gris, Freda Kahlo, Wassily Kandinsky, Paul Klee, Le Corbusier, Henri Matisse, Mies van der Rohe, Joan Miró, Amedeo Modigliani, Piet Mondrian, Claude Monet, Henry Moore, Georgia O'Keeffe, Pablo Picasso, Jackson Pollock, Auguste Renoir, Diego Rivera, Auguste Rodin, Georges Rouault, Henri Rousseau, Eero Saarinen, Maurice Utrillo, Andy Warhol, Frank Lloyd Wright, Andrew Wyeth

Writers

Edward Albee, Bertold Brecht, Truman Capote, Paddy Chayefsky, Joseph Conrad, e. e. cummings, T. S. Eliot, William Faulkner, F. Scott Fitzgerald, Robert Frost, Gregorio López Fuentes, Ellen Glasgow, Lillian Hellman, Ernest Hemingway, Aldous Huxley, A. E. Housman, Henrik Ibsen, Henry James, James Joyce, Franz Kafka, Federico Garcia Lorca, Norman Mailer, Thomas Mann, Arthur Miller, O. Henry, Eugene O'Neill, Dorothy Parker, Carl Sandburg, George Bernard Shaw, Neil Simon, Gertrude Stein, John Steinbeck, August Strindberg, Leo Tolstoi, Mark Twain, H. G. Wells, Tennessee Williams, Thomas Wolfe

Philosophers

Alfred Adler, Martin Buber, Teilhard de Chardin, John Dewey, Sigmund Freud, Eric Fromm, Mohandas K. (Mahatma) Gandhi, Carl Jung, Martin Luther King, Jr., Mao Tse-tung, Bertrand Russell, George Santayana, Jean-Paul Sartre

Social, Political, and Cultural Events

Freud's psychoanalytic theories, jazz, Einstein's relativity theories, United Nations, World Wars I and II, Russian Revolution, communism, Great Depression (United States and Europe), Korean War, Vietnam War, European Economic Community, pop art, Malcolm X, chance music and painting, dadaism, nonviolence (Gandhi), Civil Rights Movement (Martin Luther King), racial integration

Science, Technology

Ford's production-line automobile, telephone, airplane, computer, the Internet, electric automobiles, films, television, phonograph, microchip, semiconductor, laser technology, penicillin, smallpox vaccine, polio vaccine, *Sputnik*, organ transplantation, DNA research, gene splicing, cloning, computer animation

Characteristics of Twentieth-Century Music

General

Music often sounds dissonant, complex, asymmetrical, nonemotional, objective, satirical; often experimental, eclectic resources

Performing Media

Chamber orchestra and ensembles used more often than symphony orchestra; all previous media still used; electronic synthesizers and keyboards; mixed media: pre-recorded electronic sounds combined with traditional instruments; computer-generated sounds

Rhythm

Polyrhythms (layers of different rhythms), polymeters, irregular rhythmic patterns, ostinato (recurring patterns)

Melody

Wide ranges, both for voices and for instruments; fragmented, disjunct, exotic intervals and scales (Asian, chromatic, pentatonic, whole-tone, twelve-tone, quarter-tone)

Harmony

Extensive use of dissonance; polychords (two or more different chords together), clusters (chords by seconds), quartal harmony (chords by fourths); exotic, experimental sounds

Expression

All previous techniques still used; extreme effects, including silence

Texture

Polyphonic texture often used; mixes of polyphonic and homophonic; layers of ideas and sounds

Forms

All forms of the previous periods used, but highly modified; experimental forms; forms incorporate new sound sources and compositional techniques:

Musique Concrète: traditional and environmental sounds pre-recorded and manipulated on the tape recorder

Chance Music: also called aleatory—improvised, unpredictable, vague or nonspecific notation, leaving much to the performer to decide

Electronic Music: electronically produced sounds, also called synthesizer music

Computer Music: sampling of voices and instruments organized and manipulated by the computer

Igor Stravinsky (right) and Pablo Picasso, in a caricature by Jean Cocteau

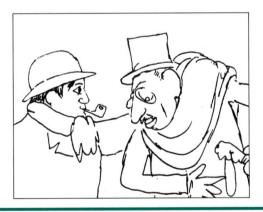

PLATE 8
Botticelli, "The Birth of Venus." (16th century)
The Birth of Venus by Italian artist Sandro Botticelli. The nude goddess steps from a scallop shell while being attended by all allegorical figures of earth and wind.
Source: Corbis.

PLATE 9
An early nineteenth-century grand pianoforte. The grand piano was made for the wife of Lord Foley, baron of Kidderminster. (See Chapter 14)
Source: The Metropolitan Museum of Art, Gift of Mrs. Henry McSweeny, 1959. Photographer: Shelda N. Collins

PLATE 10
Impression: Soleil Levant (Impression: Sunrise)
by Claude Monet, which inspired the term Impressionism in painting, poetry, and music. (See Chapter 18)
Source: Giraudon/Art Resource, New York

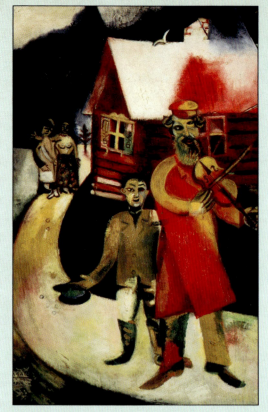

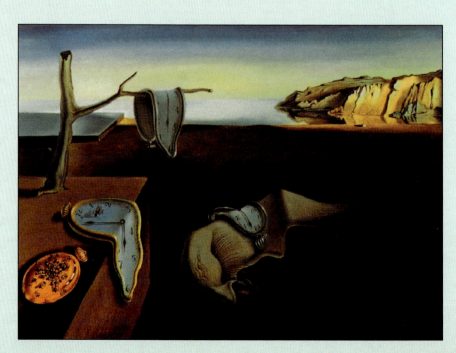

PLATE 16

The fusion-jazz group Weather Report, featuring keyboardist Joe Zawinul and saxophonist Wayne Shorter. (See Chapter 24).
SOURCE: © Andy Freeberg Photography

PLATE 17

Linares dancers from Spain. (Lucero Tena Dance Company)
SOURCE: MIRA American Ballet Theatre.
©Photographer: MIRA

Table 19.1	The Evolution of Musical Resources		
	Innovations	**Forms/Styles**	**Composers**
1600	tonal music, major-minor tonality	opera, oratorio, motet, sonata	Monteverdi
1700	traditional major and minor chords, scales, tonality perfection of the violin (craftsmen: Stradivarius)	concerto, concerto grosso sonata, cantata, oratorio	Bach, Handel Vivaldi
1750	standardized orchestra	symphony, string quartet	Haydn, Mozart
1800	orchestra expands brass valves, keyed woodwinds perfection of the piano chromatic harmony	loosening of forms descriptive/program music small piano forms, art songs realistic (verismo) opera	Beethoven, Schubert Berlioz, Mendelssohn Schumann, Chopin, Puccini
1850	expanding harmony chromaticism	concert overture, symphony, tone poem, music drama, opera	Brahms, Wagner, Verdi Strauss, Mahler, Bruckner
1880	folk songs and instruments search for new materials	nationalism, sectional forms, descriptive pieces and tone poems	Tchaikovsky, Mussorgsky, Dvořák, Smetana, Kodály Liszt,
1900	whole-tone, pentatonic, chromatic scales, expanded chords by thirds large virtuoso orchestras	Impressionism expansive symphonies and tone poems	Debussy, Ravel, Griffes Respighi Strauss, Mahler, Bruckner
1910	African-American influences polychords, polytonality, polyrhythms, dissonance atonality, 12-tone serial music	ragtime, blues, jazz, popular music ballet sectional forms symphony, songs short pieces and forms	Joplin, Irving Berlin Stravinsky Ives Schönberg, Berg, Webern
1920	back to tonality jazz elements	neoclassicism Broadway musical, popular music	Stravinsky, Prokofiev, Gershwin, Kern
1930	mix of elements jazz, environmental sounds	eclecticism process oriented, free forms	Copland, Feldman, Gershwin
1950	graphic notation natural sounds manipulated by tape recorder	chance-aleatory music *musique concrète* composer control	Cage, Stockhausen Varèse, Cage, Stockhausen
1960	multitrack recording, amplified, electronic synthesizer fusion chance-electronic athematic tonal	pop, rock, eclectic, folk, blues electronic music composer control eclectic mix of forms	Beatles, Rolling Stones Luening, Ussachevsky Subotnick, Carlos Boulez
1970	mix of resources, tonality electronic sounds, MIDI	eclecticism, fusion new romanticism	Bernstein, Barber, Babbitt, Davidovsky

1980	computer-generated sounds	eclectic, traditional and free forms	Penderecki,
	sampling, eclectic mix or elements	minimalism	Steve Reich, Philip Glass
	multicultural elements		Hovhaness, Wen-Chung
1990	computer-synthesizer non-Western scales	New Romanticism Multicultural	Del Tredici, Musgrave, Corigliano, Zwilich
2000	digital computer technologies, eclectic approaches, non-Western	free and traditional forms	Machover, Lutoslawski
	instrument sampling	fusion with world music	Takahashi, Takemitsu

Stravinsky:
Into the Twentieth
Century

Just as audiences were starting to grow comfortable with the sooth-ing "new" music of Debussy and the Impressionists, Igor Stravinsky burst onto the scene with music to jar the senses: his 1913 master-piece *The Rite of Spring*.

STRAVINSKY'S PIVOTAL POSITION

As we reflect on musical giants and assess their respective influence, Stravinsky looms as one of the dominant musical forces of the twen-tieth century. The impact of *The Rite of Spring* on composers of the twentieth century was similar to the impact of Beethoven's Ninth Symphony on nineteenth-century composers.

During Beethoven's time, the pendulum of change had begun to swing from the objectivism of the Classical period toward the subjectivism of the Romantic period. A century later, the pendulum began to swing back to objectivism.

Chapter 20

Igor Stravinsky (1882–1971)

When Igor Stravinsky was born, his father was a leading basso at the Imperial opera in St. Petersburg, Russia. As a boy, Igor showed little interest in music, which pleased the elder Stravinsky. Despite his own success in music, he urged his son to pursue a more practical career. However, soon after enrolling in St. Petersburg University, Stravinsky revealed his real interests. He eagerly dropped his studies in civil law and began studying composition with Rimsky-Korsakov at the St. Petersburg Conservatory.

In the audience at the 1908 debut of Stravinsky's first major work, *Fireworks* (*Feu d'artifice*), was his distant cousin Diaghilev, a prominent avant-garde thinker. He was so impressed by Stravinsky's music that he commissioned him to compose music for the Ballets Russes, the Paris-based dance company of Russian expatriates that Diaghilev had founded two years earlier.

Thus began a 10-year association between the great impresario and one of the most enduring composers of the twentieth century. During those years, Stravinsky composed *Firebird* (1910), *Petrushka* (1911), the monumental *The Rite of Spring* (*La Sacre du printemps*, in 1913), and other notable works.

Both Russia and France were under siege in 1914: World War I had begun. The disorder of war and his wife's illness convinced Stravinsky to escape to neutral Switzerland where he lived and worked until after the war. In 1920 France became his homeland. That was also the year Stravinsky abandoned his earlier style of composition and adopted a neoclassical idiom (see Chapter 22) for his new orchestral, instrumental, and vocal works. He served as conductor for the Ballets Russes during the company's 1925 tour of the United States.

The 1939 outbreak of World War II in Europe coincided with the deaths of his daughter, wife, and mother. So Stravinsky accepted an invitation to lecture at Harvard and moved to the United States. After a year at Harvard, the newly remarried Stravinsky settled in Los Angeles where he composed most of his remaining works. He became a naturalized American citizen in 1945.

Stravinsky began to experiment with serial music in 1955, and he did compose several fully serial works during his later years. As part of the celebration of his 75th birthday, Igor Stravinsky toured the United States, conducting his works at concerts and music festivals from coast to coast.

In his eighties, Stravinsky's health began to fail. In 1969, after several illnesses, he and his wife Vera moved into the Essex House Hotel in New York City. It was to be his final residence. Stravinsky died two years later at age 88. Following his funeral in New York, his body was taken to Stravinsky's favorite city, Venice, for a gondola procession down the Grand Canal, followed by his burial.

PRINCIPAL WORKS

Operas: *Oedipus Rex* (1927); *The Rake's Progress* (1951)

Ballets: *The Firebird* (1910); *Petrushka* (1911); *The Rite of Spring* (1913); *Pulcinella* (1920); *Les Noces* (The Wedding, 1923); *Apollo Musagetes* (1928); *The Fairy's Kiss* (1928); *Jeu de Cartes* (The Card Party, 1937); *Orpheus* (1947); *Agon* (1957)

Music-theater: *L'histoire du soldat* (The Soldier's Tale, 1918)

Orchestral Music: *Symphonies of Wind Instruments* (1920); Violin Concerto (1931); *Dumbarton Oaks* Concerto (1938); *Symphony in C* (1940); *Symphony in Three Movements* (1945); *Ebony Concerto for Clarinet* (1945); *Concerto for Strings* (1946)

Chamber Music: *Duo Concertante for Violin and Piano*

Choral Music: *Symphony of Psalms* (1930); *Mass* (1948); *Cantata* (1952); *Threni* (1958); *A Sermon, a Narrative, and a Prayer* (1961); *Requiem Canticles* (1966)

Vocal Music: *Pribaoutki* (1914); *Abraham and Isaac* (1963)

Piano Music: *Sonata* (1924); *Concerto* (1925); *Sonata for Two Pianos* (1944)

HISTORICAL PERSPECTIVE

The Rite of Spring: Its Infamous Debut in 1913

PARIS, 1912   Audiences enjoyed two new Impressionist-style ballets premiered by Diaghilev's Ballets Russes—Ravel's *Daphnis et Chloé* and Debussy's *The Afternoon of a Faun,* both choreographed by Nijinsky.

PARIS, 1913   The Téâtre des Champs-Elysées—the Ballets Russes opened its season with the premiere of Debussy's *Jeux.* But Paris audiences were totally unprepared for the unleashing of the next work, *The Rite of Spring:* "Scenes from Pagan Russia."

AUDIENCE REACTION: At first, not knowing what to make of these new sounds, many in the audience began laughing. Soon, others began heckling and protesting, trying to stop the performance. A few slaps across the faces of the protesters—some from women—and a full-fledged riot broke out. Demonstrators tore out seats. Spilling out into the Paris streets, the melée continued until the Paris police brought it under control by arresting more than forty of the rioters.

  To be fair to Stravinsky's music, the audience's disapproving reaction was compounded both by the shocking pagan rituals (see Listening Guide) and by Nijinsky's avant-garde choreography.

Cubism in Painting

Just as music departed from the predictable lines and harmonies of the nineteenth century, so did the visual arts.

Employing similar techniques around 1910, painters such as Picasso, Braque, and other artists created a style called "cubism." To grasp the essence of three musicians in costumes and masks on stage, Picasso breaks images into geometric shapes in his *Three Musicians* (see below).

Debussy (standing) and Stravinsky

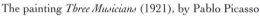

The painting *Three Musicians* (1921), by Pablo Picasso

What Was New in Stravinsky's Music?

Unprepared for what they heard, the audience was disturbed. What was this music that reached out and assaulted them? Unfamiliar with Stravinsky's new musical language, many listeners felt lost and alienated.

Even today, some people are unable to accept *The Rite*'s dissonance and "modern" techniques. Curiously, audiences seem to not mind similar dissonances and modern techniques that effectively establish a mood in films or television. Hollywood film and television composers owe a great deal to Stravinsky.

MUSICAL DOUBLE EXPOSURE   In *The Rite of Spring* and many of his other works, Stravinsky often superimposes two or more coherent ideas on each other, resulting in an entirely new idea. A double exposure in photography is the closest illustration. For instance, suppose you take a front-view snapshot of your friend. Without your knowing it, the film does not advance. Then, you snap a side-view picture. In the developed film, you see a novel effect. Although you can still recognize your friend, he or she looks different—because front and side views have been superimposed.

Stravinsky used musical double exposure through many elements:

POLYRHYTHMS.   Two or more contrasting rhythms sounded simultane-   **Polyrhythms**
ously produce polyrhythms. Even if you cannot read music, you can still
see that in the duration of each beat there are several different rhythmic
patterns. On the first beat: 2-note pattern, 6-note pattern, 4-note pattern,
and 7-note pattern. On the second beat: 4-note pattern, 6-note pattern, and
5-note pattern.

POLYMETERS.   These occur when two or more contrasting meters are   **Polymeters**
sounded simultaneously. In the following example, the upper part is in four
meter plus five meter, while the lower part is in nine meter with three
groups of three eighth notes.

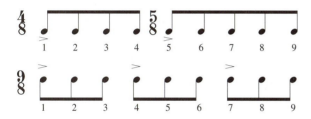

The Rite of Spring

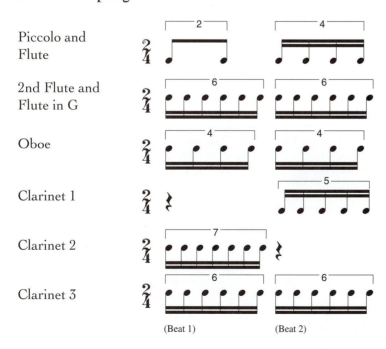

POLYCHORDS.   Two or more triads performed simultaneously, producing a   **Polychords**
novel harmony.

This is a polychord.

Polytonality

POLYTONALITY.   A section of music with parts simultaneously residing in different keys produces polytonality.

Here is the opening of Mozart's Sonata in C Major in its original form. Both upper and lower parts are in C major:

A twentieth-century treatment of the same section of the Mozart Sonata follows. This time, the upper part is in C major and the lower is in F-sharp major, producing polytonality:

Martha Graham Company dancing *The Rite of Spring,* 1984.

OTHER STRAVINSKY INNOVATIONS For centuries, music had predictable, recurring rhythm patterns—meters: for example, the three pattern of the waltz, minuet, and mazurka and the two and four patterns of the march. But does music need predictable rhythmic patterns? Stravinsky and other twentieth-century composers began employing irregular metrical patterns in their music.

CHANGING METRICAL PATTERNS. A section from *The Rite of Spring,* "Dances of Youth and Maidens," which uses constantly changing metrical patterns, follows. The patterns are difficult to predict. Imagine how difficult they are to dance to.

Changing metrical patterns

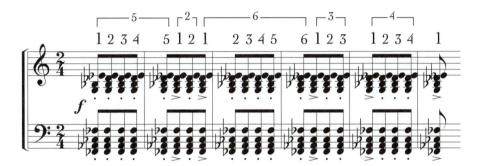

OSTINATO. Inspired by the complex rhythms of African music, Stravinsky employs recurring patterns of rhythmic and melodic ideas—an *ostinato.* Fascinated by the rhythmic energy and drive of the ostinato rhythms, he used them in his ballet music.

Ostinato

LISTENING ACTIVITY

THE RITE OF SPRING, IGOR STRAVINSKY
"SACRIFICIAL DANCE" FROM *PART II: THE SACRIFICE*

Large Form: Dance Movement from a Ballet
Detailed Form: Complex Rondo or Sectional Form
Performing Medium: Large Symphony Orchestra

Compact Disc 2, Track 33
Cassette Tape: Side D, Example 2
Running Time: 4:33

Subtitled "Scenes from Pagan Russia," the ballet presents a series of primitive scenes built around the spring fertility rites of ancient

Russia. Listen to this recording of the final section, "The Sacrificial Dance," to gain a greater understanding of this important work. Later, listen to a complete recording.

PART I: THE ADORATION OF THE EARTH

1. *Introduction: The Birth of Spring.* A group of girls is seated before the sacred mound. Each is holding a long garland. The tribal Sage appears and leads them toward the mound.

2. *Omens of Spring: Dances of the Youths and Maidens.* Youths and maidens dance around the mound in celebration of spring.

3. *Dance of Abduction.* In this frenzied ritual, one of the maidens is abducted and carried off.

4. *Spring Rounds.* Four couples remain. Each man lifts a girl on his back and, in a solemn procession, they begin making the Rounds of Spring.

5. *Games of the Rival Tribes.* Young warriors from the rival tribes display their prowess. The Sage pushes his way through the crowd.

6. *Entrance of the Sage.* The village Sage enters and assumes direction of the proceedings.

7. *Adoration of the Earth.* The dancers prostrate themselves in adoration of the mystical powers of the Earth.

8. *Dance of the Earth.* An exuberant dance in praise of the Earth's fertility.

PART II: THE SACRIFICE

1. *Introduction: Pagan Night.* The Sage and the girls sit motionless around the fire in front of the sacred mound. They will choose a girl to be sacrificed to ensure the earth's fertility.

2. *Mystic Circles of the Adolescents.* The girls dance the mystic circles until one stands, suddenly transfixed as she realizes that she is the Chosen One.

3. *Dance to the Glorified One.* In honor of the sacrificial victim, all dance vigorously, building into a frenzied climax.

4. *Evocation of the Ancestors.* Strong rhythmic dances invoke the blessings of the ancestors.

5. *Ritual Performance of the Ancestors.* Village elders perform a shuffling, swaying dance, to undulating and pulsating rhythmic patterns.

6. *Sacrificial Dance.* The Chosen One begins a frenzied dance and continues until she collapses and dies. The men carry her body

to the foot of the sacred mound as an offering to the gods of fertility.

As you listen to "Sacrificial Dance," many of Stravinsky's innovative techniques will become obvious; others may be more difficult to perceive upon your first hearing:

- polychords
- polytonality
- polyrhythms
- polymeters
- changing metrical patterns
- ostinato with driving rhythms

The complex form with many sections most closely resembles a rondo. Notice how the first motive keeps returning, which is the basic plan of the rondo. Repetitions of the first theme are modified. Several rhythm patterns are introduced, most as ostinatos.

Motive 1 (A)	Rhythmic Pattern 1	Motive 2 (B)	Rhythmic Pattern 1	Motive 2 (B)	Rhythmic Pattern 2	Ostinato Pattern	Motive 2 (B)
Ostinato Pattern	Transition	Motive 1 (A)	Rhythmic Pattern 3	Motive 3 (C)	Motive 1 (A)	Motive 3 (C)	Motive 1 (A)

LISTENING GUIDE

THE RITE OF SPRING, IGOR STRAVINSKY
"SACRIFICIAL DANCE" FROM PART II: THE SACRIFICE

| 33 | 0:00 | MOTIVE 1 | After a dissonant chord by the string section, the orchestra plays the rhythmic-melodic motive, *f;* polychords; fast tempo, unpredictable, changing meters and rhythmic patterns; ostinatos |

Violins

| | 0:29 | RHYTHM PATTERN 1 | introduction to motive 2, played mainly by strings and horns, suddenly *p;* less dissonant polychords; ostinato with changing meters |

0:41	MOTIVE 2	introduced by muted trombones, *f;* imitated by muted trumpets several times, and then by horns, while strings and horns continue ostinato

Trombones

0:52	RHYTHM PATTERN 1	in lower strings and horns, *p;* then *f;* ostinato with changing meters
1:04	MOTIVE 2	played by muted trumpet and piccolos, *f;* imitated by horns
1:19	RHYTHM PATTERN 2	full orchestra, *ff;* ostinato with changing meters, polychords
1:31	OSTINATO PATTERN	played by lower strings and horns, *p*
1:38	MOTIVE 2 OSTINATO PATTERN	played by muted trombones, alternating imitations with trumpets, *f;* while ostinato pattern 1 is played by strings and horns softly
1:47	TRANSITION SECTION	played by full orchestra, *f;* strings and flutes have fast running patterns of 5 notes to a beat, section ends with a loud chord, then short pause.
1:56	MOTIVE 1	returns, similar to opening section, *f;* repeats several times, polychords, changing meters
2:24	RHYTHM PATTERN 3	polyrhythms, triplet patterns played by timpani, duple patterns played by lower strings, changing meters, loud trombone glissandos
2:33	MOTIVE 3	played by horns, then horns and strings, changing meters

Horns

2:46	MOTIVE 3	played by trumpets and strings, ostinato rhythm in duple meter, polychords, crescendo to *ff;* then short pause
3:01	MOTIVE 1	returns, similar to beginning section, *f;* changing meters, short pause
3:12	MOTIVE 3	played by brass, then overlapping imitations throughout the orchestra, mostly duple meter, ostinato
3:32	MOTIVE 1	played by low strings, *f* then *ff;* changing meters, polychords, changing ostinato patterns, then gradual crescendo to loud chord
4:29	FINAL CHORD	flute upward run to piccolo and high strings to a loud final chord emphasized by low strings and drums

Challenge Your Expertise

Which non-European culture was the main influence on Stravinsky's use of ostinato?

LISTENING INSIGHTS

How to Listen to Twentieth-Century Music

Twentieth-century music often uses new musical language. Be patient upon your first hearing. Once you get used to the sound, you will discover the composer's intentions. Then you can begin to form a more educated opinion about this "different" music and find a place for it among your personal values.

Summary of Terms

Ballets Russes	irregular metrical	polymeters
changing metrical	patterns	polyrhythm
patterns	objectivism	polytonality
cubism	ostinato	
double exposure	polychords	

Chapter 21

Expressionism: Atonal Music

The term *Expressionism* is used to describe music, painting, and poetry developed in Vienna during the early decades of the twentieth century. The movement began as a rejection of *Impressionism*, which focused on the "outer" world. Expressionism, in contrast, centered on the "inner" world described in the writings of Sigmund Freud (1865–1939).

In music, Arnold Schoenberg led the Expressionistic movement. His colleagues, Anton Webern and Alban Berg, followed. Some of the painters associated with Expressionism include Pablo Picasso (1881–1973), Wassily Kandinsky (1866–1944), and Paul Klee (1879–1944).

End of Tonality?

In use since the 1600s, the major-minor tonal system of Western music had been bent and stretched by many composers, especially Wagner and Debussy. In 1908, it snapped. A young Viennese composer, Arnold Schoenberg, pushed tonality beyond its former limits. Disciples gathered, establishing a major movement still alive today: *atonality*.

Arnold Schoenberg (1874–1951)

Arnold Schoenberg (*shurn*-behrg) grew up in his native Vienna at the same time Brahms, Mahler, and Richard Strauss were working there. By age eight he was studying violin and soon began composing his own string chamber music—an interest that continued throughout his life.

Just after Schoenberg completed his schooling, his father died, leaving the family poor. Needing to support himself, young Arnold had to forsake his musical interests in order to earn a living in a Viennese bank.

Mostly self-taught as a composer, Schoenberg continued composing and performing in chamber music groups in his spare time. It was not until he took a position as music director for a Berlin cabaret that he was able to make his entire income as a professional musician. Finally, he returned to Vienna to teach and compose, interrupted by World War I, when he had to serve in the Austrian army.

Between 1918 and 1923 he formulated his twelve-tone method, which he used throughout most of his remaining compositions. In 1925, he was appointed professor of composition at the Berlin Academy of Arts.

Because he was Jewish, Schoenberg had to flee to the United States from Germany when Adolf Hitler seized power. Settling in southern California, Schoenberg attained citizenship and taught at both the University of Southern California and the University of California at Los Angeles. He died at the age of 77.

PRINCIPAL WORKS

Orchestral Music: *Verklärte Nacht* (Transfigured Night, 1917); *Pelleas und Melisande* (1903); Five Pieces for Orchestra (1909); Variations (1928); Violin Concerto (1936); Piano Concerto (1942); two chamber symphonies

Chamber Music: four string quartets, one string trio, one wind quintet, Octet (1922)

Operas: *Erwartung* (Expectation, 1909); *Die glückliche Hand* (The Fortunate Hand, 1913), *Von Heute auf Morgen* (From Today to Tomorrow, 1930), *Moses und Aron* (1932)

Choral Music: *Gurrelieder* (1911); *A Survivor from Warsaw* (1947)

Vocal Music: *The Book of the Hanging Gardens* (1909); *Pierrot lunaire* (1912); cabaret songs

Piano Music: Three Piano Pieces, Op. 11 (1909); Six Little Pieces, Op. 19 (1911); Five Piano Pieces, Op. 23 (1920); Suite (1923)

In Street, Berlin (1913), painted by Ernst Ludwig Kirchner

ATONALITY

Atonal, or nontonal, music contains pitches, but melodies and harmonies are carefully constructed to avoid creating tonal centers, or home keys.

Early Atonal Experiments

Strongly influenced in his youth by Brahms, Wagner, Strauss, and Mahler, Schoenberg composed his earlier works with roots in late-nineteenth-century Viennese romanticism. New directions and experiments in music always interested him, and he often discussed his ideas with his friend Gustav Mahler.

Schoenberg concluded that because music had been gradually moving away from tonality throughout the nineteenth century, he would take that idea to its logical destination: atonality. Experimenters such as Wagner, Strauss, Debussy, and Stravinsky had approached the threshold; Schoenberg made a quantum leap, and from 1908 on, many of his works are atonal.

Once he had crossed over, his Viennese colleagues followed. Throughout the twentieth century, other composers saw atonality as a progressive avenue of self-expression.

Schoenberg's Twelve-Tone System

Atonal music was an inevitable development, and Schoenberg, Webern, and Berg became absorbed by it. Even Stravinsky admired the orderly procedures and intellectual nature of Schoenberg's atonal music, and he spent some time later in life composing twelve-tone music.

By 1923, Schoenberg had formulated a theoretical system for composing atonal music that would ensure both its unique status and its departure from traditional tonal music. His system is known variously as the *serial, twelve-tone,* or *dodecaphonic* method.

Dodecaphonic music

Tone-row

The twelve-tone method is highly disciplined. At its core is an ordered set, or *tone-row*, of the twelve different tones of the chromatic scale. Because Western music has only twelve different tones within an octave, each tone-row uses all of them. Only their order is different.

Looking at a model of the keyboard. You'll notice that there are only twelve tones within an octave (See Appendix B). Using tones or pitches from a higher or a lower octave does not change the *names* of the pitches or the *order* of the row—only the *register* of the pitches.

TRANSPOSED ROWS　Keeping the series intact, entire rows and their treatments also can be transposed to higher and lower pitches, and each row will retain its integrity. This is true as well for traditional melodies and harmonies. moving a melody to a different key (higher or lower) does not change our recognition of that melody or harmony.

ENSURING ATONALITY　In Schoenberg's method, tones of the row are rarely repeated until all have been sounded, which helps ensure atonality. With all pitches having equal importance, there can be no suggestion of a tonal center around any one pitch. Repeating pitches often tends to force a tonal center.

ATONAL HARMONY   Rows can provide a source of harmony as well. Taking three or four tones from any portion of the sample tone row, we can sound them simultaneously to produce chords.

Tone Row and Chords from Schoenberg's Suite for Piano, Op. 25, First Movement

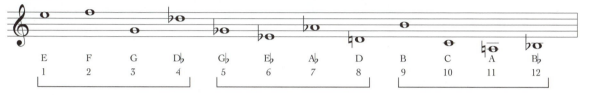

E	F	G	D♭	G♭	E♭	A♭	D	B	C	A	B♭
1	2	3	4	5	6	7	8	9	10	11	12

Although the resulting chords are dissonant, usually they are compatible with the atonal nature of the row. Since it adheres to strict principles, twelve-tone music tends to be short and concise. Webern's *Symphony*, Op. 21 (1928) lasts only ten minutes, in contrast to Gustav Mahler's Third Symphony (1896), which lasts about one hour and twenty minutes.

LISTENING INSIGHTS

How to Listen to Twelve-Tone Music

Twelve-tone-row, atonal music sounds different from most other music. For the listener, melodies often seem fragmented and difficult to follow. Unfamiliar harmonies usually are dissonant, and it is easy for a listener to feel lost.

Schoenberg and his colleagues did not expect listeners to follow the row completely through all of its transformations. Most musicians have difficulty doing this. Instead, they felt that the tone-row provided an integral infrastructure for the work that may not always be apparent in the listening.

To get the most out of the music, you have to remain totally attentive, focusing especially on the opening section. Here is where the tone-row is revealed, usually in its basic form before it undergoes transformation. This is similar to traditional forms, such as the theme and variations or rondo, which state the theme at the beginning. Though a challenge, memorizing the tone-row, or as many of the intervals as possible, will help you recognize it through its transformations.

Challenge Your Expertise

After the premiere of which ballet did a Paris theater need repair?

LISTENING ACTIVITY

SUITE FOR PIANO (1923, OP. 25), ARNOLD SCHOENBERG
FIRST MOVEMENT: RASCH (QUICK)

Large Form: Suite
Detailed Form: Highly Complex Theme and Variations
Performing Medium: Piano

Compact Disc 3, Track 5
Cassette Tape: Side D, Example 4
Running Time: 0:51

Listen to the "Praeludium" from Schoenberg's *Suite for Piano,* Op. 25. The piece starts with the entire tone-row in its original form in the upper register of the piano. After only two of the row's tones are sounded, the bass register begins an imitation using a different rhythm. Following that, the row is manipulated and transformed using retrograde, inversions, retrograde-inversions, transpositions, and harmony.

Original Form of Tone Row

Anton Webern (1883–1945)

Like his colleagues from Vienna—Schoenberg and Berg—Anton Webern (*vay*-bern) studied music there: cello, piano, and music theory. At age eighteen, after attending the Wagner Festival in Bayreuth, Webern decided to become a serious composer and musicologist.

He studied musicology at the University of Vienna and composition for two years privately with Arnold Schoenberg. To earn a living, Webern began a conducting career in 1908, working with orchestras throughout Austria.

Following his obligatory service in the Austrian army during World War I, Webern lived near Schoenberg in Vienna, turning his efforts mainly toward teaching music and composing. Using Schoenberg's twelve-tone system and experimenting with works of extreme brevity, Webern's post–war compositions became more atonal and dissonant.

In 1927, Webern was appointed conductor and adviser for Radio Austria, where he remained until the Nazi takeover in 1938. Although he differed politically with the Nazis, Webern chose to remain in Vienna throughout World War II, losing his son in battle and his home to bombs. In September 1945, only months after the war ended in Europe, Webern was mistakenly shot and killed by an American occupation soldier.

PRINCIPAL WORKS

Orchestral Music: Six Pieces for Orchestra, Op. 6 (1909); Five Pieces for Orchestra, Op. 10 (1913); Symphony, Op. 21 (1928); Variations, Op. 30 (1940)

Chamber Music: Five Movements for String Quartet (1909); Six Bagatelles for String Quartet (1913); Four Pieces for Violin and Piano, Op. 7 (1910); Quartet for Violin, Clarinet, Tenor Saxophone, and Piano, Op. 22 (1928); three string quartets

Piano Music: Variations, Op. 27 (1936)

Vocal Music: *Das Augenlicht* (Eyesight, 1935), three cantatas, several songs

Alban Berg (1885–1935)

Alban Berg (*behrg*) was born into a financially comfortable Viennese family. Although he had no training in composition as a teenager, Berg wrote many songs. After graduating from school, he took a position in Vienna as a government accountant.

A newspaper advertisement caught Berg's attention when he was nineteen: Arnold Schoenberg was inviting composers to study with him. Berg, financially secure, responded to the ad and studied with Schoenberg for the next seven years.

During World War I, Berg spent more than three years in the Austrian army. After the war, he composed one of the twentieth century's most interesting operas, *Wozzeck* (*vo*-tseck). Mostly atonal, the work captured the torment and anxiety of the common man caught in the societal and psychological upheavals between the two World Wars.

A year after *Wozzeck,* Berg wrote his *Lyric Suite* for string quartet, using a musical language that was gentler, though still atonal. He began his next opera, *Lulu,* in 1928. The main character, Lulu, is another victim of a decaying society. After shooting her wealthy husband, she is sentenced to years of degrading experiences in prison. Once released, she becomes a prostitute, murdered at the end of the opera by Jack the Ripper.

Berg's chronic ill health restricted his composing output. At 50, when he died in Vienna, he left *Lulu* not quite finished.

PRINCIPAL WORKS

Orchestral Music: Chamber Concerto (1925), Violin Concerto (1935)

Chamber Music: String Quartet (1910), *Lyric Suite* (1926)

Operas: *Wozzeck* (1925), *Lulu* (1934)

Songs: more than seventy-five songs, *Altenberg Songs* (with orchestra, 1912)

Piano Music: Sonata (1908)

Summary of Terms

atonal	Expressionism	tone-row
atonal harmony	major-minor tonality	transposed rows
atonal music	nontonal	twelve-tone method
atonality	serial music	twelve-tone music
dodecaphonic music	tonal center	twelve-tone row

Neoclassicism:
Mainstream Music

BEGINNINGS OF NEOCLASSICISM

In spite of the influence of *The Rite of Spring* (1913) on his colleagues,
Stravinsky retreated from that musical language. Perhaps it was the
public uproar at the ballet's premiere. Was the audience offended by
the pagan subject matter? Did it object to his creative choices?
Stravinsky was a working composer who had a family to support. If
the audience is not ready for musical innovations, a pragmatic composer gives them something more familiar, something that communicates an idea.

As Stravinsky contemplated his next direction, Diaghilev commissioned him in 1917 to write *The Story of a Soldier* (*L'histoire du soldat*) for the Ballets Russes. It was during World War I. With players
in the armed services, orchestras were in shambles. So Stravinsky
turned to leaner, eighteenth-century techniques and wisely scored
the music for a chamber ensemble of seven musicians. Taking his
inspiration from the Baroque and Classical periods, he integrated
the forms, idioms, and instrumental sounds of those times with his
personal compositional techniques. The result was *neoclassicism.*

289

An Approach, Not a Style Period

Generalizing about neoclassical music is difficult, because it is neither a style nor a style period. Rather, it is a creative approach to producing new and fresh music by adopting resources from former musical style periods. Composers integrated mostly tonal, prominent melodies with twentieth-century compositional techniques.

Stravinsky began using techniques from early style periods, such as the Medieval and Baroque. His ballet *Pulcinella* (1920) was based on the music of the Baroque composer Pergolesi. With his Octet (1922), Stravinsky's shift to neoclassicism was complete. By broadening the concept of neoclassicism, composers were free to incorporate techniques from any previous style period—or several style periods—within a piece.

Neoclassicism in Russia

The same year that Stravinsky was composing *The Story of a Soldier* (1917), Prokofiev had already reached the same conclusion about neoclassicism: Audiences would be more willing to accept modern techniques as long as the musical language was familiar.

HISTORICAL PERSPECTIVE

Neoclassical Approaches

When discussing and listening to these works, it is not necessary to label them Neo-Baroque if they use Baroque-period techniques, or Neo-Renaissance if they use Renaissance styles. *Neoclassical* will do.

Sergei Prokofiev (1891–1953)

Born in the Ukraine in southern Russia, Sergei Prokofiev (proh-*kohf*-yef) studied piano with his mother, who also encouraged him to compose at an early age. By age nine he had written a three-act opera. After the family moved to Moscow, his parents sent him to the Conservatory in St. Petersburg, where he studied composition with Rimsky-Korsakov.

When the turmoil of the Russian Revolution became intolerable, Prokofiev followed Diaghilev and Stravinsky to Paris. He was taken into the Russian expatriate community, which included members of the Ballets Russes. Prokofiev used Paris as his home base while traveling through post–World War I Europe and the United States.

When he decided to return to Russia in 1933, Prokofiev was greeted warmly by both the public and the government. But he soon found himself in trouble with the Stalin Regime: they accused him of writing music that was "too formalistic, too technically complicated and alien to the Soviet people." The Party Central Committee constantly pressured Prokofiev to publicly apologize for his "transgressions." Though he tried to shrug off these attacks, the stress finally affected his health. Ironically, both Joseph Stalin, his tormentor, and Prokofiev died of brain hemorrhages on the same day.

PRINCIPAL WORKS

Orchestral Music: Symphonies: No. 1 (*Classical*, 1917); No. 2 (1925); No. 3 (1928); No. 4 (1940); No. 5 (1944); No. 6 (1947); No. 7 (1952): *Peter and the Wolf* (1936); *Lieutenant Kijé Suite* (1934) from the film score; five piano concertos, two violin concertos, and a cello concerto

Chamber Music: string quartets; Flute Sonata; Violin Sonata; Cello Sonata

Piano Music: Mostly sonatas

Operas: *The Love for Three Oranges* (1921); *The Fiery Angel* (1928); *The Gambler* (1929); *War and Peace* (1944)

Ballets: *The Prodigal Son* (1929); *Romeo and Juliet* (1938); *Cinderella* (1945)

Choral Music: *Alexander Nevsky* (1939) for chorus and orchestra—from the film score

LISTENING ACTIVITY

SYMPHONY NO. 1 (CLASSICAL SYMPHONY, 1917),
SERGEI PROKOFIEV

First Movement: Allegro
Large Form: Symphony
Detailed Form: Sonata-Allegro
Performing Medium: Chamber or Symphony Orchestra

Compact Disc 3 Track 6
Cassette Tape: Side D, Example 5
Running Time: 3:37

Prokofiev composed his *Symphony No. 1* (*Classical* Symphony) during the period 1916–1917 as a modern work using Classical-period compositional techniques. Scored for an orchestra similar to Haydn's,

Prokofiev's four-movement symphony follows the typical late-eighteenth-century large form:

First Movement:	*Allegro* (fast, sonata form)
Second Movement:	*Larghetto* (moderately, slow rondo form)
Third Movement:	*Gavotte* (moderate dance in duple meter, song form and trio—similar to minuet and trio)
Fourth Movement:	*Allegro* (fast, sonata form)

Prokofiev's *Classical* Symphony is quite similar in style to most of Haydn's symphonies. In comparing the two composers' use of orchestral instruments, however, notice that Prokofiev utilizes the capabilities of modern, technically improved instruments; for example, violinists are required to play extremely high on their fingerboards (THEME 2). Woodwinds and brass also have parts that are considerably more demanding than those written in Haydn's day. Also, many of the melodies contain large leaps, requiring highly skilled performers.

LISTENING GUIDE

SYMPHONY NO. 1 (CLASSICAL SYMPHONY, 1917),
SERGEI PROKOFIEV

EXPOSITION

6   0:00   THEME 1   played by the strings and woodwinds, quickly changing dynamics, *ff; p*, crescendo, *ff; p*, key of D major, duple meter; homophonic texture

| 0:11 | THEME 1 | repeats played only by the strings and in the key of C major |
| 0:19 | TRANSITION THEME | played by flute, *p;* imitated by oboe and clarinet, *p;* then by bassoon, *p* |

| 7 | 0:46 | THEME 2 | played by first violins in dominant key, *pp;* light arpeggio accompaniment played by bassoon, theme repeated several times, then *ff;* cadence to pause (exposition is not repeated) |

Development

| 1:29 | | all three themes are used throughout the development, through a series of tonal modulations |

Recapitulation

2:26	THEME 1	played by violins, *p;* in C major (not D major)
2:35	TRANSITION THEME	played by flute in the exposition original key of D major, *p;* imitated by oboes, then viola, cellos
2:56	THEME 2	played by violins, *ff;* in D major

Coda

| 3:20 | | full orchestra, *ff;* cadence to final chord in D major |

Dimitri Shostakovich (1906–1975)

Like many other composers, Dimitri Shostakovich (shos-tah-*koh*-vich) received his earliest piano training from his mother, an accomplished pianist. At age thirteen, Shostakovich entered the Conservatory in his native St. Petersburg, focusing his studies on composition. By age 19, he had completed his first symphony. Over his lifetime, he composed fifteen symphonies and a considerable legacy of various types of music.

Communist bureaucrats in control of the arts continually assailed Shostakovich's music as "too formalistic," "too self-serving," "chaotic," "coarse and primitive," and "not subservient to the Soviet State."

To continue composing, Shostakovich, like Prokofiev, often had to sign humiliating, phony apologies. Addressing his public, he promised to do better in the future. After withstanding many years of harassment by the Stalinist bureaucrats, Shostakovich died at age 69.

PRINCIPAL WORKS

Orchestral Music: fifteen symphonies (1925–1966); piano concertos, violin concertos, cello concertos; *Festival Overture* (1954); Suite from *The Age of Gold* (1929)

Chamber Music: fifteen string quartets; Piano Quintet (1940); two piano trios

Piano Music: two sonatas; twenty-four Preludes (1933); twenty-four Preludes and Fugues (1951)

Operas: *The Nose* (1930); *Katerina Izmaylova* (1963)

Ballets: *The Age of Gold* (1929)

OTHER RUSSIAN NEOCLASSICAL COMPOSERS   A group outlook on modern composition emerged from Russia. Working independently, other composers concurred with the idea of expanded neoclassicism and incorporated techniques from previous style periods, including the recent Romantic era.

In addition to Prokofiev, the composers working in this genre include *Sergei Rachmaninov* (*1872–1943* see biography in Chapter 17), *Dimitri Shostakovich* (see biography in this chapter), *Dmitri Kabalevsky* (*1904–1987*), and *Aram Khachaturian* (*1903–1978*).

MOVING BACK TO THE MAINSTREAM

Viewed broadly, neoclassicism can be seen as an attempt to move back to mainstream music. According to mainstream composers, lack of communication with audiences runs contrary to the role of music—the tradition of

Bach, Haydn, Beethoven, Schumann, and Brahms. However interesting atonal experimental music may be to the knowledgeable musician, most audiences seem to prefer tonal music. Composers need audiences who appreciate them. Without them, there is only an empty hall.

To pigeonhole the diverse lot of twentieth-century mainstream composers into rigid categories would be misleading. Despite their differences, however, they shared a common goal: to express their musical individuality in a way audiences could understand.

United Kingdom

For a country that produced many of the greatest performers, presented some of the finest concerts, and nurtured many outstanding composers from other countries, England boasted few prominent composers until the twentieth century. Since then, a notably prolific group of English composers has surfaced.

Vaughan Williams

EDWARD ELGAR (1858–1935)   Active as a performer and composer in the latter part of the nineteenth century, Elgar wrote his most popular works beginning in the 1890s and into the twentieth century: the "Serenade for Strings" (1892), *Enigma Variations* (1899), and the "Cello Concerto" (1919). Perhaps Elgar is best known for his *Pomp and Circumstance* Marches (1901–1930), widely identified with school commencement exercises.

RALPH VAUGHAN WILLIAMS (1872–1958)   Following his interest in English folk music, Vaughan Williams composed *Fantasia on "Greensleeves"* (1934) and *English Folk Song Suite* (1923). His nine symphonies, especially *A Sea Symphony* (No. 1, 1910) and the popular *London Symphony* (No. 2, 1914), demonstrate his considerable talent for orchestration and the influence of his studies in Paris with Maurice Ravel. Vaughan Williams also wrote a sizable collection of choral music for the Church of England.

GUSTAV HOLST (1874–1934)   A contemporary and close friend of Vaughan Williams, Holst also incorporated English folk songs (Suites 1 and 2 for band) in his music. The influence of Hindu mysticism is evident in his *Choral Hymns from the Rig-Veda* (1912). Brilliantly scored for orchestra, his best-known work is *The Planets* (1914–1916).

Benjamin Britten (center)

WILLIAM WALTON (1902–1983)   Walton composed a wide variety of works: symphonies, concertos, chamber music, ballet, and even ceremonial music for coronations (*Crown Imperial*, 1937, and *Orb and Sceptre*, 1953).

BENJAMIN BRITTEN (1913–1976)   Britten was the most prolific and most famous English composer of the mid-twentieth century. His outstanding works include *A Ceremony of Carols* (1942, for choir), *Spring Symphony* (1947, for vocal soloists and chorus), and *War Requiem* (1962). Britten is one of the most important contributors to twentieth-century opera, most notably with *Peter Grimes* and *Billy Budd*. His composition *The Young Person's*

Guide to the Orchestra is often used to introduce newcomers to orchestral instruments. (Compact Disc 4, Tracks 23–44)

PERCY GRAINGER (1882–1961)   Best known for his tune "In An English Country Garden," the brilliant, eccentric Grainger was born in Australia, educated in England, and lived in the United States most of his life. His early influences were little known British folk songs, which he discovered while roaming the countryside with music pad and portable recorder.

During World War II, he was an arranger in the United States Coast Guard Band, using many of his folk song discoveries in compositions for band, for example, *Irish Tune from County Derry, Shepherd's Hey,* and *Lincolnshire Posy.*

Challenge Your Expertise

Name two composers who were forced by their government to make public apologies.

Spotlight: Outstanding Artist-Teacher
Nadia Boulanger (1887–1979)

The influence of some musicians extends far beyond their personal triumphs as composers, performers, and conductors. Such distinction belongs to Nadia Boulanger (boo-lahn-*zhay*).

Few artist-teachers have earned such high esteem, not only for their knowledge of music but also for their ability to transmit their knowledge. Despite her reputation for being austere and authoritarian, Boulanger had a sincerity and warmth of spirit that opened up the universe of music to the countless young people who sought her tutelage.

Many details of her life will remain secret until 2009, when documents entrusted to the Bibliothèque Nationale (National Library) become accessible. However, here are some of the highlights currently public.

Nadia's father, the pianist and composer Ernest Boulanger, supervised her first musical studies before she was eight years old. The following year, he enrolled her in a sight-reading/singing (solfège) class at the Paris Conservatoire (Conservatory) and hired a teacher to instruct her in organ and composition. Nine-year-old Nadia revealed a dedication and diligence unusual for a child her age. In 1897, she received First Prize in solfège.

After her husband's death in 1900, Madame Boulanger accelerated the pace of Nadia's studies. In 1901, she was in Gabriel Fauré's class in composition, that year winning Second Prize in harmony. Two years later, Nadia won First Prize in harmony, and the following year, 1904, she received First Prizes in organ, piano accompaniment, fugue, and composition. Also in 1904, Nadia became a paid musician.

By 1905, Nadia had established her career as a performer, composer, and teacher, gaining an excellent reputation for her group lessons. Then-prominent pianist Raoul Pugno and her former teachers at the Conservatory sent pupils to her. Through Pugno's recommendation, Nadia acquired her first American students, who helped her learn English.

Having Pugno as her champion significantly boosted Boulanger's career, but even his prestige was not enough to help her prevail over the sensitive politics of the French music world. Some attributed her losing the First Grand Prize of the 1908 Prix de Rome to her youth and to her sex—she was the only woman among the finalists. Others suggest that it was due to her offending one of the judges, Camille Saint-Saëns. Having ruffled his plumage, she settled for second place. However, in 1913, Boulanger did become the first woman to win the Prix de Rome's First Grand Prize.

Her youth and sex also deprived her of an appointment to the Paris Conservatory in 1910. It took thirty-five years until she became a duly appointed faculty member.

Nadia's friendship with Walter Damrosch, head of the New York Philharmonic, began in 1918. Damrosch, who had founded American Friends of Musicians in France, had come to Paris to conduct a benefit concert. Nadia performed as organist for the Third Symphony by Saint-Saëns, with whom she had finally reconciled.

After World War I, Damrosch continued his philanthropic activities in France, donating and raising substantial funds to establish several music schools. One such school, for American musicians who wanted to spend summers studying in France, opened in June 1921 in Fontainebleau Castle. With her enthusiasm and innovative techniques, Nadia revolutionized instruction in harmony.

Nadia had begun trying out her teaching concepts two years earlier in her classes in organ, harmony, and counterpoint at *École Normale de musique*. In January 1920, Nadia wrote: "My goal is to awaken my students' curiosity and then to show them how to satisfy that curiosity." So popular were her classes that enrollment was soon limited.

Aaron Copland was among the first students at Fontainebleau. The twenty-year-old Copland had enrolled in another teacher's composition class, but out of curiosity he sat in on one of Boulanger's classes. He never missed another one, hesitantly asking her for private lessons. "No composer has ever had a woman teacher. It was not Nadia Boulanger I was worried about—it was my reputation!" said Copland.

Yet he stayed on with her for three years. In return, she introduced him to important contacts, such as the newly appointed conductor of the Boston Symphony, Russian-born Serge Koussevitzky, with whom Nadia had been working closely at the time.

Nadia's personal magnetism played a great part in the success of the school at Fontainebleau, which attracted several generations of young Americans. In ever greater numbers they came to France to work with her at the school, followed by extended stays in Paris. For nearly fifty years, interrupted only by World War II, Boulanger's Paris apartment at 36 rue Ballu became a gathering place for these young musicians.

In January 1938, Nadia sailed for America. She was scheduled for forty concerts and sixty lectures and classes. From the moment she landed in New York, she was treated like a star. A high point of that tour was on February 19. Thanks to her friend Koussevitzky, Nadia became the first woman to conduct the Boston Symphony.

The following year—February 1939—Nadia was the first woman to conduct the New York Philharmonic in a sold-out performance at Carnegie Hall. The New York *Herald Tribune* music critic wrote: "One can already say of her, in the full maturity of her career, that she has enriched her time."

That same year Boulanger also conducted the Philadelphia Orchestra, after which the press noted: "The prejudice against women conductors, which lurks in the bosom of every orchestra player, breaks down instantly when one comes in contact with Mlle. Boulanger's masterful touch." Boulanger's response: "Let's forget that I'm a woman. Let's talk about music."

Fontainebleau was hastily closed at the end of August 1939. When the Nazis invaded France, Nadia requested and received a contract from the Longy School of Music in Boston in order to obtain an exit visa from France. In addition to teaching at Longy, Nadia resumed her activities as a lecturer, conductor, and soloist, mostly in New England. In 1942, she also accepted an offer from the Peabody Conservatory in Baltimore, commuting there once a week from Boston to give classes.

After the war, she came home to her beloved France. Although much of the country was rubble, her rue Ballu apartment was intact. By the summer of 1946, her life had resumed just about where it had left off, including her classes at the reopened Fontainebleau School. She also accepted an appointment to the Paris Conservatory.

In 1953, Nadia Boulanger became the undisputed head of the Fontainebleau School, where she remained for twenty-six summers. Although compulsory retirement ended her classes at the Conservatory upon her seventieth birthday in 1957, she remained engaged in diverse activities, traveling widely until her ninetieth year. However, with her health and eyesight failing in 1976, she was no longer able to give lessons.

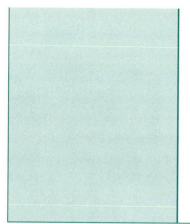

In 1977, the president of France made her a Grand Officer of the Legion of Honor, a distinction that was extremely rare for women. It was just one of the many honors bestowed upon her, including the Order of the British Empire, the Gold Medal of the Beaux-Arts Academy, and the Medal of the City of Paris.

On Nadia's 92nd birthday, Leonard Bernstein visited her in Paris. In a flash of lucidity, she recognized him, heard what he said, spoke a few words, and clung to him. He was one of the last to see her. A few weeks later, in the early hours of October 22, 1979, Nadia Boulanger died in her rue Ballu apartment.

France

ERIK SATIE *(sah-tee, 1866–1925)*   A unique composer, Satie is famous for giving intriguing, surrealistic titles to his works: *Three Pieces in the Form of a Pear, Three Flabby Preludes for a Dog,* and *Jack in the Box.*

Satie was strongly opposed to Impressionism, which had become the popular music style in his country. His clever, antisentimental music influenced many younger French composers: Honegger, Milhaud, and Poulenc.

ARTHUR HONEGGER *(ohn-ne-gehr, 1892–1955)*   Perhaps Honegger's best-known work is the oratorio *King David,* written for amateur choruses. He wrote *Joan of Arc at the Stake* for children's chorus and large orchestra. One of his most intriguing works is *Pacific 231* (1923), a musical translation of the sounds of a speeding locomotive. The "231" in the title refers to the number and placement of wheels on the locomotive as seen from the side: *2* wheels, followed by *3* wheels, followed by *1* wheel. This configuration is well known in railroad circles.

DARIUS MILHAUD *(mee-yoh, 1892–1974)*   Extremely prolific, Milhaud composed in almost every form—even film music. His *Suite provençale* (1937) and *Suite française* (1944) for orchestra are impressions of his native France. North and South America held a fascination for Milhaud, and he incorporated music from both continents into his pieces.

His ballet *La Création du Monde* (The Creation of the World, 1923) was influenced by his visit to Harlem jazz clubs in the 1920s. To avoid Nazi persecution, Milhaud left Paris in 1940 for Oakland, California, where he was a professor at Mills College until his retirement in 1971.

FRANCIS POULENC *(poo-lahnk, 1899–1963)*   Poulenc's songs (chansons) are among the most charming in the literature. His larger works include the *Mass in G* (1937, for chorus *a cappella*) and his opera *Dialogues des Carmelites* (Dialogues of the Carmelites, 1956).

Les Six, a group of six French composers. From left to right: Darius Milhaud, Georges Auric, Arthur Honegger, Germaine Tailleferre, Francis Polenc, and Louis Durey (not shown). Seated at the piano is the poet, artist, and novelist Jean Cocteau.

Germany

Nationalistic aggression during the twentieth century largely displaced creative expression in both Germany and Austria. Most composers had to leave these countries; many emigrated to the United States. These were the lands that produced Bach, Handel, Mozart, Haydn, Beethoven, Schubert, Mendelssohn, Schumann, Brahms, Wagner, and Strauss. So much for war's contribution to civilization!

PAUL HINDEMITH (*hin*-duh-mit, 1895–1963)   Hindemith stands out as Germany's most important composer and teacher in the twentieth century. Beginning his teaching career at the Berlin School of Music, from 1927 to 1937 he became the model of the artist-teacher. To escape from the Nazi regime, he came to the United States and taught at Yale University from 1940 to 1953. He then accepted a professorship at the University of Zurich.

Disturbed by the widening gap between composer and audience, Hindemith created a collection of works with a broad appeal, in contrast to pure art works. He called these compositions *Gebrauchsmusik*, or "useful music." Numerous chamber pieces fall into this category, as does his musical playlet for children, *Wir Bauen eine Stadt* (Let's Build a Town, 1930).

Hindemith used excerpts in his opera *Mathis der Maler* (Mathis the Painter, 1934) after a symphony of the same title. His outstanding ballets are *Nobilissima visione* (1938) and *The Four Temperaments* (1940). Works for more

Paul Hindemith

unusual instruments such as a saxophone, bassoon, tuba, string bass, and harp are among his notable contributions to sonata literature.

Challenge Your Expertise

Which one of *Les Six* was influenced by his visits to Harlem jazz clubs? Which of his compositions shows that influence?

The musician Sting starring as MacHeath in a 1990 Broadway production of Weill's *Three Penny Opera.*

KURT WEILL (*vile*, 1900–1950)   Close friends, Weill and Hindemith collaborated (a rare occurrence for composers) on the music for several interesting stage works. Inspired by Lindbergh's daring flight across the Atlantic is a choral piece called *Der Lindberghflug* (The Lindbergh Flight), with a text by Berthold Brecht (1898–1956).

Weill collaborated again with Brecht on the opera *The Rise and Fall of the City of Mahagonny* (1929). Written in pre-Nazi Berlin, it is a scathing commentary on twentieth-century materialism, power struggles, and sex.

The Three Penny Opera (1928) characterizes city life during the early twentieth century. One of the hit songs, "Mack the Knife," depicts modern, low-life street and cabaret people. Written in a popular chamber-opera style, *The Three Penny Opera* (1928) is based on the 1728 William Gay work *Beggar's Opera.*

When the rise of the Nazis in Germany became intolerable in 1933, Weill and his wife Lotte Lenya fled to Paris, and then, in 1935, emigrated to the United States, where Weill composed mainly for films and Broadway shows. His last work, *Lost in the Stars* (with Maxwell Anderson, 1949), is a brilliant Broadway-style musical that comments on the Apartheid problem in South Africa from the black worker's point of view.

CARL ORFF (1895–1982)   Orff based his well-known dramatic cantata *Carmina burana* (1937) on a collection of thirteenth-century student songs and poems discovered in an old Bavarian monastery. With its driving rhythms and ostinati, Orff's music has been frequently used as background music in films and television.

Italy

OTTORINO RESPIGHI (reh-*spee*-ghee, 1879–1936)   Writing in both neoclassical and impressionistic styles, Respighi distinguished himself by composing nationalistic symphonic poems: *Fountains of Rome, Pines of Rome,* and *Roman Festivals.* To create a feeling of reality in portraying the countryside on the outskirts of Rome, Respighi calls for a recording of birds to be played over the loudspeaker at performances of *Pines of Rome.*

Béla Bartók (right) with violinist Rudolph Kolisch during a rehearsal of *Music for Strings, Percussion and Celesta* (1940)

Challenge Your Expertise

What were some of the differences between The Five and *Les Six* (The Six)?

Central Europe

BÉLA BARTÓK (1881–1945)   One of the leading twentieth-century composers (See Bartók's biography on page 251). Collaborating and traveling with his friend Zoltán Kodály (koh-*dye*, 1882–1967), he collected and edited Hungarian folk music, which they both used extensively in their music.

When he emigrated to the United States in 1940, Bartók joined the hordes of artists escaping from Europe. Although suffering from leukemia and oppressed by financial problems, Bartók wrote his last and most popular works in the United States between intermittent hospitalizations. Finally, his problems were somewhat eased when he was invited to join a folk music research group at Columbia University.

Reflective of Hungarian peasant music, much of Bartók's music contains interesting dissonances. His most famous work, the Concerto for Orchestra (1943), resulted from a commission from the Boston Symphony Orchestra.

One of his last works before his death in New York in 1945 was the *Third Piano Concerto*. Gravely ill and aware of his imminent death, Bartók worked feverishly to finish the concerto so that he could leave his family less impoverished.

Hebrew Music

ERNEST BLOCH (*blohk*, 1880–1959)   An international musician, Bloch was influenced by his Jewish heritage. His popular work *Schelomo* (Solomon, 1915) is a plaintive rhapsody for cello and orchestra. *Baal Shem* (1923) is for violin and piano. And another popular work, *Sacred Service* (*Avodath Hakodesh*, 1930–1933), is for cantor (baritone), chorus, and orchestra.

Latin America

HEITOR VILLA-LOBOS (*vee*-la-*loh*-bohsh, 1887–1959)   Villa-Lobos and Darius Milhaud met in 1915 in Brazil. Milhaud, then the French ambassador's secretary, encouraged Villa-Lobos to incorporate Brazilian folk material into his music.

Of his more than 2,000 works, his *Bachianas brasileiras* are the most widely known. In this group of nine works, Villa-Lobos blended his Brazilian heritage with the style of Johann Sebastian Bach.

CARLOS CHÁVEZ (chah-vez, *1899–1978)*   Incorporating Native American folk tunes into his music, Chavez was Mexico's most outstanding composer. *Sinfonia india, Toccata for Percussion,* and the ballet *Horsepower* are among his most important works.

Challenge Your Expertise

- Name at least two composers whose works represent more than one style.
- Which composer is associated with commencement ceremonies?
- Name two composers whose works sound like an earlier style period than when they lived.

Summary of Terms

Broadway-style   neoclassicism

Chapter 23

Experimental and Technological Music

During the first half of the twentieth century, the momentum of accelerating progress swept artists toward the future. Radical changes were inevitable. Traditionalism was the past; experimentalism was the future.

Following this trend, composers have been writing works that fall into disparate categories:

- *musique concrète*
- electronic music

- computer music and mixed-media music
- aleatoric music
- chance music

MUSIQUE CONCRÈTE

French composers use the term *musique concrète* to refer to everyday sounds that they captured and manipulated with tape recorders. The techniques were startling: overdubbing, cutting and splicing, playing backward and forward, changing the speed.

Use of Tape Recordings

It was in 1942, during World War II, that the magnetic tape recorder was invented. Edgard Varèse (vah-*rehz*), a French-born musician who later emigrated to the United States, saw possibilities for using the new invention to create musical sounds. Soon, other musicians followed his lead. Lugging the clumsy portable machines, musicians headed outdoors, microphones in hand, to record the "real" (concrete) world.

For centuries, composers had tried to replicate the sounds of the world around them: Vivaldi (*The Four Seasons*), Beethoven (*Pastoral* Symphony), Mahler (Symphony No. 1), Honegger (*Pacific 231*). In *Pines of Rome*, Respighi came closest with recordings of nightingales played during live performances. Now, with the amplification ability of the tape recorder, composers could capture sounds from everywhere, no matter how puny the original source.

Music with Composer Control

By the 1950s, the composer with a tape recorder had final control over his or her music. Performers were not necessary: the composer was the performer. Pointing the microphone, the composer could choose the sound sources. Then, back in the studio, the composer could decide how to manipulate the various prerecorded sound events in order to produce the desired final tape recording.

Important *musique concrète* composers include the following:

John Cage (1912–1992)
Karlheinz Stockhausen (b. 1928)
Edgard Varèse (1883–1965)
Otto Luening (1900–1996)
Vladimir Ussachevsky (1911–1990)
Iannis Xenakis (b. 1922)

ELECTRONIC MUSIC

Electronic music refers to sounds produced on electronic oscillators and then usually recorded and stored. At first, the term *electronic music* was used to distinguish electronically produced sounds from the manipulated sounds of *musique concrète*.

As the 1960s approached, the analog electronic music synthesizer changed recording techniques. Storing individual sounds on tape was now obsolete. Instead, both natural sounds—birds, thunder, rain—and "musical" sounds could now be produced synthetically—"synthesized"—in the electronic music laboratory.

Early synthesizers had some faults. Because the music they produced was *too* precise, it sounded synthetic. Singers and instrumentalists do not perform like machines. Depending on their interpretations, live artists deliberately vary beats, tempo, pitches, and other elements of music. Realizing this, later electronic music composers used digital synthesizers to incorporate these variations into their music to "humanize" its sound.

Important electronic music composers include:

Milton Babbitt (b. 1916)	Otto Luening
Wendy (née Walter) Carlos (b. 1939)	Karlheinz Stockhausen
	Morton Subotnick (b. 1933)
Mario Davidovsky (b. 1934)	Vladimir Ussachevsky
Charles Dodge (b. 1942)	Edgard Varèse
Philip Glass (b. 1937)	Charles Wuorinen (b. 1938)
Frederick Lesemann (b. 1936)	Iannis Xenakis

COMPUTER AND MIXED MEDIA

Invented in 1942, the same year as the magnetic tape recorder, the computer may prove to be the most important development since the wheel. Musicians have become quite creative in exploring its technology for composing, scoring, and music education.

Electronic music studio

Common Terms Used in Computer Music

MIDI   An acronym for Musical Instrument Digital Interface, MIDI is a set of agreed-upon standards for use by keyboards, computers, and other devices. Standards make the sharing of information possible through a common "language." **MIDI**

SAMPLING   Using a series of numbers to represent sounds of an instrument, the sound is digitally recorded and stored on disc. A composer can recall samples of a particular sound from that disc and use it in new music. Thus, the composer can access computerized information to put together an entire ensemble of mixed instruments. **Sampling**

Music with Performer Control

ALEATORIC MUSIC   This music leaves many important decisions to the performer but is otherwise specific in its notation. "Alea" is the Latin word for one die in a pair of dice. "Aleator," Latin for gambler, suggests the risk and chance involved in playing this twentieth-century music. **Aleatoric Music**

CHANCE MUSIC   Chance music is less precise in its notation than aleatoric music. Instructions to performers are mainly general. Details (pitches, duration) happen as they will, allowing the players to create a performance that is a matter of "chance." Therefore, no two performances of the same work are identical. **Chance Music**

SILENCE   John Cage's *4:33* (four minutes, thirty-three seconds) is typical of the playfulness of chance music. To perform this work, the player comes out on the stage, sits at the piano, starts a stopwatch, and remains there in **Silence**

Jackson Pollack's painting *Number One* (1948), using elements of chance

silence, allowing the audience to fill that time with their own musical imaginations and to become aware of the sounds already present in the concert hall. Four minutes and thirty-three seconds later, the player rises and walks off the stage.

In another Cage composition, *Imaginary Landscape,* his directions call for twelve radios and "random noise assemblages." Each of the twelve radios is tuned to a different station. The performance consists of constantly changing stations. Microphones placed outside the concert hall provide random noise. A pair of loudspeakers picks up the sounds onstage.

Notation and directions in chance music are rarely conventional. With specific notes and duration left to the performer, only sound events and suggestions appear. In essence, chance music is similar to improvisational theater, where actors use only a situation or character and create dialogue at their discretion. "Action" painters, such as Jackson Pollock and Salvador Dali, who drip and throw paint on the canvas and allow things to "happen," operate in a similar way.

DECK OF CARDS   Another interesting way to make music by chance is to use a deck of cards to select materials randomly. The technique is to translate card numbers and suits into music. For instance:

Number on card determines pitches on the 12-tone scale:

card:	ace (1)	2	3	4	5	6
pitch:	C	C-sharp	D	D-sharp	E	F

card:	7	8	9	10	Jack	Queen
pitch:	F-sharp	G	G-sharp	A	A-sharp	B

king and joker = wild cards (your choice of any pitch)
Suits on card determine duration:

clubs = eighth note or eighth rest	spades = quarter note or quarter rest
diamonds = half note or half rest	hearts = whole note or whole rest

To create a chance piece, shuffle the deck, deal the cards, and assign the results to one player. Repeat the process for the other players. Then perform the piece. This may seem simplistic, but this kind of chance music can become very complicated in its execution. Because of the random nature of each shuffle of the deck, each player will have an entirely different part.

Important composers of chance music include:

Earle Brown (b. 1926)   Karlheinz Stockhausen
John Cage (1912–92)   Christian Wolff (b. 1934)
Morton Feldman (1926–89)   Iannis Xenakis (b. 1922)
Lukas Foss (b. 1922)   LaMonte Young (b. 1935)

LISTENING INSIGHTS

How to Listen to Chance and Aleatoric Music

Though serious in its philosophical position, most chance and aleatory music has a tongue-in-cheek element, leaving room for playfulness. *Process*-oriented rather than *product*-oriented, chance music may at times sound chaotic. Most of the focus for the listener is on the unusual happenings on stage and the novel sound combinations that spontaneously develop.

Pierre Boulez in 1971

Other Experimentalists

PIERRE BOULEZ *(boo-lez,* b. 1925*)*   Boulez favors an athematic (themeless) approach to atonal music. Using a variety of compositional techniques, his music is highly organized yet sounds very different from traditional music. In his words:

> After the war we felt that music, like the world around us, was in a state of chaos. Our problem was to create a new musical language.

Athematic

Karlheinz Stockhausen

KARLHEINZ STOCKHAUSEN *(shtohk-how-zen)*   An important post–World War II German composer, Stockhausen composes in a variety of styles. Extremely complex rhythms abound in his music, along with unusually detailed instructions to the performer. Already mentioned for his work in *musique concrète*, electronic music, and chance music, Stockhausen also incorporates ideas from older styles. His popular work *Gruppen* (Groups, 1955–1957), for example, is played by three orchestras located in different areas of the concert hall—influenced by Giovanni Gabrieli's sixteenth-century polychoral style (see Chapter 9).

KRYSZTOF PENDERECKI *(kris-tof pen-der-ets-kee,* b. 1933*)*   An eclectic composer, Penderecki combines musical elements from his native Poland with various "mainstream" and experimental techniques. Having witnessed Nazi persecution of the Jews in Poland, he composed music full of compassion for human suffering. You can hear this in his powerful *Threnody for the Victims of Hiroshima*.

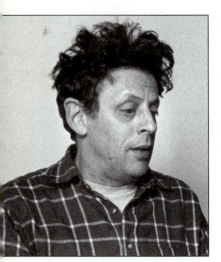

Philip Glass

PHILIP GLASS (b. 1937)   A New York-based composer, Glass has achieved popularity through his mesmerizing film music, *Koyaanisqatsi* and *Powaqqatsi*. His operas, including *Einstein on the Beach* (1975) and *1,000 Airplanes on the Roof* (1987), have won critical acclaim.

Often referred to as a *minimalist,* Glass takes bits of rhythm and pitches and repeats them over and over, while subtly changing their character. From his extensive travels, Glass has incorporated Asian, North African, and South American percussion music into his minimalist techniques.

STEVE REICH *(rysh,* b. 1936)   Also a minimalist, Reich uses ostinato to help his music evolve hypnotically, gradually—similar to a slowly changing sunset. *Musique concrète* recording techniques provide the basis for Reich's ostinati. He then moves the ostinati out of phase on other recording tracks, creating interesting polyphonic effects. His "Come Out" is an example of this technique.

Challenge Your Expertise

What might happen if the piano is not tuned before a performance of Cage's *4:33* (four minutes, thirty-three seconds)?

WHAT LIES AHEAD?

The future is difficult to predict: Today's experiment may be tomorrow's mainstream. New approaches continue to evolve as technology advances. With world migration and new media of communication, the world as a "global community" is rapidly approaching. As cultures interact, each leaves its imprint on the others. Undoubtedly, a greater mix of ethnic and diverse cultural resources will spawn new art works.

Summary of Terms

aleatoric music	electronic music	minimalism
athematic	electronic music synthesizer	mixed-media music
chance music	MIDI (Musical Instrument	*musique concrète*
computer music	Digital Interface)	sampling

Chapter 24

Music in North America

IMMIGRATION

Around the turn of the twentieth century, into the port cities of New York, Boston, and Philadelphia poured the most diverse immigrant population in the history of the world. Never before had so many people come to so relatively small an area.

Russian and Polish Jews fled czarist pogroms; earlier, the Irish, Scandinavians, and Germans, and later, the Italians were forced off their farms by crop failures. Others left their homelands to avoid persecution. To all of them, North America represented "the promised land" of freedom and limitless opportunities.

The Arts in North America

The same freedom and opportunities attracted artists. America became a refuge and a home for some of the world's greatest musicians. Gustav Mahler conducted the Metropolitan Opera and the New York Philharmonic early in the twentieth century. Later, conductors such as Bruno Walter, Fritz Reiner, and Arturo Toscanini obtained major positions. Great violinists Mischa Elman and Nathan Milstein, and pianists Artur Rubinstein and Vladimir Horowitz made their homes in the United States.

SCHOOLS OF MUSIC   To escape the Nazis and World War II, many composers found employment in America's colleges and schools of music. For example, Stravinsky taught at Harvard for a year; Arnold Schoenberg taught at both the University of Southern California and University of California, Los Angeles; Darius Milhaud taught at Mills College in California; Béla Bartók was hired as a folk-music librarian at Columbia University. Violinist Jascha Heifetz, cellist Gregor Piatigorsky, and violist William Primrose taught at the University of Southern California.

Today, many of the world's finest schools of music are in the United States and Canada, including:

Curtis Institute of Music
Indiana University School of Music
Juilliard School of Music
McGill University
New England Conservatory of Music
Northwestern University School of Music
Oberlin College Conservatory of Music
Peabody Conservatory of Music
University of British Columbia School of Music
University of Illinois School of Music
University of Miami School of Music
University of Michigan School of Music
University of Rochester, Eastman School of Music
University of Southern California, Thornton School of Music
University of Toronto School of Music

Graduates of these schools now perform in the major orchestras and opera companies around the world.

ORCHESTRAS IN NORTH AMERICA   The influx of great artists from Europe helped elevate the standards of American orchestras to a world-class level. Of the great symphony orchestras in the world today, many are in the major cities of North America:

Atlanta Symphony	Minnesota Orchestra
Baltimore Symphony	Montreal Symphony
Boston Symphony	National Symphony (Washington, D.C.)
Buffalo Philharmonic	New Orleans Symphony
Chicago Symphony	New York Philharmonic
Cleveland Orchestra	Philadelphia Orchestra
Dallas Symphony	Pittsburgh Symphony
Detroit Symphony	St. Louis Symphony
Houston Symphony	San Francisco Symphony
Indianapolis Symphony	Seattle Symphony
Los Angeles Philharmonic	Toronto Symphony

AMERICAN COMPOSERS

Amy Beach and Charles Ives were among the earliest, distinctly American composers. Although well-versed in European music, they chose to incorporate into their music American spirit, songs, and rhythms.

Amy Beach née Amy Marcy Cheney (1867–1944)

Amy Beach was born in West Henniker, New Hampshire, the only child of Charles Abbott Cheney, a paper manufacturer, and Clara Imagine Marcy Cheney. Amy quickly displayed musical precocity. As a toddler, she could sing forty tunes accurately. At age two, she improvised alto lines against her mother's melodies. At age four, she devised her own piano pieces and played hymns by ear in correct 4-part harmony. When Amy was six years old, her mother began teaching her piano, and two years later, in 1875—the year the Cheneys relocated to Boston— Amy gave her first public performance, playing a Chopin waltz and "Mamma's Waltz," her own composition, at a church musicale.

In spite of her prodigious talent, Amy had little more than a year of formal training in harmony and counterpoint. Studying theory in Germany—the usual path prescribed for serious young American musicians of the day—was not possible. In addition to the family's financial limitations, Mrs. Cheney wanted her daughter to lead a normal life.

While she was developing into one of America's brilliant young pianists, Amy taught herself composition by memorizing Bach fugues, analyzing the works of the masters, and translating orchestration treatises. After making her professional debut at 16 at the Boston Music Hall, Amy continued concertizing until 1885. Shortly after her first appearance with the Boston Symphony that year, Amy married Henry Beach, a socially prominent physician. She abruptly ended her performing career because Beach, a widower in his late 40s, did not want his young wife to be a traveling concert pianist.

It was then that Amy turned her attention to composing. With the discipline stemming from her New England upbringing, Amy steadily churned out pieces in a variety of genres, using the byline Mrs. H. H. A. Beach. Her first major work, *Mass in E♭*, received its debut performance in 1892 by the Handel and Haydn Society of Boston. Four years later, the Boston Symphony played her massive *Gaelic Symphony*, the first (performed) symphony composed by an American woman.

Amy Beach was the first American woman to succeed as a composer of large-scale music. Her music "speaks the lyrical, rich-textured, late Romantic language of the Second New England School." (Others in that "school" were a group of conservative, chiefly German-trained, young American composers who studied with John Knowles Paine, Harvard's first professor of music.)

In 1900, Beach again performed publicly, playing her own *Concerto for Piano and Orchestra in c-sharp minor*. She then returned to composing. Following her husband's death in 1910, the childless young widow decided to catch up on her life experiences. For the first time, she traveled to Europe, where she remained for nearly four years. Now billing herself as Amy Beach, she enjoyed success as both a composer and performer.

Upon returning to the United States in 1914, Amy settled in New York. She continued her performing career (reverting to the name Mrs. H. H. A. Beach to avoid confusing American audiences). She also became an unofficial composer-in-residence at St. Bartholomew's Church, where she was called "Aunt Amy."

Throughout her career, Beach received prestigious composing commissions, and all but three of her 150 opus numbers remained unpublished during her lifetime. One of those unpublished works was "Cabildo," a one-act chamber opera for voices and string trio. Because commissions for opera were sparse, it was not until 1932, while working at the MacDowell Colony in Peterborough, New Hampshire, that Amy Beach tried her hand at this genre. Composed to a libretto by Atlanta author Nan Bagby Stephens, "Cabildo" is set in a New Orleans museum and contains motifs derived from Creole folk tunes. Beach never heard her opera performed.

Amy Beach gave her last public recital in 1940 with the Brooklyn Chamber Music Society. In 1944, she succumbed to heart disease. The following year, just two months after her death, "Cabildo" reached the stage of the University of Georgia at Athens. Thirty years later, in May 1995, this last of Amy Beach's unpublished works received its first fully professional performance at Alice Tully Hall in New York's Lincoln Center.

PRINCIPAL WORKS

Mass in E♭ ("Grand Mass," 1891), *Festival Jubilee* (1893), *Gaelic Symphony in E,* Op. 32 (1896), *Sonata in A for Violin and Piano, Op. 34* (1898), *Concerto for Piano and Orchestra in c♯ minor, Op. 45* (1899), *Panama Hymn* (1915), chamber works, songs, and cantatas, including *Rose of Avontown, Chambered Nautilus,* and *Sylvania.*

Charles Ives (1874–1954)

Born in Danbury, Connecticut, Charles Ives was influenced by his father, who had been a bandmaster in the Civil War. The elder Ives gave Charles his first lessons in music.

Music inventiveness was part of their household as Ives's father experimented with new scales and quarter tones—the tones that fall between the traditional notes of the chromatic scale. In the 1880s, Charles experimented with *polytonality* (some years before Stravinsky), singing in one key and accompanying himself in another.

Once accepted at Yale, Charles majored in music. But upon graduation, he realized that he would have a difficult time earning a living as a musician. So this practical Connecticut Yankee went to New York City to find a job in the business world. Charles did extremely well in business and founded one of the New York Life Insurance Company agencies.

His wealth as a businessman made it possible for him to compose as a hobby without concern for compensation. On weekends and during vacations in his country home in Connecticut, Ives composed hundreds of works.

By the time of his death in New York in 1954, only a few of his works had had public performances. His wife Harmony later uncovered dozens of works that had been gathering dust in the couple's barn, and she arranged for their performance and publication.

Principal Works

Orchestral Music: four symphonies; First Orchestral Set (*Three Places in New England*, 1914); Second Orchestral Set (1915); *The Unanswered Question* (1906); *Central Park in the Dark* (1906); *Emerson Overture* (1907); *Washington's Birthday* (1909); *Robert Browning Overture* (1912); *Decoration Day* (1912); *The Fourth of July* (1913)

Chamber Music: String quartets and sonatas

Piano Music: Sonatas and studies

Choral Music: *Psalm 67* (1894); *The Celestial Country* (1899)

Organ Music: *Variations on "America"* (1891)

Songs: More than 150

Ives's Songs

You'll come to know Ives best through his songs. Mixing European art song tradition with American speech and temperament, Ives called for a unique sound. He expected full-voiced concert singers to use twangy American pronunciation.

Subjects for his songs range from a child's singing about his father ("The Greatest Man"), to a man's impression of a circus parade ("The Side Show"), to the reflections on the death of a cowhand ("Charlie Rutlage").

Ives's piano accompaniments are novel too. Behind the calm, tonal melodies of his songs, he relishes accompaniments in contrasting keys (bitonal or polytonal) and even employs atonality—although not the Schoenberg variety.

Ives was an experimenter. Predating Stravinsky in using polychords, polytonality, polymeters, and polyrhythms, Ives felt free to follow his creative ideas without regard for what people thought. To him, creating music was a joyful process. Just for fun, Ives worked into his music some of the popular tunes of his day, church hymns, and patriotic songs. Combined with dissonant, occasionally atonal passages, the familiar tunes seem to anchor the listener to reality, while Ives moves off into uncharted regions.

Ives's favorite holiday was the Fourth of July. He wrote several works to capture the exuberance of the occasion, including "Putnam's Camp, Redding, Connecticut" from his *Three Places in New England*, and "The Fourth of July" in the third movement of his *Holidays Symphony*.

LISTENING ACTIVITY

"CHARLIE RUTLAGE" (1921), CHARLES IVES

from "Cowboy Songs"
Large Form: Song
Detailed Form: Song Form (loose ABA)
Performing Medium: Soprano with piano

Compact Disc 3, Track 8
Cassette Tape: Side D, Example 6
Running Time: 2:55

The song "Charlie Rutlage" is pure Americana. Charlie is a California ranch hand who is accidentally killed while rounding up cattle. To enhance the mood of the story, the singer usually uses an American Western-cowboy twang, as well as song-speech—partly sung and partly spoken. To depict the accident when Charlie's horse stumbles and falls on top of him, the piano accompaniment becomes highly descriptive, employing dissonant tone clusters of sound.

LISTENING GUIDE

"CHARLIE RUTLAGE" (1921), CHARLES IVES

A SECTION

8   0:00   INTRODUCTION piano begins; quadruple meter; rhythmic syncopation; *mp*; Western popular music flavor; opening melody uses a pentatonic scale; major tonality; soprano entrance with American-cowboy twang; homophonic texture

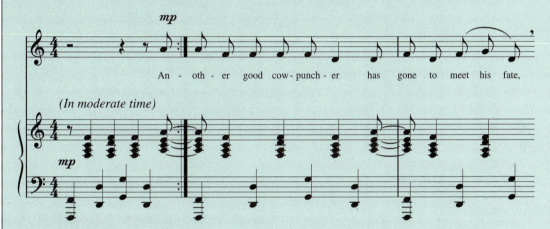

Another good cowpuncher
has gone to meet his fate,
I hope he'll find a resting place,
within the golden gate,
the golden gate.

      0:21   syncopated piano accompaniment continues; major tonality with growing dissonance; *mp*

Another place is vacant
on the ranch of the X I T,
'Twill be hard to find another
that's liked as well as he.

      0:31   mf getting louder to forte at a cadence

The first that died was Kid White,
a man both tough and brave,

      0:44   slower tempo; *p*; calmer mood

While Charlie Rutlage
makes the third to be sent to his grave,

B SECTION

      1:08   faster tempo, agitated, accelerating tempo; *f*; song-speech departs from traditional sung musical line

Caused by a cowhorse falling,
while running after stock;
'Twas on the spring round up,
A place where death men mock,

> 1:18   faster and louder; highly agitated; tone-cluster chords

He went forward one morning
on a circle through the hills,
He was gay and full of glee
and free from earthly ills;
But when it came to finish up
the work on which he went,

> 1:34   a little slower, then faster and faster; louder and louder; cadencing in crashing
> tone-cluster chords

Nothing came back from him;
his time on earth was spent.
'Twas as he rode the round up,
an X I T turned back to the herd;
Poor Charlie shoved him in again,
his cutting horse he spurred;
Another turned; at that moment
his horse the creature spied
and turned and fell with him,

> 2:01   slower and softer; polychords; melody sliding up

beneath poor Charlie died,

A SECTION (RETURN)

> 2:19   OPENING MELODY same tempo and syncopated cowboy style as the
> beginning; *p*

His relations in Texas
his face never more will see,
But I hope he'll meet his loved ones
beyond in eternity, in eternity,
I hope he'll meet his parents,
will meet them face to face,
And that they'll grasp him
by the right hand

> 2:46   gradually slower and softer; church hymn-like cadence chords

at the shining throne,
the shining throne,
the shining throne of grace.

> ### LISTENING INSIGHTS
>
> #### How to Listen to Ives
>
> Listen particularly for some of the dissonant, surrealistic sound journeys on which Ives takes you. Look for the fun in the music. Try to find the buried treasure—the hymns and popular and patriotic tunes that he has hidden everywhere. If you listen expecting traditional musical sounds, you might often feel lost. If you open your mind to the possibilities, you'll be surprised.

Ives always tried to project the American spirit he acquired during his New England childhood. His music expresses it: wonderful American holidays, full of warmth and celebration and joyful din.

POLYMEDIA   Ives enjoyed mixing media. Many of his works are surrealistic in that they juxtapose seemingly unconnected tunes and situations, much in the way events occur in a dream. His favorite experiments are combining a symphony orchestra playing in one key with a marching band playing a patriotic march, or mixing two orchestras with two conductors playing two seemingly different works on the same stage.

> ### LISTENING ACTIVITY
>
> #### *FIRST ORCHESTRAL SET* (1914): *THREE PLACES IN NEW ENGLAND,* "PUTNAM'S CAMP," REDDING, CONNECTICUT) CHARLES IVES
>
> **Large Form: Descriptive Orchestra Piece**
> **Detailed Form: Sectional Modified A B A**
> **Performing Medium: Symphony Orchestra with Extra Wind-Band Players**
>
> Compact Disc 3 Track 9
> Cassette Tape: Side D, Example 7
> Running Time: 6:14
>
> As you listen to "Putnam's Camp" from *Three Places in New England,* imagine a turn-of-the-century band playing popular patriotic music on the town square. In the nearby park, children rush about in play, shouting and laughing. The American flag unfurls everywhere, making the townspeople feel festive and patriotic.

In his preface to the music, Ives supplies a written program, which is paraphrased here:

In a Revolutionary War Memorial Park near Redding, Connecticut, a child attends a Fourth of July picnic. General Israel Putnam's soldiers spent the winter of 1778–1779 in that park. The child wanders into the woods beyond Putnam's camp ground and rests on a hillside. As the tunes of the band and the songs of the children grow fainter, the child falls asleep and dreams of the discouraged American soldiers breaking camp, marching out with fife and drum to a popular tune of their day. Suddenly, the soldiers turn back and cheer—Putnam is coming over the hills.

Waking from his dream, the child hears the songs of the children at the picnic. He runs down to join them and listen to the band.

Three sections (A B A) reflect the events in the program:

Section One (A) sets the raucous, happy mood with a quick-step march that Ives reused from an earlier piece he wrote for band. Also featured are melody fragments, including the British army's quick-step march "The British Grenadiers," contrasted with the American army's "Yankee Doodle," and also "Battle Cry of Freedom," composed by George Frederick Root (1820–1895) during the Civil War.

Section Two (B) depicts the child's dream state. First the music gradually fades to a pause. Then a surrealistic collage of tunes begins: overlapping melodic fragments of "Yankee Doodle," "The British Grenadiers," bugle calls, church hymns, and popular tunes from Ives's day.

Section Three (A) depicts the exciting celebration when the boy awakens and rejoins his friends. Polyrhythms, polytonality, and polyphonic treatment of fragmented tunes characterize the music. A short quote from "The Star Spangled Banner" brings the piece to a resounding end.

LISTENING GUIDE

First Orchestral Set (1914):
Three Places in New England, "Putnam's Camp,"
Redding, Connecticut) Charles Ives

SECTION ONE (A) FOURTH OF JULY CELEBRATION

9	0:00	MARCH INTRODUCTION	full orchestra; *ff*; allegro; changing meters, syncopation; homophonic texture
	0:10	BRITISH QUICK STEP	mainly strings, musical show style; *f*; dissonant chords

Allegro (quick step time)

10	0:26	BRITISH GRENADIERS	fife and drum tune; quadruple meter with syncopation and polyrhythms; imitations of tune fragments; polytonal; polyphonic texture

"The British Grenadiers"

	0:52	BRITISH QUICK STEP	bugle calls played by trombones and tubas; polyrhythms, syncopation; polyphonic texture
		BUGLE CALLS	
	1:03	BATTLE CRY OF FREEDOM	fragments of several tunes; polytonal

"The Battle Cry of Freedom"

Trumpet

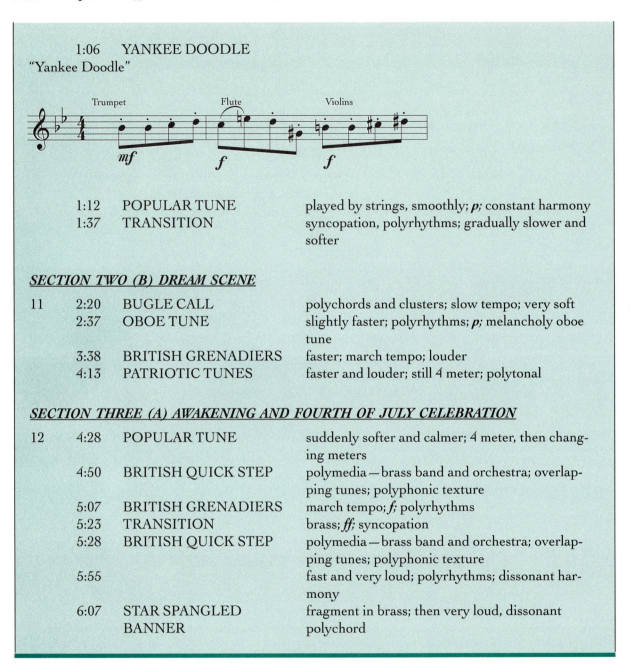

1:06   YANKEE DOODLE

"Yankee Doodle"

1:12	POPULAR TUNE	played by strings, smoothly; *p;* constant harmony
1:37	TRANSITION	syncopation, polyrhythms; gradually slower and softer

SECTION TWO (B) DREAM SCENE

11	2:20	BUGLE CALL	polychords and clusters; slow tempo; very soft
	2:37	OBOE TUNE	slightly faster; polyrhythms; *p;* melancholy oboe tune
	3:38	BRITISH GRENADIERS	faster; march tempo; louder
	4:13	PATRIOTIC TUNES	faster and louder; still 4 meter; polytonal

SECTION THREE (A) AWAKENING AND FOURTH OF JULY CELEBRATION

12	4:28	POPULAR TUNE	suddenly softer and calmer; 4 meter, then changing meters
	4:50	BRITISH QUICK STEP	polymedia—brass band and orchestra; overlapping tunes; polyphonic texture
	5:07	BRITISH GRENADIERS	march tempo; *f;* polyrhythms
	5:23	TRANSITION	brass; *ff;* syncopation
	5:28	BRITISH QUICK STEP	polymedia—brass band and orchestra; overlapping tunes; polyphonic texture
	5:55		fast and very loud; polyrhythms; dissonant harmony
	6:07	STAR SPANGLED BANNER	fragment in brass; then very loud, dissonant polychord

JAZZ: THE AMERICAN ART FORM

Turn-of-the-century New Orleans was a musical breeding ground. Several ingredients came together to produce a distinctive style of American music enjoyed throughout the world today: jazz.

Origins of Jazz

Slave trade   Prize captives for the slave trade in the 1600s and 1700s were the tribal musicians of west Africa. Understanding that music could help keep their steerage slave cargo calmer during the arduous journey across the Atlantic,

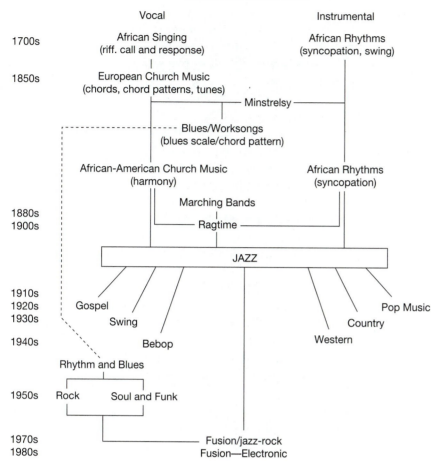

THE EVOLUTION OF JAZZ

the traders insisted that their agents select representative musicians from the tribes they raided. Once they had arrived in the Americas, music helped to prevent the deterioration of the slaves' spirits. This music was passed down through generations of African Americans, and elements of it were absorbed into the mainstream of American music.

African Singing

CALL AND RESPONSE   In call and response, characteristic of most African vocal music, a leader would sing a phrase (question), and the group would promptly repeat or answer it—comparable to a responsive reading in a religious service. Today, call and response permeates jazz, gospel, rhythm and blues, and rock music, and it is an integral part of African-American church services, both spoken or sung. The minister constantly throws out a question or stirring statement, and the congregation responds, often by saying, "Amen!"

Call and response

Riff
Ostinato

RIFF   Heard throughout African singing and instrumental groups, and later in jazz, a *riff* is a short phrase repeated over and over. It fits our definition of an *ostinato*, a repeated pattern that unifies the music. Originally, riffs or ostinatos were improvised by various members of the African percussion ensemble and then imitated by the entire ensemble. Today, *riff* may refer to any repetitive passage.

African rhythms

African Rhythms

Rhythm has often been called the "soul of Africa." Almost every African social gathering had its rhythmic accompaniment. Every tribal occasion also brought out the percussion instruments played by male members of the tribe.

Especially throughout western Africa, each percussionist had a discrete role in the ensemble. Choosing a particular instrument while still a young boy, each tribesman continued playing that instrument throughout his lifetime. Exceptional percussionists often developed into soloists, responsible for improvising new rhythmic patterns that the rest of the ensemble answered or imitated.

Syncopation

SYNCOPATION   Complexities of rhythm have always been the essence of African percussion ensembles. Playing the same rhythm hour after hour at ceremonies can be boring. To maintain interest, players created variations. *Syncopation* is a variation that accents part of the beat not usually accented. Constant use of syncopation results in a *swing* or forward motion to the music.

When musicologists first analyzed African percussion music in the nineteenth century, they could not understand it. In contrast to European music, the musicologists heard beats accented in unusual places (syncopation). They finally concluded that "Africans don't know how to keep time."

Offbeat

OFFBEAT   The fact that African percussionists did not all play continuously on the beat also disturbed early musicologists. Later, they came to learn that African percussionists have fun trying *not* to play on the beat. Great jazz players and singers have been influenced by this relaxed, *offbeat* performing. (It's not "cool" to play on the beat—that's for Lawrence Welk.)

Polyrhythms

POLYRHYTHMS   African percussion ensembles utilize *polyrhythms*—several overlays of conflicting rhythms that add interest to the music. Through the several World Expositions in Paris in the early 1900s, Debussy, Stravinsky, and others were so impressed with the use of polyrhythms that they incorporated them into their compositions.

Cakewalk

Cakewalk

Originating as an entertainment on Southern plantations, the *cakewalk* was a high-kicking dance. Slave couples competed for a prize, generally a cake. Those with the highest, proudest steps, often parodying the slave owner's pomposity, would "take the cake." On some plantations, the dancers moved with pails of water on their heads. The winner was the couple who

United States Marine Band (1880) with its leader, John Philip Sousa (1854–1932), playing cornet (with black cape, front right)

could maintain the most erect posture while spilling the least amount of water.

The cakewalk's rhythms are full of syncopation. As the dance craze became widespread, concert and military bands obliged their audiences with band arrangements of the music.

Military Bands

Military bands

At the turn of the century, American military bands, as well as the French military bands in New Orleans, influenced the beginnings of jazz. A band played at every important occasion, especially if a parade was part of the celebration. Even a funeral procession for an important person would be headed by a band.

THE FUNERAL   In New Orleans, the African-American funeral procession became a tradition. The New Orleans African-American community was a proud, distinctive society. Ultimately, their use of funeral procession bands spread into other cities—particularly to Memphis, St. Louis, and New York.

The funeral band

At the death of one of the community leaders, a band would assemble, usually playing secondhand instruments that had been traded in by the military bands. Performing mainly church hymns, these African-American-society marching bands headed the long, solemn parade of mourners through the streets.

Introduced to Europe by the New Orleans pianist and composer Louis Gottschalk (1829–1869), the cakewalk caught on in Europe as well. Even Debussy composed one, "Gollywog's Cakewalk," in 1908.

Rags

Ragged time

New Orleans funeral procession

Ragtime

Ragtime

HISTORICAL PERSPECTIVE

Rags and Ragtime

A highly popular form of entertainment between the 1890s and 1920s, ragtime helped foster the development of jazz. African-American rhythms found their way into the highly syncopated melodies of "rags." As with jazz, military bands contributed to ragtime. While syncopation is going on in the higher parts, the lower parts play a military-band style continuous bass line (*um-pa, um-pa*) in duple meter. Also borrowed from military-band marches is the form used in most rags. In fact, most rags sound like slower marches.

Having contributed to the style and form of ragtime, band music was in turn influenced by ragtime. Seizing upon the popularity of ragtime piano music, in the 1890s, military bands added ragtime pieces to their regular fare of marches to entertain the general public—especially at outdoor concerts.

For many years during the beginning of the twentieth century, ragtime became the favorite music played in saloons and bordellos throughout much of North America.

Because syncopated rhythms and duple meter characterize both ragtime and jazz, the term *jazz* became a catchall classification for those forms. However, today we make a distinction between the two. Ragtime music, especially the works composed by Scott Joplin, was intended for classically trained pianists reading and playing notes printed on sheet music. In contrast, jazz is essentially improvised—each performance is different.

Several theories exist about the origin of the name *ragtime*. One attributed the word to African-American clog dancing, which they called *ragging*. A more popular theory is that the ragged syncopation evolved into *rag'-time* (*ragtime*), and later became *rag*.

Scott Joplin (1868–1917)

Scott Joplin was part of the generation of African-American artists born just after the Civil War. Called the "King of Ragtime," he grew up in a musical family in Texarkana, Arkansas. His father, a railroad laborer, played the violin. His mother, a domestic worker, sang and played the banjo. She persuaded one of her employers to allow young Scott to play the piano while she cleaned the house, and by the time he was an adolescent, his parents had scraped up enough money to buy him a used grand piano. Although mostly self-taught, Joplin caught the attention of a German-trained local piano teacher who gave him free lessons and introduced him to European music.

Joplin's career took off in 1895, when he began singing with quartets and accompanying minstrel troupes. Then he found work playing in saloons, bordellos, clubs, and theaters around the country. In 1899, he had his first success as a composer in Sedalia, Missouri, when he published his "Maple Leaf Rag." The piece was named after the Maple Leaf Club, a gathering place for the "best and brightest young colored people of the city."

"Maple Leaf Rag" was different from other music and made Joplin famous. By 1903, people all over the world were listening to his rags, and the royalties made him wealthy. One critic proclaimed that if American music were ever to be more than a reflection of European music, Joplin's works were the beginning.

Joplin settled in New York in 1909 and began writing operas. His second, *Treemonisha,* is a parable of racial and spiritual themes. Disappointed that every opera company rejected the work, Joplin personally produced a scaled-down version in a Harlem hall. It was 1915, and he was already suffering from syphilis. The public's negative reception to *Treemonisha* was devastating to him.

By 1917, the disease had caused paralysis, dementia, and loss of speech. Just before Joplin died, composer and pianist Eubie Blake saw him trying to perform the "Maple Leaf Rag" and said he was so far gone that he sounded like a child struggling to pick out a tune. Joplin died that year at age 48.

PRINCIPAL WORKS

Rags: "Maple Leaf Rag" (1899); "The Entertainer" (1902)—used in the film *The Sting;* "The Sycamore" (1904); "Gladiolus Rag" (1907); "Sugarcane Rag" (1908); "Wall Street Rag" (1909)

Ragtime Opera: *Treemonisha* (1911)

LISTENING ACTIVITY

"THE ENTERTAINER" (1902), SCOTT JOPLIN
A RAGTIME TWO-STEP

Large Form: Piano Rag
Detailed Form: March Form Modified Song Form and Trio
Performing Medium: Piano

| **Compact Disc 4, Track 10**
| **Running Time: 4:21**

Listen to the catchy rag "The Entertainer" by the "King of Ragtime," Scott Joplin. You may remember it from the Paul Newman and Robert Redford film *The Sting* (1973), which uses the music throughout. The march form in this rag is typical of contemporaneous marches made famous by composers such as John Philip Sousa and Pat Conway.

In both marches and rags, the form contains four sections or tunes, also called *strains*. After a short introduction, section 1 is played and then repeated. This is followed by a new tune, section 2, which also is repeated. Then section 1 is played again but not repeated. The "trio" section, usually in a new key, contains two different sections, 3 and 4, each of which is repeated once. Joplin adds a brief transition between section 3 and section 4 of "The Entertainer"—a quote from section 2 that modulates the tonality back to the original key.

The following overview of the form for "The Entertainer" was used by Joplin for many of his rags:

Introduction (4 bars)	Section 1 (A) repeated (16 + 16 bars)	Section 2 (B) repeated (16 + 16 bars)	Section 1 (A) no repeats (16 bars)	*Trio* Section 3 (C) repeated (16 + 16 bars)	Transition quote from Section 2 (4 bars)	Section 4 (D) repeated (16 + 16 bars)

LISTENING GUIDE

"THE ENTERTAINER" (1902), SCOTT JOPLIN
A RAGTIME TWO-STEP

INTRODUCTION

| 10 | 0:00 | INTRODUCTION | solo piano; moderate tempo in duple meter; *f*; melody in octaves major tonality; starts high, then two descending sequences to a cadence |

Not fast

| | 0:08 | SECTION 1 (A) | upper melody syncopated with steady bass line; homophonic texture; C-Major tonality; motive; *p*; answered *f* |

| | 0:43 | SECTION 1 | repeated |
| 11 | 1:13 | SECTION 2 (B) | new tune in octaves; *f*; section is repeated with melody one octave higher; ends with a cadence |

Repeat 8va

	1:45	SECTION 2	repeated
	2:17	SECTION 1	first tune returns, upper melody syncopated with steady bass line; homophonic texture; still C-Major tonality; motive, *p*; answered *f*; ends with strong cadence; this section is not repeated

TRIO

| 12 | 2:50 | SECTION 3 (C) | new tune in key of F Major; *f*; answered in a lower sequence; still homophonic texture with upper melody syncopated with steady bass line |

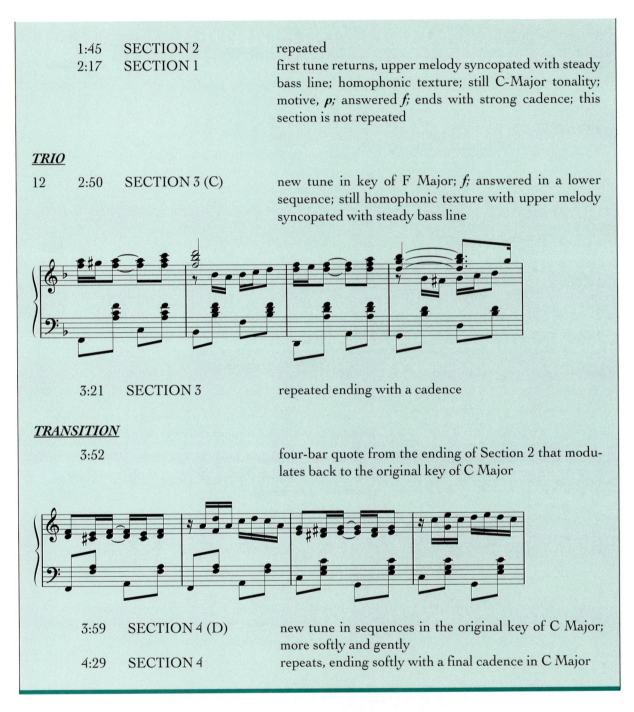

| | 3:21 | SECTION 3 | repeated ending with a cadence |

TRANSITION

| | 3:52 | | four-bar quote from the ending of Section 2 that modulates back to the original key of C Major |

| | 3:59 | SECTION 4 (D) | new tune in sequences in the original key of C Major; more softly and gently |
| | 4:29 | SECTION 4 | repeats, ending softly with a final cadence in C Major |

Church music

Influence of European Church Music

Harmony

HARMONY   Early jazz performers used the harmonies they found in the European Christian hymns. For instance, you can find the popular "When the Saints Go Marchin' In" in many turn-of-the-century Christian hymn books. This hymn and many others were used as a harmonic basis for many jazz arrangements.

When the Saints Go Marchin' In

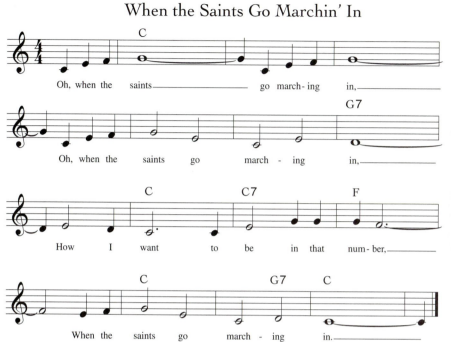

Oh, when the saints ____ go march-ing in, ____

Oh, when the saints go march - ing in, ____

How I want to be in that num-ber, ____

When the saints go march - ing in. ____

Bessie Smith (1928)

Creole Jazz Band (1923). Louis "Satchmo" Armstrong (cornet in the middle), Joe "King" Oliver (trombone on Armstrong's right), and Lil Hardin Armstrong (Armstrong's wife) at the piano).

Blues

Predating jazz, mainly through the work songs of African-American workers, the *blues* songs convey sadness.

Blues

Blues Scale and Blue Notes

BLUES SCALE AND BLUE NOTES Contributing to jazz and other jazz-related music, the blues uses a scale containing *blue notes*, which were part of the African singing tradition. Blue notes "bend" some degrees of the traditional Western scale, usually the 3rd, 5th, and 7th degrees.

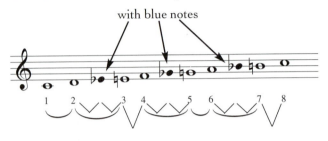

Chord pattern
12-bar blues progression

CHORD PATTERN Characteristic of blues is its use of predictable chord patterns. Called *blues progressions*, these patterns were derived from church hymns. The following is the basic 12-bar blues progression. Creative jazz musicians later developed more complex modifications.

12-Bar Blues Progression

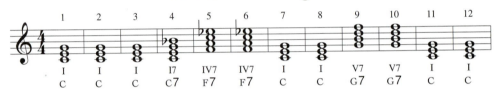

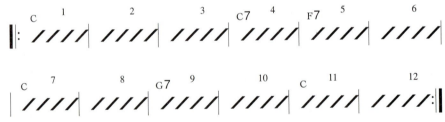

Tin Pan Alley, 26th Street, New York City, 1917.

George Gershwin

Closing the gap between the jazz idiom and classical music, Gershwin was one of America's greatest composers. He also was among the most financially successful.

Gershwin was one of those tremendous talents—like Mozart, Mendelssohn, and Chopin—whose art seemed to pour effortlessly out of him. All of them, like supernovas, lit up the world, then suddenly died—Gershwin at age thirty-nine, Mozart at thirty-five, Mendelssohn at thirty-eight, and Chopin at thirty-nine.

Gershwin had an easier life than Mozart. Almost everything he touched was successful. Writing music for radio, recordings (even piano rolls), Broadway shows, films, popular songs, and classical concert music, Gershwin achieved fame and fortune while still in his twenties.

Gershwin loved jazz. He played it. He expanded it. During his early years as a song plugger and improviser in the theater, he incorporated jazz elements into his music. Syncopation, ragtime, blues scales, blue notes, and bent tones abound in Gershwin's music.

George Gershwin (1898–1937)

George Gershwin's Russian-Jewish immigrant parents had no idea that he had musical talent when he was a child. Born in Brooklyn, New York, George seemed to be a typical street kid who excelled in sports — hockey, stickball, whatever allowed him to be physically active. But for years, without his parents knowledge, George had been taking lessons on a friend's player piano, inspired to learn music after hearing a classmate play the violin at a school assembly.

In 1910, George's mother arranged for an upright grand piano to be hoisted through the living room window of the family's Second Avenue apartment. Her intention was that the oldest son, Ira, would have lessons. No sooner was the instrument in place when George amazed his family by playing a popular song of the day. George received the lessons, to his delight and Ira's relief. Two years later, he was studying for a career as a classical pianist.

Life was economically unstable during the years leading up to World War I. Gershwin was a young teenager, and although he loved the classics, his interest was in popular music. After working one summer as a pianist at a resort in New York's Catskill Mountains, George dropped out of high school and took a $15-a-week job as a song plugger for Remick Music Company. At 16, he added to his income by making piano rolls for player pianos. Every Saturday, George traveled to New Jersey and made six piano rolls for $35 — an enormous sum for that time.

In the meantime, George was plugging his own tunes, and at age eighteen, he had his first song published, "When You Want 'Em You Can't Get 'Em — When you Got 'Em You Don't Want 'Em." That same year, another of his tunes was used in a musical revue called *The Passing Show of 1916*. Encouraged by his success, George left Remick and landed a new job as a rehearsal pianist for a show written by his idol, Jerome Kern. This was not just a job to Gershwin; it was his entry to the world of musical theater.

In 1919, Al Jolson heard Gershwin at a party playing his new song "Swanee" and asked whether he could use it in his new Broadway show. The song was a hit, selling two and a half million copies of sheet music, netting Gershwin a fortune in royalties, and making him a fixture on Broadway.

From 1920 to 1924, he composed songs for *George White's Scandals*. Then George and his brother Ira, the brilliant lyricist, wrote a succession of hit Broadway musicals (see Chapter 26).

A great controversy arose when Paul Whiteman, a noted conductor, commissioned Gershwin to compose *Rhapsody in Blue* for performance at New York City's Aeolian hall. Because the work is scored for piano and jazz band, concert hall managers and board members considered it unfit for a "serious" music venue. After lengthy negotiations, the management allowed the piece to have its premiere. So in 1924, with Gershwin himself the piano soloist with the Paul Whiteman Orchestra, jazz had its breakthrough into the concert hall.

George Gershwin was productive throughout his short lifetime. With Ira and famed author DuBose Heyward, George composed the first American folk opera, *Porgy and Bess* (1935). Although the work had a mixed reception from critics who did not know what to make of it, audiences worldwide loved *Porgy and Bess*, making it a staple of the contemporary repertoire.

George also wrote several more orchestral pieces, chamber music, piano music, and works for stage and film. Because of his work with movie studios, he also had a home in California. There he struck up a warm friendship with Arnold Schoenberg. Gershwin used another of his artistic talents—painting—to create a famous portrait of his friend.

In 1937, after performing his *Concerto in F* with the Los Angeles Philharmonic, George Gershwin was hospitalized with a brain tumor. He died a few months later at age 39.

PRINCIPAL WORKS

Orchestral Music: *Rhapsody in Blue* (piano concerto, 1924); *Concerto in F* (piano concerto, 1925); *An American in Paris* (tone poem, 1928); *Second Rhapsody* (piano and orchestra, 1931); *Cuban Overture* (1932)

Chamber Music: *Lullaby for String Quartet* (1919)

Piano Music: Preludes (1926)

Opera-Musical Theater: *Porgy and Bess* (1935)

Other Stage and Film Works: *Lady Be Good* (1924); *Tip Toes* (1925); *Oh, Kay* (1926); *Strike Up the Band* (1927); *Funny Face* (1927); *Rosalie* (1928); *Treasure Girl* (1928); *Show Girl* (1929). *Girl Crazy* (Hollywood Film, 1930); *Of Thee I Sing* (1931); *Pardon My English* (1933)

LISTENING ACTIVITY

PORGY AND BESS, GEORGE GERSHWIN
"BESS, YOU IS MY WOMAN NOW"

Large Form: Opera (Musical Theater)
Detailed Form: Three-Part Song Form (Duet)
Performing Medium: Soprano, Bass-Baritone, and Orchestra

Compact Disc 3, Track 13
Cassette Tape: Side D, Example 8
Running Time: 4:42

Written in 1935, two years before Gershwin's death, *Porgy and Bess* is his last important composition and perhaps his greatest work. After years of writing hit musicals, Gershwin's emphasis shifted to composing mainly serious concert music. However, he did not stray too far from his roots. Perhaps Gershwin heeded Maurice Ravel's advice about sticking with jazz and jazz-influenced concert music rather than trying to imitate European composers.

The 1925 novel and the later serious play *Porgy,* by South Carolinians DuBose Heyward and his sister Dorothy, interested Gershwin. He envisioned it as the basis for a distinctly American folk opera. George was excited about the project when he approached DuBose Heyward with his idea. His excitement was contagious. Heyward invited him to come to South Carolina with him, where the two began writing the opera.

Although a wealthy white man, Heyward had carefully and lovingly captured the speech rhythms and spirit of the African-American Gullah community in his play. In an effort to preserve that, DuBose wanted to be the lyricist. He later agreed that Ira Gershwin could also write some of the lyrics. George sent for his brother, and they both soaked up African-American culture in the remote islands off the coast of South Carolina. Both Gershwins attended church services and musical gatherings, and they became familiar with the distinctive Gullah dialect, speech patterns, and musical style and performance of the islanders.

Following the brilliant overture, the curtain rises on a neighborhood called Catfish Row, and we hear the music for the opening number, a haunting song titled "Summertime." The love story begins between an unlikely couple: the crippled beggar Porgy and the flamboyant street woman Bess. In their duet in Act II, "Bess, You is My Woman Now," the lovers declare their devotion to each other.

LISTENING GUIDE

PORGY AND BESS, GEORGE GERSHWIN
"BESS, YOU IS MY WOMAN NOW"

SECTION 1 (A)

13   0:00   Moderate tempo, orchestra introduction with cello solo leads into Porgy's entrance; B-flat major blues scale; complex chromatic harmonic accompaniment, syncopated rhythms

Porgy
Bess, you is my woman now,
 you is, you is
An' you mus' laugh an' sing an' dance
 for two instead of one.
Want no wrinkle on yo' brow, nohow,
because de sorrow of de past
 is all done done
Bess, my Bess!
De real happiness is jes' begun.

SECTION 1 (A)

1:19   section, main melody returns, higher key of D major.

Bess
Porgy, I's yo' woman now,
 I is, I is!
An' I ain' never goin' 'less you shares de fun
Dere's no wrinkle on my brow, no how,

SECTION 2 (B)

14   1:53   bridge section, faster, then slowing for return of main melody

Bess

> I ain' go - in'   You hear me say - in', if you ain' go - in.

> ***Bess***
> but I ain' goin'
> You hear me sayin'
> if you ain' goin'
> wid you I'm stayin'

SECTION 1 (A)

2:04   main melody and tempo returns; higher key F-sharp major

> ***Bess***
> Porgy, I's yo' woman now!
> I's yours for ever,

2:19   transition section; imitations; softer, recitative style

> ***Bess***
> Mornin' time and ev'nin' time an'
> summer time an' winter time.

SECTION 1 (A)

2:45   song repeats as a duet; D major; original tempo

Porgy	***Bess***
Bess, you is my woman now an' forever,	Porgy, I's yo' woman now,
Dis life is jes' begun	I is, I is!
	An' I ain' never goin' nowhere
Bess, we two is one now an' forever	'less you shares de fun.
Oh, Bess, don' min' dose women.	Dere's no wrinkle on my brow, nohow.
You got yo' Porgy,	
You loves yo' Porgy,	

SECTION 2 (B)

3:13   faster; then slowing back to main melody

Porgy	***Bess***
I knows you means it.	I ain' goin! You hear my sayin'
I seen it in yo' eyes, Bess.	if you ain' goin' wid you I'm stayin'.

SECTION 1 (A)

3:24   original tempo; F-sharp major

Porgy
We'll go swingin' through de years
a singin'

Bess
Porgy, I's yo' woman now!
I's yours forever.

3:38   transition section; imitations; softer; recitative style

Porgy
Hmm—
Hmm—
Mornin' time and ev'nin' time an'
summer time an' winter time.

Bess
Mornin' time and ev'nin' time an'
summer time an' winter time.
Hmm—
Hmm—

3:52   coda; orchestra with jazzy clarinet, then duet

Porgy
My Bess,
My Bess,

Bess
Oh, my Porgy,
my man Porgy,

4:07   faster, rubato till the end cadence

Porgy
From dis minute I'm tellin' you
I take dis vow:
Oh, my Bessie,
We's happy now,
We is one now.

Bess
From dis minute I'm tellin' you
I take dis vow:
Porgy,
I's yo' woman now.

LISTENING INSIGHTS

How to Listen to Eclectic Music

Eclecticism incorporates into a musical work materials, styles, and ideas from a variety of sources. The search for new materials was underway during the late nineteenth century, when nationalist composers gathered resources from within their own borders—folk songs and dances, indigenous instruments, and so on. Around the turn of the twentieth century, Debussy incorporated Asian scales and instruments that he had heard at the Paris World Exposition. Stravinsky, Prokofiev, and others incorporated into their neoclassical compositions materials and compositional methods from other style periods.

For American and Canadian composers exposed to the tremendous waves of immigration from all over the globe, incorporating the cultural influences from their new citizens was inevitable. Thus, the

United States and Canada became the first *world* communities. The rise of jazz and popular music developed in North America offered additional materials into the great mix of concert music.

Listening to the eclectic music of Ives, Gershwin, Copland, Bernstein, and others, you'll find a grand mixture of ideas: folk songs, folk-influenced songs, folk instruments, jazz and popular music melodies, harmonies, rhythms, patriotic songs, and tunes from a variety of churches—for example, the Shaker Church tune "Simple Gifts" woven into Copland's *Appalachian Spring*.

Much of the enjoyment in listening to eclectic music is in identifying the sources of the various musical resources.

Scene from *Porgy and Bess*. Krister St. Hill as Sportin' Life

Aaron Copland (1900–1990)

Like Gershwin, Aaron Copland (*cope*-land) was born in Brooklyn, New York, to recently immigrated Russian-Jewish parents. Unlike Gershwin, Copland's talent was recognized early, and he began to study music as a child. At age twenty, he went to Paris and was one of the first of many American composers to study with the famous teacher Nadia Boulanger.

Ironically, Copland had his first real exposure to jazz in Paris. Returning to the United States in 1924, Copland was determined to compose music that would be identified as "Americana" and would appeal to a wide variety of audiences.

A series of commissions from Agnes de Mille (*Rodeo*) and Martha Graham (*Appalachian Spring*) launched Copland into the ballet world, for which he produced some of the finest works of the twentieth century. Incorporating jazz and American-folk syncopations, Stravinsky's techniques, and neoclassical influences, Copland developed a highly appealing style many call American Nationalistic music.

By 1945, Copland had written the majority of his most popular compositions. He began devoting himself to conducting (mostly his own music) and teaching, spending many of his summers at the Tanglewood Music Center in Massachusetts. His most famous pupil was Leonard Bernstein.

PRINCIPAL WORKS

Orchestral Music: Symphonies: No. 1 (1928), No. 2 (1933), No. 3 (1946), *Music for the Theater* (1925), *El Salón México* (1936), *An Outdoor Overture* (1938), *Quiet City* (1940), *Lincoln Portrait* (with narrator, 1942), *Fanfare for the Common Man* (1942), Orchestral Variations (1957), *Music for a Great City* (1964), *Inscape* (1967), *Three Latin American Sketches* (1972), Piano Concerto (1926), Clarinet Concerto (1948)

Ballets: *Billy the Kid* (1938), *Rodeo* (1942), *Appalachian Spring* (1944)

Film Music: *Of Mice and Men* (1939), *Our Town* (1940), *Red Pony* (1948), *The Heiress* (1949)

Operas: *The Tender Land* (1955)

Chamber Music: Study on a Jewish Theme (1928), Violin Sonata (1943); Piano Quartet (1950), Nonet for Strings (1960), *Threnody I: Igor Stravinsky, in memoriam* (1971)

Piano Music: *Variations* (1930), Sonata (1941), Fantasy (1957), *Night Thoughts* (1972)

Songs: *Old American Songs, Twelve Poems of Emily Dickinson* (1950)

LISTENING ACTIVITY

RODEO BALLET (1942) "HOE DOWN," AARON COPLAND

Large Form: Ballet Dance Scene
Detailed Form: Modified Theme and Variations
Performing Medium: Large Ballet or Symphony Orchestra

Compact Disc 3, Track 15
Cassette Tape: Side D, Example 9
Running Time: 3:18

Copland composed his Old West ballet *Rodeo* in 1942. Agnes de Mille choreographed it and danced the leading role in its premiere.

Rodeo is about a cowgirl infatuated with the head wrangler and championship roper. To attract his attention, she shows off her skills as a rider. But none of the cowboys pays attention to her. However, when she appears in a feminine dress in the "Hoe Down" scene, near the end of the ballet, she has to fight off the competing cowboys. Finally, the head wrangler asks her to dance, and they join the other cowboys in a wild hoe down.

Notice how the syncopation and exciting dance rhythms capture the sound and spirit of country fiddlers.

LISTENING GUIDE

RODEO BALLET (1942) "HOE DOWN," AARON COPLAND

15   0:00   FIDDLE TUNE 1   played by strings and winds; *ff;* fast tempo, duple meter; D-major tonality; homophonic texture

0:03   FIDDLE TUNE 1— variation 1   played by trumpets, imitated by oboes and strings; *f* variation of tune 1

0:12   FIDDLE TUNE 1   like the beginning, *ff*

0:17   RHYTHM INTERLUDE   rhythm interlude played by strings and piano, *mf*

0:36   FIDDLE TUNE 1   similar to beginning, played by strings and clarinet, *f*

0:43   FIDDLE TUNE 1— variation 2   played by strings and woodwinds, *f*

0:57   FIDDLE TUNE 1   played by strings and woodwinds, *f*

0:59   FIDDLE TUNE 1   played by strings, imitated by woodwinds, *mf* played by full orchestra, *fff*

1:14   FIDDLE TUNE 1   similar to beginning, *f*

1:32   FIDDLE TUNE 2   played by trumpet, imitated by violins, then woodwinds, *f;* then *mf* sudden pause

2:15   RHYTHM INTERLUDE   played by strings and piano; *mf—p;* rubato tempo, then slowing to held E-flat chord

2:42   FIDDLE TUNE 1   like beginning, *f;* fast tempo again

2:49   FIDDLE TUNE 1— variation 2   played by woodwinds, *mp;* then imitated by full orchestra, *fff*

3:11   FIDDLE TUNE 1   played by strings and winds; *f;* crescendo to *ff* to *fff;* three quick final chords; played by full orchestra, *fff*

Leonard Bernstein (1918–1990)

A man of many talents, Leonard Bernstein successfully pursued six separate although related careers. Some associate him primarily with orchestral conducting. Others think of him as a composer for Broadway and the concert stage. Some remember him as a pianist, a teacher, a writer, and a television personality.

Lawrence, Massachusetts, was a thriving mill town in 1917 when Leonard's parents, Samuel and Jennie, settled there. Their families had been among the thousands of Russian immigrants who fled czarist oppression and anti-Semitism at the turn of the century. The following year, Leonard was born.

When Leonard was ten years old, he started his piano studies on an upright grand piano, a gift from Aunt Clara, Sam's sister. A year later, Leonard was playing Chopin and Bach. At age thirteen, he performed in two significant events: his first piano recital and his bar mitzvah. At his recital, his playing delighted the audience. His bar mitzvah was a turning point; Sam was so proud of his son that he gave him a baby grand to replace the upright.

In 1937, during his junior year as a music major at Harvard, Bernstein met celebrated conductor Dimitri Mitropoulos and lyricist-performer Adolph Green, with whom he would later collaborate on musicals. In October of that year, Bernstein made his professional debut as a pianist. In November he met Aaron Copland, who became his composition adviser and introduced him to renowned musicians, including Virgil Thomson and Nadia Boulanger.

Bernstein continued his studies with noted conductor Fritz Reiner at the Curtis Institute in Philadelphia. He spent summers at the Tanglewood summer school in Massachusetts, studying with Serge Koussevitzky, conductor of the Boston Symphony Orchestra. In 1942, he became Koussevitzky's assistant at Tanglewood, completed his first symphony (*Jeremiah*), and moved to New York. Following his appointment as assistant conductor of the New York Philharmonic, Bernstein was presented with the opportunity of a lifetime: to step in as a substitute for Bruno Walter at a Carnegie Hall concert. His conducting career soared.

Bernstein's first Broadway show, *On The Town* (1944), was an instant hit. In 1957, his most successful Broadway musical, *West Side Story*, opened and became a classic.

Concentrating on conducting, Bernstein served as permanent conductor of the New York Philharmonic from 1958 to 1968. After 1971, upon composing his theater piece *Mass*, he divided his efforts between composing and conducting, becoming a revered guest conductor for the world's most prestigious symphony orchestras.

Bernstein smoked. In fact, he smoked so much that he developed cancer. Yet he continued working until the end. In a funeral procession usually reserved for heads of state, a police escort blared sirens and blocked traffic for the motorcade of twenty limousines, carrying mourners from the Dakota, Bernstein's apartment building on Central Park West, to his burial place in Brooklyn, New York.

PRINCIPAL WORKS

Orchestral Music: Symphony No. 1 (*Jeremiah*, soprano and orchestra; 1943), Symphony No. 2 (*Age of Anxiety* for piano and orchestra, 1949); Symphony No. 3 (*Kaddish*, mixed chorus, boys' choir, soprano, speaker, and orchestra, 1963); *Chichester Psalms* (mixed chorus, boy soloist, and orchestra, 1965), *Songfest* (A Cycle of American Songs for Six Singers and Orchestra, 1977); Slava! (1977); *Halil* (Nocturne for Solo Flute, String Orchestra, and Percussion, 1981)

Ballets: *Fancy Free* (1944), *Facsimile* (1946), *Dybbuk* (1974)

Chamber Music: Clarinet Sonata (1942), Fanfares (1961)

Piano Music: *Seven Anniversaries* (1943), *Touches* (1980)

Stage Music: *On the Town* (1944), *Trouble in Tahiti* (1951), *Wonderful Town* (1953), *Candide* (comic operetta, 1956), *West Side Story* (1957), *Mass* (Theater Piece, 1971)

LISTENING ACTIVITY

OVERTURE TO CANDIDE (1956), LEONARD BERNSTEIN

Large Form: Musical Theater Overture
Detailed Form: Sectional Medley of Show's Tunes
Performing Medium: Musical Theater or Large Orchestra

Compact Disc 4, Track 13
Running Time: 4:22

Though the original 1956 run on Broadway of *Candide* was short lived—only seventy-three performances—the overture has remained a concert favorite. Lillian Hellman's book and Richard Wilbur's lyrics for the original production were adapted from Voltaire's classic about mindless optimism. When the show was revised in 1974, with added lyrics by Stephen Sondheim and staging by Harold Prince, the new Broadway run was highly successful.

In the musical, we accompany Candide, his frivolous fiancée Cunegonde, and his teacher Dr. Pangloss as they leave Westphalia, Germany—"The Best of All Possible Worlds"—and travel to Lisbon, Paris, Buenos Aires, and Venice. During their voyage they endure such devastations as the treachery of the Spanish Inquisition, an insurrection, a war, the rape of Cunegonde, an earthquake, the plague, and the humiliation of slavery. By the time they finally return home to Westphalia, they realize that perfection can never be attained: One must accept life's realities and try to do one's best.

Listen to Bernstein's *Overture to Candide.* The function of the overture is to set the tone, style, character, and spirit of the musical before the curtain rises. Bernstein's *Overture to Candide* is one of the most effective overtures to any musical theater work, achieving all those requirements. Although several tunes from the musical are previewed in the overture, the music focuses on the optimistic and witty tune "Glitter and Be Gay" ("If I'm not pure, at least my jewels are").

LISTENING GUIDE

OVERTURE TO CANDIDE **(1956),** LEONARD BERNSTEIN

13	0:00	INTRODUCTION MUSIC	very fast, mostly duple meter; *ff;* full orchestra; tonal with some dissonant chords; homophonic texture
	0:38	BATTLE SCENE MUSIC	duple meter; march; *f;* mainly band instruments
14	1:19	OH, HAPPY WE	low woodwinds and strings; meters changing between 2 and 3; *mf*
	1:32	OH, HAPPY WE	violins and oboes added higher
	1:44	OH, HAPPY WE	full orchestra; *f*
	2:01	OH, HAPPY WE	full orchestra; *ff*
	2:12	INTRODUCTION MUSIC	duple meter; *ff*
	2:34	BATTLE SCENE MUSIC	mostly band instruments; *ff*
	2:49	OH, HAPPY WE	melody in oboes and horns; *p*
	3:00	OH, HAPPY WE	full orchestra; *ff;* section ends with silent pause
15	3:18	GLITTER AND BE GAY	woodwind melody; *pp;* then gradually getting louder and adding more instruments
	3:31	GLITTER AND BE GAY	full orchestra, horns and woodwinds imitate one beat after flutes and violins

CODA SECTION

16	3:37	GLITTER AND BE GAY	suddenly faster and softer
	3:55	GLITTER AND BE GAY	full orchestra; _ff_
	4:07	BATTLE SCENE MUSIC	full orchestra, _fff_
	4:13	OH, HAPPY WE	horns in counterplay; two final chords, first soft, last loud

OTHER AMERICAN COMPOSERS

WILLIAM SCHUMAN _(1910–92)_   Raised in his native New York City, Schuman began a lively music career as a Tin Pan Alley songwriter and song plugger—à la Gershwin.

Coming late to classical music, Schuman did not hear his first symphony concert until he was twenty years old. The next day he changed his major at Columbia University to music. He continued composing and later taught at the Juilliard School of Music, serving as its president from 1945 to 1961.

An eclectic composer, Schuman purposely incorporated composition techniques similar to Copland's. With syncopation and other interesting rhythms, Schuman's music has a distinctly American flavor. His symphonies, ballet music (_Undertow_, 1940), and his works for band (_Chester_ Overture) are among his most popular music.

Challenge Your Expertise

- Who was the composer who supported himself during his teenage years by plugging songs and recording piano rolls?
- Whose one-act opera contains motifs derived from Creole folk tunes?

Gian Carlo Menotti (B. 1911)

An Italian by birth, Gian Carlo Menotti later became a naturalized citizen of the United States. He grew up, however, in a country town on Lake Lugano on the Swiss-Italian border. Menotti's father was a prosperous businessman, and his mother was an amateur musician.

By the time he entered the Milan Conservatory of Music at age thirteen, Menotti had written two operas. In 1928, at age seventeen, he continued his musical studies at the Curtis Institute of Music in Philadelphia, where he met his lifelong friend, composer Samuel Barber.

After graduating with honors from the Curtis Institute, Menotti began receiving commissions for opera works. In 1936, his *Amelia Goes to the Ball,* a comic opera in Italian, premiered in Italy and then played at the Metropolitan Opera in New York. It was then that Menotti decided to remain in the United States to become a citizen.

From 1958 until recently, Menotti spent most of his efforts directing the Spoleto Festival of Two Worlds, located in Spoleto, Italy.

Menotti's operas have been some of the most successful of the twentieth century. He has the distinction of having composed the first opera for television, *Amahl and the Night Visitors,* commissioned by NBC. His concerns have been to make his operas realistic and accessible to North American audiences. Caring for the voice and vocal melody, Menotti has often been compared to Puccini. Though he has composed entirely in the twentieth century, Menotti's compositional techniques have been mostly traditional, conservative, and somewhat reminiscent of nineteenth-century romanticism.

Principal Works

Orchestral Music: Piano Concerto in F (1945); *Sebastian,* ballet suite (1947); Concerto for Violin (1952)

Operas: *Amelia al ballo* (Amelia to the Ball, 1936); *The Old Maid and the Thief* (1939); *The Medium* (1945); *The Telephone* (1946); *The Consul* (1949); *Amahl and the Night Visitors* (1951); *The Saint of Bleecker Street* (1954); *Help, Help, the Globolinks* (1968); *The Hero* (1976); *Tamu-Tamu* (1973)

Cantatas, Madrigal Ballets: *The Unicorn, the Gorgon and the Manticore* (1956); *The Death of Bishop Brindisi* (1963); *Landscapes and Remembrances* (1976)

Chamber Music: Four Pieces for String Quartet (1936); Suite for Two Cellos and Piano (1973)

Piano Music: *Poemeti per Maria Rosa,* twelve pieces for children (1937); *Ricecare and Toccata on a Theme from The Old Maid and the Thief* (1953)

Ellen Taaffe Zwilich (B. 1939)

Born in Miami, Florida, Ellen Taaffe Zwilich began to study violin at an early age. After receiving both her bachelor's and master's degrees in music from Florida State University, she studied composition with Roger Sessions and Elliot Carter at the Juilliard School of Music in New York City. Zwilich was the first woman to be awarded a doctorate in composition from Juilliard.

Commissions from the San Francisco and Indianapolis orchestras and several chamber music groups gave Zwilich opportunities to compose for a variety of performing media. Her Symphony No. 1 earned her a Pulitzer Prize in 1983.

As with other North American composers, eclecticism characterizes Zwilich's music, which draws on a wide range of diverse styles. Her twentieth-century compositional techniques blended with Romantic tonality and thematic treatment have appealed to a wide range of audiences—atypical of much of contemporary music. In fact, some of her admirers call her the champion of a "new romanticism."

PRINCIPAL WORKS

Orchestral Music: *Symposium* (1973); Chamber Symphony (1979); Symphony No. 1 (1982); Symphony No. 2 (1985); *Celebration* (tone poem, 1984); Prologue and Variations (1984); *Concerto Grosso* (1985) (after Handel); *Symbolon* (1988)

Chamber Music: Sonata for Violin and Piano (1974); String Quartet (1974); String Trio (1981); Divertimento (1983); Double Quartet for Strings (1984); Concerto for Trumpet and Five Players (1984)

Vocal Music: *Einsame Nacht* (Lonesome Night, song cycle, 1971); *Passages* for Soprano and Instrumental Ensemble; several other songs

LISTENING ACTIVITY

ZWILICH, *CONCERTO GROSSO 1985*
FIRST MOVEMENT: MAESTOSO

Compact Disc 4, Track 45
Running Time: 2:41

Listen to the *Concerto Grosso 1985* by Ellen Taaffe Zwilich. It is scored for a chamber orchestra consisting of a small group of winds, harpsichord, and strings reminiscent of Baroque style period. The work was commissioned by the Washington Friends of Handel for the commemoration of George Frideric Handel's birth.

Zwilich patterned the *Concerto Grosso* on a violin sonata by Handel. The first movement contains several musical quotes from the original Handel work. The Handel sections are juxtaposed with contemporary polytonal arpeggios. To contrast Handel's style with Zwilich's unique contemporary style, she instructs the performers to perform the Handel sections in obvious Baroque style.

The composer states that the concerto is "both inspired by Handel's sonata and, I hope, imbued with his spirit." More specifically, in neoclassical style (neo-Baroque here), she uses terraced dynamics—contrasting imitations of loud and soft sections—repeated melodic phrases, and sequences.

Interestingly, at the world premiere in 1986, the Handel violin sonata was performed preceding the Zwilich *Concerto Grosso 1985*.

LISTENING GUIDE

Zwilich, *Concerto Grosso 1985*
First Movement: Maestoso

45	0:00	HELD TONES	3 long tones on the pitch D, *f;* maestoso
	0:24	ARPEGGIO THEME	intervals based on Handel's theme, 16th note, polytonal arpeggios in flutes, oboes, violins over held D, *f;* repeated *p*
	0:41	HANDEL THEME	played by violin, harpsichord continuo in Baroque style, ornamented stately melody, *mp;* duple meter
	1:02	ARPEGGIO THEME	*f;* 16th note polytonal arpeggios played by flute and violin, imitated by various instruments
	1:22	HANDEL THEME—fragments	*p;* oboe, ornamented melody over harpsichord and basso continuo
	1:38	HANDEL THEME—fragments	violins, *f;* alternating imitations with flute and oboe, oboe fragments from the Handel theme
	1:57	HANDEL THEME—fragments	*f;* woodwinds and strings, ornamented melody in Baroque style with continuo, section ends with cadence

| 2:10 | ARPEGGIO THEME | woodwinds and strings together play polytonal arpeggios |
| 2:20 | POLYCHORDS | *f;* three held polychords with harpsichord arpeggios |

Neoclassical American Composers

Following Copland's goal to create music that could be accessible to the general American population, several important American composers incorporated neoclassical influences in their music.

WALTER PISTON (1894–1976)   A contemporary of Copland, Piston studied in France with Nadia Boulanger, as well as with Paul Dukas. He is known for his books on music theory and his teaching at Harvard (Bernstein was one of his students). Piston wrote eight symphonies, numerous concertos, and chamber music works. His ballet *The Incredible Flutist* (1938) is his most popular work.

ROGER SESSIONS (1896–1985)   Born in Brooklyn, New York, Sessions wrote complicated, abstract music (without extramusical ideas attached) and twelve-tone music. He taught at Smith College in Massachusetts, Cleveland Institute of Music, Princeton University, University of California/Berkeley, and Juilliard School of Music.

Sessions' most successful students include Miriam Gideon, Hugo Weisgall, Vivien Fine, Donald Martino, and Ellen Taaffe Zwilich.

SAMUEL BARBER (1910–1981)   An eclectic, neo-Romantic composer, Barber was born in Philadelphia and studied at Curtis Institute there. Some of his most popular works are his overture for *School of Scandal* (1933), String Quartet (1936), *Vanessa* (opera, 1958), "Adagio for Strings" (1936, used in the film *Platoon*), *Medea* (Ballet, 1946), and many interesting songs.

HOWARD HANSON (1896–1981)   From 1924 to 1964, Hanson was director of the Eastman School of Music, where he also founded and conducted the Eastman Philharmonic Orchestra. Symphony No. 1 (*Nordic,* 1923) and Symphony No. 2 (*Romantic,* 1930) are two of his popular works, along with his opera *Merry Mount* (1934).

Summary of Terms

African rhythms
church music
bebop
bitonal
blue notes
blues
blues progressions
blues scale
cakewalk
call and response
chord pattern
country
eclecticism
funeral
fusion

fusion-electronic
fusion/jazz-rock
gospel
jazz-rock
military bands
minstrelsy
offbeat
ostinato
polychords
polymedia
polymeters
polyrhythms
polytonal
polytonality

pop music
quarter tones
rag
ragged time
ragtime
rhythm and blues
riff
rock 'n' roll
slave trade
song plugger
soul and funk
swing
Tin Pan Alley
work songs

Chapter 25

North American Popular Music

How does popular music fit into a study of concert music? Drawing a dividing line between classical and popular music can be difficult—especially since many popular artists have classical music backgrounds, for example, Wynton Marsalis, Herb Alpert, and Cleo Laine.

Some musicians claim that classical music is for serious listening and will be a legacy for future generations, and that popular music is for sheer entertainment, satisfying the changing tastes of today's audiences. In that case, much of Mozart's music would have been considered popular in his day. In the 1790s, Viennese from all walks of life sang tunes from Mozart's *The Magic Flute*.

Also, many popular music hits cross over into symphony orchestra "pops" concerts and summer festivals. You may find popular music on the same program as opera, ballet, and traditional orchestral music. For example, the Boston Pops Orchestra has regularly programmed music by the Beatles.

People have always used popular music to enhance their lives. Songs have helped uplift the spirit and ease the rigors of daily existence. African-American slaves in America's South sang their popular spirituals to mitigate the pain of their toil. Lonely cowboys on the vast prairies sang to relieve their boredom. Work songs accompanied the hammering of spikes into railroad ties across America. Caught in a traffic jam today, what do we do? Turn on the radio or put in a CD and listen to music.

EARLY AMERICAN POPULAR MUSIC

"Yankee Doodle," originally a British tune, became a popular song throughout the colonies during the Revolutionary War. Later, during the Civil War, "Yankee Doodle" and "John Brown's Body" ("The Battle Hymn of the Republic") were identified with the North, and Dan Emmett's (1815–1904) "Dixie" with the South. They were popular in their day and remain so.

Foster

Stephen Foster (1826–1864) wrote hundreds of popular songs in the nineteenth century. "Jeanie with the Light Brown Hair," "Oh, Susanna," and "Camptown Races"—hit songs of his day—are still sung. Foster's "My Old Kentucky Home" sold 90,000 copies of sheet music. His "Old Folks at Home" reached an all-time record, with his royalties topping $10,000, a considerable sum in the nineteenth century.

Twentieth-century technology and a host of inventions have created an unprecedented mass market for popular music. Radio, television, music videos, DVDs, compact discs, audio tape recordings, and the Internet deliver popular music to millions of people around the world.

Irving Berlin's "Alexander's Ragtime Band"

When Irving Berlin (1888–1989) wrote the popular song, "Alexander's Ragtime Band" in 1911, jazz crossed over into popular music, and for the first time, jazz style became commercially successful. Berlin intended to capture the flavor of a New Orleans street-parade jazz band and bring it to Tin Pan Alley in New York City. Within a few years of its introduction, a whole nation was singing and dancing to that tune.

Until that time, highly syncopated ragtime music, blues, and jazz had been the province of African-American musicians. They played to small audiences in their churches, social clubs, and society street parades in Memphis and New Orleans. By 1916, the new jazz style had influenced popular music, sweeping the nation.

Sheet music cover of Berlin's "Alexander's Ragtime Band"

TIN PAN ALLEY

Until the late 1930s, Tin Pan Alley was the commercial hub of American popular music. Rows and rows of four-story brownstone buildings on New York's West 28th Street housed music publishing companies and related businesses. From there they distributed their products throughout the Western world.

Where did that peculiar name come from? During the hot, stifling New York City summers, music businesses would open their windows to let in fresh air. The sounds they produced spilled out into the streets, mixing the pounding of pianos of song pluggers, squealing saxophones and blaring trumpets, and musical show singers trying out the latest tunes. The din must have reminded someone of the banging of tin pans.

THE COMMERCIALIZATION OF POPULAR MUSIC

With the wind-up phonograph of Thomas Edison and the crystal radio of Guglielmo Marconi still luxury items, no mass market had emerged for the expensive wax recordings, nor were there commercial radio stations to play "Alexander's Ragtime Band." To hear the latest Irving Berlin or George M. Cohan songs, music lovers had to go either to the theater or to a department store where song pluggers would play music to entice customers to buy the sheet music. Royalties from sheet music sales and from vaudeville and musical theater performances were the only mass market for songwriters.

Edison phonograph
Marconi Radio

Record Companies

The first African-American-owned recording company, The Black Swan Phonograph Company, started in 1921. The blues singer Ethel Waters gave the company its first big hit, "Down Home Blues."

By the late 1920s, major record companies were electronically recording and mass producing brittle shellac phonograph records that were now flat discs, eight to twelve inches in diameter. Turntables for the discs spun at 78 revolutions per minute.

Popular and affordable, phonograph records introduced musical artists and their songs to people around the world. In 1928, for instance, Al Jolson's recording of "Sonny Boy" sold 4 million copies in just four weeks! Jolson, a Russian-Jewish immigrant, made a fortune imitating African-American minstrels.

Radio Broadcasts

With the opening in 1920 of America's first public broadcast station, KDKA in Pittsburgh, mass-produced home radio sets became a hot-selling item. Disc jockeys created a new market for popular music.

Popular Music in Films

The 1927 film *The Jazz Singer*, starring Al Jolson, became the first commercially produced "talkie." With the advent of sound film, musicals became another important outlet for popular music.

America in the 1920s became the world's commercial center for popular music. Through the media of radio, sound films, and sound recordings, people everywhere could hear the music of George Gershwin, Irving Berlin, W. C. Handy, Eubie Blake, Jerome Kern, Cole Porter, Richard Rodgers, Harold Arlen, and many others.

THE SWING ERA

The big bands of the 1930s and 1940s brought popular swing music into dance halls and ballrooms. Band buses rolled around the country bringing

Benny Goodman with his big band

Billie Holiday

live music to millions from Bridgeport to Boise. Through the media and live performances, Americans heard the seventeen-piece bands of trumpeter Bunny Berrigan, pianist Fletcher Henderson, trombonist Tommy Dorsey, saxophonist Jimmy Dorsey, trombonist Glenn Miller, trumpeter Harry James, clarinetist Artie Shaw, and the American royalty: "Duke" Ellington (piano), "Count" Basie (piano), and the "King of Swing," Benny Goodman (clarinet).

Highly skilled performers staffed their bands. Audiences crowded around the bandstand to hear these popular music virtuosos. Because big bands provided music for listening as well as dancing, they gave their audiences unforgettable performances.

Each big band featured a male and a female vocalist. "Crooners" such as Russ Columbo, Frank Sinatra, Bing Crosby, Dick Haymes, Perry Como, and Vaughan Monroe launched their careers singing with the big bands. So did female vocalists: Sarah Vaughan, Helen Forest, Ruth Etting, Peggy Lee, Rosemary Clooney, Doris Day, Billie Holiday, and Ella Fitzgerald.

Popular Music and World War II

To boost the morale of English-speaking troops during World War II, Armed Forces Radio broadcast music throughout the war zones. Glenn Miller and many members of his band eventually joined the Army Air Corps. Based in London, they broadcast to all the fighting forces—on both sides of the conflict. After the Allies liberated Paris, Glenn Miller obtained a small aircraft and pilot to fly him there to relocate the Air Force band. His plane crashed in the Normandy fog, killing him and the crew.

Popular Music in Industry

To increase production during World War II, factories introduced music. Researchers studied different music throughout the day and noted its effect on production. As a result of these studies, a new branch of music emerged—*environmental* music.

Today, music is everywhere—in elevators, offices, medical and dental waiting rooms, airport lounges, restaurants, bowling alleys, shopping malls, supermarkets, lawyers' offices—even when one is on "hold" during a phone call. Environmental music companies provide sound tracks designed to increase employees' efficiency by creating a cheerful environment. Theoretically, you don't even have to listen to the music intently: It surrounds you and helps shape your mood.

Environmental music

Decline of the Big Bands

After World War II, with America focusing its economy on housing and consumer goods for the returning G.I.s and their expanding families, music retrenched. Spending priorities changed from expensive entertainment to buying automobiles, housing, furniture, and kitchen appliances. Gone was the costly big band era. Now, small groups became fashionable.

THE JUKEBOX   The jukebox, an offshoot of the record industry, was an economical replacement for live music. The "box" also made popular music available in ice cream parlors, bowling alleys, bars, and restaurants. By 1959, over a half million jukeboxes across the nation were swallowing dimes and quarters.

During and immediately after World War II, with money scarce, most young families had stay-at-home parties. They danced to radio programs such as "Juke Box Saturday Night" and "Your Hit Parade." In the 1950s, "Your Hit Parade" moved to television, where it was seen along with new dance programs such as Dick Clark's "American Bandstand" and in the 1960s, "Soul Train."

COUNTRY MUSIC

Replacing the big bands throughout America were the four- to seven-piece bands with the all-important lead singer. Guitars—acoustic, electric, and the Hawaiian steel guitars—replaced trumpets, trombones, and saxophones.

A "down-home" eclectic music became popular. Combining elements from Southern folk music (simple tunes and predictable harmony) with elements of jazz, blues, and gospel, a new sound echoed throughout the music industry. Called "country," "country-western," "country-folk," "rock-a-billy," or at times "honky-tonk," the music became popular everywhere, notably in the South and Southwest.

Country music performers can boast some of the highest-grossing albums in the popular music world. Founded in 1958, the Country Music Association (CMA) was the first trade organization created to promote a

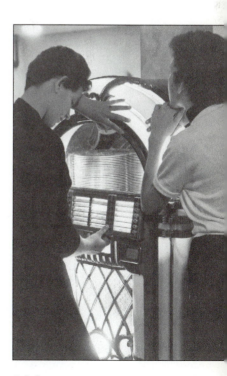

Jukebox

specific genre of music. The CMA Awards, originally broadcast on network television in 1968, was the first music-awards program. (The Grammys and the American Music Awards came later.)

Some of the artists—old-timers, and newcomers—who have contributed to the enormous success of country music include Willie Nelson, Johnny Cash, Bonnie Raitt, Dolly Parton, Wynonna, LeAnn Rimes, Garth Brooks, Tim McGraw, Conway Twitty, Charlie Daniels, Michael Martin Murphy, Trisha Yearwood, George Strait, Dwight Yoakam, Brooks & Dunn, Randy Travis, Shania Twain, Kenny Rogers, Patsy Cline, Vince Gill, K. T. Oslin, Kris Kristofferson, Loretta Lynn, Brenda Lee, Waylon Jennings, Buck Owens, Charlie Rich, Hank Williams, Reba McIntyre, Emmylou Harris, Faith Hill, Clint Black, Roy D. Mercer, Mel Tillis, Roy Orbison, Alan Jackson, Pam Tillis, Lyle Lovett, and Travis Tritt.

RHYTHM AND BLUES

Rhythm and blues (R & B), a transitional style between swing and rock, first became popular in the African-American communities in big cities such as Chicago and Detroit. Chuck Berry, "Fats" Domino, Little Richard, Muddy Waters, Otis Redding, James Brown, Ray Charles, and Aretha Franklin were the leading exponents of rhythm and blues. Using electronic amplifiers, a four-piece band could not only match but exceed the volume of the seventeen-piece band of the swing era. And did they ever turn up the volume!

R & B's influence continued to expand throughout the 1960s. Berry Gordy organized Motown Records (from "*mo*tor *town*," i.e., Detroit) to handle the careers of R & B artists. Specializing in African-American artists, Motown had its first big hit in 1964 with a recording by The Supremes, featuring Diana Ross.

Some of the artists who have recently made their marks include Kelly Price, Boyz II Men, The 2 Live Crew, Gerald Levert, Lauryn Hill, Mary J. Blige, Montell Jordan, Monica, Keith Washington, Luther Vandross, and Mariah Carey. The list grows longer every day.

ROCK 'N' ROLL/ROCK

In the mid-1950s, a relatively obscure group, Bill Haley and the Comets, recorded "Rock Around the Clock." The music was part of the score for

Ray Charles

Challenge Your Expertise

- Name several places where song pluggers worked.
- How did the term *Tin Pan Alley* originate?

the 1955 film *Blackboard Jungle,* which portrayed the inner-city, teenage subculture of the time.

The music caught on, especially with teenagers, and has remained popular through four decades. Rock 'n' roll (later "rock") was originally a music mixture of jazz, blues, rhythm and blues, folk, and country. From its early days, rock was characterized by its hard-driving beat—a departure from the subtle, syncopated rhythms and prominent melodies of the swing era. In rock, melody and text are subordinate to rhythms.

Elvis Presley

"You Ain't Nothin' But a Hound Dog," "Blue Suede Shoes," and other Elvis Presley hits added a new dimension to early rock music. A young "country boy" gyrating in leather and glittering studs, Elvis was dubbed "The King." He exuded a sensuality that teenagers could not resist. Crowding around to hear him, screaming their adulation, teenagers had found not only a music but an idol all their own. Hordes of imitators followed.

The Beatles

Something was different about those long-haired young men—the four-piece group from Liverpool, England, who made their North American television debut on February 8, 1964, on "The Ed Sullivan Show."

For their first number, the Beatles sang a rather simple love song, "I Wanna Hold Your Hand," and crowds of teenagers screamed and yelled and tore their hair in virtual hysteria. The Beatles achieved immediate popularity, and from that moment on, they arguably had a profound, lasting influence on popular music throughout the world for the rest of the decade.

Something else was different in 1964: the American consciousness had begun to change. As the Beatles' popularity spread, they verbalized the feelings many people shared toward the government, the military, and

The Beatles

industry. They sang about the absurdity of war, and we listened. Youth protested the Establishment in a twentieth-century version of romanticism.

Many of the Beatles' songs, especially those of John Lennon and Paul McCartney, have become standards, such as:

"Yesterday"   "Penny Lane"
"Michelle"   "Eleanor Rigby"
"Sgt. Pepper's Lonely
    Hearts Club Band"

It would be impossible to name every star in the pop music galaxy: there are so many talented people, and every fan has a favorite singer, songwriter, or group. For longevity, one group is notable—the Rolling Stones. Of those who have left their imprints on rock music, the Stones have been consistent favorites for more than thirty years. Only the Beatles have had more Top 40 hits. Other groups whose recordings have topped the charts are the Beach Boys, the Bee Gees, the Temptations, the Four Seasons, the Miracles, the Eagles, Bon Jovi, and KC & The Sunshine Band.

Woodstock Rock Festival

The 1969 Woodstock Festival was the largest music gathering in history. More than 300,000 people listened to Joan Baez, Janis Joplin, Jimi Hendrix, and the Jefferson Airplane, among others. An attitude of "sex, drugs, and rock 'n' roll" prevailed, but considering the size of the crowd, the festival was relatively peaceful. Rock music proved it was no passing fad; it would remain on the world scene for generations. The twenty-fifth anniversary of Woodstock was celebrated with a 1994 concert.

The Rolling Stones, featuring Mick Jagger (center)

Woodstock rock festival in
upstate New York, August 1969

Folk-Rock

Folk-rock music was a prominent part of Woodstock and many subsequent festivals. Promoting contemporary causes such as civil rights and the end of the Vietnam War, modern-day troubadours echoed the troubled, changing times.

Many artists blended folk and rock music styles. Performing for large crowds, artists took advantage of amplification systems, though folk-rock artists favored the traditional acoustic guitar over rock music's electronic instruments.

Some of the most influential folk-rock artists include:

Bob Dylan	Joni Mitchell	John Denver
Joan Baez	Simon and Garfunkel	Cat Stevens
Judy Collins	Peter, Paul and Mary	Donovan

Jazz-Rock

During the late 1960s, seven- and eight-piece rock groups began featuring trumpets, trombones, and saxophones as well as electronic and orchestral instruments. These groups include:

Chicago	Yes
Blood, Sweat & Tears	Ten Wheel Drive
Earth, Wind, and Fire	The Mothers of Invention

With performers more highly trained than those of some previous rock groups (many were college music school graduates), they were able to incorporate more complex four- and five-part harmonies. Moving toward the fusion of rock and jazz styles (jazz-rock), these groups created music that appealed to more sophisticated audiences than had earlier rock groups.

Characteristics of Live Rock Music Performances

- heavy, driving bass (usually played by amplified bass guitar and/or electronic keyboards)
- persistent ostinato in rhythms
- catchy, repetitive refrain (the "hook")
- extensive modal harmonies and tonalities, generally avoiding traditional major and minor tonalities
- live sounds augmented with electronic synthesizers and prerecorded tapes
- pyrotechnics in lighting, stage sets, and visual displays (smoke, lasers, strobes, etc.)

Summary of Terms

country	folk-rock	Marconi radio
country-folk	honky-tonk	rhythm and blues
country-western	jazz-rock	rock 'n' roll
Edison phonograph	jukebox	rock-a-billy
environmental music		

Chapter 26

Broadway Musical Theater

Ever since the Middle Ages, when the troubadours of Provence sang their poetic notions of love, song has been the vehicle for communicating romantic ideas and ideals. As all music does, song enriches the spirit with its fundamental messages: Life is worth living, love conquers all, good ultimately prevails over evil, and a rainbow may indeed lead us to a pot of gold.

As North America's contribution to world theater, the Broadway musical offers us not only optimistic messages but also an exciting, carefully constructed entertainment package. We can sit back, relax, and enjoy its art, color, universal theme, drama, believable characters, distinctive form, and demanding production.

Above all, there is an engaging story—the "book"—that can sweep us away for a couple of hours. Afterward, we leave the theater humming an enchanting new melody.

THE BROADWAY MUSICAL: ITS ROOTS

European Predecessors of the Broadway Musical

BALLAD OPERA   Starting in the first half of the eighteenth century, ballad opera differed from other opera mainly by having spoken dia-

361

Ballad opera

logue instead of the recitative between songs. Also, much of the music was from popular tunes and folk songs of the day, to which composers set new lyrics. Most ballad operas contained simple melodies with uncomplicated harmonies, designed to appeal to middle-class audiences. Similar to Greek tragedy, plots were based on familiar material.

In England, the most popular work of the eighteenth century was John Gay's *The Beggar's Opera* (1728). Included in the repertory of every touring company at that time, the work satirized Italian opera—especially works by Handel—the aristocracy, the British government and its then-prime minister, Robert Walpole. Using English for its language, *The Beggar's Opera* presented an alternative to Italian, which had been the dominant opera language. With its strong book, *The Beggar's Opera* set the standard for the form and style of musical productions that followed: The book comes first.

Exactly 200 years later, the German-born composer Kurt Weill (1900–1950) wrote his popular *Dreigroschen Opera* (*The Three Penny Opera*, 1928), a modern-setting imitation of *The Beggar's Opera.*

The year 1735 marked the production of *Flora,* the first ballad opera farce staged in North America. Without scenery, costumes, or footlights, the show played in the Charleston, South Carolina, courthouse to only the handful of people who could fit into the room.

Singspiel

Mozart took inspiration from the English ballad operas and wrote his delightful *Abduction from the Harem* in 1782 for the German *singspiel,* employing the German language.

Comic opera

COMIC OPERA   From the French, Italian, and English repertory, comic opera resembled the French *opéra bouffe* and the German operetta. In the United States, the comic opera incorporated the English emphasis on comedy over romance.

Mozart had a special flair for comic opera. His witty and charming *Le nozze di Figaro* (*The Marriage of Figaro,* 1786) and *Don Giovanni* (1787) are two of his most often performed comic operas.

Operetta

OPERETTA   Originating in Germany and the Austro-Hungarian Empire, the operetta incorporated every aspect of the late-nineteenth-century romanticism: love, idealism, adventure, and bravery. Wrapped in a trivial plot combined with appealing music and graceful dance, life in operettas was a delightful fantasy.

NORTH AMERICAN ROOTS OF THE MUSICAL

African-American influences

African-American music has been a part of North American culture since the arrival of the first slave boats. Slaves preserved their customs and culture by dancing, chanting, story-telling in pantomime, and playing instruments such as the banjo and drums. Although some plantation owners objected, most did not. Still others recognized the entertainment value for

Sheet music cover for collection of songs by James Bland

their guests and organized "minstrel shows" featuring syncopated song-and-dance performances, including a "cakewalk" competition in which the highest-strutting dancers would "take the cake."

Minstrelsy

Minstrelsy

Following the Civil War, former plantation owners assembled troupes of African-American performers to present their unique entertainment professionally. Minstrel shows of the nineteenth century became the first musical theater that originated in America. By the 1870s, these shows had become so popular that white entertainers formed their own touring minstrel companies. Wearing gaudy costumes and blackening their faces with burnt cork, the white troupes imitated the originals.

With the performers sitting in a semicircle facing the audience, the typical show had three parts:

Part 1 featured jokes and solo songs backed by the humming of the other performers.

Part 2 was similar to vaudeville and featured whatever diverse talents the minstrel performers possessed—juggling, dancing, magic, and the like.

Part 3 was usually a parody of a play or an opera. Most often it took the form of a sentimental operetta based on idealized plantation life.

North American composers—African-American and white—viewed minstrel shows as a marketplace for their original songs. They were right. When audiences liked the songs, they would buy the sheet music. Some composers became famous: Dan Emmett (1815–1904), Stephen Foster (1826–1864), and James A. Bland (1854–1911). "Dixie" was the best-known minstrel song. Written originally for banjo by *Dan Emmett*, the song later acquired new lyrics and became the battle anthem of the Confederacy.

Stephen Collins Foster (1826–1864)

Early America's most popular composer, Stephen Collins Foster, was born in Pittsburgh, Pennsylvania, on July 4, 1826, the fiftieth anniversary of the signing of the Declaration of Independence. Educated and well-to-do, Stephen's parents provided music instruction for all their children throughout their formative years. In fact, music was the primary focus in the life of Stephen's oldest sister Charlotte, an accomplished pianist, harpist, and singer. At an early age, Stephen also showed both an interest and a talent for music. His sister Henrietta taught him chords on the guitar. He learned to play both the piano and flute, and he was soon able to pick out melodies on these instruments.

Stephen was educated in a succession of private schools and studied with one of Pittsburgh's finest musicians, Henry Kleber, who exposed his eager young student to the masters, particularly Mozart, Beethoven, and Weber. Trained in music conservatories in Germany, Kleber was not only a music instructor but he performed as a tenor soloist and pianist, organized and directed a wind band, and composed popular dances.

At age nine, Foster joined the Thesbian Company, a neighborhood minstrel group. Performing what were then called "Ethiopian songs," they created a makeshift theater out of a carriage house. Most of their songs were written and often performed by African Americans, many of whom were still slaves.

In 1845, Foster began composing Ethiopian songs for a group of men who met twice a week at his house in Pittsburgh. Calling themselves Knights of the Square Table, the group practiced Foster's multipart harmony, accompanied by piano, guitar, flute, and violin. Foster promoted his songs to other groups and soon became one of the leading composers of minstrel songs. He was renowned for the finely crafted harmony of the chorus, which the entire minstrel troupe performed.

Foster was only eighteen when his first known ballad, "Open They Lattice, Love," was published. In 1849, he signed an agreement with New York music publisher Firth, Pond & Company, and at about the same time, he signed a similar contract with F. D. Benteen in Baltimore.

People were eager to buy the sheet music so that they could sing and play Foster's songs at home.

Since most composers sold their songs outright, Foster's contracts set a precedent by guaranteeing him royalties of two cents for each copy of sheet music sold. Some of his songs, such as the quick-tempo "Camptown Races," became show stoppers for African-American minstrel singers.

In addition to the more than 200 works for minstrel shows, Foster was known for his "plantation songs," such as "Old Folks at Home" (1851), "Old Black Joe," and "My Old Kentucky Home" (1853). His popular ballads include "Jeanie With the Light Brown Hair" (1854) and "Come Where My Love Lies Dreaming" (1855). "Jeanie With the Light Brown Hair" was inspired by Foster's Irish background: his great-grandfather had emigrated from Londonderry, Ireland, around 1728.

During his four-year contract with E. J. Christy, Foster conducted all his work by mail. He neither met the famous Original Christy Minstrels nor watched them perform until years later. Because the printed sheet music did not mention Foster's name, some of his most enduring songs, such as "Oh! Susanna" (1848), were initially associated with E. J. Christy. When Firth and Benteen reissued the sheet music, Foster was credited for his earlier songs.

In the two years that followed (1850 and 1851), Foster published fifteen songs with Firth and fifteen songs with Benteen. His income from royalties allowed him to compose full time. As North America's most successful songwriter of his day, he himself set his earnings at more than $15,000 during his fifteen-year career—in today's terms, approximately $1 million. However, he was plagued by alcoholism, outspent his income, and was constantly in debt. By 1857, he had taken advances on future royalties and had to sell his last works outright. In 1860, he moved to New York and began churning out songs just to earn a few dollars. "Beautiful Dreamer" (1864), written in his final days, was published posthumously. Stephen Foster died in a New York charity ward at age 38.

African-American Minstrels

Perhaps the most important of the Negro writers and entertainers who joined minstrel troupes after the Civil War was *James A. Bland* (1854–1911). A well-educated man born in the North, Bland was the son of one of the first African-Americans in the United States to receive a college education. Bland started as an entertainer, but he is best remembered for the songs "Carry me Back to Old Virginny," "In the Evening by the

Moonlight," and "Oh, Dem Golden Slippers." Unfortunately, all but thirty-eight of his songs have been lost.

FROM MINSTRELSY TO VAUDEVILLE

Toward the end of the nineteenth century, traditional black-face minstrel shows declined in popularity, and many African-American entertainers moved into vaudeville. After the success of the syncopated song "All Coons Look Alike to Me" (1890, Ernest Hogan), a new term emerged: "coon songs." These racially stereotyped songs were performed by black entertainers in white vaudeville.

Eventually, these entertainers decided to try something they called "all-Negro productions." Since African-American producers did not have access to theaters on the white vaudeville circuit, they presented some of their earliest musicals in burlesque houses. In 1896, an all-Negro show called *Oriental America* had a short Broadway run and attracted multiracial audiences. It was now clear that white theatergoers were willing to pay money to see black performers in all kinds of shows. Although Broadway did not easily open to African-American artists and producers, they slowly overcame the odds and arrived on Broadway to stay.

Will Marion Cook

Will Marion Cook (1869–1944) was a graduate of Oberlin Conservatory and became a distinguished composer, conductor, and violinist. After graduation, he pursued his advanced studies in Europe and later returned to New York to study composition with Antonín Dvořák.

In 1898, Cook composed music to lyrics by African-American poet-lyricist Paul Laurence Dunbar for a musical comedy sketch, *Clorindy, or the Origin of the Cakewalk*, which was produced at the Roof Garden of the Broadway's Casino Theatre. His first hit, *In Dahomey* (1902), was the first African-American musical to play in a major Broadway theater, followed by a European tour. The extravaganza *In Abyssinia* (1906) and the musical comedy *In Bandana Land* (1907) established Cook as a major force in African-American theater.

Robert Cole

Robert Cole (1863–1911) came to New York after his graduation from Atlanta University. He became a playwright and manager of the All-Star Company, the first African-American-owned and operated stock company, which presented his show *A Trip to Coontown* (1898), the first all-Negro musical comedy to open in New York.

Cole teamed with the Johnson Brothers in 1901. They created musical shows without minstrel scenes, coon songs, or shuffling. Instead, they offered good melodies, well-orchestrated scores, and some plot continuity.

John Rosamond Johnson

James Weldon Johnson

Composer *John Rosamond Johnson* (1873–1954) and his brother, poet-lyricist *James Weldon Johnson* (1871–1938) were Florida natives. Rosamond received his formal music training at the New England Conservatory of Music in Boston. After touring with the road company of *Oriental America*, he settled in New York to collaborate with his brother and Bob Cole. In 1901, they signed a contract with Joseph Stern and Company, the first known agreement between African-American songwriters and a Tin Pan Alley publisher.

The songs they wrote for *The Supper Club* (1902) brought them to the attention of powerful white producers Klaw and Erlanger. The Johnsons signed an exclusive three-year contract, for which they received a monthly salary, a flat fee for each production number, and royalties for each show.

After James's 1906 appointment as U.S. consul to Venezuela, Rosamond and Cole continued as a duo, writing *The Shoo-Fly Regiment* (1907) and *The Red Moon* (1909). Rosamond also composed the score for *Mr. Lode of Kole* (1909), starring renowned black vaudevillian Bert Williams.

In 1912 and 1913, Johnson was the music director of Hammerstein's Opera House in London. He returned to New York at the outbreak of World War I. In the 1920s, the Johnson brothers collaborated on two collections of Negro spirituals. Rosamond later published two collections of his popular music, *Shout Songs* (1936) and *Rolling Along in Song* (1937).

After a 10-year absence of all-black shows on Broadway, *Shuffle Along* (1921, Eubie Blake and Noble Sissle) opened at the 63rd Street Theatre. The show was an immediate success. It also made history. Not only did the show set new standards for the African-American productions that followed in the next two decades, but it also brought African-American audiences into the orchestra section of the theater—the section formerly reserved for white audiences only.

Eubie (James Hubert) Blake (1883–1983) was born in Baltimore. He   **Eubie Blake**
began to read and play music when he was six. Over the objection of Eubie's deeply religious mother, an organ salesman placed an instrument in their home. In his teens, Eubie began hanging around "bawdy houses" and learned how to play rag on the piano. At about age sixteen, he was hired as a pianist in one of the brothels and composed the first of his many rags, *The Charleston Rag*, published many years later.

Noble Sissle (1889–1975) sang in the high school glee club in his native   **Noble Sissle**
Indianapolis. He met Eubie in 1915, and they immediately joined forces. The following year they became players in James Reese Europe's Society Orchestra.* After World War I, Blake and Sissle worked as a vaudeville act, known as the Dixie Duo, performing their own compositions. They then collaborated on *Shuffle Along*.

Early Broadway Musicals

VAUDEVILLE   Vaudeville's roots go back to a fifteenth-century French vil-   **Vaudeville**
lage, Val-de-Vire, in Normandy. The villagers were famous for entertaining one another by composing and performing ballads and satirical songs.

The North American stage form of vaudeville, which flourished from 1878 to 1925, was a succession of unrelated specialty acts: singers, dancers,

---

*Mentioned as the employer of the fictional Coalhouse Walker, Jr., in the show *Ragtime* (1997).

actors, acrobats, comics, magicians, jugglers, midgets, monkeys, dogs, dancing elephants, skating bears, fire-eaters, Swiss bell ringers, xylophonists, female impersonators, and anything that was sensational and startling.

Tony Pastor

When Tony Pastor, a former minstrel showman, opened the doors of his Paterson, New Jersey, variety theater in 1865, he opened the doors to vaudeville in North America. In both his New Jersey and New York theaters, Pastor promoted family entertainment only—no smoking, no drinking, no vulgarity. E. F. Albee continued the crusade for purity, setting the moral tone for the Albee Theater in Brooklyn, the great Palace Theater in Manhattan, and the Keith circuit—a nationwide chain of vaudeville houses.

E. F. Albee

Keith circuit

Some of America's most popular songs emerged from vaudeville. "Sidewalks of New York" (1894) by vaudevillian Charles Lawlor became the unofficial anthem of New York City. Other surviving vaudeville hits include the following:

> "In the Good Old Summertime"
> "Waltz Me Around Again, Willie"
> "The Band Played On"
> "My Wild Irish Rose"
> "Sweet Adeline"
> "When You Were Sweet Sixteen"
> "After the Ball Is Over"
> "Shine on Harvest Moon"

During the early heyday of vaudeville, the popular song developed in both form and content. It matured with the influence of ragtime, blues, Tin Pan Alley, and such greats as Jerome Kern, Irving Berlin, George Gershwin, and Richard Rodgers.

Burlesque

BURLESQUE In direct contrast to the Keith "Sunday School Circuit," as vaudeville artists called the chain, burlesque was raucous, bawdy, musical sex-and-comedy-travesty entertainment. Starting around 1868, touring companies played to audiences of men eager for naughty, grown-up amusement, though performances were fairly modest in the early years. Not until the 1920s, when striptease replaced "hootchie-cootchie" dancing, did burlesque degenerate into sexual exhibitions.

Weber and Fields

Innovative "travesty" comedy—broad parody—was burlesque's real contribution to musical theater. In fact, around 1900, it was the great vaudeville team of Joe Weber and Lew Fields who decided to try out a travesty-comedy routine in burlesque. After their successful debut, Weber and Fields left the show to open their own music hall. Critics praised their shows, commenting that the combination of lavish musical numbers and outrageous travesty offered the best "musical comedy" available.

Burlesque had begun with a tradition of satire and comedy. After World War I, when the shows replaced their hallmark comedy with vulgar sexuality, burlesque had a decline from which it could never recover. Fortunately, musical theater learned its lesson from that: Never abandon comedy.

EXTRAVAGANZA AND SPECTACLE   The embodiment of extravaganza and spectacle was New York's Hippodrome Theater (1905–1935), which occupied the entire block on Sixth Avenue between Forty-third and Forty-fourth streets. Inside, as many as 5,200 paying customers could thrill to unobstructed views of floods and fires, sensational water ballets, cavalry charges of 480 soldiers on horseback, entire baseball games, and a brilliantly costumed female chorus of 280 dancers. Six hundred performers could fit comfortably on the half-acre stage.

The Great Depression affected the economics of all theatrical forms, especially the costly extravaganza. Paying customers decreased, and public taste changed at the same time, signaling the demise of the Hippodrome.

Renowned showman Billy Rose tried to revive the theater in 1935 with a spectacular production of *Jumbo* by Richard Rodgers and Lorenz Hart. The show was only a moderate success, and the era of the extravaganza was over.

THE REVUE   America borrowed the term *revue* from the French musical variety show that satirized Parisian high life. The new, more cohesive North American version was an energetic, nonbook show—usually built around star performers—featuring musical numbers, comedy acts, dramatic sketches, and specialty routines.

After its Broadway debut with *The Passing Show* in 1894, the revue grew in popularity. It reached its height equally in England and in North America between the two World Wars.

On Broadway, the longest-running annual revues included:

The Ziegfeld Follies	(1907–31)	25 editions
The Passing Show	(second series, 1912–24)	12 editions
George White's Scandals	(1919–31)	11 editions
Earl Carroll Vanities	(1923–32)	11 editions
The Greenwich Village Follies	(1919–28)	8 editions

Florenz Ziegfeld (1867–1932), whose shows epitomized glamour and extravagance, was the greatest exponent of the American revue. He dedicated each of his editions to the glorification of the American woman, packaging the show with a pace that built to climaxes and a spectacular finale.

Ziegfeld was a star maker. Through his casts paraded the celebrities of the era: Fanny Brice, Nora Bayes, Eva Tanguay, Marion Davies, Barbara Stanwyck, Ed Wynn, Marilyn Miller, Irene Dunne, and comedians W. C. Fields, Eddie Cantor, and Will Rogers.

Over the years, Ziegfeld commissioned more than 500 songs from composers such as Jerome Kern, Victor Herbert, and Irving Berlin. Berlin is the composer most identified with the Follies and its theme song "A Pretty Girl Is Like a Melody," which he wrote for the 1919 edition.

The 1992 musical *Will Rogers' Follies* is a modern revue based on Will Rogers' career with *The Ziegfeld Follies*.

Other long-running revues spawned great American composers such

Extravaganza and spectacle

Billy Rose

Revue

Ziegfeld

The Ziegfeld Follies of 1918, featuring (left to right): W. C. Fields, Will Rogers, Lillian Lorraine, Eddie Cantor, and Harry Kelly

Challenge Your Expertise

How did *Shuffle Along* make history?

as Cole Porter and Harold Rome. Between 1920 and 1924, George Gershwin wrote his first scores for *George White's Scandals*. Richard Rodgers and Lorenz Hart wrote their first complete Broadway score for *The Garrick Gaieties of 1925*. One of the songs in the score, "Manhattan," became a hit and launched their successful career collaboration.

Categories of Modern Broadway Musicals

The majority of Broadway musicals fall into the following broad classifications:

- modern operetta
- musical comedy
- musical play
- play with music
- popular opera

MODERN OPERETTA   Viennese composers Johann Strauss in *Die Fledermaus* and Franz Lehar (*lay*-har, 1870–1948) in *The Merry Widow* perfected the

Franz Lehar

form. Both operettas remain in the modern repertory. Victor Herbert, Sigmund Romberg, and Rudolf Friml refined operetta and introduced it to North American audiences.

Modern operetta

The Depression also affected operetta. Ragtime and jazz had taken the place of quaint tunes. With the emergence of Jerome Kern, George Gershwin, Cole Porter, Irving Berlin, and Richard Rodgers, the popular song had come of age. Composers were leading American musical theater into a new era.

GEORGE M. COHAN   Some of the roots of modern Broadway musical comedy are traceable to the early works of George M. Cohan (1878–1942). His "plays with music" were punctuated with songs created for singing actors rather than for full-voiced operetta singers. And Cohan's thin plots had a "hometown" flavor that Americans easily related to. *Little Johnny Jones* (1904) was Cohan's first Broadway hit, giving us such songs as "Yankee Doodle Boy" and "Give My Regards to Broadway." His other popular shows included *Forty-Five Minutes from Broadway* (1906), *The Little Millionaire* (1916), and *Little Nelly Kelly* (1922). During World War I, his song "Over There," from *The Cohan Revue of 1918*, became a symbol of patriotic fervor.

Cohan

Over There (1918) with a Norman Rockwell illustration on the cover

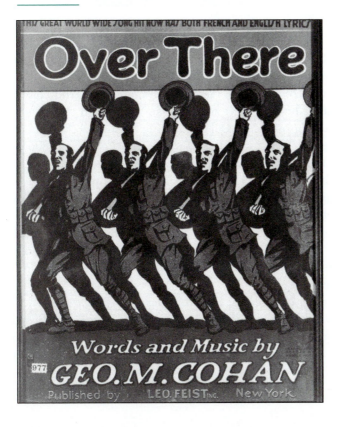

Sigmund Romberg (1887–1951)

The most prolific composer of popular musicals, Sigmund Romberg was born in Hungary and raised in Vienna, coming to America in 1909. Among his sixty operettas are *Maytime* and *Over the Top* (1917), *Blossom Time* (1921), *The Student Prince* (1924), *The Desert Song* (1926), *The New Moon* (1928), and *Up in Central Park* (1945).

His most enduring songs include "Deep in My Heart," "Serenade," and "Drinking Song" from *The Student Prince;* "One Alone" from *The Desert Song;* and "Lover Come Back to Me" and "Stout-Hearted Men" from *The New Moon.* From 1929 on, he wrote songs for motion pictures, including "When I Grow Too Old to Dream."

Victor Herbert (1859–1924)

Victor Herbert was born in Dublin, Ireland, and emigrated to the United States in 1886. He became the first important composer of the American musical stage.

From 1893 to 1898, Herbert conducted the 22nd New York Regiment band. For the next six years, he conducted the Pittsburgh Symphony, until organizing and conducting his own orchestra in 1904.

Herbert's first success, *The Wizard and the Nile* (1895), was set in Egypt. This was followed in 1898 by *The Fortune Teller,* which premiered at the Grand Opera House in Toronto, preceding its Broadway run. Set in Hungary, the operetta gave us "Gypsy Love Song," which has endured for many generations.

Legend has it that in 1899 and 1900, while simultaneously composing four operetta scores, Herbert, a great lover of food and drink, kept four bottles of wine chilled in a washtub of ice, sipping a different one with each score.

Among his greatest hits were *Babes in Toyland* (1903), *The Red Mill* (1906)—which had the first moving electric sign on a Broadway marquee—and *Naughty Marietta* (1910). Herbert also wrote musical scores for *The Ziegfeld Follies* of 1917 and 1921–24 and composed two grand operas.

Rudolf Friml (1879–1972)

Considered an infant prodigy at the piano, Rudolf Friml studied in Prague with his Czech countryman Antonin Dvořák. In 1901 and 1906, Friml was accompanist for the U.S. tours of the famous Czech violinist Jan Kubelik (1880–1940). After the second tour, Friml decided to remain in the United States, becoming a naturalized citizen in 1925.

In his more than thirty operettas, Friml's formula for success was a combination of rich melody, rousing choruses, and passionate romance.

His works include *The Firefly* (1912), *You're in Love* (1917), *Rose Marie* (1924, which featured the song "Indian Love Call"), *The Vagabond King* (1925, which included "Only a Rose" and "Someday"), *The Three Musketeers* (1928), and *Bird of Paradise* (1930).

From 1930, Friml composed for movies. He wrote the famous "Donkey Serenade" for the 1937 film version of *Firefly*.

Irving Berlin (1888–1989)

Irving Berlin came to New York's Lower East Side from his native Russia in 1892. Although he had no musical training, he taught himself to compose by picking out melodies on the black keys of the piano. He even worked as a singing waiter in Chinatown, performing his own songs.

Berlin's 1914 show *Watch Your Step* introduced ragtime into the theater. *As Thousands Cheer* (1933), which ranks among his finest works for the theater, includes "Heat Wave," the show-stopper he wrote for Ethel Waters, and the timeless "Easter Parade." For that song, Berlin did something that was common among musical composers of that time. He unearthed a tune he had written earlier titled "Smile and Show Your Dimple" and simply changed the lyrics.

Later, Berlin wrote two long-running Broadway hits—*Annie Get Your Gun* (1946) and *Call Me Madam* (1950)—both starring the great Ethel Merman. In 1999, *Annie Get Your Gun* was revived on Broadway.

Princess Theatre

JEROME KERN   Jerome Kern (1885–1945) brought a new attitude into musical theater: he insisted on a partnership between the story, or "book," and the music. Kern had been leading a revolution in musical theater even in his co-authored series of shows known as the Princess Theatre musicals. Staged in a 299-seat house, Kern's shows could be more intimate, a departure from the European operetta. And each show had a simple, modern, farce-oriented plot.

Jerome Kern (1885–1945)

The son of Eastern European immigrants, Jerome Kern developed a love for music from learning the Bohemian folk songs his mother sang to him. When he displayed his musical gifts at a young age, his family encouraged him. Kern studied piano, theory, and orchestration at the New York College of Music, and he continued his advanced training with private tutors in Germany. He then went to London where he met American impresario and producer Charles Frohman. Impressed with Kern's early songs, Frohman interpolated them in his West End musicals.

In 1904, Kern returned to New York and began his career on Tin Pan Alley, the center of the popular music business. Max Dreyfus, head of the music publishing firm of T.B. Harms, discovered Kern and hired him as a rehearsal pianist and song plugger. Kern used the opportunity to audition his own tunes. He finally succeeded in placing his ballad "They Didn't Believe Me" in the 1914 musical production *The Girl From Utah*—a British import despite the title.

Dissatisfied with the formulas of conventional musicals, Kern was determined to reinvent musical theater, revealing his vision in the intimate Princess Theatre Shows. These musicals were the first to break with the tradition of enormous, elaborately costumed companies performing on large stages amid ornate sets. The shows used contemporary settings, breezy stories, and small casts whose main characters were two lovers and a comedian.

It was in these early musicals that Kern began to refine the show song. The opening production was *Nobody Home* (1915). Later that year, the Princess had its first hit, *Very Good Eddie* (1915), a farce-comedy that was good enough to stand on its own without music. Working with librettists P.G. Wodehouse and Guy Bolton, Kern then turned out *Have a Heart* (1916), followed by two outstanding hits—the legendary *Oh, Boy!* (1917), and *Oh, Lady, Lady* (1918).

Kern hit his musical stride with *Sally* (1920, "Look For the Silver Lining"). Produced by Florenz Ziegfeld, the show opened at the New Amsterdam Theater and ran for a record 570 performances. Kern collaborated with Otto Harbach and Oscar Hammerstein II on *Sunny* (1925, "Who?"). He then teamed with Oscar Hammerstein II on the show that would revolutionize the Broadway musical.

The Kern–Hammerstein masterpiece, *Show Boat,* opened at the Ziegfeld Theater in December 1927. Their score contains one memorable song after another: "Ol' Man River," "Can't Help Lovin' That Man," "Make Believe," "Bill," and "Why Do I Love You?" Hammerstein's libretto was an adaptation of a successful Edna Ferber novel.

Despite these assets, Florenz Ziegfeld was certain the show would flop because of its controversial themes: interracial marriage, divorce, desertion, and alcoholism. Compounding his skepticism was the fact that for the first time, African Americans were featured in key roles interacting with Caucasians. Ziegfeld spared no expense in mounting the production. As the first distinguished, dramatic musical comedy, *Show Boat* became the benchmark for innovative productions.

Most critics welcomed the groundbreaking show, declaring that Kern and Hammerstein had created a timeless theater piece. Audiences overwhelmingly approved, although many did not know what to make of it. Through the years, *Show Boat* has grown more popular. Although racially based resistance in Toronto and New York preceded the 1995 revival, the show opened to acclaim and reaffirmed its appeal.

During the 1930s, Kern was primarily engaged in composing film musicals, but he did turn out a few moderately successful shows: *The Cat and the Fiddle* (1931), *Music in the Air* (1932), *Roberta* (1933, "Smoke Gets in Your Eyes," with Otto Harbach), and *Very Warm for May* (1939, "All the Things You Are"). In the midst of discussions about a new musical based on the life of Annie Oakley, Kern died suddenly of a brain hemorrhage in 1945. The producers, Richard Rogers and Oscar Hammerstein II, then offered the project, *Annie Get Your Gun* (1946), to Irving Berlin.

PRINCIPAL WORKS

Musicals: *Nobody Home* (1915); *Very Good Eddie* (1915); *Have a Heart* (1916); *Oh, Boy!* (1917); *Oh, Lady, Lady* (1918); *Sally* (1920); *Sunny* (1925); *Show Boat* (1927); *The Cat and the Fiddle* (1931); *Music in the Air* (1932); *Roberta* (1933); *Very Warm for May* (1939).

Film Scores: *Show Boat* (1931, 1951).

Challenge Your Expertise

What did Tony Pastor do to change vaudeville?

HISTORICAL PERSPECTIVE

Kern's Show Boat: The New Broadway Musical

Show Boat (1927), Jerome Kern's milestone musical produced by Florenz Ziegfeld, demonstrated that dramatic literature could merge successfully with romantic song to create good theater. The *New York Times* singled out for exceptional praise the collaborative achievement of Kern's music and Oscar Hammerstein II's book and lyrics.

Daring for its time, *Show Boat* deals with delicate and controversial subjects such as love gone sour, miscegenation (racially mixed marriages), racial prejudice, alcohol and gambling addiction, and economic troubles—a major departure from the "happy-go-lucky," "all is well with the world" musical. Yet audiences took to the integration of music and challenging story with great enthusiasm, paving the way for later musicals such as *South Pacific*, *Les Misérables*, and *Miss Saigon*.

LISTENING ACTIVITY

Paul Robeson singing "Ol' Man River" in the 1936 film version of Kern's *Show Boat*

Show Boat (1927), Jerome Kern
"Ol' Man River"

Large Form: Broadway Musical
Detailed Form: Three-part Song-form
Performing Medium: Bass Voice and Orchestra

Compact Disc 4, Track 17
Running Time: 2:17

In Act 1, the song, "Ol' Man River" introduces Joe, an African-American handyman on the *Show Boat*. Originally written for the great bass Paul Robeson (1898–1976), the son of a slave, the song functions as a *leitmotif*—a recurrent theme that represents the Mississippi River and the passage of time.

In this rare recording, we hear the role of Joe as Kern and Hammerstein had conceived it for Robeson. Robeson himself felt oppressed by racial discrimination in the United States and later sought refuge in the Soviet Union for a number of years. This 1958 recording of a live Carnegie Hall concert marks Robeson's historic return to his native United States.

As a fighter for racial equality, Robeson slightly alters Hammerstein's lyrics in the recording you will hear. For example, to avoid the stereotypical dialect associated with the African American, he replaces *"dat's de ol' man"* with *"that's the ol' man."* And in the last few lines:

> "I get weary
> An' sick of tryin',
> I'm tired of livin',
> An' skeered o' dyin'"

Robeson replaces lyrics about his personal crusade for civil rights:

> "But I keep laughin'
> Instead of cryin'.
> I must keep fightin',
> Until I'm dyin' . . ."

LISTENING GUIDE

SHOW BOAT *(1927), JEROME KERN*
"OL' MAN RIVER"

17	0:00	INTRODUCTION	piano; moderately fast; 4 meter throughout; major, mostly pentatonic scale; slowing down to cadence, emphasis on text:
	0:17	VERSE	

Dere's an ol' man
called the Mississippi.
That's the ol' man
I don't like to be.
What does he care
If the world's got troubles?
What does he care
if the land ain't free?

18	0:37	CHORUS [A]	slower, steady tempo; mostly pentatonic

That ol' man river,
That ol' man river,
He mus' know sumpin'
But don't say nuthin',

		He jes' keeps rollin',	
		He keeps on rollin' along.	
	1:00	CHORUS [A]	*same music, different text*
		He don't plant 'taters,	
		He don't plant cotton,	
		an' dem that plants 'em	
		Is soon forgotten,	
		But ol' man river,	
		He jes' keeps rollin' along.	
19	1:23	BRIDGE [B]	faster tempo; agitated; rubato; slowing to cadence
		You an' me,	
		We sweat an' strain,	
		Body all achin'	
		an' racked wid' pain.	
		Tote dat barge!	
		Lift dat bale!	
		Yo' show a little click,	
		An' you' lands in jail.	
20	1:46	CHORUS [A]	same music as [A] with new text; cadence at end
		But I keep laughin'	
		Instead of cryin'.	
		I mus' keep fightin',	
		Until I'm dyin'.	
		An' ol' man river,	
		He jes' keeps rollin' along!	

George Gershwin

Ira Gershwin

George and Ira Gershwin

The music of George Gershwin (1898–1937) and the lyrics of his brother Ira (1896–1983) were a remarkable collaboration. On December 1, 1924, at the Liberty Theater, the show *Lady Be Good* opened—with the first complete score by the Gershwin brothers produced on Broadway. Giving us both the title song "Lady Be Good" and "Fascinating Rhythm," the show was the jazz-age equivalent of Kern's Princess Theatre musicals of the preceding decade.

Because their first show with book writers Guy Bolton and P. G. Wodehouse had been a hit, the Gershwins again teamed up with them on *Oh, Kay!* (1926). That score contains several Gershwin classics: "Do, Do, Do," "Clap Yo' Hands," and "Someone to Watch Over Me." *Girl Crazy* (1930) gave us "Embraceable You," "I Got Rhythm," and "But Not for Me."

LISTENING INSIGHTS

Listening to Broadway Musical Theater Songs

Most songs in musicals contain three main elements: verse, chorus, and bridge.

Verse   Similar to the recitative in opera, the verse introduces the song (*aria* in opera) and presents story or background. The verse was even more important in early musicals such as the *revue* or *vaudeville* because these shows contained little or no story—magicians, dancers, acrobats, and comics performed between songs. When the singer took center stage, the verse provided a vehicle to engage the audience in the song. Occasionally, when the songs were performed outside the context of the show, the verse was omitted.

Chorus [A]   The chorus is the main tune or song.

Bridge [B]   A middle, usually contrasting, section of music. The tempo, mood, and style of the bridge usually contrasts the first melody.

Typical Plans for Broadway Musical Songs are:

VERSE (optional)	CHORUS (A)	CHORUS (A)	BRIDGE (B)	CHORUS (A)

or

VERSE (optional)	CHORUS (A)	BRIDGE (B)	CHORUS (A)	BRIDGE (B)

Cowboy Curly (Gordon MacRae) singing "Oh, What a Beautiful Morning" in the opening scene from the film production of *Oklahoma*

Just as *Show Boat* had brought a new maturity to the American musical stage, *Of Thee I Sing* (1931) introduced an offbeat, adult approach to musical comedy. The show was the first musical to receive the Pulitzer Prize for Drama.

The book by George S. Kaufman and Morrie Ryskind was a send-up of American political institutions and the Establishment. To complement the story, the Gershwins explored a new style of composition, producing a score that interweaves a succession of songs, recitatives, and extended musical scenes. A distinctively native form had emerged.

Cole Porter (1891–1964)

Composer-lyricist Cole Porter came from an affluent, socially prominent family in Peru, Indiana, and maintained an elegant lifestyle throughout his life. Serious musical training did not play a significant role during his childhood, but while at Yale, he composed football songs ("Bingo Eli Yale" and "Bulldog").

Ironically, Porter's wealth did not help his early Broadway career. After the flop of his 1916 composing debut, he realized he would have to learn his craft or remain a dilettante. So he went to France to study composition with Vincent D'Indy (dan-*dee*) at the Paris Conservatory.

By 1929, Porter resumed his career writing musicals. Whether or not the shows themselves were hits, many of the songs from those shows were to become classics. Porter distinguished himself and revealed his background with his witty, sophisticated lyrics. Instead of the everyday realities that other Depression-era lyricists dealt with, Porter's songs refer to wealth, luxury, and lavish spending.

In the autumn of 1937, both of Porter's legs were crushed in a horseback riding accident. One leg healed; the other did not and was eventually amputated. Following the accident, Porter continued to work, creating two of his biggest Broadway successes, *Leave It to Me!* (1938) and *DuBarry Was a Lady* (1939).

Between 1929 and 1955, Cole Porter wrote twelve Broadway musicals and several film scores. After his final Broadway outing—*Silk Stockings* (1955), an adaptation of the film *Ninotchka*—Porter focused his composing career on film scores and television specials.

PRINCIPAL WORKS

Fifty Million Frenchmen (1929, "You Do Something to Me"), *Wake Up and Dream* (1929, "What Is This Thing Called Love"), *The New Yorkers* (1930, "Love For Sale"), *Gay Divorce* (1932, "Night and Day"), *Anything Goes* (1934, "Anything Goes," "I Get a Kick Out of You," "You're the Top," "All Through the Night"), *Jubilee* (1935, "Begin the Beguine" and "Just One of Those Things"), *Leave It to Me* (1938, "My Heart Belongs to Daddy"), *DuBarry Was a Lady* (1939, "Friendship" and "Do I Love You"), *Panama Hattie* (1940), *Kiss Me Kate* (1948), *Can-Can* (1953, "I Love Paris" and "It's All Right With Me"), *Silk Stockings* (1955)

Songs Written for Films: "Let's Do It" (1928), "I've Got You Under My Skin" (1936), "In the Still of the Night" (1937), and "I Concentrate on You" (1940)

Richard Rodgers (1902–1979)

One of the most prolific and successful Broadway musical composers, Richard Charles Rodgers was born in Hammels Station on Long Island near New York City. Studying piano from the age of six, he quickly learned to improvise and play by ear. As a teenager, he attended one Broadway show after another and was particularly impressed by the operettas of Victor Herbert and the musicals of Jerome Kern.

While studying at Columbia University in 1918, he met Lorenz Hart, and they began writing musicals together. Their first collaboration, *Fly with Me*, was written for Columbia's amateur varsity production.

Rodgers and Hart's first Broadway success was *The Garrick Gaieties* (1925), a revue-type show. Between 1926 and 1930, the team produced fourteen musicals and revues.

Called to Hollywood, Rodgers and Hart continued working together on films. After a fruitful partnership for nearly thirty musicals, their collaboration ended with the death of Lorenz Hart in 1943.

A new era began in Rodgers' life when he teamed up with the great lyricist Oscar Hammerstein II. Beginning with *Oklahoma* (1943), their eighteen-year collaboration until Hammerstein's death created a legacy of nine of Broadway's greatest and timeless musicals—including *Carousel* (1945), *South Pacific* (1949), *The King and I* (1951), and *The Sound of Music* (1959).

Even though there were earlier examples of a "book show"—*Show Boat* (1927), *Pal Joey* (Rodgers and Hart, 1940), and the Gershwins' *Of Thee I Sing* (1931)—*Oklahoma!* became the benchmark for musicals in which the songs were fully integrated dramatically and served the play. Rodgers and Hammerstein believed in the importance of music in theater—that it could reinforce emotion beyond words alone. Their songs helped move the story along, establishing mood and contributing to character development and dynamic.

After Hammerstein's death, Rodgers tried writing both the lyrics and the music. But even in his collaboration with Stephen Sondheim he was never as successful as he was when he worked with his two great collaborators, Lorenz Hart and Oscar Hammerstein II. Richard Rodgers died in New York City at age 77.

PRINCIPAL WORKS

Hit Musicals, Revues, and Films from Musicals: *The Garrick Gaieties* (with Hart, 1925); *On Your Toes* (with Hart, 1936; film 1939); *Babes in Arms* (with Hart, 1937, film 1939); *Pal Joey* (with Hart and O'Hara, 1940; film 1957); *Oklahoma!* (with Hammerstein, 1943; film 1955); *Carousel* (with Hammerstein, 1945; film 1956); *South Pacific* (with Hammerstein, 1949; film 1958); *The King and I* (with Hammerstein, 1951; film 1956); *Flower Drum Song* (with Hammerstein, 1958; film 1961); *The Sound of Music* (with Hammerstein, 1959; film 1964); *Do I Hear a Waltz?* (with Laurents and Sondheim, 1965)

Original Film Scores: *Love Me Tonight* (with Hart, 1932); *State Fair* (with Hammerstein, 1945); *Words and Music* (with Hart, 1948)

Television Musicals: *Cinderella* (with Hammerstein, 1957); *Androcles and the Lion* (Rodgers and Shaw, 1967)

Television Documentary Series: *Victory at Sea* (1952); *Churchill, the Valiant Years* (1960)

Stephen Sondheim (B. 1930)

Born in New York City, Stephen Joshua Sondheim showed an early interest in Broadway musical theater. He was encouraged to pursue that interest by family friend, mentor, and neighbor Oscar Hammerstein II.

At the small, prestigious liberal arts Williams College in Massachusetts, Sondheim wrote several full-length musicals that earned him a scholarship to study for two years with the avant-garde composer Milton Babbitt.

Working with Babbitt gave Sondheim insight into contemporary sound. He mastered the inventive meters, unusual melodic intervals, and unpredictable harmonies that characterize his music.

Hammerstein passed on to Sondheim what Jerome Kern had passed on to him and Richard Rodgers: an understanding of dramatic construction. The songs in Sondheim's scores grow not only from the dramatic ideas in the story but also from the objective of giving the actor something to act—a theatrical moment. With his success, Sondheim brought another level of maturity into Broadway's musical theater.

Sondheim made his Broadway debut with incidental music to *The Girls of Summer* (1956) and as a lyricist for *West Side Story* (1957, with Leonard Bernstein). The 1962 production of *A Funny Thing Happened on the Way to the Forum*, the first for which he wrote both music and lyrics, won a Tony Award for best musical of the year. Over the years, Sondheim collaborated as lyricist with Richard Rodgers (*Do I Hear a Waltz*, 1965), and again with Bernstein in the 1974 revival of *Candide*.

Principal Works

Musicals: *The Girls of Summer* (1956, incidental music); *West Side Story* (1957, lyrics, with music by Leonard Bernstein); *Gypsy* (1959, lyrics, music by Jule Styne); *A Funny Thing Happened on the Way to the Forum* (1962, lyrics and music); *Company* (1970, lyrics and music—Tony Award); *Follies* (1971, lyrics and music—Tony Award), *A Little Night Music* (1973, lyrics and music—Tony and The Standard Awards); *Pacific Overtures* (1976, lyrics and music); *Sweeney Todd* (1979, lyrics and music—Tony and The Standard Awards); *Merrily We Roll Along* (1981, lyrics and music); *Sunday in the Park with George* (1984, lyrics and music—Pulitzer Prize); *Into the Woods* (1987, lyrics and music)

Film Music: *Stavisky* (1974); *The Seven Percent Solution* (1977); *Passion* (1994)

LISTENING ACTIVITY

A LITTLE NIGHT MUSIC (1973), STEPHEN SONDHEIM
"SEND IN THE CLOWNS"

Large Form: Broadway Musical
Detailed Form: Three-part Song-form
Performing Medium: Soprano Voice and Orchestra

Compact Disc 4, Track 21
Running Time: 3:14

Sondheim's show was one of the big hits of Broadway's 1973 season. Mozart's serenade "Eine Kleine Nachtmusik" (A Little Night Music) provided the title for this charming work. Because of its turn-of-the-century (nineteenth to twentieth) setting, period costumes, sentimental plot, and waltz-filled score, *A Little Night Music* is usually called a modern operetta, similar to those of Franz Lehar and Johann Strauss, Jr.

The story, closely based on Ingmar Bergman's film "Smiles of a Summer Night," is set in Sweden. It is about Fredrik Egerman, a middle-aged attorney, newly remarried to a teenage girl the same age as his son. After eleven months of an unsatisfying marriage during which his new wife remains a virgin, Egerman resumes an affair with his former mistress, Desirée Armfeldt—an actress whose current lover is Count Malcolm, a Swedish military officer. "Send in the Clowns" is sung in the musical by Desirée when she and Egerman meet again after years of separation.

Egerman, Desirée, Count Malcolm, and his wife meet at Desirée's mother's country estate for a brief holiday. Madame Armfeldt herself was a beautiful and notorious courtesan in her day.

By the final curtain, Egerman is relieved to learn that his wife and his eighteen-year-old son have fallen in love and have run off together. Egerman and Desirée are reunited, and the count is reconciled to being reunited with his wife.

Scene from the film version of Bernstein's *West Side Story*

LISTENING ACTIVITY

OVERTURE TO CANDIDE (1956), LEONARD BERNSTEIN

Large Form: Broadway Musical Overture
Detailed Form: Sectional
Performing Medium: Symphony Orchestra

Compact Disc 4, Track 13
Running Time: 4:22

See Chapter 24 for background on the musical *Candide* and the Listening Guide for the Overture.

Challenge Your Expertise

- Suppose Bach, Mozart, and Brahms were alive today. Who do you think would be the most likely composer of Broadway musicals?

- Although trained as a composer, Stephen Sondheim collaborated as a lyricist with which three composers?

Topol in the role of Tevye in the film production of *Fiddler on the Roof* (1971)

LISTENING ACTIVITY

FIDDLER ON THE ROOF (1964), JERRY BOCK AND SHELDON HARNICK
"SUNRISE, SUNSET"

Large Form: Broadway Musical
Detailed Form: Three-part Song-form
Performing Medium: Soprano, Baritone, Chorus, and Small Orchestra

▌▌ Compact Disc 4, Track 22
▌▌ Running Time: 3:05

Fiddler on the Roof, based on the story "Tevye and His Daughters" by Sholom Aleichem, is set in Anatevka, a *shtetl* (small ghetto-town) in turn-of-the-century Russia. Plagued by czarist pogroms, the towns-people live precariously—like a "fiddler on the roof."

"Sunrise, Sunset" is sung at the oldest daughter's wedding. Tevye and his wife Golde reflect on how their family has grown up and how quickly the years have gone by.

HISTORICAL PERSPECTIVE

Rent: A Rock Opera for the 90s

After seven years of trying to transform musical theater into something more modern, **Jonathan Larson** (1960–1996) had had no luck. No one was convinced that his notions represented the direction of the future. Then in 1989, the idea for *Rent* struck him. He called it his ". . . rock opera for the 90s."

Inspired by Giacomo Puccini's opera *La Bohème,* Larson's *Rent* updates the setting from the Left Bank of Paris at the end of the nineteenth century to the East Village of Lower Manhattan at the end of the twentieth century. The characters, although exaggerated, were based on the people in his neighborhood. He also updated the life-threatening disease. Puccini's Mimi is dying from tuberculosis, a common killer of her time. In *Rent,* Mimi and her lover Roger are HIV-positive. He is a recovering addict, but she is still using drugs.

Revision followed revision, and in 1992, while riding his bicycle through the East Village, Jon passed the New York Theatre Workshop on Fourth Street. The next day, he brought the tape of the score to NYTW director James Nicola, who loved the music. Michael Greif was brought in as the director, and the four-year process of creating *Rent* had begun.

The first preview was slated for January 25, 1996. Friends noticed that Jon seemed to be exceptionally tired, despite his excitement about the opening. During a rehearsal, he collapsed and went by ambulance to the nearest hospital. The doctors diagnosed his problem as food poisoning, pumped his stomach, and sent him home. Three days later, Jon blacked out again and was diagnosed with the flu.

Despite his sore chest and fever, Jon took a taxi to watch the dress rehearsal and another taxi home. A short time later, his roommate found him on the floor of the kitchen, next to his coat. Jon had died of an aortic aneurysm—less than two weeks before his thirty-sixth birthday.

Challenge Your Expertise

When you hear song lyrics about luxury, wealth, and extravagance, which composer-lyricist are you reminded of?

OTHER IMPORTANT BROADWAY MUSICALS

ALAN JAY LERNER (1918–86) *AND* ***FREDERICK LOEWE*** (1901–88)***:*** *Brigadoon* (1947); *Paint Your Wagon* (1951); *My Fair Lady* (1956, Tony Award); *Camelot* (1960); *Gigi* (1958 film)

FRANK LOESSER (1910–69)***:*** *Where's Charley?* (1948); *Guys and Dolls* (1950, Tony Award); *Most Happy Fella* (1956); *How to Succeed in Business Without Really Trying* (1961, Pulitzer Prize and Tony Award)

JULE STYNE (1905–1994)***:*** *Gentlemen Prefer Blondes* (1949, with Leo Robin); *Gypsy* (1959, with S. Sondheim); *Two on the Aisle* (1951, with Betty Comden and Adolph Green); *Peter Pan* (1954, with Comden and Green); *Bells Are Ringing* (1958, with Comden and Green); *Say, Darling* (1958, with Comden and Green); *Do Re Mi* (1960, with Comden and Green); *Subways Are for Sleeping* (1961, with Comden and Green); *Fade Out—Fade In* (1964, with Comden and Green); *Funny Girl* (1964, with Bob Merrill)

JERRY HERMAN (b. 1933)***:*** *Milk and Honey* (1961); *Hello, Dolly!* (1964); *Mame* (1966); *La Cage Aux Folles* (1983)

RICHARD ADLER (b. 1921) *AND* ***JERRY ROSS*** (1926–55)***:*** *Pajama Game* (1954, Tony and The Standard Award); *Damn Yankees* (1955, Tony and The Standard Award)

KURT WEILL (1900–50)***; SEE BIOGRAPHY IN CHAPTER 22:*** *The Threepenny Opera* (1928, with Berthold Brecht); *Happy End* (1929, with Brecht); *Knickerbocker Holiday* (1938, "September Song", with Maxwell Anderson); *Lady in the Dark* (1940, with Ira Gershwin); *One Touch of Venus* (1943, with Ogden Nash); *Street Scene* (1947, with Langston Hughes); *Lost in the Stars* (1949, with Maxwell Anderson)

MEREDITH WILLSON (1902–84)***:*** *The Music Man* (1957, Tony Award); *The Unsinkable Molly Brown* (1960); *Here's Love* (1963)

VINCENT YOUMANS (1898–1946)***:*** *No! No! Nanette!* (1925, with Otto Harbach and Irving Caesar)

MITCH LEIGH (b. 1928)***:*** *Man of La Mancha* (1965, Tony Award)

CHARLES STROUSE (b. 1928)***:*** *Bye, Bye, Birdie* (1963, with Lee Adams, Tony Award); *Applause* (1969, Tony Award); *Annie* (1978, with Martin Charmin)

JOHN KANDER (b. 1932) *AND* ***FRED EBB*** (b. 1932)***:*** *Cabaret* (1966; revival, 1998); *The Happy Time* (1968); *Zorba* (1968); *Chicago* (1975); *Funny Lady*

Final scene from the film production of *The Music Man*

(1975 film); *New York, New York* (1977 film); *Woman of the Year* (1981); *Kiss of the Spider Woman* (1993)

JERRY BOCK (b. 1928) *AND SHELDON HARNICK* (b. 1924): *Fiorello!* (1959, Tony Award); *Tenderloin* (1960); *She Loves Me* (1963); *Fiddler on the Roof* (1964, Tony Award); *The Apple Tree* (1966)

BURTON LANE (b. 1912): *Finian's Rainbow* (1947, with E. Y. Harburg); *On a Clear Day You Can See Forever* (1965, with Alan Jay Lerner)

TOM JONES (b. 1928) *AND HARVEY SCHMIDT* (b. 1929): *The Fantasticks* (1960); *110 in the Shade* (1963); *I Do! I Do!* (1966)

ANDREW LLOYD WEBBER (b. 1948): *Joseph and the Amazing Technicolor Dreamcoat* (1968, 1972, with Tim Rice); *Jesus Christ Superstar* (1971, with Tim Rice); *Evita* (1976, with Tim Rice, Tony Award); *Cats* (1981); *Starlight Express* (1984); *Phantom of the Opera* (1986); *Aspects of Love* (1989); *Sunset Boulevard* (1993)

MARVIN HAMLISCH (b. 1944): *A Chorus Line* (1975, with Edward Kleban, Tony Award)

HENRY KRIEGER AND TOM EYEN: *Dreamgirls* (1982)

ALAIN BOUBLIL AND CLAUDE-MICHEL SCHÖNBERG: *Les Misérables* (1985, with Herbert Kretzmer); *Miss Saigon* (1990); *Martin Guerre* (1995)

STEPHEN FLAHERTY AND LYNN AHRENS: *Ragtime* (1997, multiple awards)

ALAN MENKEN: *Beauty and the Beast* (1994)

ELTON JOHN AND TIM RICE *The Lion King* (1997, multiple awards)

MAURY YESTON: *Titanic* (1997, Tony Award)

JASON ROBERT BROWN: *Parade* (1998)

JONATHAN LARSON: *Rent* (1996, Tony Award)

FRANK WILDHORN: *Jekyll & Hyde* (1996, with Nan Knighton); *The Scarlet Pimpernel* (1998, with Leslie Bricusse); *The Civil War* (1999)

CHOREOGRAPHY BY SAVION GLOVER; CONCEIVED BY GEORGE C. WOLFE: *Bring in 'Da Noise, Bring in 'Da Funk* (1996)

Summary of Terms

African-American musicals
ballad opera
bridge
burlesque
chorus
comic opera
extravaganza/spectacle
minstrel shows

modern operetta
musical comedy
musical play
opéra bouffe
operetta
popular opera
Pulitzer Prize
revue

rock opera
Singspiel
Standard Award
Tony Award
troubadours
vaudeville
verse

"Beauty and the Beast," Broadway, New York

Chapter 27

Music in the Movies

Lights dim, curtains open, and the screen comes alive. The title and credits roll. As soon as the music begins—even before we watch the first scene—we know a great deal about the film. Music, or the absence of it, provides an important clue to what we are about to see: a mystery, a comedy, a love story, a horror movie, a swashbuckling adventure, a shoot-'em-up Western, or an action thriller.

Since silent film days, music and the movies have been inextricably linked. As an ingredient of the total entertainment, music adds impact, heightens action, deepens emotion, increases tension, reinforces comedy, and augments mystery. In other words, music gives life to the film medium and draws the audience into the story.

HOW IT BEGAN: THE SILENT ERA

In 1908, a film company in Paris, *Le Film d'Art,* created its first musically scored production, *L'Assassinat du Duc de Guise* (The Assassination of the Duke of Guise). Composer Camille Saint-Saëns readily accepted the opportunity to write the film's musical score, later developing it into a concert piece—*Opus 128 for Strings, Piano, and Harmonium.*

A year after the Saint-Saëns score, specific music suggestions accompanied movies produced by the Edison Film Company. Within five years, publishers had catalogued their music for theater orchestras, pianists, or organists, according to specific moods or dramatic situations. Giuseppe Becce's 1919 Berlin publication *Kinobibliothek* (or *Kinothek,* as it was called) is the most famous early example of these catalogs.

CATALOGUING OF EXISTING CONCERT MUSIC

Max Winkler, a clerk in the Carl Fischer Music Store in New York City, is customarily given credit for being the first cataloguer in the United States. It was 1912, and filmmakers were demanding more and more music for their productions. Winkler realized that the vast Carl Fischer library was a potential gold mine.

Fischer had enough music stored and catalogued to fit any situation a film maker needed, most of it concentrating on music for nineteenth-century-style melodrama: maestoso, agitato, misterioso, largo. Soon the designations changed from musical terms to dramatic elements: "villain lurks in the shadows" or "hero makes his entrance." Eventually, categories became even broader: sea storm, romance, children, chatter, parties, horror, humor, religious, sword fight, hunting, festival, orgies, forest fire, and almost anything a screenwriter might imagine.

So the enterprising Winkler wrote to the Universal Film Company. He offered to make up music cue sheets for all their films on one condition—that they would let him see each film before they released it. Understanding the value of this idea, Universal's publicity director gave Winkler a chance to show what he could do. Max was so successful that he eventually left his job at Fischer's to work full time in film music.

MASTERS TRANSCRIBED FOR FILM

To keep pace with the increasing market for his services, Winkler and his partner S. M. Berg began to catalogue excerpts from the great masters. Since any work not under copyright was up for grabs, Beethoven, Brahms, Bizet, Bach, Verdi, Mozart, Grieg, Tchaikovsky, and others were making their film debuts.

The composers might not have recognized their works, however. To create the desired effect, the excerpts would often undergo transformation. They would be jazzed up, slowed down, or played out of tune as needed. For example, Mendelsson's or Wagner's wedding marches, played intact, might underscore the happiness of a bride and groom. As the marriage grew rocky, the same music would be played out of tune.

Occasionally, a score might be all-Debussy or all-Tchaikovsky, but usually the production schedule and the scenario did not allow for this. Problems persisted in making smooth transitions and in synchronizing pre-existing music with the picture. Often, the music director would have to compose music to accommodate particular scenes.

Buster Keaton in a scene from the silent movie *The General*

Max Winkler

The score for D. W. Griffith's *The Birth of a Nation* (1915) established the standards for orchestration and cuing that continued throughout the silent era. A joint work by Griffith and Joseph Carl Breil, a composer/orchestra leader, the score is a melange of original music interspersed with "Dixie," "The Star Spangled Banner," and quotes from Liszt, Verdi, Beethoven, Wagner, and Tchaikovsky.

Edmund Meisel

Composer Edmund Meisel was responsible for another milestone in scoring silent films. His music was much more than background or an accessory to the picture. Each note strikes to the heart of the drama, making it a component of the film itself. For his scores, including his legendary work for the 1925 Sergei Eisenstein film *The Battleship Potemkin,* Meisel devised a distinctive system for analyzing film montages to determine the timing of music needed. His contributions earned him recognition as the master of the silent film score.

Another Eisenstein film—*Alexander Nevsky* (1938)—was screened at the Hollywood Bowl during the summer of 1989. In a live performance, the Los Angeles Philharmonic accompanied the film with a performance of Sergei Prokofiev's original score.

In 1981, after producer/director Francis Ford Coppola restored Abel Gance's four-hour silent masterwork *Napoleon,* Coppola arranged for special screenings in theaters that could accommodate a full orchestra. He had commissioned his father, composer Carmine Coppola, to write a new score for the movie. (Arthur Honegger composed the original.) Following the theatrical presentations with live music, Coppola used the new score as a synchronized sound track for the film.

THE ROLE OF MUSIC IN SOUND FILMS

A beneficial side effect of silent film music was employment opportunities for instrumental players in hundreds of theaters. With the advent of sound films in 1927, however, the music track displaced live performances, and orchestra pits became empty.

From the earliest days of sound films through the summer of 1930, the most common use of music was in the musical films of the era, such as *Rio Rita, The Street Singer,* and *The Vagabond Lover.* By 1931, a few directors had incorporated music to support love scenes or to bridge silent sequences. For the most part, though, directors felt music had to be justified by the plot; for example, it had to emanate from a visible source on screen—a theater, a nightclub, a ballroom, or an organ grinder.

HISTORICAL PERSPECTIVE

From Broadway to Hollywood

The majority of films released in 1929 were musicals, almost all of which came from Broadway.

FILM MUSIC COMES OF AGE

During the next several years, composers skilled at writing symphonic music began to receive commissions to compose film music. Each score was unique, like a work of art in any other medium, with the best scores carrying the imprint of their composers. Music had assumed a more important function: to serve the story. A 1935 *New York Times* article characterized film music as a vital element—an accentuated background for mood and action.

Here are some of the composers, usually associated with concert music, who wrote original scores for films:

Hermione Gingold and Maurice Chevalier in a scene from *Gigi*

Malcolm Arnold	Aram Khachaturian
Leonard Bernstein	Ernesto Lecuona
Benjamin Britten	Gyorgy Ligeti
Mario Castelnuovo-Tedesco	Pietro Mascagni
Aaron Copland	Sergei Prokofiev
Rheinhold Gliere	Erik Satie
Ferde Grofe	Jan Sibelius
Hans Werner Henze	Virgil Thomson
Paul Hindemith	Ernst Toch
Gustav Holst	Edgar Varèse
Arthur Honegger	Ralph Vaughan Williams
Jacques Ibert	William Walton
Dmitri Kabalevsky	

Some films with original scores also include existing concert music pieces as recurrent themes. For example, in *Platoon* (1986), we hear not only Georges Delerue's score but also Samuel Barber's *Adagio for Strings*. Mozart's Piano Concerto No. 21 K. 467 is used as the love theme in the 1967 *Elvira Madigan*.

THE HOLLYWOOD SOUND

Early in the twentieth century, attitudes toward romantic music sharply changed. Orchestras and concert management organizations began to champion the works of twentieth-century composers whose musical language took a more intellectual approach than their nineteenth-century predecessors. To make room for these new compositions, music that was accessible—understandable to general audiences—was programmed less frequently. Seeking other outlets for their music, romantic-style composers turned to Hollywood.

During the 1930s and 1940s, the lush, evocative "Hollywood Sound" enjoyed its Golden Age. The exponents of this style (such as Max Steiner, Erich Wolfgang Korngold, and Miklos Rozsa) brought to the medium an impressive music background and education. In creating the new genre, therefore, they understood the music of the past. As musicians, they stayed

Hollywood Sound

abreast of the latest developments in contemporary developments by studying the music of Ravel, Shostakovich, Frederick Delius (1862–1934), and Arnold Schoenberg. Despite the talent and impact of film composers, art music circles usually were condescending to movie music. Even Leonard Bernstein called it "ghastly."

THE CONTRIBUTION OF MUSIC TO FILM

In a 1949 *New York Times* article, Aaron Copland (*Of Mice and Men*, 1939; *Our Town*, 1940; *The Heiress* and *The Red Pony*, 1949) said: "Music can create a more convincing atmosphere of time and place. This atmosphere, musically speaking, is 'color.' Music creates a psychological element better than dialogue can." Copland also cited two other uses for music—as a neutral background that fills empty spots without our being aware of it, and as an intensifier that builds the drama and helps deliver the climax.

Music also builds and sustains momentum. Pay attention to how music is used in a James Bond thriller (score by John Barry) whenever Bond propels his high-tech vehicle either in pursuit or in flight from the villain. You'll find a similar technique in any action film released today.

Can you recall a film where certain music is associated with one character and then transferred to another character? *The Wizard of Oz* (1939, Oscar-winning score by Herbert Stothart) is one example. The melody we hear each time we see Miss Gulch riding her bicycle tells us that she is Dorothy's nemesis. In Oz, we hear the same melody when we see the witch ride her broom, leaving little doubt that Dorothy and her friends will eventually have to tangle with another nemesis.

MOVIE MUSIC OF THE GOLDEN AGE

Film scores of the Golden Age—music that might be considered "schmaltzy" today—were artfully composed and executed to create and support the images we see on the screen. In addition, they were crafted to provide clues to things we could not see: what was happening *inside* a character (confusion, loneliness, fear, falling in love), what was about to happen *to* a character (discovery, betrayal, harm), what a character was like (seductive, compassionate, timid, evil), and what the character wanted

LISTENING INSIGHTS

Listening for Associations in Film Music

As a filmgoer, imagine the elements one might associate with a minuet played on a harpsichord, a calypso tune played on steel drums, a hillbilly song played on the banjo, and a fiery dance played on Flamenco guitar.

(revenge, acceptance, mercy). A harp glissando expresses sentiment; blaring trumpets express heroism or victory.

Because of film censorship, certain types of scenes could not be depicted from the 1930s into the 1960s. So composers suggested sex and violence by featuring certain instrumentation. Thrusting strings, saxophones, or clarinets might symbolize off-camera rape. And who can forget the driving, shrill violins that composer Bernard Herrmann used to punctuate each stab of the knife in the shower scene of Alfred Hitchcock's *Psycho*?

Imagery and Music

Film music helps imagery stay in our minds. For example, early in the classic film *Gone With the Wind* (1939, score by Max Steiner), the characters Scarlett O'Hara and her father, Gerald O'Hara, are standing under a tree on Tara, their plantation. As Mr. O'Hara imbues his daughter with his philosophy, "Land is all that matters," the films theme music swells. Then the camera pulls back, and with the music soaring, we see a silhouette of Scarlett and her father, symbolizing the prosperity of the Antebellum South. Later in the film, Scarlett returns to her plantation to find her home and land ravaged by the Civil War. The moment we hear Steiner's theme again, we remember it, and our association between Scarlett and her deep attachment to Tara is complete. Used in imitation and repetition throughout the film, the recurrent theme keeps reminding us of the contrast between the glory of the past and the realities of the present.

Western movies present another set of images: the dusty streets of frontier towns, gunmen tumbling from second-story balconies, vast expanses of range land, crests of mountains lined with Indian warriors on ponies, circles of covered wagons, gunfights between outlaws and the posse. Even though these scenes might be considered clichés, a memorable Western movie can use these images in a unique or distinctive way. The score contributes to that uniqueness, as in the following films, all available on video: *High Noon* (1952, Dimitri Tiomkin), *The Magnificent Seven* (1960, Elmer Bernstein), *The Good, the Bad, and the Ugly* (1967, Ennio Morricone), and *Silverado* (1985, Bruce Broughton).

SOME OF THE GREAT FILM COMPOSERS OF THE GOLDEN AGE

MAX STEINER (1888–1971)   One of the most prolific film composers of his time, Max Steiner wrote symphonic, "wall-to-wall" scores—music that fills every moment of a film. He is known for using a "stinger chord" to punctuate the action and force the audience's attention to something specific on the screen. His outstanding scores include *King Kong* (1933), *The Informer* (1935, Academy Award), *A Star Is Born* (1937), *Gone With the Wind* (1939), *Citizen Kane* (1941), *Casablanca* (1942), *Now, Voyager* (1942, Academy Award), *Since You Went Away* (1944, Academy Award), and *Johnny Belinda* (1948).

Steiner was born in Vienna into an affluent family that boasted of its notable musicians and composers. As one story goes, it was Max's grandfather who advised Johann Strauss, Jr. to write for the theater. (Strauss later gave us such operettas as *Die Fledermaus* and *Zigeunerbaron*.)

Classically trained at the Vienna Imperial Academy, Steiner completed his music studies by the age of thirteen. Three years later, he had become an accomplished conductor. After emigrating to New York, Steiner worked with such Broadway greats as Jerome Kern, Victor Herbert, George White, Florenz Ziegfeld, and George Gershwin.

With the advent of the "talkies," Hollywood needed sound. The studios raided Broadway to supply composers, arrangers, orchestrators, copyists, music editors, and conductors to staff their expanding music departments. So Steiner went to Hollywood as an arranger-orchestrator for the 1929 musical film *Rio Rita* and became a member of the RKO music department. He composed his first complete score in 1932 for *Symphony of Six Million*—the first film to use music under dialogue.

In 1936 Steiner moved to Warner Brothers, where he remained until 1953. He then worked as a freelance composer, but as his eyesight began to fail, his productivity declined. Max Steiner completed his last film in 1965.

ERICH WOLFGANG KORNGOLD (1897–1957)   Erich Korngold's nineteen film scores include *Anthony Adverse* (1936, Academy Award), *The Prince and the Pauper* (1937), *The Sea Wolf* (1941), and *King's Row* (1942). He displayed his talent for music very early in life, and by age nine was called a genius by Gustav Mahler. Korngold later studied with Richard Strauss, intending to become a serious composer and conductor. He spoke of film composing as something to kill time until he could do something else.

Korngold was a master of swashbuckling melodies containing fanfares and fanfare-like music, a characteristic of his Academy Award-winning score for *The Adventures of Robin Hood* (1938)—one of seven scores he wrote for Errol Flynn movies. After completing *Robin Hood*, Korngold was preparing to return to his native Vienna to resume his concert music activities when he received word from his father to remain in the United States: Hitler had overrun Austria.

ALFRED NEWMAN   Movie studios themselves were training grounds for composers. Alfred Newman, an excellent pianist, never studied composition formally. Instead, he learned to write for movies by doing it. He was born in 1900, the oldest of ten children. He was a concert pianist by age seven, and by the time he was in his twenties, Newman was working on Broadway. In 1930, Irving Berlin and George Gershwin mounted a campaign to bring him to Hollywood. Newman took the opportunity and became associated with Samuel Goldwyn for ten years.

From 1940 to 1960, Alfred Newman was the Music Director at 20th Century Fox—composing, conducting, and overseeing all musical arrangements for the studio's 26 to 54 releases a year. His influence was so great that many credit him with setting the style for film music of that period.

Newman also recognized talent and was responsible for hiring noted film composers Franz Waxman, Bernard Herrmann, and David Raksin.

Alfred Newman was known for his melodic, lyrical love themes and orchestrations dominated by strings. In contrast to the wall-to-wall scores of Max Steiner, Newman's were designed to accompany the action. Among his many notable scores are *Les Misérables* (1935), *The Hunchback of Notre Dame* (1939), *How Green Was My Valley* (1941), *The Song of Bernadette* (1943, Academy Award), *Leave Her to Heaven* (1945), *Gentleman's Agreement* (1947), *Call Northside 777* (1948), *The Robe* (1953), *Love Is a Many-Splendored Thing* (1955, Academy Award), and *The Best of Everything* (1959).

In 1999, Newman Hall, a concert venue, was dedicated at the University of Southern California.

FRANZ WAXMAN (1906–1967)   Born in eastern Europe, Franz Waxman showed early musical ability, and at age seventeen enrolled in the Dresden Music Academy. He soon moved on to the Berlin Music Conservatory, earning his tuition by playing piano with a jazz ensemble. In Berlin, Waxman came to the attention of conductor Bruno Walter, who encouraged him in his career.

After writing film scores for a number of German-language films, Waxman emigrated to the United States just as the Nazis were rising to power. At the beginning of his Hollywood career, he composed the score for *The Bride of Frankenstein* (1935), which not only displayed his motivic technique but also set new quality standards for the music of horror films.

Waxman wrote in various genres. His credits include *Captain's Courageous* (1937), *A Christmas Carol* (1938), *Rebecca* and *The Philadelphia Story* (1940), *Dr. Jekyll and Mr. Hyde* (1941), *Destination Tokyo* (1944), *To Have and Have Not* (1945), *Sunset Boulevard* (1950, Academy Award), *A Place in the Sun* (1951, Academy Award), *Rear Window* (1954), *The Silver Chalice* (1955), and *Cimarron* (1960). During his later years, Waxman composed for several television series, notably *Gunsmoke*, *Twilight Zone*, and *Arrest and Trial*.

HUGO FRIEDHOFER (1902–1981)   A San Francisco native, Hugo Friedhofer began his Hollywood career as an orchestrator. Between 1936 and 1946, he orchestrated more than fifty scores for Max Steiner and worked on many others for Erich Korngold and Alfred Newman. His own composing career took off after he won an Oscar for *The Best Years of Our Lives* (1946). Through 1973, in addition to his many credits as co-composer or subordinate composer, Friedhofer was the principal composer for about seventy film scores, including *Body and Soul* and *The Bishop's Wife* (1947), *Joan of Arc* (1948), *Broken Arrow* (1950), *Vera Cruz* (1954), *Boy on a Dolphin*, *An Affair to Remember*, and *The Sun Also Rises* (1957), and *One-Eyed Jacks* (1960).

DIMITRI TIOMKIN   Perhaps the most well-known movie composer between the early 1950s and the mid-1960s was Dimitri Tiomkin. Born in the Ukraine in 1894, he enrolled in St. Petersburg Conservatory in 1912 and studied composition with Alexander Glazunov (1865–1936). Tiomkin was working as a concert pianist by 1919, but after the October Revolution in the Soviet Union, he moved to Berlin and continued his music studies with pianist-composer Ferruccio Busoni (1866–1924). In the late 1920s, Tiomkin introduced Gershwin's *Concerto in F* to Paris audiences and included Gershwin's music in his concert tours throughout Europe.

Tiomkin credited both Glazunov and Busoni for influencing his flair for dramatic scoring. He also developed the theory that film music could not only direct attention *to* the screen but also *from* the screen. For example, he believed that musical sounds could do what makeup could not—distract an audience from the performance of an aging actor trying to portray a young man in a love scene.

In his active film career from 1930 to 1971, Dimitri Tiomkin composed many memorable scores, including *Lost Horizon* (1937), *Duel in the Sun* (1946), *Red River* (1948), *High Noon* (1952, Academy Award), *The High and the Mighty* (1954, Academy Award), *Friendly Persuasion* (1956), *Giant* (1956), *The Old Man and the Sea* (1958, Academy Award), and *The Guns of Navarone* (1961).

MIKLOS ROZSA   "The music of Hungary is stamped indelibly one way or another on virtually every bar I have ever put on paper," said Hungarian-born composer Miklos Rozsa. In a Hollywood career that spanned forty-five years, Rozsa composed for a variety of film genres. His music is best associated, however, with monumental biblical and historical epics—scores that convey grandeur and pageantry.

His first Oscar-winning score was for David O. Selznick's *Spellbound* (1945). It included the piano work *Spellbound Concerto*. Rozsa's numerous credits include *The Lost Weekend* (1945), *A Double Life* (1947, Academy Award), *Madame Bovary* (1949), *The Asphalt Jungle* (1950), *Quo Vadis* (1951), *Ivanhoe* (1952), *Ben-Hur* (1959, Academy Award), *King of Kings* and *El Cid* (1961), *Sodom and Gomorrah* (1962), *Eye of the Needle* (1981), and *Dead Men Don't Wear Plaid* (1982). In his later years, Rozsa taught film composition at the University of Southern California.

THE NEXT GENERATION OF COMPOSERS

BERNARD HERRMANN   A student of Arnold Schoenberg, Bernard Herrmann introduced a twentieth-century sound to movie music. He was known for writing music that emphasized the mood and dramatic impact of a film,

Challenge Your Expertise

Why did movie studios have to establish large music departments?

such as his score for the shadowy *Citizen Kane* (1941), the otherworldly *The Ghost and Mrs. Muir* (1948), and the original, chilling *Cape Fear* (1962). At age thirty, Herrmann won an Oscar for *All That Money Can Buy* (1941).

For eleven years, Herrmann was associated with Alfred Hitchcock, composing for such thrillers as *The Man Who Knew Too Much* (1956), *Vertigo* (1958), *North by Northwest* (1959), and *Psycho* (1960). (Danny Elfman arranged and adapted Hermann's score for the 1998 remake of *Psycho*.) Some experts have suggested that Herrmann's music was essential in creating the intensity of Hitchcock's films. Despite their long collaboration, the Herrmann-Hitchcock association ended bitterly.

In 1966, Bernard Herrmann completed the score for the futuristic *Fahrenheit 451*. He then composed in Europe for a number of years, including films for director François Truffaut. In 1976, Herrmann resurfaced in Hollywood, working with young directors on his last two films: Brian de Palma's *Obsession* and Martin Scorsese's *Taxi Driver*.

ELMER BERNSTEIN (b. 1922)   With more than 200 films to his credit, Elmer Bernstein had already been in the business for a decade before he had his initial success composing a jazz score for *The Man With the Golden Arm* (1955). Building on his new reputation, he then wrote jazz scores for *Sweet Smell of Success* (1957), *Some Came Running* (1958), and *Walk on the Wild Side* (1962). Among his great Western scores are *The Magnificent Seven* (1960, Academy Award) and *True Grit* (1969). His comedies include *Thoroughly Modern Millie* (1967, Academy Award), *Airplane* (1980), *Trading Places* (1983), and *Ghostbusters* (1984). Bernstein's more recent scores include *A Rage in Harlem* and *Rambling Rose* (1991), *The Age of Innocence* (1993), *Devil in a Blue Dress* (1995), *Hoodlum* (1996), John Grisham's *The Rainmaker* (1997), and *Twilight* (1998), *The Deep End of the Ocean* (1998).

JERRY GOLDSMITH (b. 1929)   One of the most respected and prolific Hollywood composers is Jerry Goldsmith. His career began after he attended Miklos Rozsa's film composing classes at the University of Southern California in the late 1940s. Since then, the roster of his credits continues to expand in an impressive body of diverse works. His films include *Rio Conchos* (1964), *The Sand Pebbles* and *The Blue Max* (1966), *Planet of the Apes* (1968), *Patton* (1970), *Papillon* (1973), *Chinatown* (1974), *The Omen* (1976, Academy Award), *Islands in the Stream* (1977), *Coma* (1978), *Star Trek* (1979), *First Blood* (1982), *Poltergeist* (1982, Academy Award nomination), *Twilight Zone—The Movie* (1983), two more Rambo films (1985 and 1988), *Star Trek V* (1989), *Total Recall* (1990), *Forever Young* (1992), *The Ghost and the Darkness* (1996), *Air Force One, L.A. Confidential,* and *The Edge* (1997), *Deep Rising* (1998), *Star Trek Insurrection* (1998), and *The Mummy* (1999).

QUINCY JONES   With careers in both performing and record-producing that rival anyone in the industry, Quincy Jones burst onto the film scene with *The Pawnbroker* (1965). He followed that with *In Cold Blood* (1967), *For* *the Love of Ivy* (1968), *In the Heat of the Night* (1969), *They Call Me Mr. Tibbs* (1970), *The Getaway* (1972), the television series *Roots* (1977), and *The Color Purple* (1985).

DAVE GRUSIN   Dave Grusin's diverse Hollywood credits include *The Graduate* and *Divorce American Style* (1967), *Tell Them Willie Boy Is Here* (1969), *Three Days of the Condor* (1975), *Heaven Can Wait* (1978), *The Electric Horseman* and *The Champ* (1979), *Absence of Malice* and *On Golden Pond* (1981), *Reds* (1981, with Stephen Sondheim), *Tootsie* (1982), *The Little Drummer Girl* (1984), *The Milagro Beanfield War* (1988), John Grisham's *The Firm* (1993), *Selena* (1996), and *Hope Floats* (1998).

ENNIO MORRICONE   Morricone made his mark during the 1960s as the composer for Sergio Leone's "Spaghetti Westerns," so called because they were made in Italy. These films also propelled Clint Eastwood to stardom. A notable feature of his scores is the way they contribute to the overall style of those films. Morricone's tremendous output has won him admiration by his peers and his fans. More recently, he composed scores for Leone's *Once Upon a Time in America* (1984). His many other films include *The Mission* (1986), *The Untouchables* (1987), *State of Grace* (1990), *In the Line of Fire* (1993), *Bulworth* (1998) and *Lolita* (1998). He has also scored a number of foreign films, including *Cinema Paradiso* (1988), *Tie Me Up! Tie Me Down!* (1990), *Everybody's Fine* (1990), and the three *La Cage aux Folles* films (1978, 1981, 1986).

JOHN BARRY   John Barry has enjoyed a long, prestigious career. His scores include *Born Free* (1966, Oscar for title song), *The Lion in Winter* (1968, Academy Award), *Midnight Cowboy* and the song "Everybody's Talkin' 'Bout Me" (1969), and most of the James Bond films from the early 1960s through the late 1980s, including the original James Bond theme. Barry's scores for *Out of Africa* (1985) and *Dances With Wolves* (1990) both won Academy Awards. During the past decade, he wrote music for *Indecent Proposal* (1993), *The Scarlet Letter* (1995), *Swept From the Sea* (1997), and *Mercury Rising* (1998).

HENRY MANCINI   Of all Henry Mancini's film music, he may be best remembered for the *Pink Panther* theme (and the eight Pink Panther scores) and for his song "Moon River" from *Breakfast at Tiffany's* (1961). Both the song and film score won Oscars. The next year, he again took Best Song honors for the title song from *Days of Wine and Roses* (1962). The Mancini touch is an important adjunct in approximately ninety films, including *Experiment in Terror* (1962), *Wait Until Dark* and *Two For the Road* (1967), *Sometimes a Great Notion* (1971), and *Victor/Victoria* (1982).

MAURICE JARRÉ   Since appearing on the film scene in the late 1950s, Maurice Jarré has composed dozens of scores, expressing himself both in the full-scale orchestral style and the electronic style. His full-scale scores include *Lawrence of Arabia* (1962, Academy Award), *Dr. Zhivago* (1965, Academy Award), *Ryan's Daughter* (1970), *The Tin Drum* (1979), *The Year of Living Dangerously* (1982), *A Passage to India* (1984, Academy Award), *Mad Max: Beyond Thunderdome* (1985), *Fatal Attraction* (1987), *Ghost* (1990), and *Only the Lonely* (1991). In the electronic style, Jarré's most interesting work includes *Mosquito Coast* (1986) and *Gorillas in the Mist* (1988). His massive score for *Jacob's Ladder* (1990) blends both styles.

LALO SCHIFRIN During his almost-thirty-five-year Hollywood career, Lalo Schifrin has been an active conductor as well as a composer for movies and television. His films include *The President's Analyst* and *Cool Hand Luke* (1967), *Bullitt* (1968), *Dirty Harry* (1971), *Magnum Force* (1973), *The Four Musketeers* (1975), *Tank* (1983), *Sudden Impact* (1983), *The Dead Pool* (1988), *Money Talks* (1997), and *Rush Hour* (1998).

MUSIC AND THE MAGIC OF ANIMATION
The Timelessness of Walt Disney

Since the earliest days of Walt Disney Productions, music has been an essential element in the creation of animated films. Walt often remarked that music helps bring animation to life. To synchronize the sound with the animation of the film *Fantasia,* he built a state-of-the-art, stereophonic sound-dubbing theater on his studio in Burbank, California.

When we think of the Disney classics, we remember the wonderful songs that came from some of Walt's earliest films: "Whistle While You

The Rite of Spring scene from *Fantasia*

Work" and "Heigh Ho" from *Snow White and the Seven Dwarfs* (1937); the Oscar-winning "When You Wish Upon a Star" from *Pinocchio* (1940); "Some Day My Prince Will Come" and the Oscar-winning "A Dream is a Wish Your Heart Makes" from *Cinderella* (1950). For the Oscar-winning film *Mary Poppins* (1964), composers Richard M. and Robert B. Sherman not only walked off with Best Song for "Chim Chim Cher-ee," but also Best Score honors.

In the 1940 classic *Fantasia*, Walt Disney added a new dimension to the partnership of music and animation. Each animated segment is a visualization of existing concert music:

- *Toccata and Fugue in d minor*, by Johann Sebastian Bach
- *The Nutcracker Suite*, by Peter Ilyich Tchaikovsky
- *The Sorcerer's Apprentice*, by Paul Dukas (1865–1935)
- *The Rite of Spring*, by Igor Stravinsky
- *Symphony No. 6* (*Pastoral*), by Ludwig van Beethoven
- "The Dance of the Hours" from *La Gioconda*, by Amilcare Ponchielli (1834–1886)
- *Night on Bald Mountain*, by Modest Mussorgsky
- *Ave Maria*, by Franz Schubert

Frank Churchill was the principal composer of *Snow White* (1937), *Dumbo* (1941, Oscar), and *Bambi* (1942). *George Bruns*, who composed scores for live-action as well as animated films, was the principal composer for the studio's television series *Davy Crockett* (1955). His scores for animated films include *Sleeping Beauty* (1959), *101 Dalmatians* (1961), *The Sword in the Stone* (1963), *Jungle Book* (1967), and *The Aristocrats* (1970).

From the mid-1960s to the early 1980s, composer Buddy Baker contributed his sizable talent to the Disney archive. In addition to his work on live-action films, Baker wrote scores for animated films, including *Million Dollar Duck* (1971) and *The Fox and the Hound* (1981).

Let's fast-forward to the 1980s and 1990s, when Alan Menken is associated with the Disney classics. Except for the Oscar-winning score by Elton John for *Lion King* (1994, also Best Song, "Circle of Life"), Menken composed scores for many Disney releases: *Little Mermaid* (1989, Oscar), *Beauty and the Beast* (1991, Oscar), *Aladdin* (1992, Oscar), *Pocahontas* (1995, Oscar for score and for Best Song "Colors of the Wind"), *The Hunchback of Notre Dame* (1995), and *Hercules* (1997).

John Williams and the Use of the Recurrent Theme

John Williams (b. 1932) easily comes to mind as one of the most active film composers today. Since the start of his film career in 1959, Williams has written for many of Hollywood's greatest box-office successes. His credits include *Poseidon Adventure* (1972), *Towering Inferno* (1974), *Jaws* (1975, Oscar) and *Jaws II* (1979), *Star Wars* (1977, Oscar), *Close Encounters of the Third Kind* (1977), *Superman* (1979, plus the sequels), *The Deerhunter* (1978), *The Empire Strikes Back* (1980), *Raiders of the Lost Ark* (1981, Oscar) plus the two sequels (1984 and 1989), *E.T., the Extra Terrestrial* (1982, Oscar), *Empire of the Sun* (1987), *Born on the Fourth of July* (1989, Oscar), *JFK* (1991, Oscar), *Schindler's List* (1993, Oscar), two *Jurassic Park* films (1993 and 1997), *Amistad* (1997), *Saving Private Ryan* (1998), and *Episode I: The Phantom Menace* (1999).

Listen to any of the powerful recurrent themes that Williams is known for. They serve as mnemonics to help us immediately associate music with a particular character, location, or dramatic situation. For example, certain music in *Jaws*, *Star Wars*, and *Superman* evokes immediate associations in both the original films and their sequels. Think about the ominous motive in *Jaws*. Just two repeated notes arouse fear and alert us: a shark is nearby—even if we cannot see it. When we hear the heroic *Star Wars* theme playing over the opening credits and repeated as the Jedi return, we are optimistic that ultimately the "good guys" will prevail.

Williams again evokes optimism with the heroic theme of *Superman*. As soon as we hear it and see Superman flying to the rescue, we know that this larger-than-life character has come to affirm the concept of good triumphing over evil. The "Love Theme" helps us associate the music with the relationship between the Lois Lane character and the Clark Kent-Superman character.

There is a striking similarity between the "Love Theme" and a theme from Richard Strauss's symphonic poem *Death and Transfiguration*. Even the orchestral treatment of the *Superman* score is reminiscent of late-nineteenth-century composers such as Richard Strauss and Richard Wagner.

Superman originated in 1938 as a comic-book character, and the films retain a satiric, tongue-in-cheek treatment of the hero who repeatedly saves the day against seemingly insurmountable odds. However, the romantic notion about *Superman* remains. Philosopher and poet Friedrich Nietzsche (1844–1900) promoted a doctrine that glorifies the "superman," or *Übermensch*, as he called him. Therefore, Williams's choice to emulate Strauss and Wagner is consistent with the nineteenth-century concept of "superman."

MATCHING MUSIC AND PICTURES

After a film is assembled, the composer and the music director discuss the score. The composer then has a relatively short time to write precisely timed music that conveys the spirit of the picture and matches the fixed image—an image already set by writers, the director, and the actors.

Challenge Your Expertise

Which three of the following have a similar function—recurring theme, *sostenuto*, leitmotif, *idée fixe*, coda?

The Role of the Music Editor

Working with the composer, director, and film editor, the music editor makes the click track by "spotting" the picture and marking where each cue will begin and end. A hole or "click" on the film indicates a cue change, for example, when to start the "chase."

If the composer wants to catch a certain action, the music editor marks the film with a *streamer*, which looks like a vertical stripe. The streamer shows tempo changes within each cue change, for example, how fast to play the "chase music." Devised by Alfred Newman, these markings are known as the Newman System.

Film scores usually are recorded in studio dubbing theaters. The conductor works to a clock. Timing is controlled by the fixed image on the screen. With the "click track" of the film projected on a screen mounted on the back wall, the conductor can watch the film while directing the orchestra.

THE STATURE OF MOVIE MUSIC TODAY

In the past two decades, film music has soared in popularity. Aware of the public's enjoyment of film scores, conductors are including movie themes in their concert programs. During his tenure as music director of the Boston Pops, John Williams programmed at least one piece of his music in every Pops concert. His recordings with the Boston Pops have greatly contributed to the cause of film music. Since films are among the most popular forms of entertainment, targeting the film-going audience makes sense. When people enjoy a film, they remember the music and buy the recording—such as *Titanic* (1997, score by James Horner), which not only won an Oscar but also topped the pop charts and won a Grammy for the song "My Heart Will Go On" (music and lyrics by Maury Yeston).

In a *Los Angeles Times* interview, David Raksin (*Laura,* 1944; *Forever Amber,* 1947; *The Bad and the Beautiful,* 1952) noted that film composers have become recognized for their art form, not only by the public but by the

Leonardo Di Caprio and
Kate Winslet in *Titanic*

LISTENING INSIGHTS

How to Listen to Film Music

Your next trip to the movies might be an opportunity to enjoy the film at a different level. See if you can remember when the music begins and when it cuts out. When is it loud? When is it barely audible in the background? Are there extended periods without music? Which instruments are playing? Does the music tug at your heart? Does it make you smile? How does it make you feel? Do you notice the music at all?

To become fully aware of music in the movies, you need to listen. If you enjoy a score, watch the credits and notice who composed it.

Challenge Your Expertise

In filmmaking, what is the track without music called?

music world in general. Now a professor of film at the University of Southern California, Raksin was an organizer and a panelist for the Seventh Annual New Music Festival, a forum for Hollywood composers who are becoming established in the industry.

So Many Films—So Many Scores

Listing every composer with complete credits would be impossible. What follows is a brief sample of the many established composers who have been involved with some of the more popular or honored films:

JOHN BAILEY   *In the Line of Fire* (1993), *Groundhog Day* (1993), *Extreme Measures* (1996), *As Good As It Gets* (1997)

BRUCE BROUGHTON   *Young Sherlock Holmes* and *Silverado* (1985), *The Boy Who Could Fly* and *Sweet Liberty* (1986), *Betsy's Wedding* and *The Rescuers* (1990), *Honey, I Blew Up the Kids* (1992), *Homeward Bound: The Incredible Journey* (1993), *Miracle on 34th Street* (1994), *House Arrest* (1996), *Lost in Space* (1998), *One Tough Cop* (1998)

BILL CONTI   *Rocky* (1976, Academy Award), *Private Benjamin* (1980), *The Right Stuff* (1983, Academy Award), *The Karate Kid* (1984), *F/X* (1986), *Broadcast News* (1987), *Lean on Me* (1989), *Necessary Roughness* (1991), *Napoleon* (1996)

GEORGES DELERUE   *A Man for All Seasons* (1966), *The Day of the Jackal* (1973), *Silkwood* (1983), *Agnes of God* (1985), *Platoon* (1986), *Twins* and *Beaches* (1988), *Steel Magnolias* (1989), *Joe Versus the Volcano* (1990), *Rich in Love* (1993)

ANNE DUDLEY   *The Crying Game* (1992), *Knight Moves* (1993), *The Full Monty* (1996, Academy Award for Best Comedy Score), *American History X* (1998)

CLIFF EIDELMAN   *Crazy People* (1990), *A Simple Twist of Fate* (1994), *Free Willy 3: The Rescue* (1997), *One True Thing* (1998)

DANNY ELFMAN   Once the leader of the rock group Oingo Boingo, Danny Elfman found a new voice in films, such as *Beetlejuice* (1988), *Batman* (1989), *Edward Scissorhands* and *Dick Tracy* (1990), *The Nightmare Before*

Christmas (1993), *Mission: Impossible* (1996), *Flubber* (1997), *Good Will Hunting* (1997), *Men in Black* (1997), *A Simple Plan* (1998), *A Civil Action* (1998), and *Instinct* (1999)

GEORGE FENTON   *Gandhi* (1982, Oscar), *Cry Freedom* (1987), *Dangerous Liaisons* (1988), *White Palace* and *Memphis Belle* (1990), *Shadowlands* (1993), *Groundhog Day* (1993), *The Madness of King George* (1994), *The Crucible* (1996), *Dangerous Beauty* (1998), *Living Out Loud, Ever After,* and *You've Got Mail* (1998)

JAMES HORNER   *Star Trek 2* (1982), *Star Trek 3* (1984), *Cocoon* (1985), *Aliens* (1986), *An American Tail* (1986), *Glory* (1989), *Field of Dreams* (1989), *Patriot Games* (1992), *Pelican Brief* (1993), *Legends of the Fall* (1994), *Braveheart* (1995), *Apollo 13* (1995), *Courage Under Fire* (1996), *The Devil's Own* (1996), *Titanic* (1997), *Deep Impact* (1998)

MARK ISHAM   *Quiz Show* (1994), *The Net* (1995), *Last Dance* (1996), *Blade* (1998), *October Sky* (1999)

MICHAEL KAMEN   *Brazil* (1985), three *Die Hard* films (1988, 1990, 1995), four *Lethal Weapon* films (1987, 1989, 1992, 1998), *Robin Hood: Prince of Thieves* (1991), *The Three Musketeers* (1993), *Circle of Friends* and *Don Juan DeMarco* (1994), *Mr. Holland's Opus* (1995), *Jack* (1996), *101 Dalmatians* (1996), *Event Horizon* (1997), *What Dreams May Come* (1998)

RANDY NEWMAN   *The Natural* (1984), *Awakenings* (1990), *Toy Story* (1995), *Michael* (1996), *James and the Giant Peach* (1996), *Cats Don't Dance* (1997), *Pleasantville* (1998)

THOMAS NEWMAN   *Revenge of the Nerds* (1984), *Fried Green Tomatoes* (1991), *The Player* and *Scent of a Woman* (1992), *Little Women* (1994), *The People vs. Larry Flynt* (1996), *Phenomenon* (1996), *Red Corner, Oscar and Lucinda,* and *The Horse Whisperer* (1997), *Meet Joe Black* (1998)

BASIL POLEDOURIS   *Robocop* (1987), *The Hunt for Red October* (1990), *Quigley Down Under* (1990), *Les Misérables* (1997)

RACHEL PORTMAN   *Where Angels Fear to Tread* (1991), *Used People* (1992), *Benny and Joon* (1993), *Sirens* (1994), *Marvin's Room* (1996), *Emma* (1996), *Addicted to Love* (1996), *Beloved* (1998), *Home Fries* (1998), *The Other Sister* (1999)

GRAEME REVELL   *The Hand That Rocks the Cradle* (1992), *The Crow* (1993), *Spawn* (1997), *The Saint* (1997), *Phoenix* (1998)

RICHARD ROBBINS   *Remains of the Day* (1993), *A Soldier's Daughter Never Cries* (1998)

MARC SHAIMAN   *When Harry Met Sally* (1989), *A Few Good Men* (1992), *Sleepless in Seattle* (1993), *The American President* (1995), *Ghosts of Mississippi* and *The First Wives Club* (1996), *In and Out* (1997), *Simon Birch* (1998), *Patch Adams* (1998)

ALAN SILVESTRI   *Romancing the Stone* (1984), three *Back to the Future* films (1985, 1989, 1990), *Predator* (1987), *Who Framed Roger Rabbit?* (1988), *The Abyss* (1989), *Soapdish* (1991), *Eraser* (1996), *Contact* (1997), *Holy Man* (1998), *Practical Magic* (1998)

GABRIEL YARED   *Camille Claudel* (1989), *The English Patient* (1996), *The Wings of the Dove* (1997), *City of Angels* (1998), *Message in a Bottle* (1999)

CHRISTOPHER YOUNG   Christopher Young first became known for his effective electronic music in scary thrillers such as *Hellraiser* (1987). Now he composes both orchestral and electronic music. His recent films include *Tales from the Hood* and *Virtuosity* (1995), *Hard Rain* (1997), *Hush* (1998), *Urban Legend* (1998), *The Rounders* (1998), and *Entrapment* (1999)

HANS ZIMMER   *Driving Miss Daisy* (1989), *Black Rain* (1989), *Pacific Heights* (1990), *Thelma and Louise* (1991), *Backdraft* (1991), *A League of Their Own* (1992), *Cool Runnings* (1993), *Broken Arrow* (1995), *The Preacher's Wife* (1996), *As Good As it Gets* (1997), *The Thin Red Line* (1998), and *Prince of Egypt* (songs by Steven Schwartz 1998)

Summary of Terms

click track	sound film	streamers
film score	sound track	synchronized sound
motivic technique	spotting	track
recurrent theme	stinger chord	*Übermensch*
sound dubbing		

Chapter 28

Contributions of World Cultures

As new modes of transportation and electronic communication shrink the world into a "global village," as Marshall McLuhan called it, we learn about and interact with cultures different from ours.

To learn more about the music of these cultures, ethnomusicologists equipped with tape recorders and video cameras travel to some of the world's most remote areas to study the native music. This chapter covers only a sampling of that vast variety of folk and ethnic music.

Thus far, our focus has mainly been on music encountered in the North American and European concert halls. In the past century, an existing and distinctive wealth of folk and ethnic music from world cultures has influenced that main body of traditional Western concert music. Ethnomusicologists predict that ethnic influence will ultimately bring about even more profound changes in Western music.

Early Interactions

AMERICA'S CENTENNIAL   The place is Philadelphia. The year, 1876. The event, a small-scale World Exposition to celebrate the 100th anniversary of the American Declaration of Independence. In response to invitations, music groups from distant lands perform at the event, exposing large groups of Westerners for the first time to music of diverse cultures.

Evidently the interaction was dynamic, because other major European and American cities hosted World Expositions before the turn of the century:

1878 — Paris
1882 — Moscow
1883 — Amsterdam
1889 — Paris
1893 — Chicago
1897 — Brussels

The late nineteenth century was a time when nationalism was taking hold, nurturing an interest in travel and world cultures. Nationalistic music became the vogue — in 1880, Tchaikovsky premiered his musical travel adventures throughout Italy with *Capriccio italien;* in 1888, Rimsky-Korsakov introduced his *Capriccio espagnole* and his Arabian-influenced *Scheherazade.*

In 1889, for the 100th anniversary of the Revolution, the French government financed the construction of the Eiffel Tower and invited a large array of ethnic music groups to perform at the World Exposition in Paris. Musicians flocked to see and hear these groups firsthand. They were impressed, and the direction of traditional Western music began to change.

NON-WESTERN INFLUENCES IN WESTERN ART MUSIC

You have read earlier about some of the influences of non-Western music, some inspired by the international expositions, others through less direct influence:

- Asian scales and percussion instruments were used by Puccini in his operas *Madama Butterfly* (about Japan) and *Turandot* (about China); more recently, in the hit musical *Miss Saigon* (about Vietnam and Thailand), Boublil and Schönberg abundantly use Asian scales, flutes, and percussion instruments.

- African percussion ensembles inspired Stravinsky's greater use of percussion instruments and polyrhythms.

- African music contributed significantly to American jazz.

Other Changes in Western Art Music

SCALES AND TONAL MATERIAL Some composers considered traditional scales overworked. After hearing non-Western music, they began experimenting not only with Asian and African scales but also with newly devised scales and tonal systems.

In South Africa, workers at the mines perform tribal dances in the arenas provided by the mine owners. Pictured are Zulu dancers at the gold mine on the outskirts of Johannesburg.

INSTRUMENTS   Composers have been incorporating non-Western instruments into their works for some time. What follows is a brief list of instruments that you may encounter at contemporary Western music concerts:

From *Africa*

drums (various shapes, sizes, and construction material)	wood blocks
xylophone	gourds

From *Islamic North Africa and Turkey*

cymbals (various sizes, starting in the late eighteenth century)	bass drum (starting in the late eighteenth century)
triangle (nineteenth century)	timpani or kettledrums (eighteenth century)

From *South and Central America*

maracas	conga drum
timbales	claves
bongos	cowbell

From *Asia*

Korean temple blocks	Chinese gongs (tam tam, starting in the nineteenth century)
Indonesian antique cymbals	

MUSIC SOUTH OF THE SAHARA

Encompassing more than fifty countries, Africa is home to more than 500 million people who have developed hundreds of languages and religions and a wide diversity of music. In spite of the diversity, there are some similar characteristics among African musical traditions about which we can generalize.

Role of Music in African Life

Hardly a tribal or religious activity in African daily life takes place without music. Preparations for, during, and following the hunt, for instance, are all accompanied by prescribed musical activities, enhanced by dances, masks, and costumes. Puberty rites, weddings, and funerals all have their customary music.

Like much non-Western music, African music has mainly been passed orally from generation to generation. In rural areas, many African children grow up dancing and contributing their musical talents to the tribal rituals. Everyone participates, and as they grow older, a few become soloists and chant leaders. So integral is music in the life of each person that this interest continues even after a man or a woman leaves tribal life to live in the city or among other cultures.

Other Instruments

African musicians use a variety of flutelike instruments, animal horns, whistles, thumb harps, and stringed instruments in addition to instruments that have already crossed over into Western ensembles. This wide array contributes to the richness of the overall sound.

Rhythm

At the core of African music is rhythm. Melody and harmony usually are subordinate to the rhythmic drive of the music.

POLYRHYTHMS African music often employs multilayers of rhythms. Each percussionist may add a different rhythm, resulting in a highly complex polyrhythmic texture. Dancing adds more complexity to the performance. Each tribal dancer chooses from the various rhythms as the source of inspiration for movement.

CHANGING METERS AND RHYTHMS In the nineteenth century, after returning from Africa, one musicologist reported that "African percussionists don't seem to know how to keep time." Because he was unfamiliar with African rhythms, he failed to understand their sophistication. In fact, an important characteristic of African music is its changing rhythms and metrical groups.

OSTINATO This repetitive rhythmic pattern is at the core of African percussion ensemble music. The ostinato player helps keep a regular pattern moving forward, enabling other percussionists to improvise freely, often skirting around the steady beat.

IMPROVISATION African musicians strive to avoid the obvious. While some members of a percussion ensemble provide an underlying rhythmic element with a steady beat or ostinato, others are free to play "around the beat" rather than exactly "on the steady beat." After all, the beat is already there; they can feel it. Adding their own rhythmic layers is a valued form of individual expression. Focusing on one player in the group, you will hear changing, imaginative, and complex improvisations.

VOCAL MUSIC Though usually subordinate to rhythm, African singing is still quite important. Some vocal music uses words; however, most African singing employs varieties of ostinato chants.

A South African six-stringed instrument

Two African performers playing wooden drums topped with stretched skin

Microtones

The pentatonic scale predominates in African music, but some pitches—microtones—differ from Western pitches. *Microtones* fall between the tones in the traditional Western chromatic scale.

Call and response

One characteristic of much of the vocal music of Africa is the use of *call and response*, discussed previously in the chapter on jazz. One member of the tribe, designated as the leader, calls out (sings) a melodic-rhythmic phrase. The rest of the singers respond, either with an exact imitation or a short, ostinato-style answer.

Heterophony

African melodies are often performed using *heterophony*—singers and melodic instrumentalists all perform the same melody at the same time, each with a slightly different interpretation. Some add extra tones or ornaments to the melody, others slightly different rhythms; some players lag behind, while others perform their melody slightly ahead of the group. We find this African-style heterophony also in North American jazz.

Transplanted African Music

The eighteenth- and nineteenth-century slave traders transported Africans and their music to many lands, especially to the Americas. We discussed the African influence on jazz in the United States, but the music of Central and South America and the Caribbean Islands also reflects the African influence.

Calypso

Mambo and rumba

Bossa nova and conga

Reggae

The exciting rhythms of *calypso* music from Trinidad developed through the singing of African slaves living on that island. Other music emerged: the *mambo* and *rumba* in Cuba, and the *bossa nova* and *conga* in Brazil. More recently, in Jamaica, *reggae* music developed from African, calypso, and rock 'n' roll rhythms.

LISTENING ACTIVITY

IF IT COMES TO FIGHTING WITH GUNS

Ewe People of Ghana, West Africa

‖ **Compact Disc 4, Track 46**
‖ **Running Time: 4:00**

From the West African nation of Ghana, this traditional Ewe dance piece form is known as a *atsiagbekor.* On the recording you will hear the following instruments: five drums, one double bell (*gankoqui*), and several gourds, some with seeds, others with beads or rattles.

Gypsy Dancers in Spain

Music of the Romani Culture, or Gypsy Music

To understand the widespread and profound influence of Romani music, we need to trace the migration of the people we call "Gypsies." Scholars have reached consensus on the origin of the culture, both through blood tests on modern-day Gypsies and by tracing the Romani language to ancient Sanskrit and roots in Hindi, Punjabi, and related languages that are spoken in northern India.

However, the reasons for the Gypsies' migrations are not fully clear. One hypothesis is that 10,000 to 12,000 Indian musicians and entertainers were sent as a gift to the Shah of Persia in A.D. 439. The *Zot,* as they were called, later left Persia to support themselves as itinerant entertainers. The hypothesis about the second migration, about 500 years later, is that the Gypsies were a specialized group of fighting forces assembled as warriors during Muslim expansionism.

Starting from northwest India, the migrations progressed through the Persian Empire (Iran and neighboring countries), the Byzantine Empire (Turkey), the Balkans and eastern Europe, and finally into western Europe, parts of Africa, and North America. The term "Gypsies" originated in Europe, where the people mistook the wandering bands of dark-skinned people for Egyptians.

Wherever they settled, Gypsies left their mark on the culture. And because entertainment has always been an important part of Romani life, their music and dance became a permanent part of various Asian and European countries. *Takseen,* the Arabic word for improvisational playing, is characterized by the blues-like, non-rhythmic musical style of the Gypsies. Spanish flamenco music and dance is filled with Indian modalities and instruments: finger cymbals, guitar, bells, and drums. Even the hand and arm movements of flamenco dancers resemble those of Indian dancers.

In the eighteenth and nineteenth centuries, Gypsy melodies became so popular in Europe that some Romani (or Rom) musicians became touring artists. Because of their fine musicianship, many, such as the Ungaro sect in Hungary, achieved social status and became wealthy.

Throughout the years, Jews and Gypsies not only traded and shared elements of their music but also played in each other's bands. You can hear Gypsy influences in Klezmer music and in Israeli circle dances such as the *hora*. Just listen to Jerry Bock's musical score for *Fiddler on the Roof* and you will hear Gypsy music. You will also recognize it in Franz Liszt's Hungarian Rhapsodies, in Johannes Brahms's Hungarian Dances, in Antonin Dvořák's *Slavonic Dances*, in the *Roumanian Rhapsody* by George Enescu (1881–1955), in *Hungarian Rondo* by Zoltán Kodály (1882–1967), in the operettas of Emmerich Kálmán (1882–1953), in the blues of B.B. King, and more.

MUSIC OF INDIA

On a land area half the size of the United States reside 1 billion people — one-fifth of the world's population. They speak fifteen major languages, with dozens of dialects, most using different alphabets.

Raga
(*rah*-gah)

British, Islamic, and Asian conquerors of India have helped shape Indian music. *Ragas*, the melodic material of Indian music, have similar counterparts in Iranian and other Islamic Middle Eastern music. European instruments such as violins, clarinets, and harmoniums are used in Indian music. These instruments were adopted during the Raj, or English

Indian dancers and musicians

occupation. Indian instruments such as the *sitar*, hand cymbals, and drums, and some Indian scales can be traced to Asia.

Today, in any of the typically overcrowded cities, you will encounter many forms of music: Indian classical, folk, and popular. Recently, the predominant popular music has been *film music*. Its popularity reflects people's fascination with films and the songs that are part of those films, the majority of which are musicals.

Indian film music is a curious blend of East and West: energetic melodies, often based on Asian scales over Latin-American rhythms. Piercing, nasal-sounding singers are accompanied by instruments that may include a set of American dance-band drums, electric keyboards, guitars, violins, xylophone, celeste, bongos, and Indian sitar, *tabla* drums, or bamboo flute.

Most of the folk music still being performed in India has been handed down orally. Street folk musicians earn their livings accompanying acrobats, dancers, or street theater. Others may charm snakes by playing the *punji* (a form of gourd and reed bagpipe). Indian minstrels wander the countryside, singing traditional folk songs and accompanying themselves on a drum or a crude stringed instrument.

Indian Classical Music

Classical music in India is distinctively Indian. For more than 2,000 years, trained musicians working in the royal courts or religious temples developed the sound and traditions that survive today.

HINDUSTANI AND KARNATIC MUSIC   Since the thirteenth century, when Muslims invaded India and settled in the north, classical Indian music diverged into two closely related traditions: north Indian or Hindustani music, and south Indian or Karnatic music. Each style uses slightly different instruments. For instance, the *bin* of the north is called the *vina* in the south. Their sizes and tones differ slightly, but at first glance, the two instruments seem identical.

Using for its melodic material *ragas*, or groupings of pitches somewhat similar to Western scales, Indian music is mainly heterophonic, with the addition of a drone: the overall sound of Indian classical music is complex and, at first, seems very different from Western music. With increased listening, however, it may eventually become more understandable.

Side notes:
Sitar
(sih-*tar*)

Tabla

Snake charmers
Punji
Minstrels

Bin
Vina

Typical Classical Indian Musical Texture		
Melody	〜〜〜〜〜	singers (one or two)
Accompaniment and Soloists	::::::::::::::::::	stringed instruments violin, *sitar*, *sarod*, *bin*, or *vina*
Drone	————————	*tambura* (string instrument, one or two)
Rhythm	/////////////////////	*tabla* and other drums

Sarod
Tambura

Several Western contemporary musicians have incorporated Indian music elements into their style. After spending time in India, the Beatles included the sitar among their instruments and worked Indian-style melodies into their music.

More recently, jazz flutist Paul Horn recorded an album of improvisations that he performed in the Taj Mahal, the famous mausoleum in Agra, India. To blend Indian music with Western jazz, Horn modified his material closer to the *ragas* he heard in India.

LISTENING ACTIVITY

GHAZAI, BAT KARANE MUJHE MUSHKIL

India

‖ **Compact Disc 4, Track 47**
‖ **Running Time: 2:42**

From India, the piece *Ghazai, Bat Karane Mujhe Mushkil* features a female vocalist, sitar, tambura (string drone), harmonium (small organlike keyboard), and tabla (drums).

Challenge Your Expertise

What is the origin of the word "gypsy?"

MUSIC OF JAPAN

Throughout history, Japan has incorporated foreign elements into its culture. Today, a wide assortment of music performances in Tokyo include:

American-style Japanese marching bands (on parade)
Japanese kabuki theater
Japanese koto ensemble concert
European chorus concerts of Renaissance music
American popular and rock music
Japanese popular music (American style)
European classical music orchestra concerts

GAGAKU Japanese music is traceable to the third century B.C. The *gagaku* court orchestra originated in the fifth century A.D., when eighty Korean musicians came to Japan to participate in an imperial funeral. Japanese royalty was impressed by the Korean musicians and set about developing its own court orchestras. Later, gagaku orchestras performed in the Shinto temples, where they can be heard today.

Musical traditions from other parts of Asia, especially China, entered Japanese music beginning in the seventh century A.D. Many Japanese instruments originated in China, India, Korea, and Manchuria.

From ancient times to the present, an abundance of solo and chamber music has been available for Japan's most popular instruments:

koto—a stringed lutelike instrument
kokyu—a spiked fiddle
shakuhachi—an end-blown bamboo flute
various percussion instruments

Japanese koto

LISTENING ACTIVITY

NETORI (PRELUDE) *ETENRAKU IN HYOJO*

Japan

| **Compact Disc 4, Track 48**
Running Time: 3:00

The traditional Gagaku: *Netori* (prelude) & *Etenraku in Hyojo* is performed by singers and an orchestra of assorted instruments, most of which are heard on the recording:

Winds:
* *hichiriki*   double-reed bamboo oboe
* *kakura-bue*   six-holed bamboo flute
* *ryuteki*   seven-holed bamboo flute
* *sho*   mouth organ with seventeen reed pipes

Strings:
* *wagon*   six-stringed zither
* *gaku-so*   thirteen-stringed zither
* *biwa*   pear-shaped lute with four strings

Percussion
* *da-daiko*   large drum, played with thick sticks
* *tsuri daiko*   medium-sized suspended two-headed drum, played with two sticks
* *shoko*   small suspended gong, played with two sticks
* *kakko*   small two-headed drum, played with thin sticks

Japanese Scales

At the heart of Japanese pitch material are varieties of five-tone, *pentatonic scales*, most of which originated in China. For instance, the following scales used mainly in Japanese sacred music are identical to Chinese scales dating back to B.C. 2000.

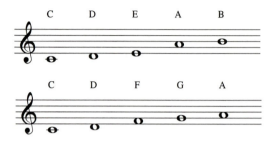

Another extensively used pentatonic scale in modern Japanese music consists of two major third gaps:

Sakura

The popular *Sakura,* or "Cherry Blossom," song uses this scale:

Theater Music

Throughout Japan's history, music usually has accompanied theatrical performances.

Kabuki performance with actors and musicians

NOGAKU Music is an important part of the traditional *Nogaku,* or *No,* musical plays. Derived from Buddhism, *No* plays feature singers accompanied by Japanese flutes and drums.

KABUKI Designed for the masses of common people, kabuki theater began developing its traditions in the sixteenth century. A colorful spectacle, kabuki incorporates acting, dancing, and music. Musical accompaniment is also an integral part of the Japanese puppet theater.

Music in Japanese Schools

Since the Meiji Restoration of 1868, when Emperor Mutsuhito modernized education, Western classical music replaced Japanese classical music in the schools. As further encouragement, talented Japanese musicians were sent to the music centers of Europe and America to study. These students brought back Western music and teaching methods to Japanese schools.

In the twentieth century, well-known music teachers such as Shinichi Suzuki continued teaching Western music to Japanese children. Through the Suzuki Method, thousands of Japanese youngsters learned in groups to play Vivaldi, Mozart, and other Western composers' violin and cello concertos. As a result, symphony orchestras around the world today employ many Japanese string players.

Suzuki Method

The Suzuki Method is now used in a number of countries, including the United States. Using the latest methods and instruments, the Yamaha Music Education Foundation teaches Western-style music to hundreds of thousands of youngsters in Japan and the United States.

Yamaha Music Education

With this history and emphasis on Western classical music, excellent symphony orchestras and opera companies thrive throughout modern Japan. Composers such as Mozart and Beethoven are as much the favorites of Japanese audiences as they are of European and American audiences. Contemporary Japanese composers are creating new music based on European principles but reflecting the venerable and diverse Japanese cultural history.

Challenge Your Expertise

Which cultures influenced Spanish flamenco music?

LISTENING ACTIVITY

Kabuki Nagauta Music Ayame-Yukata,

Japan

Compact Disc 4, Track 49
Running Time: 3:30

From Japan and the popular kabuki theater, listen to the *nagauta* music "Ayame-Yukata." Since 1652, kabuki has been performed entirely by male actors. The musicians usually are seated on the stage, facing the audience and behind the actors (see page 419). In this recording, we hear an assortment of instruments accompanying the male singer: *shakuhachi* (bamboo flutes), *koto* (stringed instruments), and *shamisen* (plucked fiddles).

Summary of Terms

Asian scales
bamboo flute
bin
bongos
bossa nova
call and response
calypso
changing meters
Chinese gongs (tam tam)
claves
conga
conga drum
cowbell
ethnic music
ethnomusicology
film music

gagaku
harmoniums
heterophony
Hindustani music
improvisation
Indonesian finger cymbals
kabuki
Karnatic music
kokyu
Korean temple blocks
koto
mambo
maracas
microtones
minstrels
nagauta

Nogaku
ostinato
pentatonic scale
punji
raga
Sakura
shakuhachi
shamisen
sitar
Suzuki Method
tabla
timbales
vina
World Exposition
Yamaha Music Education

Audience Power in the Twenty-First Century

As an *active listener*, you are equipped with the information and skills that will serve you for a lifetime. You are ready to move on to the next level of experiencing the variety of offerings in the vast world of music. You can inspire others to join you and share the joy of discovery. You are an informed member of the audience.

Fifty years ago, those of your grandparents' generation were members of the audience. They passed on the legacy to your parents, who in turn, passed it on to you. The challenge, then, is maintaining continuity. How can we ensure for succeeding generations that the work of those who came before us remains an element of our cultural future?

OUR NEW MILLENNIUM

Who could have predicted the dizzying rate of human progress over the past fifty years? Trying to imagine even a decade into the future is overwhelming, for every day, technology opens up greater possibilities for us. Music lovers might soon have unlimited, worldwide access to concerts by satellite, cable, or the Internet on a pay-per-view basis. Or they could hop on a supersonic aircraft that would transport them in a matter of hours to a live performance halfway around the globe. The new millennium—one thousand years—is almost too vast to imagine.

However, each milestone gives us an opportunity to ponder the future and to reflect on changes that occurred in the world of music at the turn of previous centuries—to look at the past 400 years of music in perspective.

Beginnings and Endings

SEVENTEENTH CENTURY Baroque-style music burst forth with great exuberance. Composers began to explore combinations of instruments with vocal soloists and ensembles. New forms included the concerto, the cantata, the oratorio, and opera. In Italy, opera houses opened to the general public. Support for the arts came from the Church, the courts, and the merchant middle class.

EIGHTEENTH CENTURY String instruments were perfected. Composers wrote instrumental concertos for emerging virtuoso performers. Although much-improved orchestras were offering subscription concerts to the general public, the main support for music came from the aristocracy.

NINETEENTH CENTURY Romanticism became dominant. Music was often associated with literature, ideas, and emotions. Predictable structure gave way to individual expression. Composers and performers attained prestige and respect, many becoming wealthy from their art. All instrument families were perfected, leading to the establishment of symphony orchestras throughout Europe. Performing arts were supported primarily by the public and the aristocracy.

TWENTIETH CENTURY The 1900s began with a rebellion against romanticism. Composers began to use new materials and sources for their music, such as atonality and irregular rhythms. Ragtime became the rage in North America, along with popular art forms such as vaudeville and musical theater. Jazz was the true American music. The popularity of rock music spread worldwide. Now a synthesizer can virtually replicate an orchestra.

What Are Today's Trends?

We might not be able to predict where we're going, but we can assess where we are. Recent studies suggest that today's younger audiences—despite higher incomes and better levels of education—demonstrate less enthusiasm than preceding generations about most "high culture" performing arts. Although popular cultures—rock music, movies, and television—are thriving, only jazz, musical theater, opera, and ballet attract people of all ages.

Most notable is opera. The number of 18- to 24-year old operagoers has increased by nearly 20 percent during the past few years—even though that age group's overall population has *decreased*. Opera companies have become more sensitive to the fact that opera is musical theater. For example, building on the success of the musical megahit *Rent,* which has been promoted as a rock version of *La Bohème,* opera companies have programmed Puccini's work in their production seasons. Young audiences, surrounded and exposed to media from infancy, enjoy the multimedia spectacle of music, words, costumes, set design, theatricality, and dance that opera provides.

Another boon to opera has been the introduction of supertitles. These English translations of the libretto projected above the proscenium make the opera accessible to the audience. Without having to memorize the entire libretto, everyone can understand the dialogue and become engaged in the story. Opera companies have discovered that an accessible production keeps an audience coming back.

Supertitles

Proscenium

Perhaps we should ask, "Will composers continue to write symphonies? If so, which orchestras will play them, and will there be audiences for the performances?"

We also should ask ourselves what we are willing to do to support art music. Will we take over the job of fund-raising? What role can an individual play in helping to ensure continuity?

BEYOND SURVIVAL

Marketing Challenges

For their very survival, performing arts organizations want to keep their audiences coming back. In an interview in the *Los Angeles Times,* Willem Wijnberger, manager of the Los Angeles Philharmonic, stated that the orchestra's continued success depends on its appeal to the great diversity in the Los Angeles area. Wijnberger sees the need to focus on community outreach, to expand educational programs for young audiences, and to target concerts for specific audiences at the Philharmonic's home at the Music Center and at the Hollywood Bowl.

Increasingly, arts organizations are making a commitment to cultural diversity in order to foster greater community support. By actively programming for people of all backgrounds, these organizations make the arts more vital, relevant, and accessible to a broader audience. As individuals, we may be able to participate in promoting our diverse cultural heritage.

Is Survival Enough?

What will it take to help performing arts organizations thrive?

According to Michael Greene, president and CEO of the National Academy of Recording Arts and Sciences (NARAS), two key federally funded arts agencies—the National Endowment for the Arts (NEA) and the National Endowment for the Humanities (NEH)—have dramatically promoted the growth of cultural organizations during the past fifty years.

Orchestra companies have increased from 110 to 230.
Dance companies have increased from 37 to 450.
Opera companies, have increased from 27 to 120.

In a May 1998 article in *Recording Academy News,* Greene stated:

Studies evidence that government support of the arts does not come at the expense of economic development. In fact, in the United States, for every $1 invested in the arts by the NEA and the NEH, the private sector further matches that with $11 of their own. Additionally, the arts employ 3.2 million individuals; nonprofit arts institutions generate $36.8 billion annually in economic activity within local communities and over $6 billion in tax revenues.

Arts organizations themselves are dynamic businesses, employers, and consumers. Recognizing the extent to which these organizations enhance our lives, some communities have built new concert halls. Others, unfortunately, face the loss of their orchestras. What might happen if government support is reduced—or discontinued?

Communication Is the Key

Your voice counts in encouraging governmental support. Let your elected officials know your opinions. When your representatives must decide whether to vote for or against support for the arts, they usually consider the priorities of their constituents. Your role is to communicate your views.

Performing arts organizations want to communicate with you to keep you coming back. In return, they need you to communicate with them. Although your support is implicit by your attendance of performances, *explicit* feedback through a letter or phone call often can be more effective in registering your personal opinion, your voice, and your vote. Let's explore some possibilities.

First, let the management know that you *want* to communicate; then mention *how* you'd like to go about it:

- by a questionnaire in the concert program
- by regular mail
- by telephone survey
- by fax
- by email

Stay in touch with the organization. Let management know what would interest you in future performances. Suggest ways in which the organization might make you feel included. Propose educational programs that would appeal to you and your family. Ask whether it would be possible for the conductor, a soloist, or a music educator to introduce and explain music that is different from what you're used to. Tell them whenever you enjoy a concert or a particular piece of music, to show that you are there—and that you care.

You have a lifetime of enjoyment ahead of you. This is only the beginning.

Summary of Terms

proscenium   supertitles

LISTENING ACTIVITY

FINALE: MARTIN BOOKSPAN, HOST

Compact Disc 4, Track 50
Cassette Tape: Side D, Example 10
Running Time: 3:00

LISTENING ACTIVITY

FINALE: MARTIN BOOKSPAN, HOST

Compact Disc 4, Track 50
Cassette Tape: Side D, Example 10
Running Time: 3:00

Music Notation

To preserve composers' creative ideas, music notation developed gradually over a span of hundreds of years. Notation makes it possible for players to recreate music accurately. Here are some of the basic concepts of modern music notation.

Pitch Notation

STAFF   This structure of five lines and four spaces holds printed notes, graphically indicating the relative highness and lowness of pitches.

CLEFS   A clef is a symbol placed on a staff line to fix the pitch notated on that line. With that reference, performers know the pitches of the other notes on the staff. There are two main clef signs:

The *G clef* or *treble* (high) *clef* is an ornate symbol that circles the line around the pitch *G*.

pitch *G* ⟶

The *F clef* or *bass* (low) *clef* contains two dots placed on either side of the "F" line to indicate the pitch *F*:

pitch *F* ⟶

GRAND STAFF   Because their ranges are limited, most instruments and voices perform music using one *clef*. Keyboards, on the other hand, use a much wider range. Therefore, their parts include both *G* and *F* clefs and are displayed on a *grand staff*.

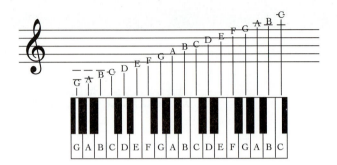

Duration or Time Notation

The shading of notes, along with stems and flags attached to them, indicates duration. Special symbols indicate the specific duration of silence or rest:

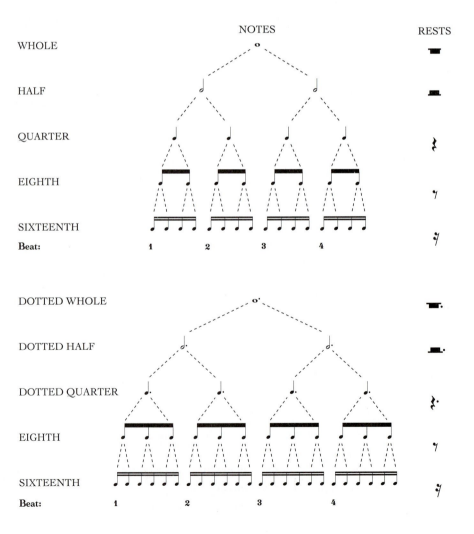

Common Scales in Music

SCALES

A scale is notated as a series of pitches proceeding upward or downward according to a prescribed pattern. With twelve different tones in Western music, a vast variety of arrangements is possible. The most commonly used scales follow:

Chromatic Scale

The scale uses all twelve of the half tones available in Western music. Each step is a half tone.

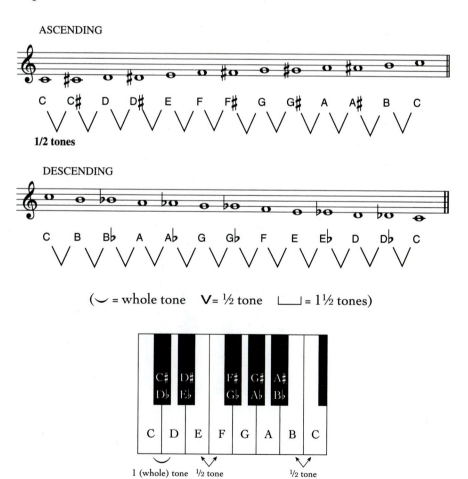

Sharp The sharp ♯ sign raises the pitch that follows it by one half tone.

Flat The flat ♭ sign lowers the pitch that follows it by one half tone.

C Major Scale

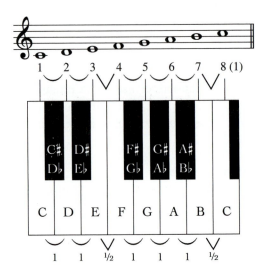

MAJOR SCALE FORMULA						
Whole,	Whole,	Half,	Whole,	Whole,	Whole,	Half
1	1	½	1	1	1	½

C Minor Scale (natural)

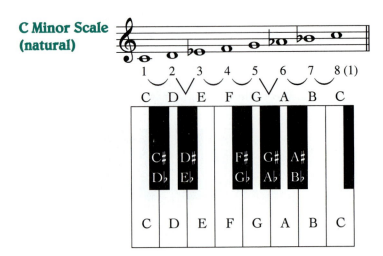

C Minor Scale (harmonic)

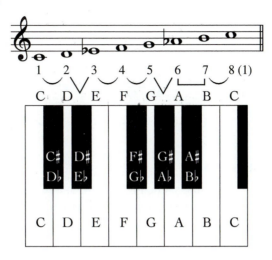

C Minor Scale (melodic)

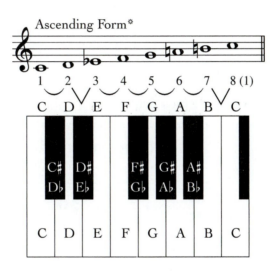

* When descending, use natural minor.

Pentatonic

(Gapped Scale) A five-tone scale used by most early music cultures. Varying forms of *pentatonic* scales are still used in Asia, Polynesia, Africa, and by the American Indians, the Celts, and the Scots. Because of the large gap between some of the tones, this scale is also known as a *gapped scale*.

C PENTATONIC SCALE (one type only)

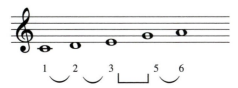

Whole-Tone

C WHOLE TONE

Blues Scale

Basically, this is a major scale with altered tones, called *blue notes*. The *blues scale* is used predominantly in jazz and popular music.

C BLUES SCALE

Hexatonic Blues Scale

The more commonly used blues scale is the six-note, *hexatonic* scale.

C HEXATONIC BLUES SCALE

Modes

Modes are scales used extensively in church music during the Middle Ages. More recent composers and modern folk, jazz, and rock musicians also employ some of the modes. The following are the ones most often used:

D DORIAN

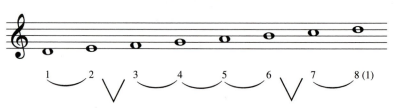

E PHRYGIAN

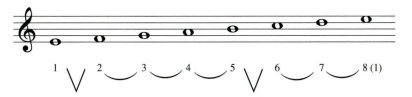

F LYDIAN

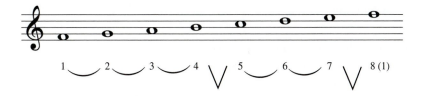

G MIXOLYDIAN

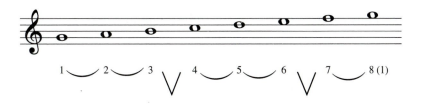

Appendix C

Writing Reports

THE SHORT CONCERT REPORT

1. Attach the program and ticket stub of the performance to your report.
2. Write a one-paragraph description of each work. Give your personal reaction to each piece. Describe the music as well as you can, using both your own words and the terms presented in this course.
3. Try to include:
   - performing medium (also special instruments and soloists)
   - general form (symphony, concerto, dance forms, etc.)
   - outstanding features of melody, rhythms, textures, style, and so on.

Other Directions

Do not copy from printed concert programs, music reviews, or record jackets. That is a breach of copyright. Take a pad and pen so you can jot down a few comments after movements or works. This will help you remember the music. If permitted, record the performance with a small, battery-operated tape recorder. That way you can write your notes later and just enjoy the performance.

Note: Most professional concerts prohibit taping.

THE LONG CONCERT REPORT

I. General Directions

  A. Ask your instructor to recommend concerts.

  B. Select one that interests you.

  C. Type your report double-spaced. Make sure your computer print-out is legible.

  D. Include a bibliography and footnotes, if necessary.

  E. Attach your program and ticket stub.

II. Pre-Concert Report

Select one major work or a group of short works scheduled on the concert.

  A. Present your research on the historical background of:

    1. the composer

    2. the composition

B. Listen to a recording and give your general reaction to the performance and specific reaction to the music regarding the composer's use of:
1. performing media
2. rhythm, tempo, meter
3. melodic materials
4. harmony and tonality
5. textures
6. form

III. Post-Concert Review
A. Include background information: date, time, place, performer(s), and musical selections.
B. Discuss your reactions to each work performed. Include both your intellectual and emotional reactions.
C. Discuss your reactions to the quality of the performance and performer(s). Also comment on the concert ritual the performers follow.
D. Compare the live concert performance of the major work with the recorded performance you researched.

Other Directions

Refrain from merely giving a play-by-play account of the concert; your printed program already gives that information.

Do not copy directly from sources. You may paraphrase researched sources as long as you cite these sources with footnotes and in a bibliography.

Jot down notes after movements or works to help you remember the performance. Try not to write during the live performance so that you will not distract yourself. If permitted, take a tape recorder to help you write your post-concert review.

THE RESEARCH REPORT

Directions

1. Choose one topic:
   • From the list of suggested research topics, choose one for your report. Or, choose an alternate topic similar to those suggested. Compare and contrast the musical selections. Use terminology you learned. Include research sources, and describe your experiences attending concerts.
2. Include biographical data on composers:
   • Explain how events in the composer's life relate to the works you have chosen to compare.
3. At the time the works were composed, what was happening in society, politics, and economics that influenced the general musical style?

- Cite specific examples from the music you selected.
4. Include information about the performer and the recording:
   - Identify the ensemble, conductor, soloists, and any other performers mentioned on the recording.
   - Identify, if possible, the date of the recording and its production label.
5. Include a bibliography:
   - Cite all sources used to research your topic—books, articles, records, and so on.
6. Be original!
   - Do not copy directly from sources such as printed concert programs, music reviews, or record jackets. Copying word for word is a breach of copyright.
   - You may paraphrase resource material as long as you properly cite sources with footnotes and in the bibliography.

Other Directions

Avoid taking notes during the performance. To help you remember the music, jot down a few comments between movements or after the work. If permitted, record the performance with a small, battery-operated tape recorder. That way you can write your notes later and just enjoy the performance.

Note: Most professional concerts prohibit taping.

SUGGESTED RESEARCH TOPICS

1. Compare and contrast an early and a late work by the same composer:
   - Haydn's Symphony No. 45 (*Farewell*, 1772) and Symphony No. 94 (*Surprise*, 1791)
   - Beethoven's Symphony No. 1 (1800) and Symphony No. 9 (*Choral*, 1824)
   - Beethoven's String Quartets Opus 18 and String Quartets Opus 135.
   - Verdi's operas *Rigoletto* (1851) and *Otello* (1887)
   - Puccini's operas *La Bohème* (1896) and *Turandot* (posthumous, 1926)
   - Mahler's Symphony No. 1 (*The Titan*, 1888) and Symphony No. 8 (*Symphony of a Thousand*, 1909)
   - Stravinsky's ballet *The Rite of Spring* (1913) and *Ebony Concerto* (1945)
2. Compare and contrast two similar works by two different composers of the same style period:
   - Bach's *Christmas* Oratorio and Handel's *Messiah* Oratorio
   - Brahms's *Academic Festival Overture* and Wagner's *Die Meistersinger von Nürnberg Overture*

- Tchaikovsky's *Nutcracker* Ballet and Falla's Suite from *The Three Cornered Hat* Ballet
- Gershwin's *An American in Paris* and Copland's *Appalachian Spring*
- Rimsky-Korsakov's *Capriccio espagnole* and Tchaikovsky's *Capriccio italien*

3. Compare and contrast two similar works by two different composers from two different style periods:
   - Haydn's Symphony No. 94 (*Surprise*) and Prokofiev's Symphony No. 1 (*Classical*)
   - Vivaldi's Concerto (*Spring*) from *The Four Seasons* and Schuman's Symphony No. 1 (*Spring*)
   - Bach's *Mass in B Minor* and Bernstein's *Mass*
   - Beethoven's Symphony No.9 (*Choral*) and Stravinsky's *The Rite of Spring*

4. Other topics:
   - Discuss the differences in orchestral music in the Classical, Romantic, and twentieth-century style periods.
   - Compare the musical contributions of Felix Mendelssohn and Leonard Bernstein.
   - Trace and discuss the development of the concert tradition from the Baroque period to the present.
   - Describe and discuss the various ways in which composers and musicians from the Baroque period to the present supported themselves.
   - Describe, compare, and contrast the different ways of listening to music of the Baroque, Classical, and Romantic style periods.

Music Listening Guide

PERFORMING MEDIUM

symphony orchestra

chamber orchestra

wind ensemble (band)

chamber music ensemble

electronic instruments

chorus (a cappella)

chorus with orchestra

solo (instrumental or vocal with orchestra)

solo (instrumental or vocal with piano)

other combinations

RHYTHM–TEMPO–METER

beat prominence: strong, weak

tempo: slow, medium, fast

meter: 2, 3, other (5, 7, etc.)

subdivision: simple (2 or 4) complex (3, 5, 7, 9)

rubato (changing)

ostinato (repetitious)

basso continuo (running bass line)

silence

MELODY

prominent

not prominent

smooth (long lines)

fragmented (short lines)

ornamented (trills, etc.)

plain (no ornaments)

imitation (repeated idea, in another
voice or instrument)

sequences (repeated idea, same voice, new
pitches)

traditional scales used: major, minor

other scales used: chromatic, pentatonic,
whole tone, tone-row, gapped

HARMONY–TONALITY

mostly consonant

mostly dissonant

major and minor chords (traditional)

polychords

quartal chords (fourths)

clusters (seconds)

major or minor tonality

polytonality

atonality

TEXTURE

monophonic (single line)
polyphonic (many independent lines)
homophonic (sounding together, also melody with accompaniment)
mixture of textures

FORM

large forms

symphony

concerto

concerto grosso

opera overture

concert overture

orchestral suite

descriptive piece

mass

oratorio

cantata

opera

chamber music (trio, quartet, quintet, sonata)

keyboard forms (sonata, fugue, nocturne, etc.)

detailed forms

strophic (A–A–A, etc.)

through-composed

free sectional

two-part (A–B, or A–A–B–B)

three-part (A–B–A)

rondo (A–B–A–C–A, etc.)

minuet and trio

theme and variations

sonata

general concept of form

developmental (repetition of ideas)

through-composed (rhapsodic, little repetition)

Challenge Your Expertise Answers

CHAPTER 3

- During the performance of a symphony, what should you do if most of the audience begins to applaud at the "wrong" time? *It's up to you whether or not to join in the applause.*
- When is a piano instead of an oboe used to "tune" the orchestra? *before a performance by a piano soloist*

CHAPTER 4

- What two things do a waltz and a minuet have in common? *They are both dances. They are both in three meter.*
- What term describes a melody or a section of the music that comes to a conclusion? *A "cadence."*

CHAPTER 5

- In terms of creating sound, what does a violin bow have in common with a pair of drum sticks? *Both are energy sources.*
- Which instrument is the smallest of the woodwinds? *piccolo*
- What do the tuba, contrabassoon, and bass viol have in common? *They all have the lowest pitch of the section.*
- Can you think of two reasons the brass section isn't in the front of the symphony orchestra? *Violins play most of main themes. The brass section plays too loudly to be in front.*
- The term "movement" on a concert program refers to which of the following?
    1. The orchestra enters and tunes.
    2. The conductor's arms are raised.
    3. A large section of a longer work is to be played.
    4. The soloist enters.

  3. A large section of a longer work is to be played.

CHAPTER 7

- What group could be considered one of the first musicians' unions? *German Meistersingers*

CHAPTER 8

- What were three purposes of stained-glass windows? *to make the church more attractive; to depict scenes from the Bible; to use as instructional tools*

CHAPTER 9

- What was Antonio Vivaldi's distinctive physical feature? *bright red hair*
- Which two Baroque-style period composers continued working after becoming blind. *Bach, Handel*
- Why is Bach's Fugue in g minor known as the "Little"? *to distinguish it from other fugues Bach wrote in that key*
- What two developments resulted in the concerto grosso? *better instruments, virtuoso performers*

CHAPTER 11

- Which is the higher number—Mozart's age at his death or the number of symphonies he composed? *number of symphonies (He wrote 41 symphonies before his death at age 35.)*
- How long did Beethoven study with Mozart? *Beethoven never studied with Mozart.*
- How did archeological discoveries in 1748 promote a renewed interest in classical art and music? *The discovery of buried ruins in Pompeii sparked a renewed interest in Greek and Roman Classical art.*
- Which Classical-period symphony ends with fewer players on stage than it begins with? *Haydn's "Farewell" Symphony*
- Why did Haydn use Italian librettos even though his audiences spoke German? *Italian was the traditional language for opera.*

CHAPTER 12

- Why did Beethoven earn more royalty income than Bach? *Bach's music was not published commercially.*

CHAPTER 14

- What was Johann Maelzel's invention, and how did it affect music performance? *Maelzel's metronome provided a standard for measuring the speed or tempo of the beat.*
- Which composer courted his loved one in a language she did not understand. *Hector Berlioz*
- Which of the following composers could have been guests at Chopin's 30th birthday party—Mendelssohn, Schubert, Liszt, Beethoven? *Mendelssohn, Liszt*

- Can you think of two composers who published their works under someone else's name? *Fanny Mendelssohn, Clara Schumann.*
- How did Mendelssohn use a combination of affluence and influence in his work with other musicians? *He raised the Gewandhaus Orchestra to a professional level by influencing the players to excel. He paid them extra from his own pocket and established a retirement fund.*

CHAPTER 15

- Who composed the most operas—Puccini, Rossini, or Verdi? *Rossini*
- What is the difference between a *castrato* and a *concerto*? *A "castrato" is a male soprano or alto singer. A "concerto" is an instrumental piece for one or more solo instruments.*
- What are at least three ways in which Wagner exerted total control? *He wrote his own librettos; composed, orchestrated, and conducted the music; designed the sets; directed the singing.*

CHAPTER 16

- Can you name two symphonies that do not have four movements? *Schubert's Unfinished Symphony; Beethoven's Pastoral Symphony*
- How are Felix Mendelssohn's travels reflected in his works? *Scottish Symphony, Italian Symphony, Hebrides Overture*
- Which opera is associated with "tobacco and bulls"? *Carmen*
- Which opera contains elephants and pyramids? *Aida*
- What sort of records did Mahler break? *length of piece (3rd Symphony), number of players called for (8th Symphony)*
- What incentives encouraged musicians to improve their skills? *more competition; higher-paying positions; better orchestras.*
- Who wrote the words for a tone poem? *No one! It is entirely an instrumental piece with no text. (However, there may be a story or program for the work that was usually written by the composer.)*

CHAPTER 17

- To which professional association did Nikolai Rimsky-Korsakov, Alexander Borodin, Mily Balakirev, César Cui, and Modest Musorgsky belong? *"The Mighty Five" or "Russian Five"*
- Which popular Russian composer worked as a law clerk? *Tchaikowsky*

CHAPTER 18

- In addition to music, which creative art forms reflect Impressionism? *mainly painting and poetry*

CHAPTER 20

- Which non-European culture was the main influence in Stravinsky's use of ostinato? *African culture and its music*

CHAPTER 21

- After the premiere of which ballet did a Paris theatre need repair? *Igor Stravinsky's Rite of Spring*

CHAPTER 22

- Name two composers who were forced by their government to make public apologies. *Shostakovich and Prokofiev*
- Which one of *Les Six* was influenced by his visits to Harlem jazz clubs? *Darius Milhaud*
- Which of his compositions shows that influence? *La Création du Monde*
- What were some of the differences between The Five and *Les Six* (The Six)? *The Five were Russian composers—all men—who promoted purely Russian music. Les Six were French, included a woman, focused on Western music.*
- Name at least two prominent composers whose works represent more than one style period. *Beethoven, Prokofiev*
- Which composer is associated with commencement ceremonies? *Edward Elgar*
- Name two composers whose works sound like an earlier style period than when they lived. *Brahms, Sibelius*

CHAPTER 23

- What might happen if the piano is not tuned before a performance of Cage's *4:33* (Four minutes, thirty-three seconds)? *Nothing would happen because the piano is not actually played.*

CHAPTER 24

- Who was the composer who supported himself during his teenage years by plugging songs and recording piano rolls? *George Gershwin*
- Whose one-act opera contains motifs derived from Creole folk tunes? *Amy Beach*

CHAPTER 25

- Name several places where song pluggers worked? *at music publishers' studios; in department stores; in theaters*

- How did the term *Tin Pan Alley* originate?   *The din from performers playing at the same time on New York City's 28th St. sounded like the banging of tin pans.*

CHAPTER 26

- How did *Shuffle Along* make history?   *The show set new standards for African American musicals, and for the first time, African-Americans were allowed to sit in the orchestra section of the theater.*
- What did Tony Pastor do to change vaudeville?   *Pastor "cleaned up" the shows and transformed vaudeville into family entertainment.*
- Suppose Bach, Mozart, and Brahms were alive today. Who do you think would be the most likely composer of Broadway musicals? *most likely Mozart, possibly Bach*
- Although trained as a composer, Stephen Sondheim collaborated as a lyricist with which three composers?   *Leonard Bernstein, Jule Styne, and Richard Rodgers*
- When you hear song lyrics about luxury, wealth, and extravagance, which composer-lyricist are you reminded of?   *Cole Porter*

CHAPTER 27

- Why did movie studios have to establish large music departments?   *With the advent of "talkies," music became more important in films.*
- Which three of the following have a similar function—recurring theme, *sostenuto*, leitmotif, *idée fixe*, coda?   *recurring theme, leitmotif, idée fixe*
- In film making, what is the track without music called?   *"click" track.*

CHAPTER 28

- What is the origin of the word "gypsy"?   *Europeans mistook the wandering bands of dark-skinned people for Egyptians (shortened to gypsies).*
- Which cultures influenced Spanish flamenco music?   *Indian and Romani cultures*

Glossary of Musical Terms

A cappella Choral music without accompaniment

Accelerando Gradual quickening of tempo

Accent Emphasis on a particular tone

Adagio Slow tempo

Aleatoric music A twentieth-century method of creating music; uses vague notation to leave many musical decisions to the performer

Allegretto Less quick than allegro; moderately fast tempo

Allegro Lively, fast tempo

Allemande A Baroque dance in moderate tempo and two-beat meter

Alto A low female voice, also called contralto

Andante Moderate, walking tempo

Andantino Slightly faster tempo than andante

Antiphony, antiphonal Music in which two or more groups are separated to create an echo effect and contrast

Arco A string instrument bowing direction where the bow is used as opposed to plucking the string

Aria An elaborate solo song with instrumental accompaniment, generally in an opera, an oratorio, or a cantata

Arpeggio Chord tones sounded in succession rather than simultaneously

Art song An elaborate solo song, usually composed to an existing poem, sung with accompaniment

Athematic Music without discernible themes or melodies

Atonality Music without tonality or key

Avant-garde A French term used to describe radical or advanced composers or other artists

Ballad A narrative-style folk song

Ballad opera A type of opera, originating in the eighteenth century, which introduced spoken dialogue between songs

Ballade (1) French trouvère poetry and songs (2) Songlike, nineteenth-century piano pieces

Bar See *measure*

Baritone A male voice with a range between tenor and bass

Bass The lowest, heaviest male voice

Basso continuo A bass line that provides a basis for a harmonic accompaniment, most often used in Baroque music

Beat The underlying basic rhythmic pulse

Bebop Originating in the 1940s, a highly innovative jazz style that features small groups of instruments

Bel canto A style of singing, particularly in Italian opera, which displays the singer's vocal agility and beautiful tone

Bin A string instrument used in the music of northern India

Blue notes Flatted or "bent" third, fifth, and seventh tones of a traditional major scale used in jazz and blues music

Blues A melancholy song originating with African-American singers

Blues progression Predictable progressions of chords in jazz and blues music, using patterns derived from church hymns

Bolero A Spanish dance in moderate tempo with three beats per measure

Bourrée A fast Baroque dance with two beats per measure

Bridge (1) A musical passage between two major sections. (2) The part of a stringed instrument that supports the strings

Buffo A singer of comic roles in Italian opera

Burlesque A raucous, bawdy, musical sex-and-comedy-travesty entertainment of the late nineteenth and early twentieth centuries

445

Cadence A melodic or harmonic progression that gives the effect of closing a section

Cadenza A virtuoso passage (sometimes improvised) played by the soloist in a concerto, usually without orchestral accompaniment

Cakewalk Originating on Southern plantations, the *cakewalk* was a high-kicking dance.

Call and response An African and African-American song style in which a leader sings phrases to which a chorus or group responds with phrases

Canon Music in which one or more lines continue to imitate one another throughout the work

Cantata Vocal music developed in the Baroque period for solo voice(s), instruments, and often a chorus; based either on a religious or secular text

Canzona A short instrumental piece popular in the sixteenth and seventeenth centuries

Castrato Castrated male soprano or alto singers, popular mainly in Italian Baroque operas

Chaconne A work featuring variations on a progression of chords repeated throughout the work

Chamber music Musical composition suitable for performances by two to eight players in a room or small hall

Chance music A twentieth-century technique using general instructions to performers, allowing them to create a performance that is a matter of chance.

Chorale A hymn tune used in the German Lutheran Church

Chord The simultaneous sounding of three or more pitches

Choreographer The person who plans the dancer's movements

Chorus (1) A group that sings choral music (2) A section of an opera or oratorio sung by the chorus (3) The refrain or main section of a song

Chromatic A scale or harmonic movement of half steps

Cine music Blend of Eastern and Western music used in popular musical films in India

Clavier A general term indicating any keyboard instrument

Coda The Italian word for "tail"; the section that brings the movement to a conclusion

Col legno A special effect in string performance where the player strikes the strings with the wooden side of the bow

Coloratura A virtuoso style of singing, usually including fast scales, arpeggios, and ornaments; often associated with a light, high soprano voice, particularly in opera

Common time A meter that consists of four beats per measure

Concert overture An overture not associated with an opera or a drama

Concertato Contrasting performing groups playing together

Concertmaster (*Konzertmeister* in German) The first chair player in the first violin section of an orchestra

Concerto A work for solo instrument(s), usually with three movements, accompanied by an orchestra

Concerto grosso A concerto for a small instrumental group accompanied by a small orchestra

Consonance A group of sounds that seems pleasing or restful

Continuo See *basso continuo*

Contrabassoon A large bassoon pitched an octave below the usual bassoon

Contralto See *alto*

Counterpoint Two or more independent melodic lines occurring at the same time

Counter subject The second theme in a fugue

Country Popular music originating in the Appalachian region of the United States

Courante A lively dance in triple meter and fast tempo

Crescendo Gradual increase in volume

Decrescendo Gradual decrease in volume, also called diminuendo

Development (1) The process of developing themes (2) The section in sonata form featuring the development of themes

Dissonance A group of sounds that seems disagreeable or unpleasant

Dodecaphonic music See *serialism*

Double stop The sounding of two different pitches simultaneously on a stringed instrument

Downbeat The accented first beat of a measure

Duet A musical work for two performers

Dynamics The various levels of intensity or loudness in music

Eclectic An incorporation of many different styles

Electronic music Sounds produced on electronic oscillators and then usually recorded and stored.

English horn An alto oboe

Etude A short, instrumental composition concentrating on a particular technical aspect of performance

Exposition The opening section of fugue and sonata forms

Fantasia A short composition in free form

Finale The concluding movement of some multimovement works and operas

Flamenco The highly rhythmic dance style of Andalusian Gypsies

Flat A sign indicating that a pitch is to be lowered by a half step

Form The structure or plan of a composition

Fortepiano See *pianoforte*

Fugue A composition in which the main subject (theme) is presented in imitation in several parts

Fusion A blend of jazz and rock music

Gagaku Ancient Korean and Japanese court orchestras

Gamelan Javanese court music

Gavotte A dance with a moderate tempo in two-beat meter

Gesamtkunstwerk Meaning "total art work" in German; Wagner used this term for his music-dramas, over which he exerted total control of the librettos, music, orchestrations, sets, and staging.

Gigue A baroque dance in compound meter with a fast tempo

Glissando A performance effect provided by rapid sliding up or down scales

Grand opera Usually serious, nineteenth-century French opera that utilizes elaborately costumed crowd scenes, large choruses, ballet, and lavish sets

Grave Very slowly and solemnly

Gregorian chant Monophonic church music of the Middle Ages named after Pope Gregory I; also called *plainchant*

Harmonics (1) Secondary tones that form a part of most tones (2) High-pitched tones that are produced on a string instrument by placing the finger lightly on a string

Harmony The simultaneous sounding of pitches

Harpsichord A popular keyboard instrument of the sixteenth through eighteenth centuries on which the strings are plucked when the keys are depressed

Heldentenor In German operas, a tenor who sings heroic roles

Hindustani music Music of northern India

Homophony, homophonic A texture consisting of a line of melody and accompaniment

Idée fixe Berlioz's name for the melody or theme used throughout all movements of his *Symphony fantastique*

Imitation The repetition of a melody or portion of a melody in another part

Impromptu A short piano composition that sounds improvised

Improvisation Spontaneous performance without notated music

Incidental music Music composed for performance in connection with, but not part of, a drama

Instrumentation The parts assigned to particular instruments in an ensemble

Interval The distance between two notes

Jazz A twentieth-century American musical style incorporating complex rhythms and improvisation

Kabuki Traditional Japanese theater incorporating acting, dancing, and music

Kapellmeister German term for music director

Karnatic music Music of southern India

Key See *tonality*

Kokyu A Japanese spiked fiddle

Koto A stringed, lutelike instrument of Japan

Largo Very slow and broad tempo

Legato Smooth, connected style of performance

Leitmotif A motive or theme associated with a particular character or an idea, used extensively by Richard Wagner

Lento Very slow

Libretto The text of an opera or oratorio

Lied (pl., Lieder) The German term for art song

Lutheran cantata A choral work, often with instruments, for the musical portion of a Lutheran church service

Lyric opera Nineteenth-century French opera emphasizing melody and romantic or fantasy-based stories

Ma non troppo A performance indication meaning "but not too much," used to qualify another term, as in *allegro ma non troppo — "fast, but not too much"*

Madrigal A secular work for small choir, popular in the Renaissance style period

Maestro de cappella Italian term for music director

Major One of the two basic scales used in Western music; see also *minor*

Mass The Roman Catholic Church's main service, frequently set to music (*Missa* in Latin)

Mazurka A Polish dance in triple meter

Measure A group of beats set off in written music by vertical lines called bar lines

Meistersinger A member of a guild of German master musicians. The guild flourished from the fourteenth to the seventeenth centuries.

Melody A series of consecutive pitches with a recognizable shape or tune

Meno Means "less" in Italian

Meter The pattern created by stressed and unstressed beats

Metronome A device (mechanical or electrical) used to indicate the exact tempo of a composition

Mezzo-soprano A female voice with a range between a soprano and an alto

Microtones Pitches falling between the semitones of the Western chromatic scale

MIDI An acronym for Musical Instrument Digital Interface; standards for use by electronic keyboards, computers, and other devices

Minimalism Twentieth-century compositional technique using the simplest musical elements, generally repeated over and over, with subtle changes in their character

Minor One of the two basic scales in Western music; see also *major*

Minstrel French poet-musician who performed throughout France during the Middle Ages

Minuet A popular dance of the seventeenth and eighteenth centuries; uses triple meter

Minuet and trio form A common Classical period form consisting of three parts: minuet, trio, minuet

Moderato Moderate tempo

Modes Scale patterns (including major and minor) derived from early church music

Monophony, monophonic A texture consisting of a single melodic line without accompaniment

Motet Sacred polyphonic music for voices, popular during the thirteenth through seventeenth centuries

Motive A short melodic or rhythmic idea

Movement A large, independent section of an instrumental composition

Music-drama Wagner's term for his German operas

Musique concrète Everyday sounds recorded and manipulated on the tape recorder

Mute A device for dampening and changing the tone of an instrument

Neoclassical A twentieth-century style that borrows compositional techniques from previous style periods

Nocturne A short, lyrical piano piece of the Romantic period that evokes feelings associated with the night

Nogaku Traditional Japanese musical plays

Notes Symbols written in musical notation to indicate pitches and rhythm

Octave An interval of eight pitches in which the first and last pitches have the same pitch name

Octet A work for eight performers

Opera A dramatic work, comedy or tragedy, set to music

Opera comique Mid-nineteenth-century French opera featuring wit and satire both in the libretto and in the music

Operetta A light opera with spoken dialogue

Opus Literally "work"; the number indicates the order in which the composer's works were written

Oratorio A large work for chorus, soloist, and orchestra, usually on a religious topic; performed without scenery, costumes, or action

Orchestration The art and technique of scoring music for an orchestra or a group of instruments

Organum Polyphonic choral church music, beginning in the ninth century

Ornament One or more tones that embellish a melody

Ostinato A short, persistently repeated melodic or rhythmic figure

Overture An instrumental introduction to a larger work

Pasticcio A cross between ballad opera and comic opera, combining a dramatic work with music by famous composers

Pentatonic scale A scale consisting of five tones

Phrase A relatively short melodic statement, similar to a clause or phrase in language

Piano (1) Keyboard instrument (2) Quiet

Pianoforte This is the complete name for the keyboard instrument usually called a *Piano*. Meaning "soft-loud" in Italian, the instrument was named *pianoforte* when it was invented in the early eighteenth century because it could play both soft and loud.

Pitch The perceived highness or lowness of a musical sound, determined by the number of vibrations per second

Più Means "more" in Italian

Pizzicato A direction to string performers to pluck rather than bow the strings

Plainchant See *Gregorian chant*

Poco A performance direction meaning "little." For example, *poco accelerando* indicates "gradually play faster"

Polonaise A Polish national dance, also used in piano pieces by Chopin

Polychord Two or more triads performed simultaneously

Polymeter Two or more contrasting meters sounded simultaneously

Polyphony, polyphonic A texture in which two or more melodies of approximately equal importance are present at the same time

Polytonality Several tonalities present at the same time

Prelude (1) A short instrumental work usually played as an introduction to a larger work (2) A short, independent instrumental work

Presto Very fast tempo

Program notes Short descriptions or background information in the printed concert program about the music, the composer, and the performers

Programmatic music Instrumental work descriptive of some nonmusical idea or object

Proscenium The front area of the stage, including the curtain, apron, and arch, that is visible to the audience when the curtain is closed

Quartet A work for four performers

Quintet A work for five performers

Raga Ancient melodic material used in Indian music

Ragtime Syncopated music composed in the 1890s, usually for piano

Rallentando Gradual slowing of tempo

Recapitulation The section of sonata form in which the themes from the exposition are heard again

Recitative A speechlike section found in operas, oratorios, cantatas, and other vocal works

Requiem The funeral Mass of the Roman Catholic Church

Revue An energetic popular entertainment show featuring musical numbers, comedy acts, dramatic sketches, and specialty routines, with no story; usually built around star performers

Rhythm The sensation of motion in music, regulated by the duration and grouping of sounds

Rhythm and blues (R & B) A transitional music style between swing and rock; first became popular in the African-American communities of large, Midwestern cities

Riff Used in African and African-American music, a riff is a short phrase repeated over and over.

Ritardando Gradual slowing of the tempo

Rock'n'roll/Rock Popular music characterized by its hard-driving beat and use of electronically amplified instruments

Rococo The highly ornamented style in music and the other arts, prevalent in eighteenth-century European courts

Rondo A form in which the main theme appears several times with contrasting sections between its appearances

Rubato A performer's slight deviation from strict rhythm for expressive effect

Sampling A series of numbers that represent sounds that have been digitally recorded and stored on computer disk

Scale A series of pitches that proceed upward or downward according to a prescribed pattern

Scherzo (1) A lively movement, usually in triple meter (2) A self-contained piano piece

Score The complete notation of a work that includes a number of parts

Secular music Nonreligious music

Sequence The immediate repetition of a melodic idea using different pitches

Serialism A twentieth-century method of composing, using tone-rows and all twelve tones of the chromatic scale

Sforzando A loud, accented tone or chord

Shakuhachi A Japanese end-blown bamboo flute

Singspiel German eighteenth-century opera with spoken dialogue

Solo A work in which one player or singer performs alone or is featured

Sonata (1) A multimovement work for piano or piano and other solo instrument (2) A Baroque piece for a small instrumental ensemble

Sonata form A large form consisting of an exposition section, followed by a development section and a recapitulation

Song cycle A group of songs with a unifying theme

Song plugger A pianist-singer who performed new songs to find customers for them

Songs without words Mendelssohn's term for melodic piano pieces, written in the style of a lied or song

Soprano The highest female voice or boy's voice

Sprechstimme A vocal style combining speaking and singing

Staccato A detached style of performing in detached, abrupt bursts

Stretto A short section mainly found in the fugue where the main subject is imitated in close succession or overlapping voices

Subject The principal melody of a fugue

Subscription concerts A series of concerts for advance-purchase subscribers

Suite (1) An instrumental work in several movements (2) Portions of a larger work, such as a ballet or opera, performed as a group

Supertitles Translations of the libretto of an opera or operetta projected above the proscenium

Swing Popular music of the 1930s and 1940s which often featured big bands

Symphonic poem Programmatic symphony in one movement; also called a tone poem

Symphony An extended, multimovment orchestral work

Syncopation Accented beats not normally expected within a particular meter

Synthesizer An electric instrument used to generate sounds

Tempo The speed of the beats in a piece of music

Tenor A male voice higher than a baritone or bass

Texture The way in which the individual parts of music are layered and woven

Theme The main melody or melodies in a piece of music

Theme and variations Form consisting of a theme, followed by a group of variations on that theme

Timbre Tone quality or color

Toccata A display piece for a keyboard instrument

Tonality A key or tonal center

Tone poem See *symphonic poem*

Tone-row music (twelve tone) See *serialism*

Tonic (key center) The specific pitch around which a piece of music is centered

Tonic chord A chord built on the first pitch of a major or minor scale

Transcription An adaptation of a musical work for a different instrument, voice, or ensemble

Transposition A piece or section of music written or performed at a pitch other than the original one

Tremolo Rapid repetition of one pitch, or rapid alternation between two tones

Triad A chord consisting of three pitches, usually separated by intervals of thirds

Trill A musical ornament consisting of rapid alternations of two tones

Trio (1) A musical work for three parts or three performers (2) The second section of a minuet and trio form

Troubadours During the age of chivalry, singing knights of the twelfth-century court in southern France.

Trouvères Noblemen in the courts of northern France who composed and sang songs during the twelfth and thirteenth centuries

Tutti An Italian performance term indicating that the entire ensemble plays

Twelve-tone music See *serialism*

Unison Performing the same pitches or melody at the same time

Variation A section of music in which the melody, harmony, or rhythm of a theme is repeated with some changes

Vaudeville A variety show featuring novelty acts as well as song and dance

Verismo Late-nineteenth-century opera that uses a realistic story, setting, and acting

Vibrato A rapid fluctuation of pitch or pulsation of tone for expressiveness

Vina A string instrument used in the music of southern India

Virtuoso A highly skilled performer

Virtuoso orchestra An orchestra consisting entirely of highly skilled (*virtuoso*) performers

Vivace Very fast, lively tempo

Whole-tone scale A scale in which the octave is divided into six whole steps

Wind ensemble A wind instrument band smaller than the traditional band

Photo Credits

Prelude: Page 1, JoAnn Falletta by Steve J. Sherman.

Chapter 1: Page 3, Yo-Yo Ma and Emanuel Ax by Steve J. Sherman. **Page 4 (top),** George Gershwin by American Society of Composers and Publishers. **Page 4 (middle),** Yo-Yo Ma, Courtesy ICM Artists, Ltd., photo by J. Henry Fair. **Page 4 (bottom),** Orchestra Hall, Minneapolis by Norman McGrath.

Plate 1, *Le Concert Champetre: La Musique (The Musicians of a Country Concert).* Anon. Italian School, 16th Century, Mus. de l'Hotel l'Allemant, Bourges, Giraudon/Art Resource, NY. **Plate 2,** *Codice Squarcilupi: Pagina Miniata,* Art Resource. **Plate 3,** A Baroque style of pulpit in Wies-Kirche, southern Germany. Photograph by the author. Zorn/August slide collection. **Plate 4,** Rose Window, Chartres, Photo Resources, Inc. **Plate 5,** Frederick the Great, King of Prussia, performing by candlelight, Archiv Fur Kunst Und Geschichte, Berlin. **Plate 6,** 18th century drawing room in the Schönbrunn Palace in Vienna. Photograph by the author. Zorn/August slide collection. **Plate 7,** Young Mozart, his father and his sister, Giraudon/Art Resource, NY. **Plate 8,** Botticelli, *The Birth of Venus.* Corbis. **Plate 9,** Grand pianoforte made for the wife of Lord Foley, baron of Kidderminster, The Metropolitan Museum of Art, Gift of Mrs. Henry McSweeny, 1959. Photograph by Sheldan Collins. **Plate 10,** *Impression, soleil levant (Impressions of the Sunrise),* Claude Monet, Giraudon/Art Resource, NY. **Plate 11,** Robert Joffrey's Production of *The Nutcracker,* H. Migdoll, The Joffrey Ballet. **Plate 12,** *The Fiddler* by Marc Chagall, Erich Lessing from Art Resource. **Plate 13,** Salvador Dali, *The Persistence of Memory* (Persistence de la memoire). 1931. Oil on canvas, 9½ × 13″. The Museum of Modern Art, NY. **Plate 14,** Vassily Kandinsky, *Painting Number 200* 1914. Oil on canvas, 64 × 31½″. The Museum of Modern Art, NY. Mrs. Simon Guggenheim Fund. Photograph © 1994 The Museum of Modern Art, NY. **Plate 15,** Picasso, Pablo. *Les Demoiselles d'Avignon.* Paris (June–July 1907). Oil on canvas, 8′ × 7′8″. The Museum of Modern Art, NY. Acquired through the Lillie P. Bliss Bequest. **Plate 16,** the fusion-jazz group *Weather Report* by Andy Freeberg. **Plate 17,** Spanish dancers by Mira.

Chapter 2: Page 5, Isaac Stern, ICM Artists Limited. **Page 6,** Marilyn Horne by Robert Cohen Photography.

Chapter 3: Page 8, John Williams conducting, Symphony Hall, Boston. Photographer: Lincoln Russell. **Page 9 (top),** Vienna Chamber Orchestra, Courtesy ICM Artists, Ltd. **Page 9 (middle),** Samuel Ramey, Courtesy Columbia Artists Mgmt., Inc. Photographer: Christian Steiner. **Page 9 (bottom),** Vienna Boys Choir, Courtesy ICM Artists, Ltd. **Page 10,** Times Square, collage. Photo: Alan Schein. The Stock Market. **Page 11,** Royal Winnipeg Ballet by KRG Sills. **Page 12,** John Williams conducting, Courtesy Boston Pops Orchestra, Photo by Lincoln Russel. **Page 15,** Riccardo Muti conducting, Philadelphia Orchestra. **Page 16,** John Williams, Courtesy of the Boston Symphony Orchestra, Inc. Photographer: Richard Feldman. **Page 17,** Sir Neville Marriner by Peter Schaaf.

Chapter 4: Page 21, Boys Choir of Harlem, Courtesy Mendola, Ltd. **Page 25,** Ahmad Jamal Trio by Steve J. Sherman. **Page 29,** James Galway, flutist. Courtesy IMG Artists. Photographer: Nick Sangiamo. **Page 30,** Itzhak Perlman, Courtesy ICM Artists, Ltd., photo by Christian Steiner.

Chapter 5: Page 32, Orchestra Performance by Steve J. Sherman. **Page 33,** Juilliard String Quartet, Courtesy ICM Artists, Ltd., photo by Peter Schaaf. **Page 35 (middle),** New York Woodwind Quintet by Peter Schaaf. Courtesy ICM Artists Ltd. **Page 35 (bottom),** Canadian Brass Quintet, Courtesy IMG Artists. Photo by Martin Reichenthal. **Page 37,** Violin Section, The Toronto Symphony. Photo by Brian Pickell. **Page 38,** Chamber orchestra woodwinds, Courtesy of The Chamber Music Society of Lincoln Center. Photo by Harry Heleotis. **Page 39,** Brass section, Courtesy of The Philadelphia Orchestra, photo by Steve J. Sherman. **Page 40,** Percussion section, Courtesy of Jay D. Zorn. Photo by Robert Millard. **Page 41,** Zubin Mehta conducting, Courtesy of the New York Philharmonic, photo by David Rentas. **Page 46,** Stradivarius violin by UPI. Courtesy of Corbis. **Page 48,** Haydn directing a court chamber orchestra. Courtesy of Corbis. **Page 56,** Painting of Mozart, Wolfgang Amadeus by Bildarchiv Preussischer Kulturbesitz. **Page 57,** Fortepiano by J. Dane. **Page 58 (middle),** Electronic synthesizer keyboard, University of Southern California, University Publications. **Page 58 (bottom),** Samuel Ramey as Attila, Courtesy of Performing Arts Library. Photo by Clive Barda.

Chapter 6: Page 61, Florentine Court Musicians of the Medici Court, A. D. Gabbiani. Art Resource, N.Y. **Page 62,** *Porgy and Bess* performance, Courtesy Houston Grand Opera.

Chapter 7: Page 64, Lute player and harpist, New York Library Picture Collection. **Page 65,** Burgos Cathedral. Photo by J. Mariani. Courtesy of Leo de Wys, Inc. **Page 69,** Lute player and harpist, New York Public Library Picture Collection. **Page 70,** Dancing in the Middle Ages, The Granger Collection. **Page 68,** Notre Dame (outside), Paris by Black Star. Photo by Joseph Modlens. **Page 71 (top),** Notre Dame (interior), Art Resource, N.Y. Photo by Alinari. **Page 71 (middle),** Statue of David, Art Resource. **Page 72,** Leonardo da Vinci sketch of an aircraft (Ornithopter), Images, Inc. **Page 73,** *Prophet Jeremiah* by Michelangelo, Sistine Ceiling, Art Resource, N.Y. Photo by Scala. **Page 74,** Palestrina title page by Bildarchiv Preussischer Kulturbesitz.

Chapter 8: Page 79, Interior church, Steinhausen, ceiling detail, Art Resource, N.Y. **Page 80 (top),** Martin Luther by Galleria Uffizi. **Page 80 (bottom),** St. Peter's, Rome, Art Resource, N.Y. Photo by Alinari. **Page 81,** Gothis Duomo, Mantua, Italy. Courtesy, August/Zorn Collection.

Chapter 9: Page 84, Baroque group painting, New York Public Library Picture Collection. **Page 85 (top),** St. Mark's Interior, Art

Resource N.Y. Photo by Alinari. **Page 85 (middle),** Exterior of the Basilica of St. Mark in Venice, Photo by Jay D. Zorn. **Page 85 (bottom),** Interior of the Basilica of St. Mark in Venice, Art Resources, N.Y. Photo by Alinari. **Page 87,** Claudio Monteverdi portrait, The Granger Collection. **Page 90,** Schutz portrait by Corbis. **Page 91,** Handel portrait, German Information Center. **Page 93,** English Baroque Soloists by Clive Barda Photography. **Page 98,** Performance of a Lutheran cantata, New York Public Library. **Page 99,** Johann Sebastian Bach, German Information Center. **Page 105,** Vivaldi portrait by Bildarchiv Preussischer Kulturbesitz. **Page 111,** Bach at the keyboard with his family, Stock Montage, Inc.

Chapter 10: Page 114, Dancing the popular Minuet at court by Corbis. **Page 115 (top, right),** Dancing the popular Minuet at court by Corbis. **Page 115 (bottom),** Pompeii. Photo by Dr. Paul Richter. Courtesy of Imapo, Inc. **Page 116,** Mansion in Munich, Photo by J. Messerschmidt. Courtesy of Leo de Wys, Inc.

Chapter 11: Page 118, Concert audience by Bildarchiv Preussischer Kulturbesitz. **Page 119 (top),** Young Beethoven. Courtesy of Corbis. **Page 119 (bottom),** Mozart portrait by Bild-Archiv Der Oesterreichischen Nationalbibliothek, Wien. **Page 129,** Mozart, age 21, Courtesy August/Zorn Collection. **Page 128,** Mozart's apartment. Courtesy of Jay D. Zorn. **Page 122,** Haydn portrait by Bild-Archiv Der Oesterreichischen Nationalbibliothek, Wien. **Page 126,** First Performance of Haydn's *Creation.* Courtesy of Bild-Archiv Der Oesterreichischen. **Page 123,** Esterhazy Palace by Bild-Archiv Der Oesterreichischen Nationalbibliothek, Wien. **Page 127,** Young Prodigy Mozart. Courtesy of Photo Resources, Inc. **Page 135,** Schonbrunn Palace in Vienna. Courtesy of Jay D. Zorn. **Page 139,** Catalog scene from Don Giovanni. Clive Barda Photography.

Chapter 12: Page 144, Beethoven drawing at age 48, The Granger Collection. **Page 145,** Beethoven portrait at the age of 49, German Information Center. **Page 148 (top),** Beethoven's studio by Bild-Archiv Der Oesterreichischen Nationalbibliothek, Wien. **Page 149,** Streicher piano factory by Bild-Archiv Der Oesterreichischen Nationalbibliothek, Wien.

Chapter 13: Page 156, *Liberty Leading the People,* Art Resource, N.Y. **Page 157,** *Liberty Leading the People,* Eugene Delacroix, Louvre/Art Resource, NY.

Chapter 14: Page 160, Schubert at piano (detail) by Bild-Archiv Der Oesterreichischen Nationalbibliothek, Wien. **Page 161,** Berlioz portrait by Corbis. **Page 162 (left),** Painting of Berlioz, Culver Pictures, Inc. **Page 162 (right),** Anonymous. Portrait of Harriet Smithson, Irish actress and wife of Hector Berlioz, 19th c. Private Collection. Art Resource, N.Y. Photo by Giraudon. **Page 170,** Schubert at piano by Bild-Archiv Der Oesterreichischen Nationalbibliothek, Wien. **Page 169,** Schubert portrait, Culver Pictures, Inc. **Page 174,** Robert Schumann by Corbis. **Page 176,** Clara Schumann portrait by Bildarchiv Preussischer Kulturbesitz. **Page 175,** Robert & Clara Schumann. Courtesy of Tony Stone Images. **Page 180,** Portrait of Chopin by Eugene Delacroix, Lauros-Giraudon/Art Resource, NY. **Page 182,** Portrait of Liszt by Charles Lehman, Lauros-Giraudon/Art Resource, NY. **Page 184,** Felix Mendelssohn portrait, The Metropolitan Museum of Art, The Crosby Brown Collection of Musical Instruments, 1901. **Page 185,** Fanny Mendelssohn portrait, Culver Pictures, Inc.

Chapter 15: Page 190, Gotterdammerung scene, Canadian Opera Company, Toronto. **Page 193 (top),** Donizetti portrait, The Granger Collection. **Page 193 (bottom),** Bellini. Photo by Scala. Courtesy of Art Resource, Inc. **Page 194,** Rossini portrait, The Granger Collection. **Page 195,** Verdi portrait, Culver Pictures, Inc. **Page 192,** Verdi

opera scene by Clive Barda Photography. **Page 200 (top),** Puccini portrait, Art Resource, N.Y. Photo by Alinari. **Page 200 (bottom),** Scene from *La Boheme,* act I, Metropolitan Opera Production, N.Y. Courtesy of Jay D. Zorn. **Page 209,** Jacque Offenbach. Courtesy of Corbis. **Page 213,** *Carmen* (San Diego), Courtesy of San Diego Opera. Photo by Ken Howard. **Page 212,** Bizet portrait by Corbis. **Page 214,** Carl Maria Von Weber, Culver Pictures, Inc. **Page 215,** Wagner portrait, Culver Pictures Inc.

Chapter 16: Page 221, Large crowd scene by Sammlungen Der Gesselschaft Der Musikfreunde in Vienna. **Page 224,** Brahms portrait, Historisches Museum Der Stadt, Vienna. **Page 229,** Mahler portrait by Bild-Archiv Der Oesterreichischen Nationalbibliothek, Vienna. **Page 236,** Strauss portrait by by Bild-Archiv Der Oesterreichischen Nationalbibliothek, Vienna.

Chapter 17: Page 240, *Nutcracker* performance by Martha Swope Associates. **Page 242,** Mussorgsky portrait by Sovfoto/Eastfoto. Photo by Tass. **Page 243,** Tchaikovsky portrait. Courtesy of Library of Congress. **Page 244 (top),** Russian Orthodox Church, St. Basil's. Photo by Galen Rowell. Courtesy of Peter Arnold, Inc. **Page 244 (bottom),** Fireworks over Lincoln Center, Photo by Chris Lee, Courtesy of The New York Philharmonic. **Page 249,** Rimsky-Korsakov portrait by Corbis. **Page 250,** Rachmaninov portrait, Culver Pictures, Inc. **Page 251,** Bartok portrait, Bartok Archive, Hungarian Academy of Sciences, Budapest. **Page 252,** Sibelius portrait by Corbis.

Chapter 18: Page 254, *Barque a Giverny,* Art Resource, N.Y. Photo by Giraudon. **Page 255 (top),** Henry VIII painting, Art Resource, N.Y. Photo by Alinari. **Page 255 (bottom),** *Les Meules,* by Claude Monet, Lauros-Giraudon/Art Resource, N.Y. **Page 257 (top),** *Rouen Cathedral, West Facade, Sunlight,* Claude Monet, Marburg/Art Resource, NY. Photo by Giraudon. **Page 257 (bottom),** Rouen Cathedral photo. Photo by Bildarchiv Foto Marburg. Courtesy of Art Resource, N.Y. **Page 256,** Debussy portrait by Corbis. **Page 258,** Eiffel Tower. Photo by Karen McCunnall. Courtesy of Leo de Wys, Inc. **Page 262,** Ravel by Corbis.

Chapter 19: Page 264, Pablo Picasso, *Guernica,* 1937. (detail) Oil on canvas, 11 ft. 5 1/2 inches × 25 ft. 5 1/4 inches. Photo by Biraudon. Centro de Arte Reina Sofia, Madrid. Giraudon/Art Resource, NY. © 1998 Estate of Pablo Picasso/Artists Rights Society (ARS), New York. Courtesy of Art Resource, N. Y. **Page 265,** Pablo Picasso, *Guernica,* 1937. Oil on canvas.11 ft. 5½" × 25 ft. 5¼ in. Photo by Giraudon.Centro de Arte Reina Sofia, Madrid. Giraudon/Art Resource, NY © 1998 Estate of Pablo Picasso/Artists Rights Society (ARS), New York. Courtesy of Art Resource, N.Y. **Page 268,** Picasso and Stravinsky in a sketch by Jean Cocteau. © 1998 estate of Pablo Picasso/Artists Rights Society (ARS), New York. Courtesy of Artists Rights Society, Inc.

Chapter 20: Page 271, In the Jean Cocteau drawing, Stravinsky plays the piano section of Le Sacre du Printemps. Courtesy of Artists Rights Society, Inc. (ARS), New York/ADAGP, Paris. **Page 272,** Stravinsky portrait. Courtesy of Culver Pictures, Inc. **Page 274 (top),** Pablo Picasso, *Three Musicians.* Oil on canvas, 1921, 70 × 87¾". Collection, The Museum of Modern Art, New York. Mrs. Simon Guggenheim Fund. Oil on canvas, 6' 7" × 7' 3¾" (200.7 × 222.9 cm.). Courtesy of The Museum of Modern Art. **Page 274 (bottom),** Debussy and Stravinsky. Courtesy of Archiv fur Kunst und Geschichte, Berlin. **Page 276,** *The Rite of Spring* performance. Courtesy of Martha Swope Associates.

Chapter 21: Page 282, *In Street, Berlin* (1913). Painted by Ernst Ludwig Kirchner. Courtesy of The Museum of Modern Art. **Page 283,** Arnold Schoenberg self-portrait. Photo by Allan Dean Walker.

Courtesy of Lawrence Schoenberg. **Page 284,** *In Street, Berlin* (1913). Painted by Ernst Ludwig Kirchner. Courtesy of The Museum of Modern Art. **Page 287,** Anton Webern portrait. Courtesy of Arnold Schoenberg Institute Archives. **Page 288,** Alban Berg (1885–1935). Courtesy of Arnold Schoenberg Institute Archives.

Chapter 22: Page 289, *The Three Penny Opera.* Photo by Nancy Ellison. Courtesy of Outline Press Syndicate, Inc. **Page 290,** Sergei Prokofiev (1891–1953). Courtesy of Archiv fur Kunst und Geschichte, Berlin. **Page 294,** Dimitri Shostakovich portrait (1906–1975). Courtesy of Sovfoto/Eastfoto. **Page 295 (top),** Vaughn-Williams portrait. Photo by Dudley Styles. Courtesy of Royal College of Music. **Page 295 (bottom),** Benjamin Britten with friends on boat. Courtesy of Tony Stone Images. **Page 296,** Nadia Boulanger portrait. Photo by UPI. Courtesy of Corbis. **Page 300 (top),** Les Six. Courtesy of Corbis. **Page 300 (bottom),** Paul Hindemith. Courtesy of Culver Pictures, Inc. **Page 301,** *The Three Penny Opera.* Photo by Nancy Ellison. Courtesy of Outline Press Syndicate, Inc. **Page 302,** Bela Bartok. Courtesy of Corbis.

Chapter 23: Page 304, Man playing synthesizer. Photo by Dan Nelken. Courtesy of Liaison Agency, Inc. **Page 306,** electronic music studio. Courtesy of University of Illinois, EMS. **Page 307,** Jackson Pollock's painting *Number One* (1948). Photo by Soichi Sunami. Courtesy of The Museum of Modern Art. **Page 309 (top),** Pierre Boulez. Photo by UPI. Courtesy of Corbis. **Page 309 (bottom),** Karlheinz Stockhausen. Courtesy of the German Information Center. **Page 310,** Philip Glass. Courtesy of Steve J. Sherman.

Chapter 24: Page 311, *Porgy and Bess* scene. Photo by Jim Caldwell. Courtesy of Houston Grand Opera. **Page 313,** Amy Beach (Mrs. H. H. A. Beach, portrait by Apeda, c. 1900. Courtesy of University of New Hampshire, Lotte Jacobi Archives. **Page 315,** Charles Ives portrait (1874–1954). Courtesy of Sony Music. **Page 325,** U. S. Marine Band, Theater Arts, Harry Ransom Humanities Research Center. **Page 326,** New Orleans Funeral Procession. Courtesy of Syndey Byrd. **Page 327,** Scott Joplin (1868–1917) . Astor, Lenox, and Tilden Foundation. Courtesy of New York Public Library at Lincoln Center. **Page 331 (top),** Bessie Smith. Courtesy of Corbis. **Page 331 (bottom),** Creole Jazz Band. Courtesy of Culver Pictures, Inc. **Page 332,** Tin Pan Alley, 28th Street, N.Y. C. Courtesy of Archive Photos. **Page 333,** George Gershwin portrait. Courtesy of Corbis. **Page 339 (top),** Porgy and Bess scene. Photo by Jim Caldwell. Courtesy of Houston Grand Opera. **Page 339 (bottom),** Aaron Copland portrait. Photo by Decasseres. Courtesy of Photo Researchers, Inc. **Page 342,** Leonard Bernstein conducting. Courtesy of Steve J. Sherman. **Page 346,** Gian Carlo Menotti portrait. Photo by John Albert. Courtesy of Culver Pictures, Inc. **Page 347,** Ellen Taaffe Zwilich. Courtesy of Steve J. Sherman.

Chapter 25: Page 351, The Rolling Stones. Courtesy of Andy Freeberg Photography. **Page 352,** Cover of Berlin's *Alexander's Ragtime Band.* Courtesy of Library of Congress. **Page 354 (top),** Benny Goodman. Courtesy of Culver Pictures, Inc. **Page 354 (bottom),** Billie Holiday. Courtesy of Culver Pictures, Inc. **Page 355,** Juke

Box. Photo by Max Tharpe. Courtesy of Monkmeyer Press. **Page 356,** Ray Charles. Courtesy of Michael Ochs Archives. **Page 357,** The Beatles at the London Palladium. Courtesy of Tony Stone Images. **Page 358,** The Rolling Stones. Courtesy of Andy Freeberg Photography. **Page 359,** Woodstock. Photo by Elliot Landy. Courtesy of The Image Works.

Chapter 26: Page 361, scene from *The Music Man.* Photo by Springer. Courtesy of Corbis. **Page 363,** Cover for James Bland songs. Courtesy of Library of Congress. **Page 364,** Stephen Foster. Courtesy of Corbis. **Page 370,** The Ziegfeld Follies. Courtesy of Culver Pictures, Inc. **Page 371,** Cover for *Over There.* Courtesy of Library of Congress. **Page 372 (top),** Sigmund Romberg (1887–1951). Courtesy of Culver Pictures, Inc. Page 370 (bottom) Victor Herbert portrait (1859–1924). Courtesy of Culver Pictures, Inc. **Page 373 (top),** Rudolf Frimi (1879–1972). Courtesy of The Granger Collection. **Page 373 (bottom),** Irving Berlin singing. Courtesy of Culver Pictures, Inc. **Page 374,** Jerome Kern (1885–1945). American composer. Portrait photo taken in the early 1900's. Courtesy of Corbis. **Page 376,** Paul Robeson. Courtesy of Culver Pictures, Inc. **Page 379,** Gordon McRae in *Oklahoma.* Courtesy of Culver Pictures, Inc. **Page 380,** Head and shoulders photo of American composer and lyricist Cole Porter (1891–1964). Courtesy of Corbis. **Page 381,** Richard Rodgers portrait. Courtesy of Culver Pictures, Inc. **Page 382,** Stephen Sondheim portrait. Courtesy of American Society of Coomposers, Authors, and Publishers. **Page 384,** *West Side Story.* Courtesy of Culver Pictures, Inc. **Page 385,** scene from *Fiddler on the Roof.* Courtesy of Photofest. **Page 387,** Scene from *The Music Man.* Photo by Springer. Courtesy of Corbis. **Page 389,** *Beauty and the Beast,* Broadway, N.Y. Photo by Alan Schein. Courtesy of The Stock Market.

Chapter 27: Page 390, *Star Wars.* Courtesy of Photofest. **Page 391,** Buster Keaton in a scene from *The General.* Courtesy of Culver Pictures, Inc. **Page 393,** Hermione Gingold and Maurice Chevalier in a scene from *Gigi.* Photo by Springer. Courtesy of Corbis. **Page 401,** The Rite of Spring scene from *Fantasia.* Courtesy of The Disney Publishing Group. © Disney Enterprises Inc. **Page 404,** Leonardo Di Caprio and Kate Winslet in *Titanic.* Courtesy of Neal Peters Collection.

Chapter 28: Page 408, Ravi Shankar. Courtesy of CBS Records. **Page 410,** Zulu dancers. Photo by Ernst Haas. Courtesy of Magnum Photos, Inc. **Page 411 (top),** Musician, South Africa. Photo by Ian Berry. Courtesy of Magnuym Photos, Inc. **Page 411 (bottom),** African musicians. Photo by Jacques Jangoux. Courtesy of Tony Stone Images. **Page 413,** Flamenco dancers. Courtesy of Jay D. Zorn. **Page 414,** Indian dancers and musicians. Courtesy of Government of India. **Page 417,** Japanese koto. Courtesy of Japan National Tourist Organization. **Page 419,** Kabuki performers. Photo by Paolo Koch. Courtesy of Photo Researchers, Inc.

Finale: Page 421, Davis Symphony Hall. Courtesy of The Stock Market. Photo by Mark & Audrey Gibson.

Index